U0127585

DECODING
NEW CONCEPT
ENGLISH

新概念英语 ③

之[全新全绎]

主编 ▸ 周成刚 翁云凯　编著 ▸ 薛 冰 蔡 颖

西安交通大学出版社
XI'AN JIAOTONG UNIVERSITY PRESS

图书在版编目(CIP)数据

新概念英语之全新全绎. 3 / 周成刚，翁云凯主编；薛冰，
蔡颖编著. —西安：西安交通大学出版社，2006（2008.4 重印）
ISBN 978-7-5605-2276-0

Ⅰ. 新... Ⅱ. ①周...②翁...③薛...④蔡...
Ⅲ. 英语—自学参考资料 Ⅳ. H31

中国版本图书馆 CIP 数据核字(2006) 第 078942 号

书　　名	新概念英语之全新全绎 3	
主　　编	周成刚　翁云凯	
编　　著	薛　冰　蔡　颖	
责任编辑	王　超　刘国洁	
封面设计	王　琳	
出版发行	西安交通大学出版社	
地　　址	西安市兴庆南路 10 号（邮编：710049）	
电　　话	(029)82668357　82667874（发行部）	
	(029)82668315　82669096（总编办）	
印　　刷	北京朝阳新艺印刷有限公司	
字　　数	508 千字	
开　　本	787mm×1092mm　1/16	
印　　张	20.5	
版　　次	2006 年 8 月第 1 版　2008 年 4 月第 5 次印刷	
书　　号	ISBN 978-7-5605-2276-0/H・596	
定　　价	38.00 元	

新东方 NEW ORIENTAL **图书策划委员会**

新概念的故事

说起《新概念英语》，只要学习英语的中国人几乎都知道。这套英语教材在中国已经流行了接近30年，还经久不衰。作为上世纪80年代进入大学学习英语专业的人，我算是最早受益于《新概念英语》的中国人之一。

20多年前，中国人学习英语没有现在这么多教材资料可以选择。我们进大学的时候，中国学生所用的英语教科书题材都很单一，课文内容大都比较枯燥乏味，多半是把发生在当时中国的事情用英语写出来作课文来讲解，使学生提不起兴趣，进而失去了对英语学习的兴趣。

可以说我对于英语学习的兴趣是被《新概念英语》这套书激发出来的。上大学时，如果没有课，我常常会骑着自行车到北大周围的书店去逛。当时只有两种书店，一是新华书店，一是外文书店。逛新华书店是找中文书，逛外文书店是找外文书。外文书店对我有着特殊的吸引力，因为在那里常常能够读到原版的在中国还没有出版的图书。当时北京海淀区五道口有一家外文书店，是我常常去浏览的地方。书店被分为里外两间，外间大一些，卖已经在中国正式出版的外语书籍和教材，里间小一些，专门销售直接影印的外国书籍，只有出示证件的中国人才能进去。就是在这家书店里，我第一次见到了影印版的《新概念英语》，随手拿起翻阅几页后就爱不释手，因为里面的课文精炼有趣，充满了英国人特有的机智幽默。当时这套书既没有翻译注解，也没有配套磁带，所以每篇课文都需要自己抱着字典一点点弄懂。但由于课文本身很有趣，所以尽管觉得吃力，我却没有产生任何厌倦情绪。我用了两个多月的时间，就把第二册到第四册的200多篇课文生吞活剥地学完了。第二年，《新概念英语》的录音磁带进入中国，那时中国流行的是英音英语，所有学英语的学生都如获至宝，把磁带买下来拼命模仿朗读。《新概念英语》在中国一下子流行开了，大学的上空好像飘满了新概念的声音。我的朋友、现任北京新东方学校校长周成刚——据他自己说——就是在没日没夜地模仿了《新概念英语》的朗读后，获得了一口标准的伦敦口音，最后被英国BBC广播公司看中，变成了BBC的记者和节目主持人。我不如周成刚有毅力，最后把自己的口音模仿得不三不四，结果只能留在中国创办新东方学校。

后来中国就有了很多《新概念英语》的版本，各种各样的注解本、翻译本，大多数粗制滥造，但却不愁没有销量，因为中国学生使用这套教材的人越来越多。再后来中国对于图书版权的管理正规化，外研社独具慧眼，买下了这套书的独家版权，对课文进行了详细的注解和翻译，并且把其中一些过时的课文进行了替换，使这套教科书再次焕发出了光辉。

1997年，新东方为新开设的基础英语培训班选择教材，第一套进入我脑海的教材就是《新概念英语》。我的另一位朋友、新东方的创始人之一王强当时正负责基础英语的教学管理工作，他和我不约而同地提出了使用《新概念英语》作为新东方常用教材的想法。从此，《新概念英语》成了新东方课堂中最常用的教材之一。为此，新东方还专门成立了新概念教学教研部门。从1997年新东方开设新概念课程以来，在新东方学习《新概念英语》的学生已经超过50万人，在新东方教师队伍中专门教《新概念英语》的老师就有两百多位。

　　在近十年的教学过程中，新东方老师们摸索出了一整套《新概念英语》的教学经验和教学法，并通过自己的努力，对该套教材的美中不足进行了弥补，比如《新概念英语》中词汇量不足、句子结构不够丰富、练习题知识面覆盖不够广泛等。新东方老师通过总结，现在终于可以把这些研究成果结集成册拿出来和大家共享了，就是大家手里的这套《新概念英语之全新全绎》。这套书所补充和诠释的肯定还有不尽人意的地方，但这是很多老师努力劳动的成果。在学习《新概念英语》时配合使用本套丛书，一定能够起到拾遗补缺的作用，使大家的英语学习变得更加容易。

新东方教育科技集团
董事长兼总裁

写给英语学习者的话

《新概念英语之全新全绎》终于和大家见面了!这是一套酝酿了很久的书,这是一套期待了很久的书,这是一套凝聚了新东方名师多年心血的英语辅导书。

有许多新东方学员曾经问过我们,为什么不出新东方老师编写的《新概念英语》(以下简称《新概念》)辅导书?是啊,新东方的学员很多,新东方的口碑不错,一期期的英语学习者在新东方进进出出,他们怀揣一个英语梦,希望通过英语学习去提高自身的竞争力,去改变自己的生活,改变自己的命运。其实,这套辅导丛书多年来一直是我们的牵挂,我们理解学员那沉甸甸的期待和寄托,新东方也没有忘记自己的责任和义务。我们始终在准备,我们始终在斟酌,我们磨砺了太久,但我们并没有犹豫,更没有放弃,而是加倍努力,潜心钻研。十年磨一剑,新东方综合能力部的名师团队今天终于把他们多年的讲课心得和体会付诸笔端,得以付梓和广大读者见面,这实在是一种欣慰,也了结了我们的一份心愿。

千千万万的中国人正在学习英语,学习的浪潮也一浪高过一浪。我们深知,世界风云变幻,世界格局在重组,世界的需求在更新,全球化的观念日益深入人心,多媒体和互联网正在缩短我们和世界的距离。今天,我们可以把世界搬上自己的办公桌,或者足不出户而知天下大事。高科技让世界变得越来越小,英语作为一种世界语言正在其中发挥着前所未有的力量和作用。我们身边的许多人已经通过英语学习获益,他们或是留洋攻读在海外就业发展,或是归国创业在国内大展宏图,他们或是把中国传统带出去,或是把西方文化请进来,但都是为了一个共同的目标:让自己成为一个真正有用的地球人。

前人的足迹和成就是我们后人的启示和榜样。今天,更多的中国人认识到了英语的重要性,他们兑现自己的承诺,走进英语课堂,踏上了他们神圣而又快乐的英语之路,一场全民学英语的热潮正在中国掀起。我相信,中国的英语学习者都熟悉《新概念》这套书,我个人对它的那种难以割舍的情感可以追溯到上个世纪80年代,当时正值中国改革开放的初期,英语学习的第一个浪潮席卷而起。读者的求知欲空前高涨,大家对知识如饥似渴,有时候甚至不加区分地吸收和接受可能得到的一切书本知识。这套来自英伦并出自大师之手的《新概念》的引进无疑给相对落后的中国英语教科书园地带来了一阵清新的西风,我自己也因此成为了她的第一批受益者。可以毫不夸张地说,我对英式英语的热爱是从《新概念》开始的。

令人惊讶的是,大浪淘沙,经过岁月的洗礼和读者一次次无情的甄选,大部分国内外的英语教科书都已被人淡忘,惟有《新概念》历久弥香,在读者的反复检验和时间的沉淀中,靠着自身的独特性、科学性和权威性一枝独秀,越来越受到广大读者的青睐和推崇。终于,《新概念》成燎原之势,在中国的东西南北风靡起来。读者趋之若鹜,人手一册,或背诵或解读,各得其需。受益者口口相传,于是这套教科书在不知不觉中已深入人心。久而久之,她也成了广大英语学习者的一位好朋友,让我们开卷有益,不仅提高了我们的听说读写能力,甚至在我们的生活中给我们启发、指导和快乐。一套英语教科书能够在海外数十年为读者津津乐道而且备受推崇,可谓是一个不小的英语奇迹。事实上,《新概念》的意义已经远远超出了教科书本身,她在中国见证的是一个时代的奋斗和对知识的渴望,她目睹的是中国经济的腾飞以及中国人走向世界的勇敢的足迹。

我们今天的读者，尤其是那些正在学习《新概念》或准备拿起或重新拾起《新概念》的朋友又如何从这套经典的教材中获得最大的收益并学有所用呢?这是我们一直在思考的,这也是我们编写这套伴侣丛书《新概念英语之全新全绎》的初衷。读者可能会问,此类图书在书店里并不少见,我们这套丛书又有什么与众不同,又有什么值得向读者推荐和夸耀的独特之处呢?

首先,正如本丛书的书名所示,这是一个专家编写队伍的"全新全绎"之作。参加本丛书编写工作的老师都是新东方的英语教学专家,他们都是出类拔萃的明星老师,执教《新概念》多年,取得了骄人的教学业绩,在广大学生和同行中皆有良好的口碑,从他们课堂里走出去的学生每年数以万计。这批青年骨干教师在讲台上授业解惑,一丝不苟,在讲台下兢兢业业,踏实做事,他们把自己全部的青春和才华都奉献给了教育事业。此外,由于他们常年拼搏在教学第一线,对广大同学学习中遇到的困难和疑点都心中有数:他们知道学生在思考什么,疑惑什么,需要什么,期待什么。他们能够对症下药,能够运用同学最能接受的语言,通过合适的渠道传递正确的信息。换句话说,他们是学员真正的良师益友。

其次,我们编写这套辅导丛书运用了独特的三位一体法。这种创新体现了新东方老师的匠心。正是抱着出精品书和畅销书的科研宗旨,编写组的全体成员反复推敲,结合中国学生的学习习惯,采纳了课内课外相结合的"巩固＋拓展＋练习"的三位一体法。我们把辅导书的整体结构分为三块,在"积累篇"中,新东方的老师们运用了新颖的解词方法,非常便于联想和记忆,可以帮助读者巩固课本上的重点内容,"拓展篇"中的全部内容不同于原文又紧扣原文,学习者可以在巩固的前提下反复操练、举一反三,又可以拓展视野、温故知新,"测试篇"更是对综合能力的检测和提高,是实战和实用的完美结合。

可以说,这套辅导丛书是我们老师的心血之作,是我们的老师用责任、经验和情感撰写的一套辅导书。我们不敢说这是最好的辅导书,但我们敢说这是一套对同学负责的书,是对得起自己良心的书。我们别无他求,只希望虔诚的读者能够从我们的字里行间感受到英语学习的快乐和奥妙,看到英语向我们打开的一片广阔而又美好的新天地。

我从开始学英语至今已有二十多年,期间接触过的英语教科书不下几十种,可惟有《新概念》这套课本让我念念不忘,书中的许多精彩篇章至今都熟谙心中。几十年后的今天,我能和我的朋友翁云凯以及我们的几位老师共同策划并完成这套辅导丛书,也算是对那段难以忘怀的英语心路历程的纪念。

谨以此丛书与那些正在奋斗的英语学习者共勉!

周成刚

新东方教育科技集团常务副总裁

丛书使用说明

亲爱的读者朋友,感谢你选择此套丛书。这套丛书包含着北京新东方学校新概念部各位名师过去十年来课堂内外的失败、成功、积淀、绽放……

丛书一套喜相逢,英语学习多少事,尽在笑谈中!

拿到这套丛书不要只顾着"看"。"看"的时候多动动笔,把疑惑标出来,把对你有用的信息摘抄下来!"看"的时候还要多动动嘴,把英文部分反复读出来,乃至背诵下来!我们建议每三个月完成一册书的学习!把书中的每一个知识点嚼碎、揉烂,把这本书变成属于你自己的《新概念英语》学习笔记!

这套丛书共分四册,采用统一的编排体系,每课结构为:

积累篇:帮助读者夯实课文内的必会知识点。

拓展篇:帮助读者补充必要的课外知识点。各分册侧重点分别为:一册——听力;二册——口语;三册——听力、阅读;四册——听力、词汇、阅读。

测试篇:依托于"积累篇"和"拓展篇"中的知识点,我们把在国内外考试中多次出现的考点以及在日常生活中经常使用的语言点进行有机整合,编撰成题,以便助你更有针对性地强化、延伸《新概念英语》各课的学习。

推荐使用方法:

第一步:把《新概念英语》课文逐字逐句地读懂,即精读课文。(注意读的时候限定时间,并圈出有疑问的地方。)

第二步:开始本套丛书"积累篇"的学习。随时到《新概念英语》课本原文中去找出相关词汇,把列出的每个知识点牢牢记住。(最好熟读所有例句)

第三步:通读相应课文的"拓展篇"。此环节可以脱离《新概念英语》课本独立完成。相对于"积累篇",本篇的知识难度有所提高,所以难免会有个别疑点出现,在得到权威解答之前,先力求记下。阅读部分也建议大家熟读,从而培养语感。

第四步:配合以上三个步骤,制作属于自己的课堂笔记。把在《新概念英语》中出现的,和在学习本书"积累篇"和"拓展篇"过程中捕获的好词、好搭配、好句型通通摘录下来,汇总、整合到一个本子上,随身携带,抽空背记。

第五步:进入每一课的测试部分。做题的时候禁止开卷,不会的就空下来,这是发现问题的最好方法。对照参考答案纠错后,尽量把每个题目都熟记。

我们编写这套丛书的初衷是希望读者能够从中感触到英语学习的紧迫性与自律性,进而把英语学习变成你生活中必不可少的一部分。没有什么比这种收获更为重要的了!丛书每位作者都已经从英语学习中受益,而且深知其中的喜悦与不易。正因为如此,我们真诚地建议你利用12个月的时间把这套丛书学完,不错过任何一课,一鼓作气,打开英语学习之门。准备好了吗?让我们开始吧!

翁云凯

Elite精英英语学习中心主任

目 录

Lesson ①. A puma at large

积累篇

Ⅰ. 振振有"词"

1. <u>Pumas</u> are large, <u>cat-like</u> animals which are found in America.

cougar 美洲狮   cheetah 猎豹   crystal-like eyes 明亮的双眸   baby-like face 稚嫩的脸庞
panther 美洲狮   leopard 豹   steel-like muscle 坚实的肌肉   home-like inn 温馨的旅馆
jaguar 美洲豹   angel-like girl 貌美的女孩

用于描述、解释的定义句型：A is+形容词+B+which从句。例：
UN is a large, international organization which deals with all kinds of affairs among nations.
联合国是处理国家间各种事务的一个庞大的、国际性组织。
A university is a kind of educational institution which instructs learners both intellectually and morally.
大学是对学习者进行智力和道德教育的教育性组织。

2. When reports came into London Zoo that a wild puma had been <u>spotted</u> forty-five miles south of London, <u>they were not taken seriously</u>.

take sb./sth. seriously 认真(严肃)对待…   spot 找到，发现(从一群人或一堆物品中)
take sb./sth. lightly 不在乎…   identify 确认(身份)
take sb./sth. too much to heart 太在意…   confirm 确认(事实)
be indifferent to... 对…满不在乎   discern 辨明
be unsympathetic to... 对…漠不关心   verify 核对(事实)
show high/low regard for... 对…很/不太关心

3. However, as the evidence began to <u>accumulate</u>, experts from the zoo <u>felt obliged to</u> investigate.

形似词辨析：   同义词辨析：
accumulate 积累   accumulate (长时间)积累   be obliged to do sth. 有必要做…
accelerate 加速，促进   amass (长时间、有意识)积累   be forced to do sth. 被迫做…
exacerbate 恶化   assemble 组装   be compelled to do sth. 被迫做…(外因驱使)
exaggerate 夸张   gather 收集(将混乱物件归拢)   be impelled to do sth. 被迫做…(内因驱使)
exasperate 惹怒   collect 收集(多作为收藏)   It is incumbent upon sb. to do sth.
aggregate 收集；集合   pile up 堆积   有责任做…
                     hoard 囤积

1

4. <u>It is disturbing to think that</u> a dangerous wild animal is still <u>at large</u> in the quiet country side.

用于描述人对某个事件产生想法的常用句型:	at large 在逃的
It is disturbing to think that...想到…令人心神不定。	show one's heels 逃跑
It is worrying to think that...想到…令人焦虑不安。	take to one's legs 逃窜
It is irritating to think that...想到…令人恼火至极。	make off (*fml.*) 溜掉
It is comforting to think that...想到…令人备感欣慰。	take flight (*fml.*) 溜走
It is exciting to think that...想到…令人激动异常。	betake oneself to flight (*fml.*) 逃跑

Ⅱ. 现身说"法":同位语从句

When reports came into London Zoo that a wild puma had been spotted forty-five miles south of London.(彩色字体部分为reports的同位语从句)
当伦敦动物园接到报告说在伦敦以南45英里处发现一头野生美洲狮。

比较:同位语从句与定语从句的区别

1. 同位语从句与中心词是等值的关系;定语从句与先行词是修饰与被修饰的关系。

2. 同位语从句里的that不作语法成分,但一般不省;定语从句里的that在从句中作主语或宾语,作宾语时可省。

3. 识别秘笈:同位语从句中去除that,剩余部分仍是完整的句子;而定语从句中去除that,剩余部分则不是完整的句子。例:

The first case of bird flu that was reported in Thailand captured the attention of officials with WHO.
(定语从句)泰国报道的首例禽流感病例受到了世界卫生组织官员的关注。

There are signs that China is speeding up her economy.(同位语从句)
有迹象表明中国正在加快经济建设的步伐。

常连接同位语从句的名词有:news, faith, report, sign, belief, fact, opinion, idea, suggestion等。

Ⅲ. 说"文"解"字"

1. Pumas are large, cat-like animals which are found in America.

译文:美洲狮是一种体形似猫的大动物,产于美洲。

解析:本句妙点就在彩色字体部分。按照汉语思维,读者对"产于"第一反应的英文对应词是be produced in,该词多指机械产品的生产;而are found in却表现了动物飘忽不定的特点,英汉差异,可见一斑。此外,该句型可作为描述性句型加以模仿。例:

Giant pandas are large, bear-like animals which are found mainly in Sichuan province, China.
大熊猫是一种体形似熊的大动物,主要产于中国四川。

2. When reports came into London Zoo...

译文:当伦敦动物园接到报告……

解析:这里运用了拟人修辞法,生动鲜活性跃然纸上,本句重点是reports,按照英文行文规律,重要信息一般前置,这与下列文字相比,显然更加流畅:When London Zoo received reports...

3. ...experts from the Zoo felt obliged to investigate...

译文：动物园的专家们感到有必要进行一番调查。

解析：这里"有必要"没有用felt forced to，而用felt obliged to，区别主要在于：前者表受外因所迫，后者则多指义务感和责任感，即具有"在其位，谋其政"的含义。模仿句型：

Each citizen feels obliged to bring up the young and take care of the old.

每个公民都有抚幼养老的义务。

4. ...a puma will not attack a human being unless it is cornered.

译文：美洲狮除非被逼得走投无路，是决不会伤人的。

解析：本句中will not和unless构成双重否定，其用意在于突显美洲狮有别于其他猛兽，即："人不犯我，我不犯人"。若换作a puma will attack a human being only when it is cornered，则强调意味顿失。模仿例句如：

One will not offend his superior unless he is cornered.

一个人除非被逼到绝路，否则是决不会顶撞上司的。

5. ...puma fur was found clinging to bushes.

译文：灌木丛中发现了粘在上面的美洲狮毛。

解析：本句的重点在于英汉互译过程中主、被动语态的灵活应用。英文的被动式常常作汉语的主动式处理，反之亦然。这也是英语科技文体的一大特色。例：

English is spoken in various parts of the world. 世界很多地方说英语。

6. The experts were now fully convinced that the animal was a puma.

译文：专家们如今已经完全肯定那只动物就是美洲狮。

解析：原文没有采用be sure、believe 等常规词，主要是由于这些词主观性较强，而be convinced 则注重客观，更符合原文推理紧凑、逻辑缜密的特点。试比较：

I believe he can fulfill the mission.（我的主观想像）

I'm convinced he can fulfill the mission.（客观事实使然）

我相信他能完成这项任务。

拓 展 篇

Ⅰ.英语趣园

The London Zoo is Britain's best-known zoo. It's a national zoo, and one of the most famous and prestigious collections in the world. It is the primary home of the Zoological Society of London which was founded in 1826. It occupies thirty-six acres of a Royal Park, less than two miles from the center of the city of London.

Ⅱ.听力快车

Englishman, 25 years old, about 8 _____ tall, average build, walks with a slight _____, pale appearance, red brown hair, almost invisible small _____, speaks through the nose, cannot pronounce the letter "s", cannot speak _____, has last been seen in a brown suit of clothes. Reward — £25.00 _____.

III. 补充阅读

Focus on the appositive clause while reading the passage.

The declaration of independence

By Thomas Jefferson

We hold these truths to be self-evident, that all men are created equal, that they are endowed by their Creator with certain unalienable Rights, that among these are Life, Liberty and the pursuit of Happiness. That to secure these rights, Governments are instituted among Men, deriving their just Powers from the consent of the governed — that whenever any Form of Government becomes destructive of these ends, it is the Right of the People to alter or to abolish it, and to institute new Government, laying its foundation on such principles and organizing its powers in such form, as to them shall seem most likely to effect their Safety and Happiness. Prudence, indeed, will dictate that Governments long established should not be changed for light and transient causes; and accordingly all experience hath shewn, that mankind are more disposed to suffer, while evils are sufferable, than to right themselves by abolishing the forms to which they are accustomed. But when a long train of abuses and usurpations, pursuing invariably the same Object evinces a design to reduce them under absolute Despotism, it is their right, it is their duty, to throw off such Government, and to provide new guards for their future security — Such has been the patient sufferance of these Colonies; and such is now the necessity which constrains them to alter their former Systems of Government.The history of the present King of Great Britain is a history of repeated injuries and usurpations, all having in direct object the establishment of an absolute Tyranny over these States. To prove this, let facts be submitted to a candid world.

He has refused his Assent to Laws, the most wholesome and necessary for the public good.

He has forbidden his Governors to pass Laws of immediate and pressing importance, unless suspended in their operation till his Assent should be obtained; and when so suspended, he has utterly neglected to attend to them.

He has refused to pass other Laws for the accommodation of large districts of people, unless those people would relinquish the right of Representation in the Legislature, a right inestimable to them and formidable to tyrants only...

◆▶ 测 试 篇 ◀■

I. 单项选择

1. Both parties promised to _____ the contract to be signed the following day. (CET-6 98/6)

   A. keep with B. tangle with C. adhere to D. devote to

2. Mark often attempts to escape _____ whenever he breaks traffic regulations. (CET-4 95/6)

   A. having been fined B. to have been fined C. being fined D. to be find

3. At the party we found that shy girl _____ her mother all the time.

   A. depending on B. coinciding with C. adhering to D. clinging to

4. The pursuit of leisure on the part of the employees will certainly not _____ their prospect of promotion.

   A. spur B. further C. induce D. reinforce

5. _____ energy under the earth must be released in one form or another, for example, an earthquake.

   A. Accumulated　　B. Gathered　　C. Assembled　　D. Collected

6. The second book was _____ by August 1952, but two years later, the end was still nowhere in sight.

   (CET-6 95/6)

   A. completed　　B. to have completed　C. to complete　　D. to have been completed

7. Many people believe we are heading for environmental disaster _____ we radically change the way we live.

   A. but　　B. although　　C. unless　　D. lest

8. A: May I have the loan?

   B: _____ you offer good security.

   A. Provided　　B. Unless　　C. Although　　D. Even if

9. My purse was found _____.

   A. missing　　B. missed　　C. losing　　D. lost

10. Scientists have reached the conclusion _____ the temperature on the earth is getting higher and higher.

    A. when　　B. but　　C. that　　D. for that

Ⅱ. 翻译

11. 飞碟是一种明亮得像碟子一样的物体，常在天空被看到。(be found in)

12. 当消息传到国家博物馆，在西安市以南45公里处发现一座古墓，立刻受到有关方面的重视。(when news came into)

13. 当我一想到一只大型猫科动物在逃遁，我不由得不寒而栗。(when the idea came to me that..)

14. 消息传到演播室，全国90%以上的人正在收看春节联欢晚会。(news came into...)

15. 无论这个花花公子走到哪里，他身后都留下了一串破碎的心。(wherever he went...)

答案

拓展篇

　　Englishman, 25 years old, about 8 inches tall, average build, walks with a slight stoop, pale appearance, red brown hair, almost invisible small moustache, speaks through the nose, cannot pronounce the letter "s", cannot speak Dutch, has last been seen in a brown suit of clothes. Reward— £25.00 dead or alive.

测试篇

1-5 CCDBA　　　　　6-10 DCAAC

11. UFOs are bright, saucer-like objects, which can be found in the sky.

12. When news came into National Museum that an ancient tomb had been spotted 45km south of Xi'an, it was taken seriously.

13. When the idea came to me that a wild cat was still at large, I was disturbed.

14. News came into the studio that over 90% of the population were watching Spring Festival Entertainment Show.

15. Wherever he went, the playboy left behind him a trail of broken hearts.

Lesson 2 Thirteen equals one

积累篇

Ⅰ. 振振有"词"

1. Our vicar is always raising money for one cause or another.

raise funds for... 为…筹集资金
raise the wind for... 为…筹集款项
make a collection for... 为…筹集款项
pass the hat around 募捐
donate...to... 向…捐赠
contribute...to... 向…捐助
patronize sb./sth. 赞助某人/某事

连缀使用的短语：
one... or another 这样那样的…
one...the other 这个…那个（两者）
some...others 一些…另一些
this...or that 这个…那个（两者）
either...or... 或是…或是
neither...nor... 既不…也不…

2. In the torchlight, he caught sight of a figure whom he immediately recognized as Bill Wilkins, our local grocer.

英文中与光线搭配的介词用in:
in the torchlight 借着电筒光
in the sunlight 阳光下
in the moonlight 月光下
in the candlelight 烛光下
in the spotlight 聚光灯下；引人注目
in the twilight 晨光下

表"看"的词组：
catch sight of... 看到
catch a glimpse of... （偶然）瞥见
catch a glance of... （迅速）扫视
take a peek at... 扫视
take a squint at... 看一看
take a peep at... 偷偷看

recognize A as B 把A认成B
regard A as B 把A当作B
refer to A as B 把A作为B
imagine A to be B 把A想像成B
think of A as B 把A想像成B
mistaken A for B 把A错当作B

3. One night, however, our vicar woke up with a start.

vicar（英国国教）教区牧师　　　with a start 吃惊
clergyman（英国国教）牧师　　　in surprise 惊奇
priest（基督教）牧师　　　to one's surprise 惊奇
missionary 传教士　　　with astonishment（*fml.*）吃惊
bishop 主教　　　be astonished at...（*fml.*）对…吃惊
pope 教皇　　　be astounded at...（*fml.* 语气强）对…震惊
be amazed at...（文雅）对…惊奇

4. Thirteen is not as good as one.

as good as...和…一样好，该词组意义广泛，不可一概而论。例：

as good as gold（小孩）乖巧　　　as good as a play 非常有趣
as good as one's word 信守承诺　　　We are as good as ruined.
as good as dead 行尸走肉　　　我们几乎破产了。

Ⅱ.现身说"法"：现在完成进行时

I've been coming up here night after night for weeks now.（彩色部分运用了现在完成进行时）我好几星期每晚都要到钟楼上来。

1）构成模式：sb. have/has been doing sth.
2）基本用法：表示动作从过去某时开始一直延续到现在或距现在不远的时间。其动作是否延续下去，则依上下文而定。该时态多用于延续动词，如：stay、wait、study、learn、live、stand等。例：
She is ill. She's been lying in bed for several weeks. 她病了。已卧床几周了。（动作会继续下去）
What have you been doing all this time? 你一直在干什么？（动作可能继续下去）
I've been reading all the afternoon. 整个下午我都在看书。（动作不再继续下去）
I've been working on this abstruse problem ever since last year.
自从去年以来，我一直在钻研这个深奥的问题。
3）该时态中所表示的动作并非一直不停地进行，也可表断断续续地重复。书中例句即是此用法。例：You've been saying that for years. 这话你已经说了多年了。

Ⅲ.说"文"解"字"

1. Our vicar is always raising money for one cause or another, but he has never managed to get enough money to have the church clock repaired.
译文：我们教区的牧师总是为各种各样的事筹集资金，但始终未能筹足资金把教堂的钟修好。
解析：1）该句子运用了一个经典句型：sb. is always doing sth., but...（某人总在做某事，却……），含蓄表达了说话者不满和抱怨的口吻。例：

Many people are always complaining, but they seldom do anything practical.

许多人总在抱怨，但很少有人做点实际的事情。

2）句中的have sth. done也是常用结构，意即：（让某人）去做某事。试比较：

have sb. do sth.（让某人做某事）　　　　　make sb. do sth.（让某人做某事）

get sb. to do sth.（让某人做某事）　　　　　get sth. done（自己完成某事）

2. The clock was striking the hours!

译文：那钟正在报时！

解析：请注意彩色字体的英文与汉语的差异。strike用法之灵变可见一斑。下面是关于该词的其他非常规用法：

1）strike oil 大发横财

2）strike home 被理解，领悟；例：

At first he didn't recognize the name, but then it suddenly struck home.

起先他想不起这个名字你是谁，但后来突然记起来了。

3）strike the flag 认输

His financial situation is growing more precarious, but he will not strike the flag.

他的经济状况江河日下，但他并不想认输。

4）strike the right note 说到点子上；做事恰到好处

3. But the clock struck thirteen times before it stopped.

译文：但是钟敲了13下才停。

解析：请注意before一词的灵活运用，不要一成不变地译作"在…之前"。例：

I'll come back before you know it. 我很快就回来。

It was not long before he told us about it. 他很快就告诉了我们这件事。

Duty comes before pleasure. 先尽义务，再谈享受。

Pride goes before a fall. 骄兵必败。

▌ 拓 展 篇

Ⅰ.英语趣园

The Archbishop of Canterbury is the Primate of All England, that is to say, he is the spiritual leader of the Church of England. After him, the Archbishop of York is called the Primate of England and under these two archbishops come a number of bishops. England is divided into 42 districts called dioceses, each with a bishop in charge and a cathedral as the central church. A diocese is divided into smaller districts called parishes. These vary in size, a large town having a number of parishes and a village being a single parish. Each parish is in the care of a priest, who is called either a vicar or a rector. A vicar with a large parish may have an assistant priest called a curate to help him.

Ⅱ.听力快车 🎧

The House of Lords consists of about _____ members, most of whom（about _____）are hereditary peers of the realm. In addition, there are about 325 non-hereditary peers: the 2 _____ of Canterbury and of York, with the 24 _____ of the Church of England; 10 Lords of Appeal and 9 retired Lords of Appeal, appointed for life, to help in the judicial functions of the House of Lords; and about _____ life peers and peeresses, created under the Life Peerages Act 1958.

Ⅲ.补充阅读

How the British worship

The Church of England (or the Anglican Church) is the "national" church in England, established by law. In spite of this, it runs its own affairs and does not receive any money from the state since it owns stocks and shares and a great deal of land and other properties.

Many people would say that the Church of England today is both Protestant and Catholic; there is certainly a great variety of beliefs and practices within the Church. A look at some church notice-broads might confuse anyone unfamiliar with the difference between high church and low church. A look inside the churches would probably add to the confusion. A visitor entering a high church at, say, ten o'clock on a Sunday morning might find a high (sung) mass in progress and think he had entered a Roman Catholic Church (the name Anglo-Catholic is sometimes used for this kind of church). The church would probably be highly decorated, the priests would be wearing various kinds of robes, people would light candles to the Virgin Mary and go to the priests for confession. By contrast, a low church service would be as simple as possible; there would be no ceremony, no candles, no private confessions and the church would look rather bare. It would seem to have more in common with the nonconformist churches. Between these two extremes there are churches with more or less ceremony, depending mainly on the views of the vicar in charge. Some Anglican priests have broken away from tradition to the extent that in some services they introduce new religious songs, composed by young people who accompany them on guitars in the church. They also use the church as a place where people can discuss the problems of everyday life; in other words, these priests want the church to become a meeting place in a wider sense, not simply for the more traditional type of religious service.

◼▷ **测 试 篇** ◁◼

Ⅰ.单项选择

1. A completely new situation will _____ when the exam system comes into existence. （CET-4 95/6）

   A. rise   B. arise   C. raise   D. arouse

2. Many difficulties have _____ as a result of the change over to a new type of fuel. （CET-4 93/6）

   A. risen   B. arisen   C. raised   D. aroused

3. By law, when one makes a large purchase, he should have _____ opportunity to change his mind.

   （CET-4 00/6）

   A. accurate   B. urgent   C. excessive   D. adequate

4. A budget of five dollars a day is totally _____ for a trip round Europe. （CET-6 99/1）

   A. inadequate   B. incapable   C. incompatible   D. invalid

5. I was about to _____ a match when I remembered Tom's warning. （CET-4 03/6）

   A. rub   B. hit   C. scrape   D. strike

6. _____ the danger from enemy action, people had to cope with a severe shortage of food, clothing, fuel, and almost everything. (CET-4 03/6)

    A. As far as   B. As long as   C. As well as   D. As soon as

7. A man escaped from the prison last night. It was a long time _____ the guards discovered what had happened. (CET-4 93/6)

    A. before   B. until   C. since   D. when

8. Scientists say it may be five or ten years _____ it is possible to test this medicine on human patients. (CET-4 95/6)

    A. since   B. when   C. after   D. before

9. _____ it or not, his discovery has created a stir in the scientific circles. (CET-4 97/1)

    A. Believe   B. To believe   C. Believing   D. Believed

10. The project _____ by the end of 2000 will expand the city's telephone network to cover 1,000,000 users. (CET-4 99/6)

    A. accomplished   B. being accomplished

    C. to be accomplished   D. having been accomplished

Ⅱ. 翻译

11. 她总是自私自利。（look after No.1）

12. 我从网上下载了一些好听的音乐。（have sth. done）

13. 听到枪声，Joe看到两只鸟儿飞走了。（doing...,）

14. 只有当你把一个单词重复到7遍的时候，你才能把它记住。（before）

15. 读书除了需要用眼睛以外，还要用脑。（as well as）

 答 案

拓展篇

    The House of Lords consists of about <u>1160</u> members, most of whom（about <u>840</u>）are hereditary peers of the realm. In addition, there are about 325 non-hereditary peers: the 2 <u>Archbishops</u> of Canterbury and of York, with the 24 <u>senior bishops</u> of the Church of England; 10 Lords of Appeal and 9 retired Lords of Appeal, appointed for life, to help in the judicial functions of the House of Lords; and about <u>280</u> life peers and peeresses, created under the Life Peerages Act 1958.

测试篇

1-5 BBDAD   6-10 CADAC

11. She is always looking after No.1.

12. I have some wonderful music downloaded.

13. Hearing the shooting, two birds were seen flying away by Joe.

14. You have to repeat a word 7 times before you can memorize it.

15. Read with mind as well as with eyes.

Lesson ③. An unknown godess

积累篇

I.振振有"词"

1. Some time ago, an interesting discovery was made by archaeologists.

> make an interesting discovery of...发现了有趣的…
> 该词组将动词discover名词化，前加make，是写作中常用的句型扩展手段。其他类似用法：
> make a close study of...对…做仔细研究（将动词study名词化）
> make a detailed analysis of...对…做详尽分析（将动词analyze名词化）
> make a comprehensive summary of... 对…做详细总结（将summarize名词化）
> make an exhaustive investigation of... 对…做深入调查（将investigate名词化）

> archaeologist 考古学家
> architect 建筑学家
> naturalist 博物学家
> zoologist 动物学家
> botanist 植物学家
> agronomist 农业学家
> ornithologist 鸟类学家
> entomologist 昆虫学家
> ecologist 生态学家

2. An American team explored a temple which stands in an ancient city on the promontory of Ayia Irini.

> explore 探索
> investigate 调查
> probe into 调查
>
> inquire into 探询
> reconnoitre 侦察
> scrutinize 仔细查看

> stand 矗立（常指较高物体）
> lie 位于（常指海拔较低的物体，如河流）
> be situated in...坐落于

> be located in...坐落于
> be sited in...坐落于（多指人为因素）

> ancient 古老的
> primitive 原始的
> pristine 太古代的
>
> prehistoric 史前的
> unprecedented 史无前例的

3. The city at one time must have been <u>prosperous</u>, for it enjoyed a high level of <u>civilization</u>.

prosper (*v.*) 繁荣
prosperity (*n.*) 繁荣
例：promote economic prosperity 促进经济繁荣
prosperous 繁荣的
thriving 兴旺的
flourishing 昌盛的
affluent 富足的

civil 公民的
例：civil rights 公民权
civil engineering 土木工程
civilize 使文明
例：Education civilizes man. 教育使人文明。
civilian 平民
civility 礼貌，谦恭
civilization 文明

Ⅱ. 现身说"法"：情态动词表猜测语气

The city at one time must have been **very prosperous...** （彩色部分可概述为情态动词 must＋动词完成式，表示对过去情况的推测。）这座古城肯定一度很繁荣……

英语的情态动词中，可表推测的包括：may/might, can/could 和 must，其中 could 比 can，might 比 may 更显委婉。形式表现为：may/might+动词原形、can/could+动词原形，must+动词原形（这些均表示对现在情形的推测，其语气从 may 到 must 逐渐增强）；或：may/might+动词完成式，can/could+动词完成式，must+动词完成式（这些均表示对过去情形的推测，其语气从 may 到 must 逐渐增强）。例：

What he says may/might be true. 他的话或许是对的。

A situation like this can/could occur from time to time. 这种情况可能会时时发生。

The mistake must lie with him. 这一定是他的错。

He seems very indolent this morning. He may/might have stayed up last night.

今早他显得很懒散，可能昨晚熬夜了。

Ⅲ. 说"文"解"字"

1. ..., an interesting discovery was made by archaeologists on the Aegean Island of Kea.

译文：……在爱琴海的基亚岛上，考古工作者有了一项有趣的发现。

解析：请注意英汉互译时运用的不同句式：英语说明文被动式居多，而汉语多译为主动式。原因在于英文表达总将信息重点前置，而汉语则将其后置。

2. ... it enjoyed a high level of civilization.

译文：……它曾享有高度的文明。

解析：1）若 enjoy 以人作主语，则是"喜欢，享受"之意。若以非生命物体为主语，则作"拥有"讲，可看作 have 的替换表达。例：

China enjoys a long and glorious history of over 5,000 years.

中国拥有 5,000 多年悠久灿烂的历史。

2）boast 与 enjoy 用法相近。以人作主语，表"夸耀，吹嘘"，以非生命物体作主语时等同于 enjoy。例：

The university boasts a team of well-trained teachers.

这所大学拥有一支训练有素的教师队伍。

3. The temple which the archaeologists explored was used as a place of worship from the fifteenth century B.C. until Roman times.

译文：考古学家考察的这座庙宇从公元前15世纪直至罗马时代一直是祭祀祈祷的场所。

解析：这个句子还可衍生出下面的形式：

The temple which the archaeologists has not been used as a place of worship since Roman times.

考古学家考察的这座庙宇从罗马时代以来就不再作为祭祀祈祷的场所了。

这种根据原文推导深层含义的形式在各类考试中都会涉及，望多加注意。

4. Its missing head happened to be among remains of the fifth century B.C.

译文：而她那身首异处的脑袋却恰巧是在公元前5世纪的废墟里找到的。

解析：sb. happen to do sth.表示"某人碰巧做某事"，而sth. happen to sb.则表示"某人遇到某事"。例：

He happened to meet an old friend of his. 他碰巧遇到了一个老友。试比较：

Robbery has never happened to him. 他从未遇到抢劫的事。

Robbery has never occurred to him. 他从未想过抢劫的事。

5. ..., they were amazed to find that the goddess turned out to be a very modern-looking woman.

译文：他们惊奇地发现那位女神原来是一位相貌摩登的女郎。

解析：1) turn out to be与prove（to be）同义，表示"原来是，结果是"，但前者中的to be不可省，而后者中的to be可省。其反义表达为seem（to be），appear（to be）（似乎是，看起来是）。例：

He seems to be very generous, but turns out to be quite stingy. 他看似大方，实则非常吝啬。

2) modern-looking是复合形容词，意为"相貌摩登的"。此类构造的表达还有：

good-looking 相貌英俊的   plain-looking 相貌平平的

earthy-looking 相貌土气的   interesting-looking 相貌丑陋的委婉表达

6. ... she was wearing a full-length skirt which swept the ground...

译文：……她身穿一条拖地长裙……

解析：1) be wearing看似动态，实则表状态。类似表达有：be dressed in, be clad in。

2) 表动态"穿戴"的表达有：put on, dress oneself in, don。

▌ 拓 展 篇

Ⅰ. 英语趣园

Anthropologists study people and primates（such as chimps），researching their cultural, physical, and social development over time. Archaeologists investigate history by finding and studying the remains and objects a society leaves behind.

Ⅱ. 听力快车 🎧

When the gods were assembled, the goddess of Discord appeared in their midst and threw down a _____, on which were written the words, "For the _____." This apple was at once claimed by Juno (the goddess of women and marriage), by Minerva (the goddess of wisdom), and by Venus (the goddess of beauty), for each of these goddesses believed herself to be the most fair. But at last they agreed Paris should be asked to decide their _____. Each in turn offered him a precious gift if only he would award the apple to her. Juno offered him _____; Minerva _____; but Venus the world's most lovely woman as his _____. He finally awarded the apple to Venus, which caused the terrible Trojan War.

III. 补充阅读

A stolen Buddha head finds its way back home

from *N.Y. Times*

For 1,300 years the Akshobhya Buddha, one of four large statues of Buddha at the Four Gate Pagoda in China's Shandong Province, sat solemnly looking eastward, face locked in a beatific expression.

In 1997, the Buddha lost its head. A gang of thieves, staging the second of two robbery attempts, swaddled the head in blankets and cut its throat with a diamond saw. Next, wielding a sledgehammer, they literally knocked it off its torso.

The thieves were caught soon afterward and the ringleader was sentenced to life in prison, but the trail of the 159-pound head itself went cold. The Four Gate Pagoda, built in 611 during the Sui dynasty as part of the Shentong Monastery, was closed to the public as the Chinese government dealt with this embarrassing blow to its efforts to protect a site that had long been a top priority for historic preservation.

That might have been the end of yet another dispiriting tale of cultural vandalism, a plague that has struck China just as it has many other countries. But then, in February the Buddha head turned up in Taiwan, as a gift from loyal disciples to the Buddhist master Sheng-Yen, the 73-year-old founder of the Dharma Drum Mountain Buddhist Association, based in Taiwan, and also of the Chan Meditation Center in Elmhurst, Queens.

Alarmed by the gash in the Buddha's neck, Master Sheng-yen started an investigation. "If there is a head, there must be a torso," was his first thought, as he later described it.

He summoned Lin Bao Yao, a scholar at the Taipei National University of Arts, who studied the piece and traced it to Shandong province in eastern China, and to the Sui dynasty, a precursor to the illustrious Tang dynasty. Experts from Shandong Province were able to confirm that this was the Akshobhya Buddha from the Four Gate Pagoda.

Apparently, the discovery was something of a shock for inhabitants of the region, who were never told back in 1997 that one of their Buddhas was missing its head.

The scholarly police work was a stroke of luck for the Akshobhya Buddha, whose name in Sanskrit means "imperturbable." For Master Sheng-yen, whose worldwide movement of a reported one million disciples is dedicated to the protection of the spiritual environment, it was, as he said later, like "winning the lottery."

"I was so happy," said master Sheng-yen, who was born in China but since 1978 has lived mostly in New York and has opened a retreat in Pine Bush, upstate. "If it had not been presented to us as a gift, maybe it would have been another 200 years before it went back to its place of origins."

On Dec.17, in a ceremony the Akshobhya Buddha was solemnly returned to its torso — this time affixed to the shoulders by a steel rod, in part to prevent future thefts. The event was frontpage news on both sides of the Taiwan Strait.

▶ 测 试 篇 ◀

Ⅰ.单项选择

1. They are trying to _____ the waste discharged by the factory for profit. （CET-4 04/1）
   A. expose   B. exhaust   C. exhibit   D. exploit

2. The police are trying to find out the _____ of the woman killed in the traffic accident. （CET-4 03/1）
   A. evidence   B. recognition   C. status   D. identity

3. We'd like to _____ a table for five for dinner this evening. （CET-4 02/6）
   A. preserve   B. reserve   C. retain   D. sustain

4. Many people like white color, as it is a _____ of purity. （CET-4 02/6）
   A. symbol   B. sign   C. signal   D. symptom

5. In my opinion, he's _____ the most imaginative of all the contemporary poets. （CET-4 02/6）
   A. in all   B. at best   C. for all   D. by far

6. By the time you get to New York, I _____ for London. （CET-4 02/1）
   A. would be leaving   B. am leaving   C. have already left   D. shall have left

7. By the time he arrives in Beijing, we _____ here for two days. （CET-4 01/6）
   A. have been staying   B. have stayed   C. shall stay   D. will have stayed

8. If the building project _____ by the end of this month is delayed, the construction company will be fined. （CET-4 01/6）
   A. to be completed   B. is completed   C. being completed   D. completed

9. He came back late, _____ which time all the guests had already left. （CET-4 99/6）
   A. after   B. by   C. at   D. during

10. My train arrives in New York at 8 o'clock tonight. The plane I would like to take from there _____ by ten. （CET-4 99/1）
    A. would leave   B. will have left   C. has left   D. had left

Ⅱ.翻译

11. 香港享有高度的自治权。（enjoy a high level of）
12. 新东方的第二教区就在附近，周围就是便利的公共汽车和轻轨设施。（with）
13. 自由女神像象征着自由与民主。（to be a symbol of）
14. 中国古代的铜钱，外圆内方，象征着天圆地方。（represent）
15. 既当爹又当娘的日子，比他想的要难得多。（turn out to be）

答 案

拓展篇

　　When the gods were assembled, the goddess of Discord appeared in their midst and threw down a golden apple, on which were written the words, "For the fairest." This apple was at once claimed by Juno (the goddess of women and marriage), by Minerva (the goddess of wisdom), and by Venus (the goddess of beauty), for each of these goddesses believed herself to be the most fair. But at last they agreed Paris should be asked to decide their rival claims. Each in turn offered him a precious gift if only he would award the apple to her. Juno offered him power; Minerva wisdom; but Venus the world's most lovely woman as his bride. He finally awarded the apple to Venus, which caused the terrible Trojan War.

测试篇

1-5 DDBAD　　　　6-10 DDABB

11. Hong Kong enjoys a high level of autonomy.

12. The second area of New Oriental School is just near here with convenient bus stop and easy light rail access.

13. The Statue of Liberty is a symbol of democracy and liberty.

14. The round bronze coin of ancient China with a square hole in the center represents the belief that heaven was round and the earth was square.

15. To be both a father and mother turned out to be more difficult than he had thought.

Lesson The double life of Alfred Bloggs

积 累 篇

I.振振有"词"

1. <u>These days</u>, people who do <u>manual</u> work often receive far more money than people who work in offices.

用于描述一般或普遍状况的常用时间状语表达形式：	manual 体力的	形似或音似词辨析：
these days 如今	physical 体力的	menu 菜单
nowadays 目前	corporeal 身体的	manure 粪肥
presently 时下	mental 脑力的	mature 成熟的
currently 当今	spiritual 精神的	manor 庄园
for the time being 眼下	intellectual 智力的	mantle 覆盖

2. **People who work in offices** <u>are frequently referred to as "white-collar workers"</u>:

white-collar workers 白领工人	pink-collars 粉领人士（尤指工作高雅的
blue-collar workers 蓝领工人	女士，如模特、空姐等）
golden-collars 金领人士	gray-collars 灰领人士（尤指服务行业）

可用于描述、解释或下定义的常用表达形式：

refer to A as B 把A称做B

regard A as B 把A看做B

call A B　　　 把A叫做B

name A B　　　把A命名为B

3. Such is human nature that **a great many men** are often willing to sacrifice higher pay for the privilege of becoming white-collar workers.

用于描述人性特点的句型:

Such is human nature that a lot of people want to follow others for feeling safe.

许多人都想追随他人以获得安全感,这是人之本性。

Such is human nature that many people always crave what they don't have.

许多人总是渴望自己没有的东西,这是人之本性。

be willing to do 乐于做…	sacrifice A for B 为B舍弃A
be glad to do 高兴做…	sacrifice A to do B 舍弃A去做B
be voluntary to do 愿意做…	do B at the price of A 以A为代价做B
be ready to do 愿意做…	do B at the cost of A 以A为代价做B
be prepared to do 愿意做…	do B at the expense of A 以A为代价做B

4. When he got married, **Alf** was too embarrassed to say anything to his wife.

get/be married to sb. 与…结婚(表状态)	形似词辨析:
marry sb. 嫁给/迎娶…(表动作)	embarrassed 尴尬的
marry above oneself 与比自己地位高者结婚	embarrassment 尴尬之事
marry beneath oneself 与比自己地位低者结婚	embezzlement 贪污
The father married his daughter. 父亲将女儿嫁出去了。	embellishment 装饰品
The Father married them. 神父为他们证婚。	embattlement 战斗
	ambassador 大使

II. 现身说"法":主谓一致

For the simple reason that they usually wear a collar and tie **to go to work.**
就是因为他们通常穿着硬领衬衫、系着领带去上班。

彩色部分如果用作主语,谓语动词应用单数,因为该词组只在首个名词前加冠词a,将其作为一个整体看待。但若在第二个名词也加a,则变成了两个概念,谓语动词要用复数:

A collar and tie is important to men. 衬衫和领带对于男士很重要。

A collar and a tie were found in the car. 在车里找到了一件衬衫和一条领带。

类似的例子:

A knife and fork is essential in western food culture. 西方文化中刀叉的地位很重要。

A knife and a fork are available for the game. 游戏过程中可以用一把刀和一把叉。

A clerk and secretary is needed in the company. 公司需要一名书记员兼秘书。

A clerk and a secretary are needed in the company. 公司需要一名书记员和一名秘书。

The owner and editor of the newspaper is to attend the conference. (CET-4 02/6)

这家报纸的创办者兼编辑将要出席会议。

The owner and the editor of the newspaper are to attend the conference.

这家报纸的创办者和编辑将要出席会议。

Ⅲ.说"文"解"字"

1. **These days, people who do manual work often** receive far more money **than people who work in offices.**

   译文：如今，从事体力劳动的人比坐办公室的人收入高出许多。

   解析：1）receive more money是常用短语，意为"赚钱"，receive也可替换为earn、make。far用于比较级前表程度，为程度副词。其他类似词汇有：much、still、even、slightly、any、a lot、a little、a bit、a good deal等。例：

   He is much older than last year. 他比去年老多了。

   This winter is slightly warmer. 今年冬天稍微暖和点。

   2）该句是一个典型的模仿句型，用于描述两种人物的对比。例：

   These days, people who work in filmdom often receive far more money than ordinary people. 如今，影视界的人比普通人收入高出许多。

2. **This can give rise to curious situations,** as it did in the case **of Alfred Bloggs who worked as a dustman for the Ellesmere Corporation.**

   译文：而这常会引起种种奇怪的现象，在埃尔斯米尔公司当清洁工的艾尔弗雷德·布洛格斯就是一个例子。

   解析：该句的难点是指代词it和did的准确含义。it指代上一句中that从句的内容，而did替代give rise to curious situations. 此外，注意in the case of 和in case of 之间的区别：前者意为"就…而论"，而后者意为"以防，万一"。

3. **He will be earning only** as much as he used to.

   译文：他将来挣的钱只有现在的一半。

   解析：as much as是一个常见的表同级比较的短语，意为"与…一样多"。表比较的常用公式有：

   1）twice + 名词：是…的两倍；比…大一倍。

   He is twice my age. 他的年龄比我大一倍。

   2）n times + as...as：是…的n倍。

   The earth is 49 times as large as the moon. 地球的大小是月球的49倍。

   3）n times +比较级+than：是…的n倍。

   The earth is 48 times larger than the moon. 地球的大小是月球的49倍。

   4）n times + 名词：是…的n倍。

   The earth is 49 times the size of the moon. 地球的大小是月球的49倍。

拓 展 篇

Ⅰ.英语趣园

White usually means something good. A white-collar job, for example, is the kind of job many people seek. It is a job where you work at a desk using your brain instead of your muscles. You wear a shirt with a white collar, as opposed to the manual laborer or factory worker who wears overalls. White-collar workers might commit "white-collar crimes", especially fraud.

II. 听力快车 🎧

_____

_____

_____

_____

III. 补充阅读

The red, yellow and white roads

On reading the title, you may feel quite puzzled. "What does it mean?" You may ask. To be frank with you, when a friend used this phrase, I also didn't know what to make of it until she explained to me.

"The red, yellow, and white roads" is a popular phrase among senior students in Chinese colleges. In their last year in college, students begin to consider their future jobs. It is time for them to decide whether they will be officials, businessmen, or intellectuals. These choices, by and large, are generalized as the "red", "yellow", and "white" roads.

The red road is considered to be the most promising one. Red in China is the color connected with communism. The one who chooses to follow this road will, first of all, join the Communist Party. A diploma and a Party card will make it much easier for him to be promoted, than one without the two documents, first as section chief, and then as head of a department. Gradually he will climb up the social ladder. The red road seems to provide a good chance for one to achieve his political goal.

The second path is the yellow road. Yellow may remind us of gold. To be wealthy is the goal. Positions in joint ventures are the most desirable for people who have chosen this road. Though they may have to work hard, they get good pay. Aside from that, those graduates who know foreign languages may have more opportunities to go abroad than people working elsewhere. On the whole, this is a profitable road.

Lastly comes the white road. The color is not so delightful as the first two. People who choose this road will work very hard to become graduate students, and to be successful in the world of knowledge. It is an arduous road without many concrete and immediate benefits. Just like the color itself, the road is very clean and pure.

The three roads reflect some characteristics of our society and show, in a way, what young people are thinking and dreaming of. It is good to know that young people are very practical now. But it is also rather disappointing to find that knowledge which is vital to our modernization is placed last. People are so obsessed by power and money that knowledge is devalued.

▶▶ 测 试 篇 ◀◀

I. 单项选择

1. The authors of the United States constitution attempted to establish an effective national government while preserving _____ for the states and liberty for individuals. （考研01）

   A. autonomy   B. dignity   C. monopoly   D. stability

2. As your instructor advised, you ought to spend your time on something _____ researching into. (考研94)

    A. precious   B. worth   C. worthy   D. worthwhile

3. In the meantime, the question facing business is whether such research is _____ the cost.   （考研97）

    A. worth   B. worth of   C. worthy   D. worthwhile

4. What a lovely party! It's worth _____ all my life.   （CET-4 02/6）

    A. remembering   B. to remember   C. to be remembered   D. being remembered

5. The ship's generator broke down, and the pumps had to be operated _____ instead of mechanically.

    （CET-4 02/1）

    A. manually   B. artificially   C. automatically   D. synthetically

6. The owner and editor of the newspaper _____ the conference.   （CET-4 02/6）

    A were attending   B. were to attend   C. is to attend   D. are to attend

7. The boy spent as much time watching TV as he _____ studying.   （CET-4 02/1）

    A. does   B. had   C. was   D. did

8. Don't let the child play with scissors _____ he cuts himself.   （CET-4 03/6）

    A. in case   B. so that   C. now that   D. only if

9. —Are you on holiday? —No, but I'd love _____.

    A. to   B. to do   C. to be   D. to go on holiday

10. I left for the office earlier than usual this morning _____ traffic jam.   （CET-6 91/6）

    A. in line with   B. for the sake of   C. in case of   D. at the risk of

Ⅱ. 翻译

11. 乔丹被大家叫做"飞人"乔丹。（be referred to as）

12. 这个人年龄太大不适合做她的丈夫。（too... to）

13. 此乃人之本性，那就是我们都喜欢不花钱白捞。（such is human nature...）

14. 众所周知，地球的体积是月球体积的49倍。（49 times as large as...）

15. 你最好给你的文件做个备份，以防电脑死机。（in case of...）

 答 案

拓展篇

    "White" is not so delightful in Chinese as it is in English. People who choose the white road will work very hard so as to become graduate students, and to be successful in the world of knowledge. It is an arduous road without many concrete and immediate benefits. Just like the color itself, the road is very clean and pure.

测试篇

1-5 ABAAA   6-10 CDACC

11. Jordan is referred to as Air Jordan.

12. He is too old to be her husband.

13. Such is human nature that we all love to get something for nothing.

14. It's well known to all that the volume of the earth is 49 times as large as the moon's.

15. You'd better back up your files in case of a crash.

Lesson 5. The facts

积累篇

I. 振振有"词"

1. Editors of newspapers and magazines often go to extremes to provide their readers with unimportant facts and statistics.

statistics（单）统计学	economics（单）经济学
statistics（复）数字	economics（复）经济情况
politics（单）政治学	logistics（单）物流学
politics（复）政治活动	logistics（复）物流状况

statistics 统计数字
database 数据库
digit（0到9任何一个）数字
number（任何）数字
volume 流量

digital camera 数码相机
digital TV 数码电视
digital transmission 数码传输
digitalization 数字化

描述不同做事方式的常用句型：
go to extremes to do...走极端做某事
take a lot of risks doing...冒险做某事
be reckless to do...不计后果做某事
take great pains to do...费力做某事
have great difficulty（in）doing sth. 做某事很困难

go to extremes 走极端
Extremes meet. 物极必反。
never overdo or undo 做事适度
the golden doctrine of "half and half" 中庸之道
keep neutral 保持中立

2. The article began: "Hundreds of steps lead to the high wall which surrounds the president's palace."

用于介绍文章、信件内容的常用句型：
The article/letter begins:
The article/letter goes:
The article/letter says:
The article/ letter reads:
The article/letter writes:
The article/letter is as follows:
The article/letter goes like this:

描述"数百、数千、数万…"等的固定表达式：
hundreds of...数百…
thousands of...数千…
tens of thousands of...数万…
hundreds of thousands of...数十万…
millions of...数百万…
tens of millions of...数千万…
hundreds of millions of...数亿…
billions of...数十亿…

3. ... but he <u>took a long time to</u> send them.

> 花时间做事的常用句型：
> sb. take some time to do...
> It takes sb. some time to do...
> sb. spend some time (in) doing...
> sb. spend some time on sth.

Ⅱ. 现身说"法"：倒装

> Not only had the poor man been arrested, but he had been sent to prison as well.（该句使用了倒装结构）那个可怜的记者不仅被捕了，而且还被送进了监牢。

倒装结构分为两种：完全倒装和部分倒装。前者指谓语结构完全移到主语之前；后者指部分谓语移到主语之前，而剩余部分仍在主语之后。

1) 完全倒装的形式主要有以下几种：

① 表时间或方位的状语放在句首，如now、then、away、down、up、out、in等。

Away went my chance of winning! 我失去了取胜的机会！

② 地点副词here、there 置于句首，若主语为代词，则使用正常语序。

Here comes the train. 火车来了。

Here he comes. 他过来了。

③ There be 句型的倒装，there之后还可接appear、stand、exist、remain、seem等动词。

There is a hotel in the vicinity. 附近有家宾馆。

There seems (to be) something about it. 事情好像不大对头。

2) 部分倒装的形式主要有以下几种：

① 具有否定意义的词或词组置于句首，如not、not only、never、seldom、hardly、no sooner、little等。

Little did I see of her recently. 最近我很少见到她。

② only+状语/状语从句位于句首。

Only in this way can you solve this problem. 只有用这种方法你才能解决这个难题。

③ so+形容词/副词/名词词组置于句首。

So clumsy was the man that he always could not solve any problem independently.

·他很笨拙，经常无法独自解决问题。

④ If引导的虚拟语气从句中，若有had、were、should这样的功能词，可将其置于句首，省略if。

Were he alive today, he would be pleased to see the changes.

如果他今天仍健在，看到这些变化会开心的。

Ⅲ. 说"文"解"字"

1. When the article arrived, the editor read the first sentence and then refused to publish it.

译文：稿件寄来后，编辑看了第一句话就拒绝予以发表。

解析：1) arrive在本句中是拟人用法，这是英文的惯常思维，以使语言生动形象。熟练掌握这种技巧有助于提升写作能力。例：

The milk arrived at the doorstep. 牛奶送到了门口台阶上。

2）refuse to do sth. 意为"拒绝做…"，属于暗含性的否定表达，在写作中常可替代直接否定短语，即 do not want to do sth. 其他例子如下：

fail to do sth. 替代 do not do sth.

deny doing sth. 替代 do not admit doing sth.

object to doing sth. 替代 do not agree to do sth.

2. **Meanwhile, the editor was** getting impatient, **for the magazine would soon** go to press.

译文：在此期间，编辑越来越不耐烦，因为杂志马上要付印。

解析：1）getting 在此表示"越来越…"，含有"逐步、渐进"之意。去掉该词，则意义有所不同。例：

He was getting impatient. 他越来越不耐烦。（动态）

He was impatient. 他很不耐烦。（静态）

2）go to press 意为"付印"，go to the press 则是"参加记者招待会"。一般而言，如果某个词组有不加the和加the两种结构，则前者表示该词组的引申义，后者表示表层义。试比较：

go to school 上学（引申义），go to the school 去学校（表层义）

go to church 作礼拜（引申义），go to the church 去教堂（表层义）

go to hospital 住院（引申义），go to the hospital 去医院（表层义）

go to prison 住监牢（引申义），go to the school 探监（表层义）

3. **...he had been arrested** while counting **the 1,084 steps** leading to the fifteen-foot wall which surrounded the president's palace.

译文：就在他数通向15英尺高的总统府围墙的1,084级台阶时，被抓了起来。

解析：while引导时间状语从句，其后省略了he was. 这是常用的省略模式。其方法是：如果从句的主语和主句的主语相同，且从句中有be动词，则从句的主语和be可省略，该法则适用于时间状语词while、when、as、once，条件状语词if、unless, 让步状语词though、however、whether 等。例：

Though（he was）late, he slipped into the classroom. 尽管迟到了，他还是溜进了教室。

Unless（you are）working hard, you can not win. 除非努力，否则你不会成功的。

拓 展 篇

I . 英语趣园

Pulitzer Prizes

Pulitzer Prizes are series of 21 awards for outstanding achievements in drama, letters, music, and journalism. They were established by the will of Joseph Pulitzer, publisher of the **New York World**. They have been awarded annually since 1917 by Columbia University on recommendation of the Pulitzer Prize Board. A newspaper photography award was made for the first time in 1942, and an award for a musical composition for the first time in 1943. Between 1970 and 1979, prizes for commentary, criticism, and feature writing were added. The value of the prizes for journalism and the arts is $3,000（originally $500）; for public service deserving praise, a gold medal is awarded instead.

Ⅱ. 听力快车

Magazines provide a wide variety of _____ . For example, they may _____ current events and fashions, _____ foreign affairs, or _____ how to repair appliances or prepare food. Subjects addressed in magazines _____ business, culture, hobbies, medicine, religion, science, and sports. Some magazines seek simply to _____ their readers with fiction, poetry, photography, cartoons, or articles about TV shows or motion-picture stars. Thousands of magazines are _____ in the United States and Canada.

Ⅲ. 补充阅读

There is an essential difference between a news story, as understood by a newspaperman or a wire-service writer, and the newsmagazine story. The chief purpose of the conventional news story is to tell what happened. It starts with the most important information and continues into increasingly inconsequential details, not only because the reader may not read beyond the first paragraph but because an editor working on galley proofs a few minutes before press time likes to be able to cut freely from the end of the story. A news magazine is very different. It is written to be read consecutively from beginning to end, and each of its stories is designed, following the critical theories of Edgar Allen Poe, to create an emotional effect. The news, what happened that week, may be told in the beginning, the middle, or the end; for the purpose is not to throw information at the reader but to seduce him into reading the whole story, and into accepting the dramatic（and often political）point being made.

▶ 测 试 篇 ◀

Ⅰ. 单项选择

1. A word processor is much better than a typewriter in that it enables you to enter and _____ your text more easily.　　　　　　　　　　　　　　　　　　　　　　　　　　　　　　　（CET-4 05/6）

   A. register　　　　B. edit　　　　　　C. propose　　　　D. discharge

2. The president promised to keep all the board members _____ of how the negotiations were going on.

   　　　　　　　　　　　　　　　　　　　　　　　　　　　　　　　　　　（CET-4 01/6）

   A. informed　　　　B. inform　　　　C. be informed　　　D. informing

3. The design of this auditorium shows a great deal of _____ .We have never seen such a building before.

   　　　　　　　　　　　　　　　　　　　　　　　　　　　　　　　　　　（CET-6 03/6）

   A. invention　　　　B. illusion　　　　C. originality　　　D. orientation

4. On that day we set out early _____ the beautiful sandy beach after a hasty breakfast.

   A. on　　　　　　　B. round　　　　　C. for　　　　　　D. at

5. I don't allow _____ in my drawing room. I don't allow my family _____ at all.

   A. to smoke...smoking　　　　　　　B. to smoke... to smoke

   C. smoking... to smoke　　　　　　　D. smoking... smoking

6. Not only _____ , but I help him.

   A. he helps me　　　B. does he help me　　C. he does help me　　D. he help me

7. "Not until science became prominent _____ abolished." Some people argue. （CET-6 89/6）

    A. did slavery come to   B. slavery to

    C. had slavery come to   D. that slavery come to

8. While _____ he joined in voluntary labor on a project.

    A. being there   B. there   C. be there   D. was there

9. Don't smack when _____ .

    A. be eating   B. eating   C. to eat   D. is eating

10. Unless _____ he wouldn't do it.

    A. be urged   B. to be urged   C. urged   D. is urged

Ⅱ. 翻译

11. 网上聊天，总的来说，只要不过分，就没什么不好。（carry sth. to extremes...）

12. 教师不仅是知识的传授者，而且要为人师表。（not only...but...as well）

13. 条条大路通罗马。（lead to...）

14. 在回家的路上，他被抢了。（while on the way home...）

15. 地球在自转的同时还围绕着太阳转动。（surround...）

  案

拓展篇

    Magazines provide a wide variety of <u>information, opinion, and entertainment</u>. For example, they may <u>cover</u> current events and fashions, <u>discuss</u> foreign affairs, or <u>describe</u> how to repair appliances or prepare food. Subjects addressed in magazines <u>include</u> business, culture, hobbies, medicine, religion, science, and sports. Some magazines seek simply to <u>entertain</u> their readers with fiction, poetry, photography, cartoons, or articles about TV shows or motion-picture stars. Thousands of magazines are <u>published</u> in the United States and Canada.

测试篇

1-5 BACCC   6-10 BAABC

11. Chatting on line, on the whole, is no harmful if it's not carried to extremes.

12. The teacher is not only a knowledge transmitter, but a model to follow as well.

13. Every road leads to Rome.

14. While on way home, he was robbed.

15. The earth rotates while it surrounds the sun.

Lesson **6.** **Smash-and-grab**

积 累 篇

Ⅰ.振振有"词"

1. The <u>expensive shops</u> in a famous <u>arcade</u> near Piccadilly were just opening.

关于shop的不同表达：
an expensive shop 高档商店
a secondhand shop 二手店
a luxury shop 奢侈品店
a five-and-dime shop 小杂货店
an antique shop 古董店

arcade 拱形门廊（arc: 弧 ; ade: shade）
arc lamp 弧光灯
archway 拱道；牌楼
Arctic 北极
Arch of Triumph 凯旋门

2. It <u>came to a stop</u> outside <u>the jeweller's</u>.

动词变为动词词组是写作中常用的扩展手段：
stop→come to a stop
end→come to an end
succeed→come to a success
fail→come to a failure

某种从业者转化为其工作场所的变通公式：从业者→从业者's
jeweller（珠宝商）→jeweller's（珠宝店）
baker（面包师）→baker's（面包房）
barber（理发师）→barber's（理发店）
chemist（药剂师）→chemist's（药店）
butcher（屠夫）→butcher's（肉店）

3. The men <u>scrambled</u> back into the car and it <u>moved off</u> at a fantastic speed.

形似词辨析：
scramble 逃窜   humble 谦卑的
crumble 弄碎   ramble 漫步
grumble 埋怨   tumble 跌倒
                  stumble 结巴

与off搭配的常用短语：   see off sb. 送别
move off 走开   fight off tears 强忍泪水
take off sth. 脱掉   laugh off an embarrassment
turn off sth. 关掉   对尴尬一笑了之

Ⅱ. 现身说"法"：独立主格

> ...a large car, with its headlights on and its horn blaring, roared down the arcade.（彩色部分是with引导的独立主格结构。）一辆大轿车亮着前灯，鸣着喇叭，呼啸着冲进了拱廊街。

独立主格结构不是主谓完整的简单句，而只是一个短语，其一般公式为：名词/名词短语/代词＋不定式/-ing分词/-ed分词/形容词/副词/介词短语，在名词前也可加with。例：

He said that he had had his own love,（with）his eyes misting.
他说自己已经有了心上人，这时他的眼睛湿润了。

He lay in the bed,（with）his teeth set, his hands clenched, his eyes looking straight up.
他躺在床上，咬着牙，握着拳，眼睛盯着前方。

Ⅲ. 说"文"解"字"

1. Mr. Taylor, the owner of a jewellery shop was admiring a new window display.

译文：泰勒——一家珠宝店的老板，正在欣赏着新布置的橱窗。

解析：1）admire本指"仰慕"，宾语一般为人。这里活用作"欣赏"。例：

Whenever traveling by train, he likes to admire the view of the countryside through the train window. 只要乘火车旅行，他总喜欢透过车窗观赏乡村的风景。

> 联想记忆：
> feast one's eyes on...大饱眼福　　　　　　　　feast one's ears on...大饱耳福

2）window display意为"橱窗展"。

> 联想记忆：
> on display 在展出　　　　　　　　　　window shopping 只看不买
> shop around 四处转转

2. One of the thieves was struck by a heavy statue, but he was too busy helping himself to diamonds to notice any pain.

译文：一个窃贼被一尊很重的雕像击中，但由于他忙着抢钻石首饰，竟连疼痛都顾不上了。

解析：1）help oneself to sth. 意为"自便"。例：

She helped herself to my food without my permission. 她没问我就吃起我的东西。
be busy doing sth.: 忙于做…

2）类似用法：be busy with sth., busy oneself doing sth., be occupied with, be swamped with sth. 例：

She was too busy helping herself to the delicious food to notice that a thief helped himself to her handbag. 她只顾吃美食，没注意窃贼正在偷她的手包。

I'm now swamped with marking examination papers. 我现在忙着评阅试卷。

拓 展 篇

I.英语趣园

The French philosopher, Jean Jacques Rousseau, once described a "bluestocking" as a woman who will remain unmarried as long as there are sensible men on this earth, for a bluestocking is a woman who is more interested in learning and an academic career than in marriage and bringing up children. The word was coined in 18th century London. Groups of men and women met in the evening to discuss books and culture. They decided to replace evening of empty, meaningless talk with intelligent discussion. The members of the group dressed very simply, to show their dislike for the fancy evening clothes of the time.

II.听力快车

True or False Questions.

1. The three men are discussing their plan for a bank robbery.
2. The three robbers don't think dustbin day is a good day for their robbery.
3. They plan to take away 15,000 pounds.
4. If two of them wear motor-cycle helmets, the bank clerks would be suspicious.
5. If Jim goes back and pretends to wake up with everyone else in the bank, people will think he is the thief.
6. One of them will wait in a dustcart in front of the bank.
7. They plan to take away the money together with rubbish.

III.补充阅读

Burglaries

The figures for burglaries have risen alarmingly over the last few years and are now quite appalling.

A house is burgled in Britain now about every two minutes, and over the past three years the number of burglaries reported to the police has risen by approximately 50,000 to well over 400,000 this year. The insurance companies report that last year alone household burglary losses rose by 27 percent over the previous year to £138.2 million, and I believe one or two insurance companies are refusing to provide burglary coverage in what we might call high-risk areas.

There are, nevertheless, half a dozen measures which can be taken against burglaries, which I will briefly outline for you. It really only requires some basic common sense and a small outlay, combined with a little knowledge of the way a burglar thinks and operates. You have to put yourself in his position, really. Most burglars are opportunists looking for an easy break-in, so don't make things simple for them. Don't advertise the fact you're out or away, or be careless about security. Even if you're just popping out for a quarter of an hour, don't leave doors and windows open or unlocked. A burglary can take less than ten minutes.

This time element leads me to my second main point, where a house is hard to get into and will take a long time to do so because you've fitted good locks and bolts on your exterior doors and windows or even burglary alarms, the chances are that the burglar will move on to somewhere easier. There are plenty of these, I can assure you. Milk bottles left on the doorstep, papers by the front door, garage doors wide open, curtains drawn in the daytime or un-drawn at night are all indications. For comparatively little you can buy a programmed time-switch that'll turn on and off a light at appropriate times.

Not all burglaries happen while you are out, of course. You should always be wary of callers at the door who say, for example, that they've come to read the gas meter; always check their credentials, and if in doubt don't let them in. It's also a good idea to keep a record of serial numbers on electrical equipment, radios, TVs and so on, or even to take photographs of valuable jewellery, antiques or pictures.

Any further tips I may not have mentioned can always be obtained from your local police station, where you should ask to speak to the Crime Prevention Officer.

In the final analysis when it comes to fitting security systems and the like you've really got to strike a balance between the cost of what you spend on installing the system and the value of the property you're trying to protect.

▶ 测 试 篇 ◀

Ⅰ.单项选择

1. The _____ of airplane engines announced a coming air raid.　　　　　（CET-4 03/6）
   A. roar　　　　　B. exclamation　　　　C. whistle　　　　D. scream
2. The neighborhood boys like to play basketball on that _____ lot.　　　（CET-4 02/6）
   A. valid　　　　　B. vain　　　　　C. vacant　　　　D. vague
3. They have decided to _____ physical punishment in all local schools.　　（CET-6 02/6）
   A. put away　　　B. break away from　　C. do away with　　D. pass away
4. Being somewhat shortsighted, she had the habit of _____ at people.　　（CET-6 97/1）
   A. glancing　　　B. peering　　　　C. gazing　　　　D. scanning
5. The apartment will fall _____ next week.
   A. empty　　　　B. blank　　　　　C. hollow　　　　D. vacant
6. _____ a man who expresses himself effectively is sure to succeed more rapidly than a man whose command of a language is poor.　　　　　　　　　（CET-4 97/6）
   A. Other things being equal　　　　　B. Were other things equal
   C. To be equal to other things　　　　D. Other things to be equal
7. All flight _____ because of the terrible weather, they had to go there by train.　　（CET-4 02/1）
   A. having been canceled　　　　　　B. had been canceled
   C. having canceled　　　　　　　　D. were canceled
8. All the tasks _____ ahead of time, they decided to go on holiday for a week.　　（CET-4 01/6）
   A. had been fulfilled　B. were fulfilled　　C. having been fulfilled　　D. been fulfilled
9. All things _____, the planned trip will have to be called off.
   A. considered　　B. be considered　　C. considering　　　　D. having considered
10. So many directors _____, the board meeting had to be put off.　　　（CET-4 01/1）
    A. were absent　　B. been absent　　　C. had been absent　　　D. being absent

Ⅱ.翻译

11. 我看见一个男士，大衣没系扣子，松松地垂下来。（...with overcoat....）
12. 她真是个美人儿，金黄的头发，烫了波浪卷儿，玉指尖尖，涂了红色，粉面如桃，双目炯炯。

（...hair, ...nails, ..., face..., eyes...）

13. 没人能逃脱法律的制裁。（get away with）

14. 晚上，有人破门而入，偷走了些值钱的东西。（help themselves to...）

15. 我无事可做，于是便四处闲逛。（wander）

拓展篇

1. T 2. F 3. F 4. T 5. F 6. F 7. T

Dustbin day robbery

Gentleman Jim has worked out a plan to rob a bank. He's telling his gang, Fingers Jones and Ginger Robertson about the plan.

Fingers: Let's see. You're going to walk up the counter and you're going to start writing a cheque. Then you're going to open the canister of nerve gas, and everyone will go to sleep instantly.

Jim: That's right. This gas will put anyone to sleep for exactly three minutes.

Fingers: And while everyone is asleep, you're going to go round to the manager's desk and steal all the money?

Jim: Exactly. I've worked it out very carefully. There should be about ￡50,000 in used bank notes.

Ginger: Sounds great. There's only one thing. If you open the gas, you'll go to sleep too, won't you?

Jim: I have thought of that. I'll wear a motorcycle helmet, with an oxygen mask inside. If I wear a helmet, no one will be able to recognize me afterwards, either.

Ginger: I think it's risky. If the bank clerk sees you take out a gas canister, he won't wait. He'll push the alarm button straight away.

Fingers: I've just had an idea. If I came into the bank when you were standing at the counter, no one would even look at me. Then, if I threw the can of nerve gas, they wouldn't guess that we were connected.

Ginger: Yes, that might be better. Are you going to wear a helmet, too?

Fingers: No. It would look very suspicious if two people were wearing motorcycle helmets. I'll just open the door, throw in the gas canister, and leave Gentleman Jim to rob the bank.

Jim: I like that idea. Right, we'll do that. Any other problems that you can see?

Ginger: What are you going to do with the money? If you walk out with ￡50,000 under your arm, somebody will surely notice you.

Jim: You'll be sitting in a get-away car, waiting for me outside the bank.

Ginger: But there is a police station just fifty yards away. If I park a car outside the bank, the police would probably come and ask me to move.

Fingers: Well, what do you suggest? He can't just walk around the town. He'll be carrying ￡50,000 in bundles of bank notes.

Jim: Just a minute! I've thought of something. What day is this robbery?

Fingers: Monday.

Jim: Monday! You know what happens on Monday, don't you? It's dustbin day!

Ginger: So?

Jim: So, can you think of a better way of moving the money? If you saw a man pick up ￡50,000 and put it into a car, what would you think?

Fingers: I'd think he was a thief.

Jim: Exactly. But if you saw a man pick up a dustbin and put it into a lorry, what would you think?

Fingers: I'd think he was a dustman. Hey! That's clever!

Ginger: And if the £50,000 was in the dustbin, I could pick up the money and nobody would notice. That's brilliant.

Fingers: Is there a dustbin?

Jim: Oh yes, several. They put the dustbins out every Monday. They'll be standing there, outside the bank.

Fingers: But if you put the money in a dustbin, it'll stink. We'll never be able to spend it if it smells like that.

Jim: We don't have to put it in a dustbin. We can put it in a black plastic bag. They often have black plastic bags for rubbish nowadays. If I carry one in my pocket, I can pull it out after you've thrown the gas. OK? Let's run through the plan once more.

Ginger: You go into the bank with a motor-cycle helmet on, and a black rubbish bag in your pocket.

Fingers: I come in a few minutes later. I open the door, throw in the open gas canister, and then go... where?

Jim: I've hired a room in the building right opposite the bank. Go up in the lift to the top floor and keep a look out. When you get there, radio Ginger, and tell him to come.

Ginger: In the meantime, everyone in the bank has gone to sleep, except you. You take the money, and put it in the plastic bag.

Jim: I come out, and put the bag with the rubbish, and then go back into the bank.

Ginger: Go back?

Jim: Oh yes. If everyone woke up and I wasn't there, they'd know I was one of the thieves. No, I'll go back and pretend to wake up with everyone else.

Fingers: That's a really clever touch.

Ginger: I drive a dustcart and wait in the cul-de-sac behind the bank until Fingers contacts me. Then I come and pick up the rubbish, including the £50,000.

Jim: I can't think of any problems, can you?

测试篇

1-5 ACCCD　　　　6-10 AACAD

11. I saw a man with an unbuttoned overcoat hanging loose about him.

12. She is a knockout, hair golden and waved, nails red and pointed, face pink, eyes flashing.

13. Nobody can get away with law.

14. Some people broke in during the night and helped themselves to something valuable.

15. With little work to do, I wandered around.

Lesson **7.** Mutilated ladies

积累篇

I. 振振有"词"

1. When you <u>rescued</u> your trousers, did you find that the <u>note</u> was whiter than white?

> rescue 营救（人）
> salvage 抢救（货物、财产）
> redeem 赎救（人）
> release 释放（人）
> emancipate 解放（人）
> liberate 解放（人、地方）

> note 纸钞（又称bank note）
> coin 硬币
> cash 现金
> currency 货币
> fund 资金
> capital 资本
> asset 资产

2. The Bank of England has a team called Mutilated Ladies which <u>deals with</u> claims from people who <u>fed their money to a machine</u> or their dog.

> feed sth. to sb. 喂某人…
> feed sb. on sth. 喂某人…
> feed on sth. 以…为食
> feed one's face 吃饭
> well-fed, well-bred 吃得饱，有礼貌

> deal with sth. （一般）处理
> cope with sth. （成功）处理
> handle sth. （巧妙）处理
> tackle sth. （艰难）处理，治理
> attend to sth. 照看

3. A recent case <u>concerns</u> Jane Butlin whose <u>fiancé</u>, John runs a successful furniture <u>business</u>.

> concern 与…有关，牵涉到
> be concerned with...与…有关
> be concerned about...关注，关心
> cause great concern 引起极大关注
> to whom it may concern （信函封面）致有关人士
> concerning 关于

> business（可数）公司，商店
> business（不可数）商业，业务
> spirit 精神；spirits 情绪
> snow 雪；snows 雪地
> confidence 信心
> confidenccs 秘密

> fiancé 未婚夫   wife-to-be 准妻子
> fianceé 未婚妻   husband 丈夫
> bridegroom 新郎   bestman 伴郎
> bride 新娘   bridesmaid 伴娘

33

Ⅱ. 现身说"法"：条件从句

> **So long as** there is something to identify, we will give people their money back.
> 只要以后东西可识别，我们就会把钱还给人们。

1) so long as（或as long as）在这里引导条件状语从句，表示相对宽松的语气。例：

So long as you can prove you are right, you can stick to it.

只要你能证明自己是对的，就可以坚持。

As long as you can make yourself understood in English, don't be afraid to make mistakes.

只要别人能懂得你的英语，就不要怕犯错。

2) provided/providing 也可引导条件状语从句，但含义和if有所不同：前者表示的条件是说话者希望出现的结果，而后者则无此限制。例：

Provided your offer is satisfactory, we'll sign the contract with your company.

如果出价合理，我们将和贵公司签订合同。（可用if替代）

We shall cancel the contract if you fail to comply with the provisions.

如果贵方违反条款，我们将取消合同。（if 不可用provided/providing替代）

联想记忆：一些特殊的条件表达法

1. 祈使句+and...= if 从句＋主句。例：

   Give it a try and you will know whether it is feasible.

   If you give it a try, you will know whether it is feasible.

   尝试一下，你才会知道是否可行。

   A few more things of this and I will give up.

   If there are a few more things of this, I will give up.

   这种事再多点，我就要放弃了。

2. 祈使句＋or/or else= unless 从句＋主句。例：

   Get round to it or you will lose the golden opportunity.

   Unless you get round to it, you will lose the golden opportunity.

   抓紧点时间，否则你会错过这个难得的机会的。

Ⅲ. 说"文"解"字"

1. Has it ever happened to you? Have you ever put your trousers in the washing machine...?

   译文：你遇见过这样的情形吗？你有没有把裤子塞进洗衣机……？

   解析：英文文章有时以问句作篇首句，借此唤起读者的注意力。因此，我们在创作英文篇章的过程中，也可尝试此法。例：

   Why does a shortage of natural resources befall our planet?

   为何我们的星球会面临自然资源短缺的局面？

   Why, you may wonder, spiders should be our friends?（《新概念英语》4册2课）

   你或许想知道，为何蜘蛛会是我们的朋友？

2. Dogs, it seems, love to chew up money!

译文：狗似乎很喜欢咀嚼钱币！

解析：该句在文中的地位不甚重要，之所以添加的原因是西方文化对于狗的情有独钟。因此，英文中对狗的溢美之词俯拾皆是。仅举几例权作资证：

help a dog over a stile 助人于危难之时　　　　die dog for sb. 为某人效犬马之劳

work like a dog 拼命工作　　　　　　　　　　a big dog 大人物

Every dog has its day. 凡人皆有得意时。

3. Imagine their dismay when they found a beautifully-cooked wallet and notes turned to ash !

译文：可以想像他们发现一只煮得好看的钱包、钞票已化成灰烬时的沮丧心情。

解析：彩色部分是一个复合形容词，在文中起幽默效应。这是英文中惯常使用的方法，即在危急环境中努力表现幽默色彩，起烘托气氛、化解紧张的作用，被称为guillotine humour（断头台式幽默）。

此外，该句也可作为典型句式加以模仿：

Imagine her dismay when she found all her efforts were in vain.

可以想像她发现自己的心血化为泡影时的沮丧心情。

Imagine his exultation when he received an offer from Harvard.

可以想像他收到哈佛录取通知的狂喜之情。

拓 展 篇

Ⅰ. 英语趣园

What is the British monetary system?

British currency is the pound sterling. The pound（£）is made up of 100 pence（p）. The most common coins in circulation are of 1p, 2p, 5p, 10p, 20p, 50p and £1 and £2. Notes are issued in denominations of £5, £10, £20 and £50, and £100 in Scotland and Northern Ireland.

Historical figures on current banknotes

£5 - Elizabeth Fry —The images on the back of the note are related to the life and work of this social reformer. The main illustration shows Elizabeth Fry reading to prisoners at Newgate. In recognition of her work she was awarded the key to the prison and this is used in the design of the banknote.

£10 - Charles Darwin—As a young man Darwin was employed as the naturalist on board the ship HMS Beagle, an illustration of which is depicted on the back of the note. Also pictured is an illustration of Darwin 's own magnifying lens and the flora and fauna that he may have come across on his travels.

Ⅱ. 听力快车

_____, paper money and bank notes spread widely. The bulk of the money in use came to consist not of actual gold or silver but of fiduciary money —_____. _____or as the transferable book entries that came to be called deposits. From fiduciary paper money promising to pay gold or silver,_____—that is, notes that are issued on the "fiat" of the sovereign, are specified to be so many dollars or francs or yen.

III. 补充阅读

The earliest coins in China

Of the various currencies used in ancient China, the round bronze coin with a square hole in the center was by far the most common. The earliest coins in this form, known as Qin ban liang, were a product of China's first centralized kingdom, the Qin dynasty, established by Qin Shi Huang in 221 B. C. Before the Qin dynasty, Chinese currency had taken many forms. Coins shaped like various items of clothing, farm implements, or knives were in circulation, but they were costly and hard to produce, and difficult to carry and transport. The new coins were a great improvement—they were relatively simple to cast and could be strung together for ease of transportation. The new coins also had a particular philosophical significance to the ancient Chinese, who made the coins to symbolize their belief that heaven was round and the earth was square, and that heaven sheltered the earth and all things in the universe were united. This concept of unity was important to the Qin emperors, who ruled over a unified China and believed their power great enough to spread to the four corners of the earth.

The coins also had great aesthetic appeal. They were thought to represent the relationship between man and nature. Commonly found in nature, the circle represents freedom, comfort, and ease; whereas the square is seen as something man-made, a symbol of law, order, and restraint.

All these factors combined to keep the coins in circulation for more than 2,000 years, only in the twentieth century did they cease to be legal tender.

▶ 测 试 篇 ◀

I. 单项选择

1. All their tempts to _____ the child from the burning building were in vain. （CET-4 04/1）
   A. regain   B. recover   C. rescue   D. reserve

2. Researchers at the University of Illinois have determined that the _____ of a father can help improve a child's grades. （CET-4 03/9）
   A. involvement   B. interaction   C. association   D. communication

3. I had just posted the letter when I remembered that I hadn't _____ the cheque. （CET-4 03/9）
   A. imposed   B. involved   C. enclosed   D. contained

4. The lawyer advised him to drop the _____, since he stands little chance to win. （CET-4 02/1）
   A. event   B. incident   C. case   D. affair

5. The story that follows _____ two famous characters of the Rocky Mountain gold rush days.
   A. concerns   B. states   C. proclaims   D. relates

6. Once they had fame, fortune, secure futures; _____ is utter poverty. （CET-6 91/6）
   A. now that all is that   B. now all that is left
   C. now all which is left   D. now all what is left

7. As it turned out to be a small house party, we _____ so formally. （考研98）
   A. needn't dress up   B. did not need have dressed up
   C. did not need dress up   D. needn't have dressed up.

8. Talk to anyone in the drug industry, _____ you'll soon discover that the science of genetics is the biggest thing to hit drug research since penicillin was discovered. （考研 00）

   A. or　　　　　　　　B. and　　　　　　　C. for　　　　　　　D so

9. _____ he works hard, I don't mind when he finishes the experiment. （CET-4 98/1）

   A. As soon as　　　B. As well as　　　C. So far as　　　D. So long as

10. A wallet has been found and can be _____ at the manager's office.

   A. claimed　　　B. proclaimed　　　C. reclaimed　　　D. acclaimed

Ⅱ. 翻译

11. 办公软件将人们从繁复的工作中解脱出来，从而节省了大量时间。（rescue...from）

12. 永远不要对自己绝望。（despair of...）

13. 老百姓喜欢把钱放在银行里以妥善保管。（...for safekeeping）

14. 只要一牵扯到英语，我就擀面杖吹火——一窍不通。（when... is concerned....）

15. ——你谈过恋爱吗？

   ——我还小，谈恋爱的事儿甚至还没想过（too... to...）。

拓展篇

　　In the late 18th and early 19th century, paper money and bank notes spread widely. The bulk of the money in use came to consist not of actual gold or silver but of fiduciary money—promises to pay specified amounts of gold and silver. These promises were initially issued by individuals or companies as bank notes or as the transferable book entries that came to be called deposits. From fiduciary paper money promising to pay gold or silver, it is a short step to fiat paper money—that is, notes that are issued on the "fiat" of the sovereign, are specified to be so many dollars or francs or yen.

测试篇

1-5 CACCA　　　　　6-10 BDBDA

11. Office software rescue people from tedious work to save a lot of time.

12. Never despair of yourself!

13. Ordinary citizens would like to put money in the bank for safekeeping.

14. When English is concerned, I'm like a babe in the woods.

15. ——Has love ever happened to you?

　　——No, it hasn't. It has never occurred to me even, for I'm too young to think about it.

Lesson 8. A famous monastery

积 累 篇

I.振振有"词"

1. But each year, the dogs <u>are still sent out</u> into the snow whenever <u>a traveler</u> is <u>in difficulty</u>.

send out sb. to do 派遣某人做…
dispatch sb. to do 派遣某人做…
expatriate sb. 遣送某人（回国）
convey sth. 传递（信息，等）
hand out sth. 分发…

traveler 游客
tourist 游客
sight-seer 观光者
excursionist 出游者
holiday-maker 度假者
hiker 远足者

in+名词表某种生活状态：
live in happiness 生活幸福
live in luxury 生活奢华
live in debt 债务累累
live in misery 生活悲惨

2. There are still a few people who <u>rashly</u> <u>attempt to cross</u> the Pass <u>on foot</u>.

-ash结尾的词具有"猛烈碰撞"之意：
smash 摔碎   crash 撞击
mash 捣碎   clash 冲突
splash 泼溅

attempt to do 试图做…
endeavor to do 尽力做…
strive to do 努力做…
do one's utmost to do 竭尽全力做…
spare no efforts to do 不遗余力做…

出行方式表达法：
on foot 步行
by sea/ship 乘船
by air/plane 乘飞机
by land 走陆路

3. For they <u>are allowed to</u> <u>wander</u> outside the enclosure.

请注意："得到许可做某事"不可说：get allowance to
do, 因为allowance表"津贴"之意。可用以下短语表示：
get permission to do
get the license to do
get the green light to do
get the nod to do

roam 漫游
ramble 流浪
stroll 溜达
saunter 闲逛

squander 漂泊
mill around 来回打转
hang around 四处游荡

Ⅱ. 现身说"法"：让步状语从句

But each year, the dogs are still sent out into the snow whenever a traveler is in difficulty. （whenever在该句中引导让步状语从句）
但每年还要派狗到雪地里去帮助遇到困难的旅行者。

一般而言，以-ever结尾的几个词whenever, wherever, whatever, whichever, however引导让步状语从句时可用no matter+when, where, what, which, how 替换。

★★★ 注 意 ★★★

whatever, whoever, whichever既可作关系副词引导让步状语从句，也可作关系代词引导定语从句。前者中whatever可替换为no matter what，而后者中what则可替换为anything that，依此类推，whoever=no matter who或whoever=anyone who; whichever=no matter which 或 anything that。例：

I like whatever you give me. （定语从句，whatever=anything that）我喜欢你给的任何东西。

Whatever happens, do not surrender. （状语从句，whatever=no mater what）

无论发生什么，决不要屈服。

Whoever feeds him will be his master. （定语从句，whoever=anyone who）受人恩惠，听人使唤。

Whoever has done it, we all must learn a lesson from it. （状语从句，whoever=no matter who）

无论是何人所为，我们都要以此为戒。

Ⅲ. 说"文"解"字"

1. At 2,473 metres, it is the highest mountain pass in Europe.

译文：它海拔2,473米，是欧洲最高的山口。

解析：at+...metres 是固定短语，意为"海拔…米"。实际上，这是一种省略模式，完整形式为：at+...metres above sea level. 表示"海拔"还可用the altitude of...is...。例：

The altitude of the mountain is 1,000 metres. 那座山海拔1,000米。

此外，表方位的还有以下短语：

The region is at around 400 latitude North. 该地区大致位于北纬40度。

The region is at around 400 longitude East. 该地区大致位于东经40度。

2. The temperature drops to -30°...

译文：气温下降到零下30度……

解析：to在本句中表程度，与by意义不同，后者表幅度。例：

The temperature rises to 20°. 气温升到了20度。

The temperature rises by 20°. 气温上升了20度。

-30° 读作30 below zero 或 minus 30 或 30 minus.

联想记忆

1. 数字的表达：分数词以基数词和序数词组成，其中基数词表分子，序数词表分母，分子若大于1，分母必须用复数。例：

$\frac{1}{6}$ one-sixth $\frac{4}{9}$ four-ninths $10\frac{4}{7}$ ten and four-sevenths

2. 读小数时，数字只用基数词：

13.47 thirteen point forty seven   0.39 zero thirty nine

3. The monks prefer winter to summer **for they have more privacy.**

译文：僧侣们喜欢冬天胜过夏天，因为在冬天，他们享有更多的清净时光。

解析：prefer A to B 表示"宁要A不要B"。例：

He prefer classical novels to pop ones. 他喜欢古典小说胜过流行小说。

上面的表达式还可扩展为：

1）prefer doing A to doing B 宁愿做A不做B。例：

The young girl preferred staying in her hometown to going to the big city.

那年轻女孩宁可呆在家乡也不愿去大城市。

2）prefer to do A rather than do B 宁愿做A不做B. 例：

He preferred to fail in the course than beg that abominable teacher.

他宁肯不及格，也不愿去恳求那个令人反感的老师。

3）would rather do A than do B 宁愿做A不做B. 例：

He would rather die than disgrace himself. 他宁死不受辱。

拓展篇

Ⅰ.英语趣园

According to the New Testament, Jesus, who was betrayed by Judas, was crucified on the cross but returned to life 3 days after. So Easter celebrates the resurrection of Jesus Christ, which falls sometime between Mar 22 and Apr 25, the 1st Sunday after the 1st full moon. The best-known Easter symbol is an egg; for all living creatures, life begins in the egg.

Ⅱ.听力快车

Westminster Abbey (used to be the church in the _____), a very large _____ in Westminster, London, was first built on the 11th _____. Almost all_____ since William the Conqueror have been crowned in the Abbey and many famous people are buried there.

Ⅲ.补充阅读

Around 1050 AD, Saint Bernard founded a monastery high in the Swiss Alps, with the Saint Bernard Pass in the valley below. The pass was a popular route for travelers and pilgrims as well as many traders. These traders were the first to bring dogs to the Saint Bernard Monastery, doing to until 1125. For the next four hundred years the pass was largely abandoned and few travelers passed the monastery. No new dogs entered the Saint Bernard Monastery, and it was during this time that the Saint Bernard breed arose.

C. Keller, a scientist, first bred the Saint Bernard from the Roman "Molossian" dog. The Molossian is said to have came from the Tibetan Mastiff. The first Saint Bernards were kept at the monastery as guard dogs. The first written account of a Saint Bernard, however, was not made until

1703 by Prior Balalu. In his writing, he spoke of the cook inventing an exercise wheel for the dog to run on, which in turn would turn the cooking spit. The Saint Bernard Pass had become popular again by then, and the dogs helped feed the 20,000 travelers that passed through each year. There are other mentionings of the Saint Bernards in later passages, including a dog that was lost in a blizzard and a bill for the repair of a dog collar.

All writings about the dogs mention their large size. Dogs then were relatively smaller than they are today, so the Saint Bernards of the past were probably much smaller. The coloration of their coats has always been stated as white with red-brown patches. Dogs of this coloration are very common in Switzerland, hence the saying "there is more of something than red dogs."

The monks soon began using the Saint Bernards to rescue people trapped in the cold Alpine wilderness. The shaggy dense coat of the Saint Bernard protects it from the cold and allows it to spend large amounts of time in severe conditions. The Saint Bernards also have a keen instinct for predicting bad weather, like snowstorms and avalanches, which was very useful to the monks.

The first mention of the Saint Bernards being used in rescuing does not appear in writing until 1750, although it likely began before then. The dogs first began working with the mountain guides who led people across the Saint Bernard Pass. The dogs had an incredible sense of direction during the heavy snows and helped guide travelers to the safety of the monastery. It was not until later that excursions of the dogs alone are mentioned. The infamous barrel attached to the collar of the legendary Saint Bernard is only a legend; barrels filled with alcoholic beverages were an invention of storytellers.

Saint Bernards are divided into two categories, both of notable size. The short hair variety has a thinner smooth coat and is also known by the name of Stockcar. The other variety is the long hair, the most common of the two. Both divisions of Saint Bernards have thick muscular bodies and are generally sturdy hardy animals. Saint Bernards have very large heads and are prone to drooling due to their large saggy lips.

Saint Bernards are gentle and calm dogs and make great pets. A Saint Bernard requires plenty of exercise and does not do well in hot weather, but for the right family they can make a wonderful addition.

▶ 测 试 篇 ◀

I.单项选择

1. Although we had told them not to keep us waiting, they made no _____ to speed up deliveries. （考研92）
   A. trial   B. attempt   C. action   D. progress

2. Some day software will translate both written and spoken language so well that the need for any common second language could _____. （考研01）
   A.descend   B. decline   C. deteriorate   D. depress

3. In addition to the rising birthrate and immigration, the _____ death rate contributed to the population growth. （CET-6 03/6）
   A. inclining   B. increasing   C. declining   D. descending

4. They had to eat a (n) _____ meal, or they would be too late for the concert. （CET-6 05/6）
   A. temporary   B. hasty   C. immediate   D. urgent

5. Every culture has developed _____ for certain kinds of food and drink, and equally strong negative attitudes toward others. （CET-4 04/1）

    A. preferences   B. expectations   C. fantasies   D. fashions

6. _____ the enormous flow of food from the entire globe, these countries have for many years not felt any population pressure. （CET-4 03/9）

    A. Thanks to   B. By means of   C. In line with   D. With regard to

7. The residents, _____ had been damaged by the fire, were given help by the Red Cross. （CET-4 02/6）

    A. all of their homes   B. all their homes   C. whose all homes   D. all of whose homes

8. The Social Security Retirement Program is made up of two trust funds, _____ could go penniless by next year. （考研97）

    A. the larger one   B. the larger of which   C. the largest one   D. the largest of which

9. Living in the central Australian desert has its problems, _____ obtaining water is not the least. （考研94）

    A. of which   B. for what   C. as   D. whose

10. We grow all our own fruit and vegetables, _____ saves money, of course. （CET-6 93/6）

    A. which   B. as   C. that   D. what

Ⅱ. 翻译

11. 台湾海峡连接着大陆与台湾。（connect）

12. 海拔5895米，迄利马扎罗是非洲最高的关隘。（at... meters）

13. 我宁愿吃药也不愿意打针。（prefer A to B）

14. 既然你想留学，不妨试试雅思吧。（now that）

15. 不要妄图考试作弊。（vainly attempt to do...）

答 案

拓展篇

    Westminster Abbey（used to be the church in the monastery）, a very large gothic church in Westminster, London, was first built in the 11th century. Almost all British kings and queens since William the Conqueror have been crowned in the Abbey and many famous people are buried there.

测试篇

1-5 BBCBA   6-10 ADBAA

11. Taiwan Strait connects Taiwan to Mainland.

12. At 5,895 meters, Kilimanjaro is the highest mountain pass in Africa.

13. I prefer taking medicine to having an injection.

14. Now that you want to study abroad, you may as well try IELTS.

15. Don't vainly attempt to cheat at exam.

Lesson 9. Flying cats

I.振振有"词"

1. Cats never fail to <u>fascinate</u> <u>human beings</u>.

> fascinate 迷住
> enthrall 强烈吸引
> captivate 深深吸引
> bewitch 诱惑
> allure 诱惑
> appeal to sb. 吸引

> human being 人类（可加复数s）
> human race 人类（总称，不加复数s）
> humanity 人类（侧重人性，不加复数s）
> mankind 人类（侧重文明、文化，不加复数s）
> man 人类（侧重政治意义，只用单数。如：Man will prevail. 人类必胜。）

2. They can be friendly and <u>affectionate</u> towards human beings, but they <u>lead mysterious lives</u> of their own.

> 表达某种生活方式的句型：
> lead/live a mysterious life
> 过着神秘的生活
> live a luxurious life 生活奢侈
> live a miserable life 生活凄惨
> live a wretched life 生活悲惨

> affectionate 柔情似水的
> passionate 激情似火的
> amiable 和蔼可亲的
> companionable 和善的
> cordial 热情的
> tender 温柔的

3. A cat's <u>ability</u> to <u>survive</u> falls <u>is based on</u> fact.

> ability（身体或智力）能力
> capability（较强）能力
> faculty（官能）能力
> competence（很强）能力
> curious talent 特异功能
> proficiency 熟练性

> survive sth. 从…中幸存
> survive sb. 比某人活得长
> survival of the fittest 适者生存
> outlast 比…活得长
> outlive 比…耐久

> be based on 基于…
> be based in 总部位于…
> be located in 位于…
> be situated in 坐落于…
> be sited in 安置在…
> settle in 定居于…

4. Of course, New York is an ideal place for such an interesting study, because there is no shortage of tall buildings.

> ideal 最理想的（无比较、最高级）
> 其他无比较、最高级的形容词：
> 表极限、主次：perfect, excellent, favorite, superior, inferior, extreme
> 表独一无二：unique, sole, sheer, single
> 表几何形状：round, square, straight, angular

> have a shortage of 缺乏…
> have a scarcity of 缺乏…
> be short of 缺乏…
> be scarce of 缺少…
> be lacking in 缺少…
> be in need of 匮乏…
> be in want of 缺乏…

Ⅱ. 现身说"法"：双重否定

> **Cats** never fail to **fascinate human beings.**
> 猫总能引起人们的极大兴趣。

句子中出现两个具有否定意义的词，这就是双重否定。其主要目的是表达强烈的肯定语气。例：

Nothing is impossible to a willing mind. 世上无难事，只怕有心人。

Nor is the city without its moments of beauty. (《新概念英语》3册41课) 城市不是没有美妙时光的。

There is no sky in June so blue that it does not point forward to a bluer, no sunset so beautiful that it does not waken the vision of a greater beauty. (《新概念英语》4册24课) 六月蔚蓝的天空总使人遐想一个更加蔚蓝的苍穹，美丽的落日总能令人憧憬更加绚烂的景象。

There is no place where grows no sweet grass. 天涯何处无芳草。

★★★ 注意 ★★★

双重否定不可滥用，以下句子是错误的：

They seldom could not arrive on time.

The villagers survived the flood without scarcely any loss of property.

可见，否定词一般不能与半否定词连用。

Ⅲ. 说"文"解"字"

1. They can be friendly and affectionate towards human beings, but they lead mysterious lives of their own as well.

译文：它们或许对人友好，充满柔情。但是，它们又有自己神秘的生活方式。

解析：can在这里表猜测，与后面的but相互呼应，形成英文行文中一个特定构式，can也可用may替换，即：can/may...but...，其中can/may后的内容为铺垫预设，but后的内容则是重点，这也符合汉语思维。熟练掌握这种用法对于提升写作的整体谋划大有裨益。例：

They may have used wood and skins, but these have rotted away. (《新概念英语》4册1课)

他们或许用过木头和兽皮，但这类东西早已腐烂殆尽。

He may be conceited, ill-mannered, presumptuous or fatuous, but I do not turn for protection to dreary clichés about respect for elders...（《新概念英语》4册5课）

他或许狂妄自负，举止无理，傲慢放肆，愚昧无知，但我不会用应当尊重长者这些陈词滥调来为我自己辩护。

2. One of the things that fascinates us most about cats is the popular belief that cats have nine lives.

译文：最令我们感兴趣的一件事情就是一种普遍的说法——猫有九命。

解析：cats have nine lives是夸张说法（hyperbole），一种常见的修辞手段。适时运用这种方法会起到幽默诙谐、形象风趣之功效。例：

A cat has nine lives and a woman has nine cats. 一猫有九命，一女有九猫。（实指女性坚强刚毅）

以下是几个运用夸张的英文句子：

I could sleep for a whole year. 我能睡上一整年。

I can eat a horse. 我饭量极大。

3. It seems that the further cats fall, the less they are likely to injure themselves.

译文：似乎猫跌落的距离越长，就越不会受伤。

解析："the+比较级，the+比较级"是一常见句型，意为"越…，就越…"。其变化过程是：把一个正常语序的句子中作状语或表语的比较级置于句首，再添加the。请注意："the+比较级，the+比较级"结构中两部分之间不能加and。因此，上面的句子恢复原状后即：

It seems that cats fall further and they are less likely to injure themselves.

类似的变化过程：

A man is richer and he is greedier. 变为：

The richer a man is, the greedier he is. 人越富有，就越贪婪。

Your success is bigger and your fame is bigger. 变为：

The bigger your success is, the bigger your fame is. 你越成功，就越有名气。

拓 展 篇

Ⅰ.英语趣园

According to Brewer's *Dictionary Of Phrase and Fable*, a cat is said to have nine lives because it is "more tenacious of life than many animals". Nine, a trinity of trinities, is a mystical number often invoked in religion and folklore. The cat was once revered in Egypt, and this is probably where its nine lives began. As cats seem able to escape injury time and time again, this mystical number seemed suited to the cat. Cats are intrepid explorers and fearless acrobats. After all, a creature with nine lives can afford to take risks.

People always think that due to the speed, cleverness and flexibility of cats, they can stay alive in most difficult situations when other animals would have been killed. Cats always seem to land on their feet after a fall. As the cat falls, an automatic twisting reaction begins and the cat maneuvers its head, back, legs and tail to lessen the impact. Cats, it seems, have an instinct for physics. Don't try this at home, though. Cats aren't all that tough; they don't always land the right way up, which is why your average pussy cat jumping from the garden fence will occasionally come home limping, bruised or fractured because of a badly timed fall. Still, studies on cats falling from skyscrapers suggest that up to 90% survive, albeit with broken bones and sore paws. The distance is crucial. Too much and the cat will splat, just as we non-feline mortals would. Too little and the cat doesn't have time to correct itself.

II. 听力快车

The famous 18th century Irish writer, Jonathan Swift, is said to be responsible for the widely used phrase, "_____". It may come from the idea that_____. "To let the cat out of the bag" means to_____. The expression comes from an old tradesman's trick of_____. A smart buyer, of course, would look inside the bag and learn the truth when the cat jumped out.

III. 补充阅读

A dog's eye view of man

If man has benefited immeasurably by his association with the dog, what, you may ask, has the dog got out of it? His scroll has, of course, been heavily charged with punishments: he has known the muzzle, the leash, and the tether. He has suffered the indignities of the show bench, the tin can on the tail, the ribbon in the hair, his love life with the other sex of his species has been regulated by the frigid hand of authority, his digestion ruined by the macaroons and marshmallows of doting women. The list of his woes could be continued indefinitely. But he has also had his fun, for he has been privileged to live with and study at close range to the only creature with reason, the most unreasonable of creatures.

The dog has got more fun out of man than man has got out of the dog, for the clearly demonstrable reason that man is the more laughable of the two animals. The dog has long been bemused by the singular activities and the curious practices of men, cocking his head inquiringly to one side, intently watching and listening to the strangest goings-on in the world. He has seen men sing together and fight one another in the same evening. He has watched them go to bed when it is time to get up, and get up when it is time to go to bed. He has observed them destroying the soil in vast areas, and nurturing it in small patches. He has stood by while men built strong and solid houses for rest and quiet, and then filled them with lights and bells and machinery. His sensitive nose, which can detect what's cooking in the next township, has caught at one and the same time the bewildering smells of the hospital and the munitions factory. He has seen men raise up great cities to heaven and then blow them to hell.

■▷ 测 试 篇 ◁■

I. 单项选择

1. The boy's foolish question _____ his mother who was busy with housework and had no interest in talking.

(CET-6 05/12)

    A. intrigued   B. fascinated   C. irritated   D. stimulated

2. The circus has always been very popular because it _____ both the old and the young.   (CET-6 03/9)

    A. facilitates   B. fascinates   C. immerses   D. indulges

3. Astronauts are _____ all kinds of tests before they are actually sent up in a spacecraft. （CET-6 02/6）

    A. inclined to   B subjected to   C. prone to   D bound to

4. Some plants are very _____ to light; they prefer the shade.   （CET-4 04/1）

    A. sensible   B. flexible   C. objective   D. sensitive

5. Many scientists remain _____ about the value of this research program.   （CET-6 02/1）

    A. skeptical   B. stationary   C. spacious   D. specific

6. Without facts, we cannot form a worthwhile opinion for we need to have factual knowledge _____ our thinking.   （CET-6 91/6）

    A.Which to be based on   B. which to base upon

    C. upon which to base   D. to which to be based

7. Life insurance is financial protection for dependents against loss _____ the bread-winner's death. （考研99）

    A. at the cost of   B. on the verge of   C. as result of   D. for the sake of

8. Although a teenager, Fred could resist _____ what to do and what not to do.   （考研98）

    A. to be told   B. having been told   C. being told   D. to have been told

9. According to Darwin, random changes that enhance a species' ability _____ are naturally selected and passed on to succeeding generations.   （考研98）

    A. for surviving   B. of surviving   C. on surviving   D. to survive

10. The _____ the monkey climbs, the more you'll see his behind.

    A. high   B. higher   C. highest   D. highness

Ⅱ.翻译

11. 我看书的时候必做笔记。（never...without）

12. 友谊要建立在信任的基础之上。（be based on）

13. 你学的越多，你就知道你不知道的更多。（the more...the more...）

14. 人们普遍认为，彗星会给人类带来灾难。（there's a popular belief...）

15. 最让老外着迷的事是中国五千年来的历史。（one of the things that....）

 答 案

拓展篇

    The famous 18th century Irish writer, Jonathan Swift, is said to be responsible for the widely used phrase, "It is raining cats and dogs". It may come from the idea that a thunderstorm sounds like a cat-and-dog fight. "To let the cat out of the bag" means to tell the truth of a long and well-kept secret. The expression comes from an old tradesman's trick of hiding a cat in a bag and trying to sell it as a pig. A smart buyer, of course, would look inside the bag and learn the truth when the cat jumped out.

测试篇

1-5 CBBDA   6-10 CCCDB

11. I never read without taking notes.

12. Friendship is based on confidence.

13. The more you know, the more you know you don't know.

14. There's a popular belief that comet can bring about disaster.

15. One of the things that fascinates foreigners most about China is its five-thousand-year history.

Lesson 10. The loss of the *Titanic*

积累篇

I. 振振有"词"

1. The great ship, *Titanic*, sailed for New York from Southampton.

titanic 本指"体积巨大无比"之意。
其他表体积之大的词有：
colossal 庞大的
giant 巨大的
gigantic 硕大的
enormous 巨大的

sail for A from B 从B驶向A（用于船只航行）
leave B for A 从B去A（任何方式）
be bound for... 去往…（任何方式）
head for...奔向…（可抽象使用），例：
China is heading for urbanization.
中国正进入城市化进程。

2. She went down on her first voyage with heavy loss of life.

go down 沉没
submerge 淹没
drown 溺水
flood 充水
dive 跳水
plunge（慌乱）跳水

on her first voyage 初航
on her maiden voyage 首航
on her virgin voyage 处女航
on her test voyage 试航
on her trial voyage 试航

heavy loss of life 重大伤亡
heavy casualties 重大伤亡（尤指战争）
death toll 事故伤亡
cause harm/detriment to...对…造成伤害
sustain injury 受伤

3. After the alarm had been given, the great ship turned sharply to avoid a direct collision.

give an alarm 发警报
sound an alarm 发警报
sound a siren 发警报
sound a false alarm 发假警报
alarmist 无事自扰者

turn sharply 急速转弯
swerve sharply 急速转弯
veer sharply 急速转弯
change the course（船）改变航向
diversion of traffic 交通改道
divert attention from...转移注意力

collision 碰撞
表示"碰撞"的词组：
A collide with B（运动物体的）碰撞
A crash into B（运动物体）碰撞（静止物体）
knock over 车撞人

Ⅱ. 现身说"法":单复数

> While the *Titanic* was sailing across the icy waters of the North Atlantic, a huge iceberg was suddenly spotted by a lookout.(water意为"水",但加-s则意为"水域,海面")
>
> "泰坦尼克"正行驶在北大西洋冰冷的海面上。突然,瞭望员发现了一座冰山。

英文中有许多名词单复数的意义迥异。试看以下例证:

advice 建议—advices 通知   age 年龄—ages 很长一段时期

air 空气—airs 氛围;神态   arm 胳膊—arms 武器

glass 玻璃—glasses 眼镜   authority 权威—authorities 政府,当局

time 时间—times 时代   manner 方法—manners 礼仪;风俗

minute 分钟—minutes 会议记录   paper 纸张—papers 论文;报纸

people 人民—peoples 民族,种族   quarter 四分之一—quarters 住所

wood 木头—woods 森林   sand 沙子—sands 沙滩

snow 雪—snows 雪地;积雪   spirit 精神—spirits 情绪

Ⅲ. 说"文"解"字"

1. At that time, however, she was not only the largest ship that had ever been built, but was regarded as unsinkable.

译文:当时,这艘轮船不仅是造船史上建造的最大船只,而且也被认为是不可沉没的。

解析:1)not only...but... 意为"不仅…而且…",其后的谓语动词用复数。该词组还可替换为 not only...but also..., not only...but...as well。

2)regard as后可接形容词、名词或介词短语。例:

This fundamental research is regarded as of great value. 这项基础研究被认为极具价值。

2. Even if two of these were flooded, she would still be able to float.

译文:即使有两个船舱进水,船仍可漂浮在水面上。

解析:even if表让步,意为"即使,纵然",与even though 同义。

> **联想记忆**
>
> as if = as though 似乎,好像   only if 只有
>
> if only 只要…就好了(后接虚拟语气)

3. Suddenly, there was a trembling sound from below.

译文:突然,从下面传来一声轻微的颤音。

解析:一般而言,from后接名词或名词短语。但也可接表方位的副词或介词短语,例:

from above 从上面   from outside 从外面

from inside 从里面   from abroad 从国外

from behind the door 从门后面

4. The order to abandon ship was given and hundreds of people plunged into the icy water.

译文:弃船的命令发了出去,数百人跳进了冰冷的海水里。

解析：1）abandon ship 中间不能加a或the，这是一个固定表达。事实上，和"船"相关的很多短语都不加冠词或定冠词。例：

jump ship 潜逃；跳槽（换工作） 　　on board ship 在船上

dress ship 给船挂满旗帜　　　　　　about ship（对舵手发的指令）抢风掉转航向

2）ship 的代词常用she。

3）英文中表天气的形容词多以-y结尾，例：

icy 冰冷的	snowy 下雪的	rainy 下雨的
windy 刮风的	foggy 大雾的	sunny 阳光灿烂的
cloudy 阴云密布的		

拓 展 篇

Ⅰ. 英语趣园

Titans, the first gods who ruled the world, were children of the Uranus（Heaven）and the Gaia（Earth）and led by Cronus. Zeus, the son of Cronus, rebelled against his father and eventually defeated the Titans. Titanic, the largest ship in the world when she was built, and supposedly unsinkable, struck an iceberg in the North Atlantic on her maiden voyage in April 1912. A film was made in 1997 about the sinking of the Titanic, which was one of the most expensive films that had ever been made. As a result, it won 11 Oscars. The two main characters are Leonardo Dicaprio and Kate Winslet.

Ⅱ. 听力快车

The Titanic Historical Society, Inc.（THS）is ＿＿＿＿＿＿＿ for all things Titanic and White Star Line related. ＿＿＿＿＿＿＿, the THS was the first and is the largest global organization ＿＿＿＿＿＿＿ and the White Star Line. They invite all to ＿＿＿＿＿＿＿＿＿, a unique collection of personal items donated by ＿＿＿＿＿＿＿＿＿＿＿＿＿ from Titanic, Olympic, Britannic and White Star Line ships. They also offer the opportunity to purchase Titanic collectibles and mementos through our online Museum Shop.

Ⅲ. 补充阅读

Ship

Ships are one of the oldest and most important means of transportation. Every day, thousands of ships cross the oceans, sail along seacoasts, and travel on inland waterways. Trade among countries depends heavily on ships. For example, ships carry wheat from Canada to Germany and machinery from Germany to Chile. They haul copper from Chile to Japan and Japanese automobiles to the United States. Ships transport American corn to Ethiopia, coffee from Ethiopia to France, and French plastics to Canada.

Many kinds of ships are used to carry the world's trade. Giant tankers haul petroleum, soybean oil, wines, and other liquids. Refrigerator ships carry fresh fruits, meats, and vegetables. Vessels called dry bulk carriers haul such cargoes as grain, ore, and sand. General cargo ships transport everything from airplane engines to zippers. Passenger liners carry travelers across the oceans and vacationers on cruises to the Mediterranean and Caribbean seas and other warm areas.

For several thousand years, people have been drawn by the mysteries of the sea and by its promise of adventure. More important, people have sailed the seas to explore, to settle, and to conquer. In 1492, Christopher Columbus braved the unknown waters of the Atlantic Ocean in three small sailing ships and reached the New World. During the 1500's, Spanish ships carried conquerors to Latin America. The conquerors soon won control of much of the region for Spain. An old trading ship called the Mayflower brought the first Pilgrim settlers to North America in 1620. From the 1600's to the 1800's, big sailing ships called East Indiamen carried passengers and goods across the oceans. The world quickly became smaller as steamships crossed the seas in a fraction of the time that sailing ships needed. Thus, ships have brought countries and peoples closer and made them dependent economically on one another.

Throughout history, nations have become rich and powerful by controlling the seas in war and peace. When countries have lost that control, they have declined. Today, ships are as important as ever to a country's prosperity and strength. The United States, the world's leading trading nation, depends largely on ships for its imports and exports. The economies of Great Britain, Japan, Germany, and many other countries would soon be badly crippled if there were no ships to bring in food and raw materials and to carry out manufactured goods. All the great trading nations try to have a large merchant marine. A merchant marine consists of the commercial, or merchant, ships of a country.

▪▶ 测 试 篇 ◀▪

I. 单项选择

1. It's reported that thirty people were killed in a _____ on the railway yesterday. （CET-6 04/1）
   A. collision   B. collaboration   C. corrosion   D. confrontation

2. The lost car of the Less was found _____ in the woods off the highway. （考研91）
   A. vanished   B. abandoned   C. scattered   D. rejected

3. The morning news says a school bus _____ with a train at the junction and a group of policemen were sent there immediately. （CET-6 97/1）
   A. bumped   B. collided   C. crashed   D. struck

4. These figures are not consistent _____ the results obtained in previous experiments.
   A. to   B. with   C. for   D. in

5. My favorite radio song is the one I first heard on a thick 1923 Edison disc I _____ at a garage scale. （考研01）

   A. trifle with   B. scraped through   C. stumbled upon   D. thirsted for

6. Many patients insist on having watches with them in hospital, _____ they have no schedules to keep. （CET-4 04/1）

   A. even though   B. for   C. as if   D. since

7. _____ the storm, the ship would have reached its destination on time. （CET-4 03/6）
   A. But for   B. In case of   C. In spite of   D. Because of

8. The millions of calculations involved, had they been done by hand, _____ all practical value by the time they were finished. （CET-4 01/6）

    A. Had lost   B. would lose   C. would have lost   D. should have lost

9. Rod is determined to get a seat for the concert _____ it means standing in a queue all night.

                                                            （CET-4 01/6）

    A. provided   B. whatever   C. even if   D. as if

10. Things might have been much worse if the mother _____ on her right to keep the baby. （CET-4 02/1）

    A. has been insisting   B. had insisted   C. would insist   D. insisted

Ⅱ. 翻译

11. 我一直把Mary当成小妹妹看待。（regard... as...）

12. 这个开飞车的司机，猛打方向盘，险些撞上了那个孩子。（turn sharply）

13. 他尴尬得都没把自己的工作告诉老婆。（so... that）

14. 即便他是总统本人，也得讲道理。（even if...）

15. 甚至按照现代标准来衡量，144米高的大金字塔仍是有史以来建造过的最高的建筑物之一。（Even by modern standard, ...）

拓展篇

    The Titanic Historical Society, Inc. (THS) is the premier information source for all things Titanic and White Star Line related. Formed in 1963, the THS was the first and is the largest global organization dedicated to preserving the history of RMS Titanic and the White Star Line. They invite all to visit the Titanic Museum, a unique collection of personal items donated by survivors and their families, historical documents and memorabilia from Titanic, Olympic, Britannic and White Star Line ships. They also offer the opportunity to purchase Titanic collectibles and mementos through our online Museum Shop.

测试篇

1-5 ABBBC   6-10 AACCB

11. I always regard Mary as my little sister.

12. The speeding driver turned sharply, narrowly missing the kid.

13. He was so embarrassed that he didn't tell his wife about his job.

14. Even if he were the President himself, he would listen to reason.

15. Even by modern standard, the 144m Great Pyramid is one of the highest buildings that had ever been built.

Lesson **11.** Not guilty

积累篇

Ⅰ.振振有"词"

1. Customs officers are quite tolerant these days.

customs（复数）海关
custom（单、复均可）习俗
custom（单数）顾客
custom-made 定做的
hand-made 手工的
half-made 半成品的
ready-made 现成的
man-made 人工的

易混淆的形似词：
tolerant 宽容的
tolerable 凑合的
considerable（数量、程度）相当大的
considerate 体贴入微的
impressive 令人印象深刻的
impressionable 思想不稳定的

2. ... when you are going through the Green Channel and have nothing to declare.

go through的用法相当广泛：
go through the Green Channel 过免税通道
go through one's luggage 查验行李
go through a magazine/novel 浏览
go through thick and thin 历经甘苦
go through the motions 得过且过；混日子
go through formalities 办手续

channel 通道
canal 运河
canoe 独木舟
canon 教规
TV channels 电视频道
The English Channel 英吉利海峡
channels of communication 交流的渠道

Ⅱ.现身说"法"：由should表示的虚拟语气

You should have declared that. 你本应该申报的。

sb. should have done sth. 属于虚拟语气的一种，表示该做而未做的事情，含有建议或责备、不满的意味。It is (high/about) time that...的意义相同，但从句中动词形式用过去式，且后面很少用时间短语。例：

You should have submitted the document last week. 你上周就应把文件交上来。

It is high time that you submitted the document. 你早该把文件交上来。

更多示例如下：

You shouldn't have been following him so closely; you should have kept your distance. (CET-4 00/6)

53

你不应该和他那么亲密；你应该保持距离。

It's high time that such practices were ended. 这样的做法早该结束了。

It is about time two parities put an end to their controversy. 双方早应该结束这场争论了。

III. 说"文"解"字"

1. **But they can still stop you when you are going through** the Green Channel **and have nothing to declare.**

   译文：但是，当你通过绿色通道，没有任何东西需要申报时，他们仍可以拦住你。

   解析：the Green Channel 指海关专供没有携带征税物品进关的旅客所走的通道。

   > green词义浩瀚，不胜枚举，例：

a green winter 暖冬	a green eye 嫉妒的
green with envy 十分嫉妒的	a green wound 未愈的伤口
green thumb 园艺技能	a green hand 生手
green-fingered 具有高超园艺技能的	green as grass 幼稚的；无经验的
in the green wood 处于最佳状态	

2. **Even really honest people** are often made to feel guilty.

   译文：甚至是非常老实的人也常被弄得有罪似的。

   解析：sb. be made to do sth. 是由make sb. do sth. 转化而来，(该结构省略了不定式中的to)，但被动表达中要加to。have、let及感官动词see、hear、notice、feel 由主动变被动时，方法相同。例：
   She made the little boy cry. → The little boy was made to cry (by her). 她把小男孩弄哭了。
   I noticed him doze off. → He was noticed to doze off (by me). 我注意到他在打盹。

3. **The hardened professional smuggler,** on the other hand, is never troubled by such feelings.

   译文：另一方面，职业走私犯总能处之泰然。

   解析：on the other hand 意为"另一方面"，一般与on (the) one hand 连用，但后者常可省略。因此，原文补全后应是：Even really honest people, on (the) one hand, are often made to feel guilty. The hardened professional smuggler, on the other hand, is never troubled by such feelings.
   be never troubled by sth. 根据情境可灵活处理为"处之泰然"。事实上，英文中比较惯用的表达为 play it cool或be as cool as cucumber。

4. **Even if he** has five hundred gold watches hidden in his suitcase.

   译文：即使他在手提箱里藏匿了500只金表。

   解析：本句并不是通常所见的have sth. done （让某人做某事）的含义，因为这不符合逻辑。而是hidden作后置定语，即其前省略了that (which) are. 且has一词是实意动词，作"拥有"解。因此整句应为：Even if he has five hundred gold watches (that/which are) hidden in his suitcase.

5. **He asked,** looking me in the eye.

   译文：他直盯着我的眼睛问道。

   解析：该短语不可望文生义，其意为：look straight into my face. 例：
   Can you look me in the eye and tell a lie? 你能看着我而说谎吗？

○ 有关eye的几个常用短语

1）do sb. in the eye 开某人的玩笑

2）be in the public eye 很受关注

Pop stars are always in the public eye, for they are trend-setters.

明星通常很受关注，因为他们是引领时尚者。

3）one in the eye for sb. 令某人失望的事

If Joan wins the case, it will be one in the eye for Jack—he looks down upon women lawyers.

如果琼赢得官司，这将令杰克倍感失望——他向来瞧不起女律师。

4）throw dust in sb.'s eyes 故意蒙骗某人

Don't try to throw dust in his eyes—he is nobody's fool. 别想蒙骗他——他精得像猴。

6. **Would you** mind unlocking **this suitcase please?**

译文：请打开这个箱子好吗？

解析：对该句的回答需注意：如表不乐意，应回答Yes; 而表乐意时，则应回答No/Not at all, 等，因为回答是针对mind一词而作的。此外，该句中mind前加上my，则表示句中所提动作unlock this suitcase由问话者而非听话者来完成。

7. **The officer** went through **the case** with great care.

译文：那个官员仔细查看了那只箱子。

解析：1）go through在这里表examine, 而在前文go through the Green Channel 则表本义"走过"。由此看来，该词组含义宽广，用法多变，例：

go through a magazine/novel（浏览）　　　　　go through thick and thin（历经甘苦）

go through the motions（得过且过；混日子）　go through formalities（办手续）

2）with great care是carefully的同义表达，但前者更加正式，也是写作中扩展句型和相互替换的常用手段。其他类似表达有：

with delight与delightedly　　　　　　　　with a smile与smilingly

with attention与attentively　　　　　　　with confidence 与 confidently

with pride 与 proudly

■　拓 展 篇

I . 英语趣园

There are many idioms connected with the color "green". For example, to be inexperienced, from which comes the phrase "to be as green as grass" —to be naive; to be blessed with luck in the growing of plants and flowers—have a green thumb; to feel extremely envious—to be green with envy; to give permission to go ahead—give the green light. Dollars are called greenbacks because that's the color of the backside of the money.

II . 听力快车

Have you anything to declare?

Customs officer: Is this all your luggage, sir?

David: Yes.

C: _____?

D: I have some small gifts for friends and here is a carton of cigarettes.

C: One carton of cigarettes is your_____ allowance. May I have a look at the gifts?

D: They are in this suitcase.

C: _____?

D: It's soybean.

C: I'm sorry, but agricultural products are not allowed to be brought into the country, especially seeds.

D: It's for eating not for planting.

C: That's not allowed, I'm sorry.

D: Sorry, I don't know that because this is my _____.

C: That's all right.

Ⅲ. 补充阅读

The World Trade Organization (WTO) created by the Uruguay Round of negotiations for revision of the General Agreement on Tariffs and Trade (GATT) is expected to come into operation on January 1, 1995.

The major features of the United States GATT implementing legislation signed by President Clinton on December 8, 1994 relating to intellectual property include:

1) The term of all new patent applications filed on or after June 8, 1995 will be 20 years from the earliest U.S. filing date claimed (including in PCT cases the International filing date which is deemed to be a U.S. filing date for this purpose). Thus, for applications that are already on file it is necessary to consider promptly whether any divisional or continuation applications are likely to be required and, if appropriate, such applications should be filed before June 8, 1995. For patents granted or applications filed before that date, the term is the greater of 17 years from grant or 20 years from the earliest U.S. filing date.

2) Assuming that the January 1, 1995 date for the start of the WTO is correct, dates of invention on or after January 1, 1996 in any WTO member country may be relied upon in proceedings before the United States Patent and Trademark Office, provided that certain conditions are met.

3) After January 1, 1996 copyright protection will become available in the United States for certain works that either never had such protection or which had lost it.

The major immediate impact abroad is that, from the date on which the World Trade Organization comes into effect, all countries that have ratified the GATT TRIPS Agreement and whose patent laws have limitations on the subject matter that can be protected that are incompatible with the Agreement must start to permit filing of patent applications relating to inventions previously in the prohibited classes. However, depending on the country's degree of economic development, there may be no obligation to grant patents on such applications for another five or ten years. The implementation of other provisions such as the extension of patent terms may be delayed up to January 1, 1996.

测 试 篇

Ⅰ.单项选择

1. You will not be _____ about your food in time of great hunger. （CET-4 03/6）
   A. special   B. particular   C. peculiar   D. specific

2. Having a（n） _____ attitude towards people with different ideas is an indication that one has been well educated. （CET-6 05/6）
   A. analytical   B. bearable   C. elastic   D. tolerant

3. Now the cheers and applause _____ in a single sustained roar. （CET-6 05/6）
   A. mingled   B. tangled   C. baffled   D. huddled

4. I don't mind _____ the decision as long as it is not too late. （CET-4 00/1）
   A. you to delay making   B. your delaying to make
   C. your delaying making   D. you delay to make

5. This is not an economical way to get more water; _____ it is very expensive. （CET-4 04/6）
   A. on the other hand   B. on the contrary   C. in short   D. or else

6. A good many proposals were raised by the delegates, _____ was to be expected. （CET-4 04/1）
   A. that   B. what   C. so   D. as

7. _____ can be seen from the comparison of these figures, the principle involves the active participation of the patient in the modification of his condition. （考研99）
   A. As   B. What   C. That   D. It

8. The careless man received a ticket for speeding. He _____ have driven so fast. （CET-4 03/1）
   A. can't   B. wouldn't   C. shouldn't   D. mustn't

9. You _____ her in her office last Friday; she's been out of town for two weeks. （CET-4 96/1）
   A. needn't have seen   B. must have seen   C. might have seen   D. cannot have seen

10. Some women _____ a good salary in a job instead of staying home, but they decided not to work for the sake of the family. （CET-4 00/1）
    A. must make   B. would make   C. should have made   D. could have made

Ⅱ.翻译

11. 因为超速，一个警察把我给拦住了。（stop sb.）
12. 我过安检的时候，被弄得像是有负罪感一般。（be made to feel guilty）
13. 不要讲吃讲穿。（be particular about...）
14. 众所周知，台湾是中国的一部分。（As is known...）
15. 一股寒气扑面而来。（be greeted by）

拓展篇

Have you anything to declare?

Customs officer: Is this all your luggage, sir?

David: Yes.

C: Have you anything to declare?

D: I have some small gifts for friends and here is a carton of cigarettes.

C: One carton of cigarettes is your duty-free allowance. May I have a look at the gifts?

D: They are in this suitcase.

C: What's in this plastic bag?

D: It's soybean.

C: I'm sorry, but agricultural products are not allowed to be brought into the country, especially seeds.

D: It's for eating not for planting.

C: That's not allowed, I'm sorry.

D: Sorry, I don't know that because this is my first time abroad.

C: That's all right.

测试篇

1-5 BDACB   6-10 DACCD

11. A cop stopped me for speeding.

12. I was made to feel guilty when I went through the security check.

13. Don't be particular about food and clothes.

14. As is known to all, Taiwan is part of China.

15. I was greeted by a freezing cold.

Lesson Life on a desert island

Ⅰ.振振有"词"

1. <u>Most of</u> us have <u>formed an unrealistic picture</u> of life on a desert island.

most of 大多数	unrealistic 不现实的	form a picture 形成一种想法
many of 许多	idealistic 理想主义的	take a picture 照相
both of 两者	romantic 浪漫的	draw a picture 画画
not all of 不是所有的	quixotic 爱幻想的	give sb a picture of...给某人描述…
neither of 两者都不	starry-eyed 爱空想的	have a clear picture of...对…了如指掌
none of 一个也不	fanciful 虚幻的	make a lovely picture 构成美丽的景色

the majority of 大多数	反义词汇联想记忆:
the minority of... 少数…	realistic 现实的
minority groups 少数民族	materialistic 务实的
ethnic groups 少数民族	pragmatic 实用的
be in a pitiful minority 可怜巴巴的少数	rational 理性的
be still in minority 尚未成年	businesslike 务实的
	down-to-earth 实事求是的

Ⅱ.现身说"法"：wish与虚拟语气

Two men who recently spent five days on a coral island wished they had stayed there
longer. 最近，两个人在一座珊瑚岛上呆了5天，他们真希望在那儿多呆些日子。

一般而论，wish所带的宾语从句是虚拟语气句型，即用于表达难以实现或与事实相反的情形，具有较强的感情色彩。可分别表示对现在、过去和将来的虚拟。

1. 对现状表示的愿望，从句谓语动词用过去时。（be动词用were）

   I wish I were a bird, flying to your side. 我想变成一只鸟，飞到你身旁。

2. 对过去发生的事情表示遗憾、后悔，从句谓语动词用过去完成时或would/could+现在完成时。

   I wish you had lent me a hand. 我真希望你能帮我一把。

   The view was wonderful. I wished I had had a camera, I would have taken some photos.

   景色太棒了。我真希望有一架照相机，那样就可以多拍几张照片了。

3. 对将来发生的事情的期盼、祝愿，从句谓语动词用would/could+动词原形。

   I wish that I could go abroad for further studies. 我希望能出国深造。

   注：若将本句中的wish改为wished，谓语时态保持不变。

Ⅲ.说"文"解"字"

1. We sometimes imagine a desert island to be a sort of paradise where the sun always shines.

译文：我们有时想像荒岛是终日阳光普照的天堂。

解析：1）imagine A to be B意为"把A想像成B"，用法与以下短语相当：think of A as B, see A as B, take A as B, regard A as B。只是前者动词搭配不定式，而后者搭配介词as。

2）sort of的用法与kind of相当，意为"某种"，其后可接名词、动词、形容词等，表示对所修饰之词的含义减弱、降低之意。a sort of paradise 即指有点paradise的意境和味道，但并非完美的paradise。试看下面几例：

He is a musician→ He is a sort of musician.（他有点像音乐家）

He is lazy→ He is sort of lazy.（他有点懒惰）

I like the novel→ I sort of like the novel.（我有点喜欢这本小说）

2. Life there is simple and good.

译文：那里的生活简朴又美好。

解析：there is 并不是通常意义的there be 句型，而是there 作后置定语修饰life, is 为表语动词。

3. The other side of the picture is quite the opposite.

译文：另一种想法恰恰相反。

解析：这是一个表转折的句子，句法功能相当于however或but. 但前者的妙处在于更富有延展性，是写作中拓展篇幅、词义替换的变通手段。

4. They were taking a badly damaged boat from the Virgin Islands to Miami to have it repaired.

译文：他们架着一条严重损坏的小船从维尔京群岛去往迈阿密修理。

解析：badly不可望文生义。它不是由bad直接推导的表面义，而是表示程度，可理解为"非常、极度"。以下是几个词义容易混淆的副词：

1）I haven't surfed the net lately. 最近我没上网。（不是"迟到"）

2）You can get this sample free. 你可以免费得到这个样品。（不是"自由的"）

3）I'm pretty certain about it. 对此我是相当有把握的。（不是"漂亮的"）

4）The criminal was justly punished. 罪犯得到了正义的惩罚。（不是"刚刚"）

5）I clear forget about it. 我完全忘了这事。（不是"清楚的"）

6）She arrived at 9 o'clock sharp. 她准9点到了。（不是"锋利的"）

7）The man scolded his son sharply. 那人严厉地训斥儿子。（不是"锋利的"）

5. As one of them put it, "ate like kings".

译文：正如其中一位所言，"吃得像国王一样好"。

解析：1）本句中put 不作"放置"讲，因为后面没有表示方位的地点状语。即：若put作"放置"讲，一般模式是：put sth. in/on..., put在这里解释为express或describe。例：

Every man is a poet when in love, as Plato put it. 恰如柏拉图所言，人在热恋时才思奔涌。

联想记忆

put it another way 换言之	put it simply 简而言之
put it precisely 准确而言	put it bluntly 坦率而言

2）短语eat like kings 可改写为live like kings, 意为"生活富贵"。

联想记忆

live like beggars 生活窘困　　　　　　　　live a hand-to-mouth existence 生活无着落

live like fighting cocks 吃香的喝辣的

■ 拓 展 篇

I. 英语趣园

Defoe, Daniel,（1660-1731）, a British writer, his best-known works are the novels Robinson Crusoe, and Moll Flanders. Robinson Crusoe, the main character in the book Robinson Crusoe.His ship sinks, he manages to reach a desert island（=a small tropical island with no people living on it）where he builds a home. Later he meets a black man whom he calls Man Friday, who becomes his servant and friend. They are both finally discovered by a British ship and taken home.

II. 听力快车

Miami, a city in the southeast of Florida in the USA, is popular with _____, known as _____ and _____. Florida is known as sunshine state, for it's _____ sunlight. In 1508, Pounce de Leon Juan _____ Puerto Rico and discovered Florida in 1513 in search of _____. Florida means _____ in Spanish.

III. 补充阅读

Friday's new life

An excerpt from *Robinson Crusoe*

Now that there were two of us on the island, I had to grow enough corn to feed us both. To do this, I needed more ground to plant seeds in. I chose a place and showed Friday how to get the ground ready for planting. He began to work very happily. When the ground was cleared, we put up a fence around it.

That was my happiest time on the island. Friday was an honest, loyal and loving servant. He did everything that I asked him to do. When he learned some English, we should talk together at night.

I taught Friday how to shoot a gun. He became very good at this.

I taught him how to milk the goats, and make butter and cheese.

I showed him how to make baskets.

Actually, I taught him everything that I had had to learn for myself! Soon he was as good at these things as I was.

I told him the story of how I got to the island. He wanted to see the pieces of the old ship, so we walked down to the beach. These pieces still lay where they had been washed onto the beach, long ago.

When he saw the old ship, he said, "Me see this kind of boat. It came to my country."

At first I did not understand this. But as we talked, I learned that some years ago, a ship had crashed into the rocks near the mainland, which was close to the island. Friday and his people had rescued seventeen white men from this ship.

"What did you do with them?" I asked.

"They live, they dwell at my nation," Friday said.

It turned out that for four years the white men had lived with Friday's people.

"Your people don't eat these men?" I asked.

"No! My people not eat other men! Only bad savages do that," Friday said. "My people make white men their brothers."

Not long after that day we were standing on the top of a hill. Suddenly Friday looked out to sea and said, "Oh, I happy! There see my country, my nation!"

He sounded very happy to see his own country again. I took him to the other side of the island, where I kept the canoe I had made before he came.

"Is this boat big enough to take us to your country?" I asked.

Friday shook his head.

A few days later, I took him to the place where, years before, I had made a boat that was too big and heavy to get into the water. The old pieces of that boat were still there. I asked Friday if this kind of boat would be big enough to take us.

He nodded. "Would carry enough food, drink, other things," he said.

"All right," I said. "Let's start building another one!"

Friday found a good tree and began to chop it down. After I showed him how to use an axe, he completed the job very well.

When the inside of the boat was finished, we pushed it into the water. That job took us almost two weeks, because the boat was so heavy. Then, I put a very tall thin tree on the boat for the mast. Then I made a sail from old pieces of cloth.

While I made these things, Friday made a fence around the boat in the shallow water, to keep too much water from coming in. We made a dock so that we could tie the boat up. Next, we covered the boat with tree branches to keep the rain off. Now there was nothing more to be done, but to wait for November and December. I thought that if we went to sea during these months, the weather would be good, so we could reach Friday's country...

测 试 篇

I.单项选择

1. It took a lot of imagination to come up with such a(n) _____ plan. （CET-6 05/1）

   A. inherent   B. ingenious   C. vigorous   D. exotic

2. The public opinion was that the time was not _____ for the election of such a radical candidate as Mr. Jones. （考研97）

   A. reasonable   B. ripe   C. ready   D. practical

3. He has gone to the post office to _____ a parcel that has come to him.

   A. pick   B. gather   C. bring   D. collect

4. A monkey is _____ at a few years old, but a human being isn't till at least 16. Which of the following four words is wrong?

   A. grown-up   B. ripe   C. adult   D. mature

5. Sawdust is not a waste product; it is the main _____ of particleboard, from which some furniture is made.

    A. element   B. ingredient   C. component   D. factor

6. Jack wishes that he _____ business instead of history when he was in university.   （CET-4 01/4）

    A. had studied   B. study   C. studied   D. had been studying

7. Sometimes I wish I _____ in a different time and a different place.   （CET-4 00/1）

    A. be living   B. would live   C. were living   D. would have lived

8. Neither his parents nor he _____ at home now.

    A. are   B. is   C. will be   D. is to be

9. Neither of the young men who had applied for a position in the university _____.   （CET-4 98/1）

    A. has been accepted   B. have been accepted

    C. was accepted   D. were accepted

10. The organization had broken no rules, but _____ had it acted responsibly.   （CET-4 96/1）

    A. neither   B. so   C. either   D. both

Ⅱ. 翻译

11. 许多人对婚姻形成了不切实际的看法。（form an unrealistic picture of）

12. 我希望能年轻10岁。（wish）

13. 我这学期的学习负担很重。（be loaded with）

14. 正如Shakespeare 所说，女人，你的名字是弱者。（As Shakespeare put it...）

15. 不成功便成仁。（either... or）

答·案

拓展篇

    Miami, a city in the southeast of Florida in the USA, is popular with tourists, known as tourist resort and retirement center. Florida is known as sunshine state, for it's flooded with sunlight. In 1508, Pounce de Leon Juan took control of Puerto Rico and discovered Florida in 1513 in search of Fountain of Youth. Florida means feast of flowers in Spanish.

测试篇

1-5 CBDBB   6-10 DCBCA

11. Many people sometimes form an unrealistic picture of marriage.

12. I wish I were 10 years younger.

13. I'm loaded with heavy academic work this semester.

14. As Shakespeare put it: woman, your name is frailty.

15. Either make or break it.

Lesson ⑬. "It's only me"

Ⅰ.振振有"词"

1. Mrs. Rechards <u>sent her children to school</u> and <u>went upstairs</u> to her bedroom.

"去上学"的不同方式：
send sb. to school 打发某人去上学
take sb. to school 带某人去上学
drive sb. to school 开车送某人上学
rush sb. to school 匆匆送某人去上学

dispatch sb. to...派遣某人去…
fetch sth. 把…取来
convey sth. 传递…
transmit sth. 传送…
communicate sth. 传递…
forward sth. 递交…

go upstairs 上楼
go downstairs 下楼
upstair room 楼上的房间
downstair room 楼下的房间

live on the ground floor〈英〉住在一层
live on the first floor〈美〉住在一层
storey（楼的）层数
five-storey building 五层高的楼
skyscraper 摩天大楼
edifice 大厦
mansion 雄伟建筑

2. Mrs. Rechards realized that it must be the man from the <u>Electricity Board</u> who had come to <u>read the metre</u>.

read the metre 查电表
read a riddle 猜谜
read one's palm 看手相
read one's mind 猜心思
read sb. a lesson 教训某人

Electricity Board 供电局
Board of Directors 董事会
Workers' Union 工会
Students' Union 学生会
Experts Panel 专家小组

Ⅱ.现身说"法":将来进行时与过去将来进行时

For in the evening she would be going to **a fancy-dress party with her husband.**
因为晚上她要和丈夫去参加化装舞会。

　　将来进行时的基本意义是表示在将来某一时间正在进行的动作。它一般表示离现在较近的未来，且常与表将来的时间状语连用（本句中的in the evening）。过去将来进行时的基本用法和将来进行时相似，表示在过去将来某一时间正在发生的动作，常与表过去将来的时间状语连用。

💬 将来进行时一般用于以下几种场合：

1. 表事情的正常发展，是由客观情况决定的（而不是个人意愿决定的）。例：

I'll be seeing Mary this afternoon. 今天下午我将见到玛丽。

2. 与某个动词连用，表紧随其后发生的动作。例：

If we don't hurry, the game will be starting by the time we arrive.

如果不赶紧，我们到的时候，比赛就会开始了。

3. 用于客气地询问他人的计划、打算，以表明不想影响其决定。例：

Will you be needing anything else? 您还需要什么吗？

Will you be going out tomorrow? If not, can you give me a hand?

你明天出去吗？如果不出去，能帮个忙吗？

Ⅲ. 说"文"解"字"

1. **She** intended to dress up as **a ghost.**

译文：她打算装扮成鬼的模样。

解析：1）intend to do sth. 是一常用短语，表"打算做…"，比plan to do sth., be going to do sth. 等更具有主观意愿性。

> **联想记忆**
>
> tend to sth. 倾向于做…   mean to do sth. 想做…
>
> aspire to do sth. 渴望做…   determine to do sth. 决定做…
>
> resolve to do sth. 决心做…

2）dress up as 意为"打扮成…"，而make up as指"化装成…"，disguise as指"伪装成…"。例：

He made up as an old lady in the drama. 在戏里，他化装成了一位老太太。

The bad guy disguised as a policeman to swindle. 那个坏家伙扮成了警察到处行骗。

2. **Though the** costume consisted only of **a sheet, it was very** effective.

译文：尽管化装服仅由一个被单制成，却十分逼真。

解析：1）costume 意为"演出服装"，如颁奖仪式中的 award for best costume（最佳服装奖）。以下是关于服饰的几个常用词汇：

plumage 漂亮服装   tuxedo 燕尾服   camouflage 迷彩服

jeans 牛仔装   shapesuit 塑身衣   cheongsam 中式旗袍

2）一般而言，副词作修饰语要置于被修饰成分的前面或后面。但如果动词词组由副词修饰，则该副词可以置于词组中间，consist only of 和下文中的come straight in即是此理。这是写作中可以尝试的灵活手段。其他范例：

He went carefully through the case. 他仔细查看了箱子。

She looked everywhere for her lost dog. 她四处找寻走失的狗。

The student listened attentively to the teacher. 学生聚精会神地在听老师讲课。

3）effective一词多义，但在本句中指"效果逼真的"。由此看来，熟悉常见词汇的新义对于句型、篇章的理解至关重要。下面列举一个常见词在不同语境中的不同含义：

a reliable assistant（可靠的助手）   a reliable company（具有诚信度的公司）

a reliable watch（走得很准的手表）   reliable evidence（可信的证据）

3. There was a knock on the door.

译文：有人在敲门。

解析：本句中knock为名词，后面可接on或at，但若knock作动词，其后必须用at。

> **联想记忆**
>
> pound on the door 嘭嘭地捶门   tattoo on the door 笃笃地敲门

4. Mrs. Rechards realized that it must be the man from the Electricity Board who had come to read the metre.

译文：理查兹夫人这才意识到一定是供电局的人来查电表了。

解析：一般而言，it多用作指代非生命物体。本句中it显然指人，其原因是根据环境无法准确判断认得面容或身份。这是it的灵活用法。此外，it还可指代小孩，例：

How cute a baby! Is it a boy or girl? 多可爱的小家伙！是男孩还是女孩啊？

拓 展 篇

Ⅰ.英语趣园

In the Halloween party, all the guests are paired off except for one boy or girl who is given a broom or a mop as a partner. Prepare the broom or mop in advance with a paper-bag cover on which you have drawn a face. Whenever the piano or phonograph music stops, everyone changes partners. The person with the broom drops it and tries to find a live partner. The music starts again, and the person left over after the others are paired off must dance with the broom or mop.

Ⅱ.听力快车

Halloween party games and fun

Give each guest a crayon and a brown paper bag with holes cut for the eyes and nose. The bags should be big enough to _____ Every one at the party draws a face on his bag. Give a prize of the funniest, _____, and so on. Your parents or elder brothers and sisters can be the judges. The same bags worn backward may be used in blindfold games, such as the following:

Pinning the nose on the witch

_____

Potato race

Hunting for nuts

Broom dance

Ⅲ.补充阅读

Ancient origins

Halloween's origins date back to the ancient Celtic festival. The Celts, who lived 2,000 years ago in the area that is now Ireland, the United Kingdom, and northern France, celebrated their new year on November 1. This day marked the end of summer and the harvest and the beginning of the dark, cold winter, a time of year that was often associated with human death. Celts believed that on the night before the New Year, the boundary between the worlds of the living and the dead became blurred. On the night of October 31, they celebrated Samhain, when it was believed that the ghosts of the dead returned to earth. In addition to causing trouble and damaging crops, Celts thought that the presence of the otherworldly spirits made it easier for the Druids, or Celtic priests, to make predictions about the future. For a people entirely dependent on the volatile natural world, these prophecies were an important source of comfort and direction during the long, dark winter.

To commemorate the event, Druids built huge sacred bonfires, where the people gathered to burn crops and animals as sacrifices to the Celtic deities.

During the celebration, the Celts wore costumes, typically consisting of animal heads and skins, and attempted to tell each other's fortunes. When the celebration was over, they re-lit their hearth fires, which they had extinguished earlier that evening, from the sacred bonfire to help protect them during the coming winter.

By A.D. 43, Romans had conquered the majority of Celtic territory. In the course of the four hundred years that they ruled the Celtic lands, two festivals of Roman origin were combined with the traditional Celtic celebration of Samhain.

The first was Feralia, a day in late October when the Romans traditionally commemorated the passing of the dead. The second was a day to honor Pomona, the Roman goddess of fruit and trees. The symbol of Pomona is the apple and the incorporation of this celebration into Samhain probably explains the tradition of "bobbing" for apples that is practiced today on Halloween.

By the 800s, the influence of Christianity had spread into Celtic lands. In the seventh century, Pope Boniface IV designated November 1 All Saints' Day, a time to honor saints and martyrs. It is widely believed today that the pope was attempting to replace the Celtic festival of the dead with a related, but church-sanctioned holiday. The celebration was also called All-hallows or All-hallowmas （from Middle English Alholowmesse meaning All Saints' Day）and the night before it, the night of Samhain, began to be called All-hallows Eve and, eventually, Halloween. Even later, in A.D. 1000, the church would make November 2 All Souls' Day, a day to honor the dead. It was celebrated similarly to Samhain, with big bonfires, parades, and dressing up in costumes as saints, angels, and devils. Together, the three celebrations, the eve of All Saints', All Saints', and All Souls', were called Hallowmas.

■▶ 测 试 篇 ◀■

Ⅰ. 词汇

1. Showing some sense of humor can be a（n）_____ way to deal with some stressful situations.

（CET-4 05/6）

    A. effective   B. efficient   C. favorable   D. favorite

2. The European Union countries were once worried that they would not have _____ supplies of petroleum.

（CET-4 02/6）

    A. proficient   B. efficient   C. potential   D. sufficient

3. She cut her hair short and _____ herself as a man.   （CET-6 00/6）

    A. decorate   B. disguise   C. fabricate   D. fake

4. It is our _____ policy that we will achieve unity through peaceful means.   （CET-4 00/1）

    A. consistent   B. considerate   C. continuous   D. continual

5. They took _____ measures to prevent poisonous gases from escaping.   （CET-4 96/1）

A. fruitful   B. beneficial   C. valid   D. effective

6. I have heard both teachers and students _____ well of him.   (CET-4 99/6)

   A. to speak   B. spoken   C. to have spoken   D. speak

7. You can't be _____ careful when you drive a car.   (CET-4 97/6)

   A. very   B. so   C. too   D. enough

8. He moved away from his parents, and missed them _____ enjoy the exciting life in New York. (CET-4 91/6)

   A. enough to   B. too much to   C. very much to   D. much so as to

9. You can't be _____ careful in making the decision as it was such a critical case.   (CET-6 90/6)

   A. very   B. quite   C. too   D. to

10. The mother said she would _____ her son washing the dishes if he could finish his assignment before supper.   (考研95)

   A. let down   B. let alone   C. let off   D. let out

II. 翻译

11. 二氧化碳是由碳和氧组成的。（consist of）

12. 中国由56个民族组成，而其中的55个少数民族多生活在边远地区，不到总人口的5%。（consist of）

13. 两年前，我回到了阔别了10年之久的家乡。（ago, before）

14. 没看见这块石头，她险些被绊倒。（not seeing...）

15. 你如此美貌与聪慧，让我如何不爱你。（too...not to...）

拓展篇

Halloween party games and fun

Give each guest a crayon and a brown paper bag with holes cut for the eyes and nose. The bags should be big enough to <u>fit over the head</u>. Every one at the party draws a face on his bag. Give a prize of the funniest, <u>the fiercest, the prettiest</u>, and so on. Your parents or elder brothers and sisters can be the judges. The same bags worn backward may be used in blindfold games, such as the following:

Pinning the nose on the witch

<u>Ducking for apples</u>

Potato race

Hunting for nuts

Broom dance

测试篇

1-5 ADBAD   6-10 DCBCC

11. Carbon dioxide consists of carbon and oxygen.

12. China consists of 56 peoples while its 55 minorities live primarily in remote areas and make up only about 5% of the population.

13. Two years ago, I visited my hometown, which I had left 10 years before.

14. Not seeing a stone, she all but tripped down.

15. You are too beautiful and gifted not to make me fall in love with you.

Lesson 14. A noble gangster

Ⅰ.振振有"词"

1. If the money was not paid promptly , the gangsters would quickly put a man out of business by destroying his shop.

promptly 立即地（正式）	gangster 强盗（团伙作案）	put sb. out of business 使某人破产
speedily 迅速地	bandit 歹徒	sb. go bankruptcy 破产
instantly 立刻地	robber 抢劫犯	one's business collapse 破产
swiftly 迅捷地	shoplifter 商店盗窃犯	one's business land on rocks 破产
directly 立刻地	pickpocket 扒手	one's business goes to the dogs 破产
instantaneously 立刻地	burglar 入室盗窃犯	one's business fails 破产
	highwayman 车匪路霸	

形似词辨析：

instantaneous 立刻的
simultaneous 同时的
simultaneous interpretation 同声传译
spontaneous 自发的
spontaneous movement 自发运动

burgle 入室盗窃
burglar 窃贼
pick pocket 偷包
smuggle sth. 走私
pirate sth. 盗版
traffic drugs 贩毒

2. An Englishman, Sir John Hawkwood, made the remarkable discovery that people would rather pay large sums of money than have their life work destroyed by gangsters.

would rather do A than do B	宁愿做A不做B
prefer A to B	宁要A不要B
prefer to doing A to doing B	宁愿做A不做B
prefer to do A rather than do B	宁愿做A不做B
choose A rather than B	选A不选B
not A but B	不是A而是B

3. He soon <u>made a name for himself</u> and came to <u>be known to the Italians as</u> Giovanni Acuto.

> make a name for oneself 出名
> make one's mark in sth. 出人头地
> rise in the world 飞黄腾达
> make a noise in the world 名噪一时
> set the world on fire 大出风头
> hit the headline 占据头条

> be known as 被称为
> be referred to as 被叫做
> be regarded as 被认为是
> be named after 以…命名
> be fashioned after 根据…设计

II. 现身说"法": would rather 之用法

> People would rather pay large sums of money than have their life work destroyed by gangsters. 人们情愿拿出大笔钱, 也不愿毕生的心血毁于歹徒之手。

1) would rather在这里作情态动词, 其后要用动词原形, 结构为would rather do...than do...

2) would rather 还可引导虚拟语气句型, 与would as soon, would prefer, would sooner用法相同, 结构为would as soon/prefer/sooner sb. did/had done sth., 表示"希望"或"委婉的责备", 谓语动词用过去时指当时或将来的情况, 用现在完成时指过去的情况。例:

I would rather you went abroad. 我希望你出国。

She would as soon chose to study medicine. 她希望学医。

She would sooner have left before her friend arrived. (She did not leave before her friend arrived)
她宁愿在朋友来之前离开。

试比较:

I would rather you accepted his apology. 我宁愿你接受他的道歉。

I would rather accept his apology than quarrel with him. 我宁愿接受道歉也不愿和他争吵。

III. 说"文"解"字"

1. There was a time when the owners of shops and businesses in Chicago had to pay large sums of money to gangsters in return for "protection".

译文: 曾经有一个时期, 芝加哥的店主和商行老板们不得不拿出大笔的钱给歹徒以换取"保护"。

解析: 1) there was a time when...是写作常用句型, 其意义类似于once, 可相互替换, 但前者更有利于扩展篇幅。例:

There was a time when Iraq was fairly prosperous. 伊拉克曾经相当富有。

2) in return for... 在句中作目的状语, 意为"为了换取…", 可用in exchange for...替换。例:

He kisses up to his superior in return for his favor. 他巴结上司以期得到对方的恩宠。

2. As long ago as the fourteenth century, an Englishman, Sir John Hawkwood, made the remarkable discovery...

译文: 早在14世纪, 英国人约翰·霍克伍德爵士就有过非凡的发现。

解析: 1) 在the fourteen century前加as long ago as表示强调。事实上, 英文中同级比较短语as...as都有此意义。例:

He earns 4,000 a month. → He earns as much as 4,000 a month. (他每月的工资多达4,000元)

The pagoda is 150 metres. → The pagoda is as high as 150 metres. (这座塔高达150米)

2) Sir 在本句的意思不是"先生"，而是"爵士"。这是一种国王封号，被册封为knight（骑士）或baronet（从男爵）后即可拥有此名。

注：Sir 作"爵士"之意时，其后接人的全名或名，这与Mr. 用法不同。试比较：

Sir John Hawkwood 或 Sir John（约翰·霍克伍德爵士）

Mr. John Hawkwood 或 Mr. Hawkwood（约翰·霍克伍德先生）

> **联想记忆**：常见的英国贵族封号
>
> Duke 公爵　　　　Marquis 侯爵　　　　Earl 伯爵
>
> Viscount 子爵　　Baron 男爵

3. **The Florentines gave him** a state funeral **and had a picture painted which was** dedicated to the memory of **"the most valiant soldier and most notable leader..."**

译文：佛罗伦萨人为他举行了国葬，并为他画像以纪念这位"骁勇善战的战士、威名远扬的头领"。

解析：1) state 作"国家"解时多含政治意义。例：

state visit 国事访问　　　　state banquet 国宴　　　　state affairs 国事

the State Council 国务院　　Secretary of State（美）国务卿

2) sth. is dedicated to sb. 意为"以某物献给某人"，而sth. is dedicated to the memory of sb.则多指词此人已离世。类似短语有：

sth. is in honor of sb.　　sth. is in recognition of sb.　　sth. is in remembrance of sb.

■ 拓 展 篇

Ⅰ. 英语趣园

HAWKWOOD, SIR JOHN （d. 1394）, an English adventurer who attained great wealth and renown as a condottiere （a leader or a member of a troop of mercenaries, especially in Italy） in the Italian wars of the 14th century.

Ⅱ. 听力快车

Renaissance, French for "_____", perfectly describes the _____ and _____ changes that occurred in Europe from the fourteenth through the sixteenth centuries.

During the _____ known by this name, Europe emerged from the economic _____ of the Middle Ages and experienced a time of financial growth. Also, and perhaps most importantly, the Renaissance was an age in which _____, _____, _____, and _____ thought turned in new directions.

Ⅲ. 补充阅读

Condottiere was the leader of mercenary soldiers in Italy in the 14th and 15th centuries, when wars were almost incessant there. The condottieri hired and paid the bands who fought under them. They dealt directly with the cities or states that requested their services and were responsible solely to them. They fought for the highest bidder, passing easily from one lord to another; this game proved dangerous and even fatal to more than one. Some condottieri had small states of their own, either inherited or acquired. The most famous were the Attendolos（founders of the Sforza family）, Colleoni, Carmagnola, and Sir John de Hawkwood.

测 试 篇

I . 单项选择

1. Although I had been invited to the opening ceremony, I was unable to attend ＿＿＿ such short notice.
（考研99）

   A. to   B. in   C. with   D. on

2. Since it is late to change my mind now, I am ＿＿＿ to carrying out the plan.　（考研96）
   A. obliged   B. committed   C. engage   D. resolved

3. We should ＿＿＿ our energy and youth to the development of our country.　（CET-6 02/1）
   A. dedicate   B. cater   C. ascribe   D. cling

4. If any man here does not agree with me, he should ＿＿＿ his own plan for improving the living conditions of these people.　（考研94）

   A. put on   B. put out   C. put in   D. put away

5. The precious manuscripts were hopelessly ＿＿＿ by long exposure in the cold, damp cellar.

   A. damaged   B. destroyed   C. harmed   D. ruined

6. In fact, Peter would rather have left for San Francisco than ＿＿＿ in New York.　（CET-4 02/6）
   A. to stay   B. stayed   C. staying   D. having stayed.

7. Wouldn't you rather your child ＿＿＿ to bed early?　（CET-4 00/1）
   A. go   B. went   C. would go   D. goes

8. We'll put off our sports meet until next week ＿＿＿ the weather is fine.
   A. since   B. as   C. when   D. while

9. Although punctual himself, the professor was quite used ＿＿＿ late for his lecture.　（CET-4 98/1）
   A. to have students   B. for student's being   C. for student's to be   D. to student's being

10. What a shame that no one has put that old deserted mansion ＿＿＿ .
   A. of use   B. to use   C. in use   D. out of use

II . 翻译

11. 两点的时候，他回来了。（when）

12. 我不图回报。（in return for）

13. 我宁愿这世界上从来没有过汽车。（would rather）

14. 谨以此片献给那些为了祖国和人民利益抛头颅，洒热血的骁勇善战的战士们。（be dedicated to）

15. 古时候，长城是用来抵御外敌的。（be used to do）

拓展篇

Renaissance,French for "rebirth," perfectly describes the intellectual and economic changes that occurred in Europe from the fourteenth through the sixteenth centuries.

During the era known by this name, Europe emerged from the economic stagnation of the Middle Ages and experienced a time of financial growth. Also, and perhaps most importantly, the Renaissance was an age in which artistic, social, scientific, and political thought turned in new directions.

测试篇

1-5 DBADD   6-10 BBCDB

11. It was 2 o'clock when he came back.

12. I want nothing in return for my help.

13. I would rather there were not any car in the world!

14. The film was dedicated to the memory of those valiant soldiers who sacrificed for the interest of the country and its people.

15. In ancient times, the Great Wall was used to protect against enemies.

Lesson **15.** Fifty pence worth of trouble

积 累 篇

I. 振振有"词"

1. Mum or dad, of course, <u>provide a regular supply of</u> <u>pocket money</u>.

> provide a regular supply of sth. 提供…稳定的供应
> cut the supply of 削减…供应
> cut off the supply of 切断…的供应
> supply sb. with sth. 提供某物给某人
> provide sth. for sb. 提供某物给某人
> ply sb. with sth. 不断供给

> pocket money 零花钱
> lucky money 压岁钱
> mad money 私房钱
> beer money（男性）零花钱
> pin money（男性）零花钱
> glove money 贿赂

2. If fifty pence pieces are not <u>exchanged for</u> sweets, they <u>rattle</u> for months inside money boxes.

> exchange A for B 用A交换B
> trade A for B 用A交换B
> do A in return for B 为了换取B而做A
> do A in exchange for B 为了换取B而做A
> 例：He bought his girlfriend a necklace in exchange for her love.
> 为了得到女友的爱，他给她买了一条项链。

> rattle 物体碰撞发出的声响
> 例：The leaves are rattling in the spring
> breeze. 树叶在春风中哗啦啦地作响。
> A rattlesnake will bite its own tail when it
> is cornered. 狗急跳墙。

II. 现身说"法"：advise 与虚拟语气

> **I gave him fifty pence and** advised **him to save it.** 我给了他50便士让他存起来。

advise sb. to do sth. 是一常见结构，意为"建议某人做…"。advise 可引导虚拟语气句型，表示"建议、命令、要求某人做…"，其后的宾语从句中使用情态动词should。若省略should则更显正式，多见于美国英语。例：

My father advised that I（should）pursue a master degree after graduation.

父亲建议我毕业之后攻读硕士。

The doctor advised that she（should）have treatment at an early date. 医生建议她早日接受治疗。

注：英语考试中常常省略should。

联想记忆：引导虚拟语气，与advise用法相同的其他动词

demand	instruct	propose	recommend	suggest
commend	ensure	request	require	decide
order	ledge	intend	decree	determine
instruct	grant	resolve	urge	desire

Ⅲ. 说"文"解"字"

1. **But** uncles and aunts **are always a source of extra** income.

译文：但是，叔舅婶姨也是孩子们额外收入的来源。

解析：1）相比而言，中国文化更加注重人际关系，伦理纲常。因此，种类繁多的敬称、尊称应运而生。而西方文化强调个性、平等，直呼其名的现象比比皆是，称呼语也就相对贫乏。如uncle可指"叔、舅、姑父、姨夫、伯父"等，而uncle可指"婶、姨、姑、舅母、伯母"等。

2）income 本指工作收入，这里用于儿童是一种幽默表述。

2. With **some children, small sums** go a long way.

译文：对于有些孩子，少量的钱可以花上很长时间。

解析：1）with 在本句中表示关系，相当于for。例：

be angry with sb. 对某人发怒　　raise a question for sb. 向某人提问

have influence for sb. 对某人有影响

◯ **with比较特殊的用法**

①with 作"尽管，虽然"解：

With all her faults, I like her. 尽管她有种种缺点，我还是喜欢她。

②with 作"在…看来"解：

The housing shortage is very much with us today. 我们目前住房十分紧张。

③with 作"作为…的成员"解：

I got a job with a publishing house. 我在一家出版社找了份工作。

④with 作"由…负责，处理"解：

It rests with you to decide. 这事由你决定。

2）go a long way 本指"走了很长的路"，这里显然是拟人用法。例：

Budget your money and it will go a long way. 精打细算就会细水长流。

With him, hundreds of money goes a short way. 对他来说，几百块钱花不了几天。

3. Instead he bought himself fifty pence worth of trouble.

译文：他却给自己买了50便士的麻烦。

解析：instead 相当于but或however，表转折。实际上，这是一种承前省略的用法，instead 之后省略了of，目的在于简洁。补全后的完整句子为：Instead（of saving it）he bought himself fifty pence worth of trouble. 再举一个例子：

I advised him to study medicine. Instead（of studying medicine）he chose English as his major. 我建议他学医。他却选择主修英文。

拓 展 篇

Ⅰ. 英语趣园

Pierre Werner is generally accepted as the father of the euro. A common currency for Europe was hinted at in the European Union's founding treaty signed in Rome in 1957, but Mr. Werner later became its most public advocate; more than that, a zealot. He had first suggested a common currency for Europe back in 1960, but had to wait for 42 years before it was launched as real notes and coins in 2002.

Ⅱ. 听力快车 🎧

Choose the best answer for each of the following questions.

1. What did the speaker and his nephew do last week?

    A. They kicked a football into the garden.

    B. They played for over an hour with a football.

    C. They stood between two apple trees.

    D. They were busy in the garden for more than an hour

2. A schoolboy may get an offer from a scout if he is an

    A. incredible player   B. outside player

    C. experienced player   D. exceptional player

3. What does an apprentice footballer promise at 18?

    A. Becoming a promising football player.

    B. Working or a professional football club.

    C. Searching for new amateur players.

    D. Doing more schoolboy international matches.

Ⅲ. 补充阅读

My little niece, a ten-month-old baby, is the loveliest child I have ever seen. Her face is like a red apple and her eyes are like bright stars. When you carry her in your arms, she likes to put her arms around your neck. All the grown-ups in the family love her very much and often try to make her smile. But quite often it is she who makes us laugh. Once I winked at her and she smiled. When I did it again, she watched me attentively. Then she tried to imitate. While we closed one eye to wink, she closed both eyes at the same time, and then quickly opened them again. And that was her way to wink. We all burst into laughter. When we looked at her again, she was staring at us, puzzled, as if she was asking: "What are you laughing at?"

⏩ 测 试 篇 ◀

Ⅰ.单项选择

1. As I'll be away for at least a year, I'd appreciate _____ from you now and then telling me how everyone is getting along.

   A. hearing   B. to hear   C. to be hearing   D. having heard

2. People appreciate _____ with him because he has a good sense of humor.   （CET-4 98/1）

   A. to work   B. to have worked   C. working   D. having worked

3. When traveling, you are advised to take traveler's checks, which provide a secure _____ to carrying your money in cash.   （考研96）

   A. substitute   B. selection   C. preference   D. alternative

4. The mayor _____ the police officer a medal of honor for his heroic deed in rescuing the earthquake victims.   （CET-4 05/6）

   A. rewarded   B. awarded   C. credited   D. prized

5. The bank is offering a _____ to anyone who can give information about the robbery.   （CET-6 04/6）

   A. reward   B. bonus   C. prize   D. compliment

6. Nowadays many rural people flock to the city to look for jobs on the assumption that the streets there are _____ with gold.   （CET-6 05/6）

   A. overwhelmed   B. stocked   C. paved   D. overlapped

7. Many in the credit industry expect that credit cards will eventually _____ paper money for almost every purchase.   （CET-4 03/9）

   A. exchange   B. reduce   C. replace   D. trade

8. The ball _____ two or three times before rolling down the slope.   （CET-6 03/1）

   A. swayed   B. bounced   C. hopped   D. darted

9. Professor Hawking is _____ as one of the world's greatest living physicists.   （CET-6 02/6）

   A. dignified   B. clarified   C. acknowledged   D. illustrated

10. The education _____ for the coming year is about $4 billion, which is much more than what people expected.   （CET-6 97/1）

    A. allowance   B. reservation   C. budget   D. finance

Ⅱ.翻译

11. 雨点乒乒乓乓地砸在玻璃上。（rattle）

12. 吸烟对某些人来说，可能是种享受，但却是他人烦恼的来源。（be a source of）

13. 只有大约十分之一的发明最终能成为商品。（find its way）

14. 他悬赏2000美金以寻找他下落不明的儿子。（reward）

15. 我喜欢听储蓄罐里的硬币叮叮当当落下的清脆的声音。（money box）

拓展篇

1.B   2.D   3.B

Last week I bought a football for my little nephew. He was delighted with it, and ran out into the garden kick it about. Two apple trees substituted for goal posts and I had to act as a goalkeeper. He kept me busy there for more than an hour and he is only five. Every boy has a natural impulse to kick a football about. And famous football stars are the gods of those little boys. How many dream that one day they will be gods too—professional footballers? If a schoolboy plays very well, he may find himself in an important match, a schoolboy international for example. The big clubs send "scouts" to these events to look for promising young players. An outstanding boy may be invited by a "scout" to register with the club that he represents as an "associated schoolboy".

Clubs may register schoolboys over the age of 13, although they are not allowed to play in matches until they have reached the official school-leaving age. But they are well coached and trained. When one of these boys leaves school, he may, if he wishes, become an apprentice footballer to the team he has been associated with. Thus he is taught his job in the same way as any other apprentice; moreover, he is paid while he is being taught. At 18 the apprentice is compelled to make up his mind whether to become a professional or to return to being an amateur. This decision has to be very carefully considered.

测试篇

1-5 ACDBA   6-10 CCBCC

11. The raindrops rattle the windowpane.

12. Smoking, which may be a pleasure for some people, is a serious source of discomfort for their fellows.

13. Only about one out of ten inventions will finally find its way on the shelf in the shop.

14. He offered a reward of $2000 for his missing son.

15. I like to listen to the coins landing with a merry jingle in the money box.

Lesson **16.** Mary had a little lamb

积累篇

I. 振振有"词"

1. She <u>kept it tied</u> to a tree in a field during the day and went to <u>fetch</u> it every evening.

> keep it tied 它被绑着
> keep sth./sb. done/doing 是一个固定结构，意
> 为：使某物/某人…。用done还是doing要根据
> sth./sb.是动作的执行者还是承受者而定。例：
> keep the door closed 让门紧闭着
> keep the fire burning 让火着着

> fetch sth. 去取某物
> deliver sth. 运送某物
> transport sth. 运输某物
> convey sth. 传送某物
> bring in sth. 带来某物
> send for sb. 去请某人

2. He told him he <u>had better return it</u> or he would call the police.

> sb. had better do sth. 是常用句型，意为："某人
> 最好做某事"，表建议。其他类似句型有：
> sb. may/might as well do sth. 某人不妨做某事。
> 比较：sb. may/might well do sth. 某人有理由/
> 满可以做某事。

> or在该句中不表选择，而表条件，引导从句，
> 大致相当于if not，是对前面主句内容的否定。
> 因此，其完整叙述为：if he did not return it.
> otherwise在用法上与or相同。

3. Dimitri <u>apologized to Aleko for</u> having <u>accused</u> him.

> apologize to sb. for sth.
> be apologetic to sb. for sth.
> make an apology to sb. for sth.
> 为某事向某人道歉
> be remorseful for sth. 为某事懊悔
> be repentant for sth. 为某事后悔

> accuse sb. for sth.
> 因为某事指责某人
> bring an accusation against sb.
> 起诉某人
> be under an accusation 被指控
> be under an accusation 被指控

> be under an accusation 被指控
> charge sb. with sth. 因为某事指责某人
> denounce sb. for sth. 因为某事斥责某人
> condemn sb. for sth. 因为某事谴责某人
> impeach sb. for sth. 因为某事弹劾某人

II. 现身说"法"：-ed分词作宾语补足语

She kept it tied **to a tree in the field during the day...**（本句的tied作宾语补足语）
她白天将它拴在地里的一棵树上。

-ed分词作宾语补足语一般用于以下几种情形：

1. 置于表示"致使"意义的动词之后，如 get、make、have、keep等。例：
   The reporter tried to make the scandal known by the public. 这位记者试图让公众了解这个丑闻。
   Our government keeps us informed of the latest development of our country.
   政府使我们了解了国家的最新发展。

2. 置于表示"希望、要求"等意义的动词之后，如 want、wish、order、like等。例：
   He liked this proposal（to be）favored by his superior. 他希望这项提议受到上司的重视。
   He ordered such an unfair provision（to be）deleted. 他要求去除这项不公正的条款。

3. 置于表示感觉和心理状态的动词之后，如 see、hear、feel、find、think等。例：
   I found him greatly changed. 我发现他变化很大。
   He felt his skin scratched by the thorn. 他觉得皮肤被刺划伤了。
   Nobody thought the game lost. 没有人认为比赛输了。
   The man saw the little boy scared. 那人发觉小孩很害怕。

III. 说"文"解"字"

1. **One evening, however, the** lamb **was** missing.
   译文：然而，一天晚上，那只羊羔失踪了。
   解析：1）英文中-mb结尾的词b不发音。例：
   　　　　　dumb　　numb　　plumb　　tomb　　comb　　womb
   　　　2）英文中关于"羊"的习语
   　　　　　The old woman is mutton dressed like a lamb. 那个老太太是个老来俏/装嫩。
   　　　　　He is a lamb. 他很温顺。
   　　　　　He is a black sheep. 他是害群之马/败家子。
   　　　　　He is a goat. 他是个色狼。
   　　　　　He often gets my goat. 他经常惹我生气。
   　　　　　separate sheep from goats 区分好人与坏人
   　　　3）missing与lost是同义词，但前者还表示"离开原位的，不在原处的"，例：
   　　　　　a missing tooth 掉了的牙齿（不是"丢失的"）
   　　　　　Five students were missing from class today. 今天5个学生没来上课。（不是"丢失的"）

2. **He told him he had better return it** or **he would call the police.**
   译文：他告诉他最好把羊交还。否则就要报警。
   解析：or在这里引导虚拟语气，实际上是一种暗含性的条件从句，相当于if he did not return it.
   　　　otherwise的用法与or相同。例：
   　　　I was ill that day. Or/Otherwise I would have done you a favor.
   　　　那天我病了。否则我会帮你忙的。（or/otherwise=if I had not been ill）

Society needs education, just as education needs society. Or/Otherwise, what would become of civilization? 社会需要教育，如同教育需要社会一样。否则，文明将会怎样？（or/otherwise=if society did not need education）

3. It was true that **he had just bought a lamb,...** but **his lamb was black.**

译文：诚然，他刚买了只羊… 但他的羊是黑色的。

解析：It is true that...表示让步，相当于although/though. 类似用法的还有：

While it is true that..., 主句   While it is true that..., it is also true that....

While..., 主句   Granted that..., but...

例：While it is true that you may be right, you can not be so supercilious.

尽管你或许是对的，但你不应那么傲慢。

While this competition may induce efforts to expand territory at the expense of others, it can not be said that war-like conflict among nations is inevitable. 尽管这样的竞争可能会引发损害他人利益的扩张领地的行为，但这不并不意味着国家间类似于战争的冲突不可避免。

拓 展 篇

Ⅰ. 英语趣园

Cattle rustler is a profession in the West involving in the stealing of branded cattle and altering the brand. In the very early west, cattle rustling was almost accepted as a way to build up one's livestock, which is how many a cattle rancher got his start.

Ⅱ. 听力快车 🎧

Mary had a little lamb

Mary had a little lamb,
Little lamb, little lamb.
Mary had a little lamb,
Its fleece was white as snow.
And everywhere that Mary went,
Mary went, Mary went,
Everywhere that Mary went,
The lamb was sure to go.
It followed her to school one day,
School one day, school one day.
It followed her to school one day,
That was against the rule.

It made the children laugh and play,
Laugh and play, laugh and play,
It made the children laugh and play,
To see a lamb at school.
Why does the lamb love Mary so,
Mary so, Mary so?
Why does the lamb love Mary so?
The eager children cry.
Why, Mary loves the lamb, you know,
Lamb, you know, lamb, you know.
Mary loves the lamb, you know,
The teacher did reply.

Ⅲ. 补充阅读

As late as the 1880s a man in the Far West could be hanged for stealing a horse, yet get no more than five years in jail for robbing a bank. Ever since the pioneers went west into the unknown, they depended entirely on their horses and their guns. If a man lost his horse or his gun in the deserts, mountains or forests of Nevada, Arizona or eastern California, he stood no chance. Hunger, thirst, a grizzly bear, a mountain lion, or hostile Indians would finish him off sooner or later. A frontiersman had to be tough, brave and resourceful in those days.

Deserts, mountains and forests are still the frontier between teeming Californian cities and the sparsely populated wilderness of Nevada and eastern California. Even today, Nevada has hardly more than 500,000 inhabitants, most of whom live in the cities of Las Vegas and Reno.

In 1849 gold was discovered in California in the mountains near San Francisco. So started the famous Gold Rush of the 49ers across the vast, unexplored wilderness that lay west of the Mississippi. Whole families perished. One small group of 49ers, looking for a short cut across the Sierra Nevada Mountains, happened to enter the infamous Death Valley. It was lucky for them it was winter, for in summer Death Valley is about the hottest and most desolate place on earth. As it was, one of the group died of thirst, and it was the 49ers who gave the valley its grim name.

Later, in 1865, after the Civil War, disillusioned soldiers, unable to find work, followed in the footsteps of the 49ers. They did not find much gold, but they found rich pastures for cattle. It was they who founded the USA's great food industry, and they worked with the vigor and courage of the early pioneers and with a faith fortified by the Bible.

The colonization of the West was given a tremendous impetus by the building of he Transcontinental Railroad, one of the greatest engineering feats of all time. Congress decided that the laying of the tracks should begin from the East and the West at the same time. So the building of this railroad, lined with poles for the first east-west telegraph system, developed into a race. The Easterners, moving across the plains, progressed faster, for they did not have to tunnel through giant mountains or bridge gaping canyons. The two railroads linked up in Utah on July 10,1867. There was great excitement, and a special ceremony to mark the occasion.

The completion of the railroad not only joined the cities of the east with California, it also brought prosperity to the isolated farmers of the plains, and to the ranchers who were now able to send their cattle to the slaughterhouses in freight cars. In fact, the new railroad became an essential life-line for a nation which now stretched 3,000 miles from the Atlantic to the Pacific Oceans.

Some Americans feel that the frontier spirit no longer exists in the USA. But it still expresses itself in a number of ways. Americans do not like being without work, and they will travel hundreds of miles in search of a job, showing a courage and an enterprise which is unusual in most of the older European countries. Then there is the exploration of outer space. President John Kennedy in a speech to the nation, spoke of this "New Frontier." The frontier spirit certainly played a part in putting the first men on the moon, the most recent of all frontiers to be crossed.

◆▶ 测 试 篇 ◀◆

I . 单项选择

1. The soldier was _____ of running away when he enemy attacked.　　　　　　　（CET-4 97/6）
   A. scolded　　　　　B. charged　　　　　C. accused　　　　　D. punished

2. The police accused him of setting fire to the building but he denied _____ in the area on the night of the

fire.　　　　　　　　　　　　　　　　　　　　　　　　(CET-6 96/1)

A. to be　　　　B. to have been　　　C. having been　　　D be

3. Some teenagers harbor a generalized resentment against society, which _____ them the rights and privileges of adults, although physically they are mature.　　　　(考研93)

A. deprives　　　B.restricts　　　C. rejects　　　D. denies

4. American women were _____ the right to vote until 1920 after many years of hard struggle. (CET-4 91/6)

A. ignored　　　B. neglected　　　C. denied　　　D. refused

5. She felt that her husband's conduct was _____.

A. shameful　　　B. ashamed　　　C. shameless　　　D. shamed

6. When she saw the clouds she went back to house to _____ her umbrella.　(考研90)

A. carry　　　B. fetch　　　C. bring　　　D. reach

7. Having decide to rent a flat, we _____ contacting all the accommodation agencies in the city.

(CET-4 98/1)

A. set about　　　B. set down　　　C. set out　　　D. set up

8. It's through learning that the individual _____ many habitual ways of reacting to situations.

(CET-6 98/6)

A. retains　　　B. gains　　　C. achieves　　　D. acquires

9. Not until the game had begun _____ at the sports ground.　　(CET-4 00/6)

A. had he arrived　　　　　　B. would he have arrived

C. did he arrive　　　　　　D. should he have arrived

10. Until then, his family _____ from him for 6 months.　　(CET-4 97/1)

A. didn't hear　　　　　　B. hasn't been hearing

C. hasn't heard　　　　　　D. hadn't heard

Ⅱ.翻译

11. 我注意到一大堆蜗牛正在我心爱的花木上爬来爬去。（prize plants）

12. 我的钱包不见了。（be found missing）

13. 冬天，你最好多穿一点。（had better）

14. 不亲眼见到我决不相信。（not...until...）

15. 底特律被誉为汽车之城。（acquire a reputation as...）

答 案

测试篇

1-5 CCDCA　　　　6-10 BADCD

11. I noticed that a number of snails were taking a stroll on some of my prize plants.

12. My purse was found missing.

13. You'd better keep warm in winter.

14. I won't believe it until I saw it.

15. Detroit has acquired a reputation as Motor City.

Lesson The longest suspension bridge in the world

Ⅰ.振振有"词"

1. He <u>described it as</u> "a very <u>agreeable</u> situation <u>located within</u> two small hills..."

describe A as B　把A描述成B
perceive A as B　把A想像成B
refer to A as B　把A称作B
feel A as B　　　把A看作B
accept A as B　　把A看作B

be located in...位于
be situated in...坐落于
be sited in...位于（多指人为因素）

be based in...总部位于
stand 矗立

agreeable 宜人的；可口的
impressionable 思想不稳定的，易受影响的
impressive 有感染力的，令人印象深的
susceptible 易受感动的

2. Though Verrazano is <u>by no means</u> considered to be a great explorer, his name will probably remain <u>immortal</u>.

一般而言，m打头的形容词的反义词前缀是im。
mortal 必死的；绝症的
immortal 永垂不朽的
moral 有道德的
immoral 可耻的
moderate 适度的
immoderate 过度的

by no means 决不
by any means 不惜任何代价
by fair means or foul 不择手段地
by all means（回答用语）当然可以
by means of...使用…
beyond one's means 入不敷出

3. It has been <u>estimated</u> that if the bridge <u>were packed with</u> cars...

estimate 估算
overestimate 高估
underestimate 低估
make a guess at...猜测
compute 计算
calculate 计算

be packed with 塞满了…
be crowded with 挤满了…
be thronged with 挤满了…
be packed to capacity 拥挤不堪
be crowded like a warren of rabbits 极度拥挤

II. 现身说"法": 介词+which/whom引导定语从句

Verrazano, an Italian about whom little is known, sailed into New York Harbour in 1524...(彩色部分属于定语从句"介词+关系代词"的用法)

1524年, 一位鲜为人知的意大利人维拉萨诺驾船驶进了纽约港。

一般而言, 该介词在句中的用法可依据以下规律判断:

1. 介词与定语从句中的谓语动词构成短语动词, 如speak of、hear of、read of、deal with、depend on 等。这些介词既可放在句末, 也可前置。但若是固定的动词词组, 则不可将介词前置, 如look at、look for 等。例:

The man with whom I work is very hospitable and sincere. 与我共事的那个人非常好客真诚。

I really love the book of which you've spoken of. 我特别喜欢你提到的那本书。

2. 看介词是否与先行词构成搭配, 即介词短语或介词词组。例:

1) He described it as "a very agreeable situation located within two small hills in the midst of which flowed a great river." 他对该港作了如下描述: "周围环境非常宜人, 位于两座小山之间, 一条大河流淌其间。"

解析: which指two small hills, 因此in the midst of which复原后即是in the midst of two small hills.

2) The resulting situation-in which most people would not be working in their jobs for more than two or three short days a week-could hardly continue to be one in which employment was still regarded as the only truly valid form of work. 最后的情形是: 多数人一周的工作时间不会超过两三天, 这将使得就业不再被认为是惟一有效的工作方式了。

解析: 此例中的which指the resulting situation, 因此, in which复原后就是in the resulting situation.

3) The American economic system is, organized around a basically private-enterprise, market-oriented economy in which consumers largely determine what shall be produced by spending their money in the marketplace for those goods and services that they want most. 美国的经济体系是以私有企业为构架的市场经济, 在这种体系中, 消费者通过在市场上购买最需要的商品或服务极大地决定了该生产何种产品。

解析: 此例中的which指market-oriented economy, 因此, in which复原后就是in market-oriented economy.

III. 说"文"解"字"

1. He described it as "a very agreeable situation located within two small hills in the midst of which flowed a great river."

译文: 他对该港作了如下描述: "周围环境非常宜人, 位于两座小山之间, 一条大河流淌其间。"

解析: 彩色部分运用了倒装结构, 原因是前面有介词短语有in the midst of.... 一般而言, 在使用不及物动词的句子中, 如果将说明方位的状语放在句首时, 往往使用倒装。例:

In the far distance came the roaring of a fire engine. 远处传来了消防车的轰鸣声。

By the riverside stands a respectable old man. 河边站着一位可敬的老者。

2. These alone took sixteen months to build.

译文: 仅这些就花了16个月才建成。

解析: 1) alone作定语时只能置于所修饰的名词之后。此外, -able或-ible结尾的形容词多属于此种用法，以下是一些例证：

a person responsible 负责人（注意：a responsible person 有责任心的人）

a sight visible 可见的景象　　　　a canal navigable 可通航的运河

the best possible 尽可能好的方式　　the largest sum of money available 能拿到的最大一笔钱

the most democratic form of college imaginable 能想像到的最民主的大学形式

2）sb. take+时间+to do sth.是一常用句型，意为："花…时间做某事"。类似用法的句型还有：

It takes sb.+时间+to do sth.　　　　sth. cost sb.+时间

sb. spend+时间+（in）doing sth.　　sb. spend+时间+on sth.

3. It has been estimated that if the bridge were packed with cars...

译文：据估计，若桥上摆满了汽车……

解析：彩色部分是一常用句型，可用于写作的开篇，其他类似结构有：

It is said that... 据说…　　　　It is reported that... 据报道…

It is recounted that... 据记载…　　It is rumoured that... 据谣传…

拓 展 篇

Ⅰ. 英语趣园

Giovanni Da Verrazzano

Giovanni da Verrazzano was born in Tuscany, Italy in 1485 and died in 1528 in the Lesser Antilles. He was a Florentine explorer sailing under the French flag. Without question, He was the first European to enter New York Bay in 1524.

Virtually unknown, Verrazzano was raised from obscurity by the efforts of John N. LaCorte, founder of the Italian Historical Society of America, who was instrumental in having the bridge spanning the entrance to New York Harbor at the narrows and joining Staten Island and Brooklyn named The Verrazzano-Narrows Bridge.

Ⅱ. 听力快车 🎧

In _____, Dutch settlers purchased _____ Island from local Indian chiefs and built town of ____ in 1664. It was captured by the English and renamed _____.

Ⅲ. 补充阅读

Suspension

Of all the bridge types in use today, the suspension bridge allows for the longest spans. At first glance the suspension and cable-stayed bridges may look similar, but they are quite different. Though suspension bridges are leading long span technology today, they are in fact a very old form of bridge. Some primitive examples of suspension bridges use vines and ropes for cables.

The development of metals brought the use of linked iron bars and chains. But it was the introduction of steel wire ropes that allowed spans of over 500m to become a reality. Today the Akashi

Kaikyo Bridge boasts the world's longest center span of any bridge at 1,991 meters.

A typical suspension bridge is a continuous girder with one or more towers erected above piers in the middle of the span. The girder itself it usually a truss or box girder, though in shorter spans plate girders are not uncommon. At both ends of the bridge large anchors or counter weights are placed to hold the ends of the cables.

The main cables are stretched from one anchor over the tops of the tower(s) and attached to the opposite anchor. The cables pass over a special structure known as a saddle. The saddle allows the cables to slide as loads pull from one side or the other and to smoothly transfer the load from the cables to the tower.

From the main cables, smaller cables known as hanger cables or hanger ropes are hung down and attached to the girder. Some suspension bridges do not use anchors, but instead attach the main cables to the ends of the girder. These self-anchoring suspension bridges rely on the weight of the end spans to balance the center span and anchor the cable.

Thus, unlike normal bridges which rest on piers and abutments, the girder or roadway is actually hanging suspended from the main cables. The majority of the weight of the bridge and any vehicles on it are suspended from the cables. In turn the cables are held up only by the tower(s); there is an incredible amount of weight that the towers must be able to support.

As explained in the cable stayed bridge section, steel cables are extremely strong yet flexible. Like a very strong piece of string, it is good for hanging or pulling something, but it is useless for trying to push something. Long span suspension bridges, though strong under normal traffic loads, are vulnerable to the forces of winds. Special measures are taken to assure that the bridge does not vibrate or sway excessively under heavy winds.

The most famous example of an aerodynamically unstable bridge is the Tacoma Narrows Bridge in Washington State, USA.

▶ 测 试 篇 ◀

I. 单项选择

1. For the new country to survive, _____ for its people to enjoy prosperity, new economic policies will be required. (考研97)

   A. to name a few   B. let alone   C. not to speak   D. let's say

2. Mobile telecommunications _____ is expected to double in Shanghai this year as a result of a contract signed between the two companies. (CET-4 02/1)

   A. capacity   B. potential   C. possession   D. impact

3. He soon received promotion, for his superiors realized that he was a man of considerable _____. (CET-4 02/6)

   A. ability   B. future   C. possibility   D. opportunity

4. According to the American federal government, residents of Hawaii have the longest life _____: 77.2 years. (CET-4 01/6)

   A. scope   B. rank   C. span   D. scale

5. The microscope and telescope, with their capacity to enlarge, isolate and probe, demonstrate how details

can be _____ and separated from the whole. （CET-6 05/1）

    A. radiated   B. extended   C. prolonged   D. magnified

6. In India more than one hundred languages are spoken, _____ which only fourteen are recognized as official. （CET-4 03/9）

    A. of   B. in   C. with   D. within

7. We have been told that under no circumstances _____ the telephone in the office for personal affairs. （CET-4 99/6）

    A. may we use   B. we may use   C. we could use   D. did we use

8. The doctors don't _____ that the patient will live much longer. （CET-6 04/1）

    A. monitor   B. manifest   C. articulate   D. anticipate

9. The goals _____ he had fought all his life no longer seemed important to him.

    A. for that   B. for which   C. with that   D. with which

10. You will want two trees about 10 feet apart, from _____ to suspend your tent.

    A. there   B. them   C. which   D. where

Ⅱ. 翻译

11. Vasco da Gama, 葡萄牙人, 关于此人知之甚少, 但在1498年的时候, 他首先发现了印度。（about whom）

12. 仅仅凭MBA培训本身是不足以使你成为成功的管理者的。（...alone...）

13. 珠穆朗玛峰高达8844米。（rise to a height of）

14. 无论如何你也不能相信他。（by no means...）

15. 我正在开会。（in the middle of）

 答·案

拓展篇

    In 1626, Dutch settlers purchased Manhattan Island from local Indian chiefs and built town of New Amsterdam in 1664. It was captured by the English and renamed New York.

测试篇

1-5 BAACD   6-10 AADBC

11. Vasco da Gama, a Portuguese about whom little was known, first discovered India.

12. The MBA training alone does not promise you a successful manager.

13. Everest rises to a height to 8844 m.

14. By no means can you trust him.

15. I was in the middle of a meeting.

Lesson Electric currents in modern art

积累篇

Ⅰ.振振有"词"

1. Even people who <u>take no interest in</u> art cannot have <u>failed to notice</u> examples of modern sculpture <u>on display</u>.

on display 在展出
make a display of sth. 展示…
make a poor exhibition of oneself 出丑
make a spectacle of oneself 出洋相
make a poor show of oneself 出洋相
make an excellent show of oneself 出彩

take interested in 对…感兴趣   be engrossed with…对…痴迷
be interested in…对…感兴趣   be crazy about…对…疯狂
be absorbed in…对…着迷   be keen about…对…热切
be fascinated with…对…痴迷

在正式表达中，常用间接否定代替直接否定，如：
fail to do 替代 don't do
deny doing 替代 don't admit doing
object to doing 替代 don't agree to do

2. Oddly shaped forms that are suspended from the ceiling and move <u>in response to</u> <u>a gust of wind</u> <u>are quite familiar to</u> everybody.

sth. is familiar to sb.某物对于某人来说很熟悉
sb. is familiar with…对…很熟悉
familiarize oneself with 熟悉...
be acquainted with 对…很熟悉
acquaint oneself with 熟悉…

in response to 随着；对…回应
The response was tremendous. 反响很强烈
cause tremendous sensation 引起极大轰动
make a positive feedback to 对…做出积极反馈

a gust of wind 一阵风   a burst of applause 一阵掌声
a burst of anger 一阵发怒   a burst/spasm of emotion 感情的迸发
a burst of laughter 一阵大笑

3. The <u>spheres</u> had been <u>magnetized</u> and attracted and <u>repelled</u> all the time.

sphere 球体
hemisphere 半球
the northern/southern /western/eastern hemisphere
北/南/西/东半球

magnetize 磁化　　　有磁力的；有魅力的
magnet 磁铁；有影响　magnate 大亨
力的人或物　　　magnificent 壮观的
magnetic

repel 排斥；厌恶
dispel 消除
expel 驱逐

be impelled to do（内因）被迫做
be compelled to do（外因）被迫做

II. 现身说"法"：not only...but...as well 与主谓语一致

These peculiar forms not only seemed designed to shock people emotionally, but to give them electric shocks as well!

这些奇形怪状的展品不仅是为了给人感情上的强烈刺激，而且还想给人电击似的！

一般而言，由 not only...but...as well（包括两种变体 not only...but also, not only...but...）连接的并列主语所使用的谓语动词的单复数要依据最靠近的名词来决定，即就近原则。例：

Not only his classmates but his girlfriend has donated some money as well.

不仅他的同学，而且他的女友也捐了款。

Not only the switches but also the wiring has been replaced. 不仅开关，而且旧电线都换掉了。

与此用法相同的结构还有：

either...or... 或者…或者…　　　neither...nor... 既不…也不…

例：Either you or he is to blame. 要么怪你，要么怪他。

Neither he nor you are wrong. 他和你都没错。

> **补充**
>
> 1. every（each, many a, more than one）后面加名词作主语，或者 every/each...and...做主语，谓语要用单数。例：
>
> Every means has been tried but without much result. 每个方法都试过了，但几乎没什么效果。
>
> Every boy and every girl has to be checked. 所有的男孩女孩都要接受检查。
>
> 2. Enough of..., most of..., half of..., (a) part of..., plenty of..., 分数/百分数+of...等结构作主语的谓语单复数取决于 of 之后的名词。例：
>
> 45 percent of the workers are well-trained. 45%的工人都经过良好的培训。
>
> Most of the earth's surface is sea. 地球表面的大部分是海洋。

III. 说"文"解"字"

1. Even people who take no interest in art cannot have failed to notice examples of modern sculpture on display in public places.

译文：即使是对艺术不感兴趣的人也不会注意不到在公共场所展示的现代艺术品。

解析：彩色部分是否定与猜测相结合的用法，意为"不可能不…"。

cannot+have+过去分词表对现在的推测, 意为"不可能…"。cannot也可换用could not, 表示"过去不可能…"。例:

Anyone who loves animals cannot have tolerated such atrocity toward them.

任何喜欢爱护动物的人都不可能容忍这种对待动物的残忍行为。

He could not have done such a thing. He is not a stupid guy. 他不可能做这种事。他根本不傻。

2. In spite of this, some people—including myself—were surprised by a recent exhibition of modern sculpture.

译文: 尽管如此, 最近举办的一次现代雕塑展还是让许多人(包括我在内)大吃一惊。

解析: 1) including myself在句中作some people的同位语。可连接同位语的标记词还有: such as, such...as..., for example, for instance, that is, in other words, so to speak, for short等。

2) 在阅读过程中遇有破折号, 可先将其间的内容略去不读, 搜寻主干句, 以加快阅读速度。

3. These peculiar forms not only seemed designed to shock people emotionally, but to give them electric shocks as well!

译文: 这些奇形怪状的展品不仅是为了给人感情上的强烈刺激, 而且还想给人电击似的!

解析: 请注意emotionally在汉语中译成了短语"给人感情上的", 形成英汉互译的不对称。实际上, 这是经常使用的一种变通手法, 即英文中的副词常可译为汉语中的短语, 甚至句子, 反之亦然, 以使语言更加顺畅自然。例:

Since I come from a poor family, I'm now heavily burdened physically and mentally in the modern society. 我来自穷苦人家, 在如今的社会里感到身体上负荷过重, 精神上压力很大。

The history of Chinese thought can be conveniently divided into three main periods. (胡适)

为了方便起见, 中国思想史可以分为三个主要历史时期。

Politically and economically, the U.S. is a superpower. 美国在政治上和经济上都是超级大国。

■ 拓 展 篇

I.英语趣园

Ice lantern art

In the far north of China, ice sculpture, or bingdiao, is an art form ideally tailored to the long winter months.

The ice lanterns of Harbin derive their name from the age-old fishermen's tradition of using hollowed-out blocks of ice as lamp shades to shield their candles from the wind. These ice lanterns were the forerunners of today's art form. Integrated with the art of lantern making, ice lanterns became ice sculpture.

II.听力快车

One of the central occupations of the ＿＿＿＿＿ is the observation of the human beings. Painters and sculptors ＿＿＿＿＿; writers ＿＿＿＿＿ about human experience; ＿＿＿ give melodic contours to the human spirit; historians and philosophers ponder the essential qualities of the ＿＿＿＿＿. And in our own lives, in our own ways, we spend a great deal of our energy and attention on our fellow creatures, being in families and other kinds of relationships, observing people with ＿＿＿＿＿ in the course of the day, thinking about and forming our own character—deciding what kind of person we wish to be — as we grow.

III. 补充阅读

Harbin international ice snow festival

"Harbin" is transliterated from Manzu language —"Alejin", which means reputation & fame. This area is one of the main areas of activities for the northern nations in the ancient times.

Harbin is praised as "a pearl under the swan's neck" by its unique city view and natural scenery. It attracts more and more tourists by its natural feature ice and snow resources in recent years.

Harbin is a cradle of the Chinese snow and ice art and the Harbin lantern is well known both at home and abroad.

The industrious and ingenious residents of Harbin make full use of the richly endowed snow and ice resources and create the exquisite and varied ice lantern art works with natural ice blocks from Songhua River.

Harbin Ice Lantern Show, the earliest and the largest of its kind in the world has now become a traditional large-scale and open air ice lantern art exhibition initiated in the year of 1963. The Ice Lantern Festival takes place in Zhaolin Park. Originally named Daoli Park in 1946. It was renamed Zhaolin Park in honor of General Li Zhaolin, a national hero assassinated by the Kuomintang operatives during the Anti-Japanese War. And now becomes a world famous snow and ice tourist resort.

In the natural environment with a lot of ice and snow, Harbin people put emphasis on investigation of ice and snow resources from the cultural point of view.

The ice people of Manchuria produce large scale ice sculptures in may shapes and forms, such as illuminated ice pagodas, bridges, lanterns, human figures, palaces. Made of ice blocks chainsawed from the frozen Songhua River, ice artists create sculptures of the U.S. Capitol, a Russian church and other sights stand over 40 feet tall. Using ice as a medium, they turn their city into a shining crystal palace. Harbin becomes an icy fantasyland.

◆▶ 测 试 篇 ◀■

I. 单项选择

1. The famous scientist _____ his success to his hard work. (CET-6 00/6)

   A. imparted   B. ascribed   C. granted   D. acknowledged

2. The beam that is _____ by a laser differs in several ways from the light that comes out of a flashlight.

   (CET-4 03/9)

   A. emitted   B. transported   C. motivated   D. translated

3. In order to keep the line moving, customers with lengthy _____ are required to do their banking inside.

   (CET-6 04/1)

   A. transit   B. transactions   C. turnover   D. tempos

4. Retirement is obviously a very complex _____ period; and the earlier you start planning for it, the better.

   (CET-6 03/6)

   A. transformation   B. transmission   C. transaction   D. transition

5. His face _____ as he came in after running all the way from school. (CET-6 03/9)

A. flared   B. fluctuated   C. fluttered   D. flushed

6. When she heard the bad news, her eyes _____ with tears as she struggled to control her emotions.

                                                              （CET-6 04/1）

A. sparkled   B. twinkled   C. radiated   D. glittered

7. Her jewelry _____ under the spotlights and she became the dominant figure at the ball.   （CET-6 03/1）

A. glared   B. glittered   C. blazed   D. dazzled

8. San Francisco is usually cool in the summer, but L.A. _____.

A. is rarely   B. rarely is   C. hardly is   D. is scarcely

9. The average family _____ four members at most is a great deal smaller than it used to be.

A. which now consist of   B. which now consists of

C. who now consist of   D. who now consists of

10. America's rapid industrial progress has been due to its readiness to adopt new _____ and to interchange information.

A. ideas   B. intentions   C. thoughts   D. views

Ⅱ. 翻译

11. 即便是最笨的学生也不可能没通过这么简单的考试。（can't have failed to do）

12. 前面立了块牌子，上面写着"不许停车"。（which says）

13. 警察针对一系列的走私活动采取了措施。（in response to）

14. 你看起来很面熟。（look familiar）

15. 世界小姐笑盈盈地接过了这顶金灿灿的桂冠。（gleaming smile）

 答 案

拓展篇

One of the central occupations of the arts and humanities is the observation of the human beings. Painters and sculptors create images of the human form; writers tell stories or compose poems about human experience; musical artists give melodic contours to the human spirit; historians and philosophers ponder the essential qualities of the human civilization and nature. And In our own lives, in our own ways, we spend a great deal of our energy and attention on our fellow creatures, being in families and other kinds of relationships, observing people with curiosity and interest in the course of the day, thinking about and forming our own character—deciding what kind of person we wish to be—as we grow.

测试篇

1-5 BABDA   6-10 DBBBA

11. Even the stupidest student can't have failed to pass such an easy exam.

12. There stands a sign which says "No parking".

13. The police took actions in response to a series of smuggling.

14. You look familiar.

15. With a gleaming smile, Miss World accepted the glittering tiara.

Lesson 19. A very dear cat

积累篇

I. 振振有"词"

1. Mrs. Eleanor Ramsay, a very <u>wealthy</u> old lady, has <u>shared a flat with</u> her cat, Rastus, for a great many years.

wealthy 富有的
affluent 富裕的
prosperous 繁荣的
copious 富饶的
opulent 阔绰的
luxurious 奢侈的

share a flat with 与⋯合租
take up one's abode with 与⋯同住
under one's own roof 在自己家里
under sb.'s roof 在别人家里
under the same roof 在同一房屋里；在同一部门里

2. Rastus <u>leads an orderly life</u>. He usually <u>takes a short walk</u> in the evening...

lead an orderly life 过着规律的生活
lead a double life 过着双重生活
lead a wretched life 过着悲惨生活
lead a luxurious life 过着奢华的生活
lead a leisurely life 过着悠闲的生活
lead a rushed life 过着忙碌的生活

take a short walk 稍微散会儿步
take a long walk 散步很久
go for a walk 散步
go for a stroll 溜达
take a stroll 溜达
be on a walking tour 徒步旅行

3. Mrs. Ramsay received an <u>anonymous</u> letter. The writer stated that Rastus was <u>in safe hands</u>.

anonymous 匿名的
synonymous 近义的，同义的
antonymous 反义的
pseudonymous 假名的

be in safe hands 很安全
be in safety 很安全
be safe and sound 安然无恙
be free from danger 没有危险

Ⅱ. 现身说"法"：considering与独立主格

> Considering **the amount she paid, he was dear in more ways than one!**
> 想到她所花的那笔钱，他的珍贵就具有双重意义了！

considering在这里引导独立主格结构。当独立主格结构的主语表泛指时，如we、you、one，主语可省略，以下是此类构造的常见例子：

talking of...说到…	speaking of...谈到…
judging from...从…判断	generally speaking 一般而言
strictly speaking 严格说来	allowing for...考虑到…

例：Allowing for his poor performance, we'd better find a replacement.

　　鉴于他表现太差，我们最好找个替换人选。

　　Judging from his strange behaviour, he was not telling the truth.

　　从他怪异的表现看，他显然没说实话。

Ⅲ. 说"文"解"字"

1. Rastus leads an orderly life.

译文：拉斯特斯的生活很规律。

解析：1）orderly是形容词。英文中名词后加-ly则变为形容词。例：

　　　friendly, worldly, daily, yearly, fatherly, motherly, beastly

　　2）lead...life为固定表达，意为"过着…的生活"。也可将lead换为live。

2. But fearing that she would never see Rastus again—the letter had made that quite clear—she changed her mind.

译文：但是她又怕再也见不到拉斯特斯了——这一点，信上说得很明白——于是改变了主意。

解析：1）make...clear是一常用短语，clear也可换作explicit. 例：

　　　She made it clear/explicit to the man that she had no intention of befriending him.

　　　她清楚地告诉这个男人自己不想和他交朋友。

　　　You should made it clear/explicit to us how you think of this plan.

　　　你应该明白地告诉我们你对这项计划的看法。

　　2）change one's mind意为"改变主意"。以下是关于mind的一些常用短语：

bear...in mind 牢记…	bring...to mind 回忆…
close one's mind to...对…置若罔闻	put...out of one's mind 把…抛在脑后
make up one's mind 下定决心	read one's mind 猜某人的心思
know one's own mind 有决断力	

3. Mrs. Ramsay was sure that the kidnapper would keep his word.

译文：拉姆斯太太相信绑架者会信守诺言的。

解析：请注意keep one's word中word为单数。试比较以下单复数的不同用法：

break one's word 失信	eat one's words 收回前言

have a word with...和···说话

have words with...和···吵架

better than one's word 比答应的还好

beyond words 难以言表

in a word 总而言之

in other words 换言之

4. Considering the amount she paid, he was dear in more ways than one!

译文：想到她所花的那笔钱，他的珍贵就具有双重意义了！

解析：more...than...结构既常用，又常考，值得掌握。试看下列例句：

He is more brave than intelligent. 他有勇无谋。

He is more of a literary worker than of a governor. 与其说他是管理者，不如说他是文人。

拓 展 篇

I.英语趣园

Pun

The Pun, a unique figure of speech, is a play on words, or more specifically, a play on the form and meaning of words, for a witty or humorous effect. There are many words in the English language which are sounded or spelled alike but which have different senses or connotations. There are also words with the same spelling that carry more than one meaning. It is with this peculiarity of difference that we play a "game" on that word for humorous effect. Let's see some sample uses of puns.

1. A: What do liars do after death?

   B: Lie still.

2. The BERD is in hand. (BERD stands for Bank of Reconstruction & Development in Europe)

II.听力快车

_____ are real dangers for companies operating both overseas and in _____ markets. They are often overlooked by management on the grounds that "_____", but the damage this can inflict on a business can be very severe—as the annual roll call of corporate and individual _____ around the world testifies.

III.补充阅读

How to kidnap a child

Congratulations! You have embarked on a great adventure. Kidnapping a child is probably unlike anything you have done before. If you are a first-time kidnapper you may be hesitant; perhaps you have lingering scruples. It is true you will probably do irreparable harm to your own child. Children of divorce more often become involved in drugs, alcohol, and crime, become pregnant as teenagers, perform poorly in school, join gangs, and commit suicide.

But look at the advantages! You can be rid of that swine you live with, with all his tedious opinions about child rearing. YOU call the shots! What could be more rewarding? And a little extra cash each month never hurts, eh?

Few people realize how easy abduction is. It happens 1,000 times a day, mostly by parents! So if you're thinking, "I could never get away with it," wake up! Millions do. In fact many only realize the possibility when they become victims. Then they invariably say, "If only I had known how easy it is I would have done it myself!" So don't be caught off guard. Read on, and discover the exciting world of child kidnapping and extortion.

If you are a mother the best time to snatch is soon after you have a new child or pregnancy. Once you have what you want, you will realize that the father is no longer necessary (except for child support).

A father should consider snatching as soon as he suspects the mother might. Once she has the child, you have pretty much lost the game. You will always be at a disadvantage, but it is in your interest (as it is in hers) to snatch first. Preventive snatching may not look good (and unlike her, it can be used against you). But hey, you have the kid. If you hit the road, it could take years to track you down.

Surprise is crucial for an elegant abduction. Wait until the other parent is away, and clean the place out thoroughly. Take all the child's effects, because if you don't grab it now you will never get it, and you will never be forced to return any of it. The more you have, the better "home" you can claim to provide. You also want to achieve the maximum emotional devastation to your spouse. Like the terrorist, you want to impress with how swift, sudden, and unpredictable your strike can be.

And now you can do what you like! You can warehouse the kids in daycare while you work (or whatever). You don't have to worry about brushing hair or teeth. You can slap them when they're being brats. You can feed them fast food every night. If they become a real annoyance you can turn them over to the state social services agency. You are free!

▷ 测 试 篇 ◁

I . 单项选择

1. In the factory, suggestions often have to wait for months before they are fully _____.　　（考研91）

   A. admitted　　　　B. acknowledged　　C. absorbed　　　　D. considered

2. They are considering _____ before the prices go up.　　　　　　　（CET-4 89/1）

   A. of buying the house　　　　　　　　B. with buying the house

   C. buying the house　　　　　　　　　D. to buy the house

3. It's very _____ of you not to talk aloud while the baby is asleep.　　（CET-4 04/1）

   A. concerned　　　　B. careful　　　　C. considerable　　　D. considerate

4. Gradually the heavy footstep _____ .

   A. disappeared　　　B. vanished　　　　C. faded　　　　　D. died away

5. Children were fascinated to see that the magician made a big and tall elephant _____ in a flash.

   A. fade　　　　　　B.vanish　　　　　C. die　　　　　　D. yield

6. While crossing the mountain area, all the men carried guns lest they _____ by wild animals. （CET-4 03/1）

    A. should be attacked B. had been attacked C. must be attacked D. would be attacked

7. We booked rooms at the hotel _____ we should find no vacancies on our arrival.   （CET-4 03/9）

    A. whenever   B. if   C. since   D. lest

8. He was punished _____ he should make the same mistake again.   （CET-4 01/6）

    A. unless   B. lest   C. if   D. provided

9. He ran away lest he _____ .

    A. would be seen   B. be seen   C. could be seen   D. might be seen

10. The mad man was put in the soft-padded cell lest he _____ himself.   （CET-4 98/1）

    A. injure   B. had injured   C. injured   D. would injure

Ⅱ. 翻译

11. 走自己的路，让别人去说吧。（follow one's own course）

12. 请尝试用多种方法解题。（in more than one way）

13. 绑匪绑架此人之后，索要高达一百万的赎金。（hold sb. for ransom）

14. 我觉得她一个人回家不安全，惟恐她会被抢劫。（for fear that...）

15. 鉴于阁下的询问，我们的答复如下……（considering/regarding）

拓展篇

Kidnap Extortion and Detention are real dangers for companies operating both overseas and in domestic markets. They are often overlooked by management on the grounds that "it won't ever happen to us", but the damage this can inflict on a business can be very severe — as the annual roll call of corporate and individual victims around the world testifies.

测试篇

1-5 DCDDB   6-10 ADBBA

11. Follow your own course, and let people talk.

12. Please try to solve the problem in more than one way.

13. The kidnappers held the man for a staggering high ransom of $1 million.

14. It's not safe for her to go home alone, for fear that she be kidnapped.

15. Regarding your recent inquiry, our replies are as follows...

Lesson 20. Pioneer pilots

积累篇

I. 振振有"词"

1. On July 19th, 1909, <u>in the early morning</u>, Hubert Latham <u>took off</u> from the French <u>coast</u>...

in the early morning 一大早	take off 起飞	coast 海岸
at dawn 黎明	depart 起飞	beach 海滨
at daybreak 破晓	land 降落	shore 河岸
the day breaks 天亮了	domestic departures 国内出发	sands 沙地
at dusk 黄昏	international departures 国际出发	coastal city 沿海城市
at late night 深夜	international flights 国际航班	seaport city 港口城市
at midnight 子夜	domestic flights 国内航班	inland city 内陆城市

2. Latham <u>made another attempt</u> a week later and had <u>got within half a mile of</u> Dover.

make an attempt to do 努力做…	get within half a mile of...离…尚有半英里
make an effort to do 尽力做…	get beyond half a mile of...超过…半英里
make an endeavor to do 竭力做…	get within an inch of success 几乎成功；功亏一篑
spare no effort to do 不遗余力做…	get within an ace of winning 几乎成功；功亏一篑
do one's utmost to do 竭尽全力做…	be a far cry from...离…相差甚远
strive to do 尽力做…	

II. 现身说"法": as if 与虚拟语气

It looked as if there would be an exciting race across the Channel.
看来会有一场飞越海峡的激烈竞争。

1. 一般而言，在 look、feel、seem 等词之后用 as if/as though 引导的表语从句要用虚拟语气，其中的谓语动词用一般过去时或过去完成时（be 动词用 were）。例：

   It seemed as if/ as though the bad weather would last forever. 这种糟糕的天气好像会持续下去了。

   He felt as if/as though he had used up all his energy. 他觉得好像已经用完了全身力气似的。

2. 有时 as if/as though 引导的方式状语从句中用虚拟语气说明在某种假设的情况下做某事，从句中用一般过去时或过去完成时。例：

He behaved as if/as though he were superior. 他那样子好像他就高人一等。

The woman treated the homeless boy as if/as though he were her own child.

那位女士似乎把那个流浪儿当作了自己的亲骨肉。

3. as is/as though引导的从句中的情形是根据现在迹象作出的判断、推测，发生的几率较大，则用陈述语气。例：

Dark clouds are gathering. It looks as if/as though it is going to rain. 天上阴云密布，似乎要下雨了。

It seems as if/as though he has made up his mind. 似乎他已经下了决心。

III. 说"文"解"字"

1. He had traveled only seven miles across the Channel when his engine failed and he was forced to land on the sea.

译文：他只在海峡上空飞行了7英里，引擎就出了故障，他只好降落在海面上。

解析：1）seven miles在句中作状语。英文中表距离、长度等概念的名词短语可作状语，跟在不及物动词之后，这是一种比较特殊的用法。例：

One cat, Sabrina, fell 32 storeys, yet only suffered from a broken tooth.

一只名叫萨伯瑞娜的猫从32层的高楼坠下，然而只摔断了一颗牙。

I walked a long distance before arriving at the station. 我走了很远才到达车站。

2）fail一词在本句中意为"出故障"，而非"失败"。熟词生义是阅读理解中的一大障碍，因此，多查字典、语境猜词是这方面快速提升的必由之路。试看以下几例fail的灵活用法：

The day slowly failed. 白昼渐去。

The roses failed for the lack of water. 玫瑰因缺水而凋零。

His thesis failed in consistency. 他的论文缺乏一致性。

When we demanded his help, he failed us. 当我们需要他帮助时，他令我们失望。

The company failed due to poor management. 由于经营不善，这家公司倒闭了。

The patient's heart failed. 病人的心脏停止了跳动。

2. The "Antoinette" floated on the water until Latham was picked up by a ship.

译文："安特瓦奈特"号在海上漂流，随后莱瑟姆才被一只船救起。

解析：1）float on the water意为"在海上漂流"，相关表达有：

float down stream 顺流而下　　　　　　　　ride the waves 乘风破浪

float in the breeze 风中飘扬

2）pick up也是一词多义，试看下列用法：

pick up a foreign language 学习一门外语　　　　pick up sb. on the street 街上偶遇某人

My radio can pick up VOA. 我的收音机可以接收到VOA.

pick up sb.（车）接某人

3. It looked as if there would be an exciting race across the Channel.

译文：看来会有一场飞越海峡的激烈竞争。

解析：It looked as if...可作为写作句型加以模仿，例：

It looked as if his side had gained the upper hand in the negotiation.

看来他这一方在谈判中占了优势。

拓 展 篇

I. 英语趣园

Louis Blériot was born in Cambrai, France on July 1, 1872, and studied engineering in Paris. He was an inventor, an aircraft designer, and a pilot. He is best known for his flight over the English Channel on July 25, 1909, the world's first flight over a large body of water in a heavier-than-air craft.

II. 听力快车

The wright brothers

Wilbur Wright was born in Dayton, Ohio. His brother Orville was born four years later. Through out their lives, they were best friends. As Wilbur once said, "_____."

Today, the Wright brothers'_____. Many visitors to the museum arrive in Washington on big jet airplanes. They look at the Wright brothers' plane with its_____, wooden controls, and tiny engine. They wonder at the changes in the world since Wilbur and Orville Wright began the_____.

III. 补充阅读

Once American flying not only fell behind automotive progress, but also lagged behind European aviation. This was particularly annoying to many aviation enthusiasts in the United States, the home of the Wright brothers. The Wrights made the first powered, controlled flight in an airplane on December 17 1903, on a lonely stretch of beach near Kitty Hawk, North Carolina. Ironically, this feat was widely ignored or misinterpreted by the American press, until 1908. Impressed by the Wrights, the Europeans began a rapid development of aviation.

At the inaugural meeting of the American Aeronautical Society, in 1911, some of its members discussed a national laboratory with federal patronage. The Smithsonian Institution seemed a likely prospect, based on its prestige and equipment. But the American Aeronautical Society's dreams were frustrated by continued infighting among other organizations which were beginning to see aviation as a promising research frontier, including universities like the Massachusetts Institute of Technology, as well as government agencies like the US Navy and the National Bureau of Standards.

The difficulties of defining a research facility were compounded by the ambivalent attitude of the American public toward the airplane. While some saw it as a mechanical triumph with a significant future, others saw it as a mechanical fashion, the behaviors of the "birdmen" and "aviatrixes" of the era tended to underscore the foolhardiness of aviation and airplanes. Fliers might set a record one month and fatally crash the next. Calbraith P. Rodgers managed to make the first flight from the Atlantic to the Pacific coast in 1911 （19 crashes, innumerable stops, and 49 days）, but died in a crash just four months later. Harriet Quimby, the attractive American aviatrix （she flew wearing specially designed clothes）, was the first woman to fly across the English Channel in 1912. Returning to America, she died in a crash off the Boston coast within 3months.

◄► 测 试 篇 ◄►

I．单项选择

1. George had difficulty in swimming across the lake, but he finally succeeded _____ his 4th attempt.
   A. in   B. on   C. at   D. by

2. When Jack was 18 he _____ going around with a strange set of people and staying out very late.
   A. took to   B. took for   C. took up   D. took on

3. He speaks English so well that he is often _____ a native.
   A. regarded as   B. thought as   C. taken for   D. respected as

4. Important people don't often have much free time as their work _____ all their time.
   A. takes away   B. takes over   C. takes up   D. takes in

5. The teacher was using many new words and the children could not _____ what he tried to _____.
   A. take in...get across   B. make out... get over
   C. work out... pass on   D. figure out...come to

6. Tom submitted 35 articles to the magazine _____ one was accepted.
   A.while   B. if   C. since   D. before

7. A man escaped from the prison last night. It was a tong time _____ the guards discovered what had happened.
   A. before   B. until   C. since   D. when

8. Scientists say it may be 5 or 10 years _____ it is possible to test this medicine on human patients.
   （CET-4 95/6）
   A. since   B. when   C. after   D. before

9. They decided to chase the cow away _____ it did more damage.   （CET-4 90/1）
   A. in case   B. until   C. before   D. after

10. "May I speak to your manager Mr. Williams at 5 o'clock tonight?" "I'm sorry. Mr.Williams _____ to a conference long before then."   （CET-4 00/6）
    A. will have gone   B. had gone   C. would have gone   D. has gone

II．翻译

11. 天都黑了，我们才到山脚下。（before）
12. 大钟敲了13下才停。（before）
13. 减肥课程使她看起来年轻了10岁。（take 10 years of）
14. 林登伯格是第一个不着陆飞越大西洋的人。（fly across）
15. 他看起来好像喝醉了。（look as if）

拓展篇

The wright brothers

Wilbur Wright was born in 1867 in Dayton, Ohio. His brother Orville was born four years later. Through out their lives, they were best friends. As Wilbur once said, "From the time we were little children, Orville and I lived together, played together, worked together, and thought together."

Today, the Wright brothers' <u>first airplane hangs in the Air and Space Museum in Washington</u>. Many visitors to the museum arrive in Washington on big jet airplanes. They look at the Wright brothers' plane with its <u>cloth wings</u>, wooden controls, and tiny engine. They wonder at the changes in the world since Wilbur and Orville Wright began the <u>modern age of flight</u>.

测试篇

1-5 BACCA   6-10 DADCA

11. It was getting dark before we arrived at the foot of the mountain.

12. The bell stuck 13 times before it stopped.

13. The slim course took 10 years off her.

14. Lindbergh was the first person to fly across the Atlantic Ocean without stopping.

15. He looked as if he were drunk.

Lesson **21** Daniel Mendoza

积 累 篇

Ⅰ.振振有"词"

1. <u>In those days</u>, <u>boxers</u> **fought with** <u>bare</u> fists for <u>prize money</u>.

in those days 过去 these days 现在，目前 at present 当前 presently 如今 currently 时下 for the time being 眼下	boxer 拳击手 pugilist（职业）拳击手 wrestler 摔跤手 gladiator 角斗士 knight 骑士 warrior 武士 swordsman 剑客	bare 裸露的 bare-fisted 不戴手套的 bare-handed 赤手空拳的 bare-headed 不戴帽子的 bare-faced 厚颜无耻的
boxing 拳击 shadow boxing 太极拳 kick boxing 搏击 martial art 武术 taekwondo 跆拳道 karate 空手道 judo 柔道 yoga 瑜伽	prize money 赏金 fine 罚金 compensation money 赔偿金 consolation money 抚恤金 ransom 赎金 bonus 奖金 scholarship 奖学金	近义词辨析： bare（身体或其他部分）裸露的 naked（身体全部或部分）裸露的 nude（全部）裸露的 bald 秃顶的 barren 贫瘠的 vacant 空缺的 hollow 中空的

2. <u>In his day</u>, **Mendoza** <u>enjoyed tremendous popularity</u>.

in one's day 在某人全盛时期 in one's heyday 在某人鼎盛时期 in one's golden day 在某人黄金时期 in the pride of one's life 在某人辉煌时期 Every dog has its day. 凡人皆有得意时。	enjoy tremendous popularity 人气很旺 have a lot of prestige 声誉很高 win considerable fame 获取极大名声 achieve great eminence 赢取极大声名

3. He was so <u>extravagant</u> that he was always <u>in debt</u>.

extravagant 奢侈的
profligate 恣意挥霍的
luxurious 奢侈的
prodigal 挥霍的

be in debt 欠债
be over head and ears in debt 债台高筑
be up to one's eyes in debt 债务累累

extravaganza 盛大演出
gala 大型演出
carnival 嘉年华
spectacle 壮观景象
feast 盛大活动
celebration 庆祝活动

be in+n 可表示一种状态，具有动感效果
be in trouble 身处困境
be in love 身处热恋
be in the red（公司）出现赤字
be in red 穿着红色衣服

II. 现身说"法": It引导的强调句

It was not until his third match in 1790 that he finally beat Humphries and became Champion of England.
直到1790年他们第3次对垒，门多萨才终于击败了汉弗莱斯，成了全英冠军。

1. It 强调句的用法是：将要强调的内容置于 It be 和 that 之间，当强调某人时，可用 who/that; 在非正式英语中，也可出现 which/when/where。例：

    It is only in the seas and rivers, and sometimes lakes, where mud and silt have been continuously deposited, that bodies and the like can be rapidly covered and preserved. (强调地点状语)(《新概念英语》4册) 只有在泥沙不断淤积的江河、湖泊里，尸体之类的东西才能被迅速地覆盖并保存下来。

    It is almost always due to some very special circumstances that traces of land animals survive. (强调原因状语)(《新概念英语》4册) 几乎总是由于某些特殊的条件，陆地动物的残骸才被保存下来。

    If this facilitates forgery, it is the bank which will lose, not the customer. (强调主语)(《新概念英语》4册) 如果这种做法便利了伪造，受损失的不是储户，而是银行。

2. It be...who/that...强调句的识别技巧：

    如果一个句子中将It be, that/who去掉之后，句子仍结构完整，且意思保持不变，则该句是强调句。

    例：It was the man who/that broke the record. 是那个人打破了记录。

    去掉It be, that/who后变为 the man broke the record, 句子仍是正确的。

比较：It be+时间状语+that...与It be+时间名词+when/before/since 的区别

It was about 9 o'clock in the morning that the banked was robbed. (强调句)

It was about 9 o'clock in the morning when the banked was robbed. (定语从句)

大约早上9点这家银行遭劫。

It was two months ago that he dropped off school. (强调句)

It was two months ago when he dropped off school. (定语从句)

两个月前他辍学了。

III. 说"文"解"字"

1. He was adored by rich and poor alike.

译文：他受到穷人和富人的一致拥戴。

解析：rich and poor是固定词组，意为"穷人和富人"。也可在rich和poor前加the, 即the rich and the poor。但是，如果rich和poor单用时，则前面必须加the, 即the rich或the poor。用法相同的还有：

young and old 年轻人与老年人   the young and the old 年轻人与老年人

the young 年轻人   the old 老年人

2. In fact, Mendoza soon became so successful that Humphries turned against him.

译文：事实上，门多萨不久就名声大振，致使汉弗莱斯与他反目成仇。

解析：turn against sb. 意为"与某人反目成仇"。以下是一些近义表达：

be hostile to sb. 敌视某人

be at odds with sb. 与某人有矛盾

come into antagonism with sb. 与某人结仇

3. Mendoza met Humphries in the ring on a later occasion and he lost for a second time.

译文：门多萨与汉弗莱斯再次在拳击场上较量，门多萨又输了一场。

解析：1）ring在这里作"拳击场"解。该词作"球场"之意时多指圆形或用绳索围起的场地。

🔘 关于"场地"的不同表达

football pitch 足球场   golf court 高尔夫球场

squash court 壁球场   badminton court 羽毛球场

playground 操场

2）on... occasion是一固定表达，意为"在…场合"。例：

On a formal occasion men are expected to wear suits and women dress.

在正式场合，男士应该着西装，女士应该着套装。

On no occasion will China be the first to resort to nuclear weapons.

在任何场合中国都不会首先使用核武器。

> **比较**：for a second time 与 for the second time
>
> 前者强调"又一次"，后者强调"第二次"。例：
>
> He lost the game for a second time. 他又一次输掉了比赛。（包含遗憾、不满等语气）
>
> He lost the game for the second time. 他第二次输掉了比赛。（不含引申义）

4. After he was defeated by a boxer called Gentleman Jackson, he was quickly forgotten.

译文：他在被一个叫做杰特曼·杰克逊的拳击手击败之后，很快就被遗忘了。

解析：Gentleman在这里不作"绅士"讲。因为如果作"绅士"解只能单用，不能在其后接人名。所以该词在本文只是人名。以某种怪异的名称作人名是西方的一种习惯，汉语做处理时应采用音译。例：

Tiger 泰格尔（本意"老虎"）   Woods 伍兹（本意"树林"）

Fox 福克斯（本意"狐狸"）   Butcher 布彻（本意"屠夫"）

拓 展 篇

Ⅰ.英语趣园

The Marquis of Queensberry rules

John Graham Chambers, a member of the Amateur Athletic Club（AAC）, wrote these rules in 1865, but they weren't published until 1867, with the patronage of John Sholto Douglas, the eighth Marquis of Queensberry.

Chambers intended the rules for amateur boxing matches, such as those conducted by the AAC. They weren't used until 1872, at a London tournament that was truly amateur: no prizes were awarded, and no betting was allowed.

Ⅱ.听力快车

_____ —that is, professional boxing for prize money—was ____ in England, but the authorities allowed bouts under the new rules. As a result, they gradually began to___ the old London____, even in professional matches.

Ⅲ.补充阅读

Boxing—legalized murder?

Forty-two boxers have died in American rings. These fatalities became one-day sensations in the newspapers. Boxing commissions viewed all this with alarm and mentioned tests to be conducted by certified doctors with the most modern brain-wave recorders. Soon, the excitement died down. Boxing went on and more boxers kept getting hit in the head, and sometimes died.

Death in the ring is bad enough. But for every death there are hundreds of other tragedies. These are the young men who literally have had their brains knocked out. Their cases get no publicity. They are the living dead of pugilism: the victims of boxing's occupational disease: punch-drunkenness.

Only recently have scientists begun to realize the appalling ruin that boxing causes in the brain. New discoveries at the United States Naval Hospital in Bethesda, Md., and by Dr. Ward C Halstead of the University of Chicago, have revealed the causes and effects of brain injuries from head blows. The findings are frightening.

Brain injuries don't heal

The most important parts of civilized man's brain are the frontal lobes. Here function the lifelines of civilized activity: the highest biological intelligence, the finest coordination, restraints and self-control. Head blows in boxing, therefore, injure that part of the brain most necessary to intelligent living.

Brain injuries do not heal, as do hurts in other parts of the body. A broken leg can be set. A ruptured spleen responds to surgery. A black eye clears up. But the brain, once damaged, never recovers. The destruction of brain cells is permanent.

Impairment of thinking powers, self control, speech, gait and emotional stability result. Just how many ex-fighters, professional and amateur, who are so afflicted, exist in the United States today, nobody knows. But their number runs into the thousands and increases yearly.

Hundreds of these men are on relief, supported at public expense, because they cannot make a living. And there are thousands of others of whom few people know about. They are being taken care of by family or friends, or they may work at menial jobs, which require little intelligence. The vast number of such cases, previously diagnosed as something other than punch drunkenness, is just now becoming apparent to medical science.

This toll of brain ruin, of course, dose not take into account such trademarks of pugilism as the broken nose, the cauliflower ear, deficient sight, the broken eardrum and the fractured jaw. These are bad enough; yet, they are as nothing compared to a damaged brain.

Every fighter a victim

No fighter escapes some degree of brain injury. It is inevitable. The more a man boxes, the worse his condition becomes. Sixty out of every hundred boxers suffer sufficient brain injury to slow them up noticeably. Five out of every hundred become out-and-out punch drunks. A pugilist may win every bout of his career and still lose the final round. He may become "slaphappy", a "stumblebum" or "punchy". Those are the three degrees of punch drunkenness into which fighters themselves classify the mental degeneration of retired boxers.

Make no mistake about it; boxing is the only sport in which punch drunkenness commonly occurs. It is the only pastime in which the entire object is to deliver such punchyment to the opponent. And don't forget this: Boxing is the only sport in which to confess injury and retire causes spectators to deride you.

Why, then, if this so-called sport is so dangerous, is it not abolished? I believe it should be; at least in high schools and colleges and for amateurs generally. This view is supported by the recorded vote of fifty percent of the college directors of physical education in the country; by virtually all state offices of public instruction; by the national association of physical educators; and by every medical man who has given the subject serious study.

It is pertinent to note that the United States Military Academy is seriously considering the removal of boxing from its intercollegiate program.

▶ 测 试 篇 ◀

Ⅰ.单项选择

1. Executives of the company enjoyed an ＿＿＿＿ lifestyle of free gifts, fine wines and high salaries.

（CET-6 04/1）

   A. exquisite　　　　B. extravagant　　　　C. exotic　　　　D. eccentric

2. Within 10 years they have turned the ＿＿＿＿ hill into green woods. 　　（CET-6 03/9）

   A. vacant　　　　B. barren　　　　C. weird　　　　D. wasteful

3. He tried to hide his ＿＿＿＿ patch by sweeping his hair over to one side. 　　（CET-6 04/6）

   A. barren　　　　B. bare　　　　C. bald　　　　D. bleak

4. Individual sports are run by over 370 independent governing bodies whose functions usually include ＿＿＿＿ rules, holding events, selecting national teams and promoting international links. 　　（CET-6 02/6）

   A. drawing on　　　　B. drawing in　　　　C. drawing up　　　　D. drawing down

5. Many people think of deserts as ＿＿＿＿ regions, but numerous species of plants and animals have adapted to live there. 　　（CET-6 99/6）

A. virgin   B. barren   C. void   D. wretched

6. Without any hesitation, she took off her shoes, _____ up her skirt and splashed across the stream. (CET-6 05/12)

A. tucked   B. revolved   C. twisted   D. curled

7. _____ she first heard of the man referred to as a specialist. (CET-4 90/6)

A. That was from Stephen   B. It was Stephen whom

C. It was from Stephen that   D. It was Stephen that

8. _____ that the trade between the two countries reached its highest point. (CET-4 89/1)

A. During the 1960's   B. That it was in the 1960's

C. It was in the 1960's   D. It was the 1960's

9. Difficulties and hardships have _____ the best qualities of young geologist. (考研91)

A. brought out   B. brought about   C. brought forth   D. brought up

10. Italy _____ Argentina 3 _____ 1.

A. beat...to   B. won...to   C. beat...against   D. win...against

Ⅱ.翻译

11. 清官难断家务案。（settle a quarrel）

12. 迈克·乔丹是篮球史上最传奇的人物之一，被大家叫做"飞人乔丹"。（one of the...）

13. Thomas Jefferson起草了《独立宣言》。（draw up）

14. 曼德拉为改善南非黑人的境况做出了巨大的贡献。（did much to...）

15. 伏明霞在她的鼎盛时期很有名，深受国内外的欢迎。（in her day...）

 答 案

拓展篇

Prize fighting—that is, professional boxing for prize money—was generally forbidden in England, but the authorities allowed bouts under the new rules. As a result, they gradually began to replace the old London Prize Ring Rules, even in professional matches.

测试篇

1-5 BBCCB   6-10 ACCAA

11. Even the upright official will find it hard to settle a family quarrel.

12. One of the legendary figures in basketball history is Michel Jordan, who is known to us all as Air Jordan.

13. Thomas Jefferson drew up the *Declaration of Independence*.

14. Mandela did much to improve the situation of the black people in South Africa.

15. In her day, Fu Mingxia enjoyed tremendous popularity. She was adored by home and abroad.

Lesson 22. By heart

积累篇

I.振振有"词"

1. Some plays are so successful that they run for years on end.

play 戏剧, 广播剧等	run（戏剧等）上映	on end 连续地
drama 戏剧, 广播剧等	shoot a film 拍片	at a stretch 连续地
opera 歌剧	premiere 首映	in a row 连续地
Peking Opera 京剧	film synopsis 影片简介	without a let-up 不停顿地
screenplay 剧本	filmstill 剧照	at one setting 一口气
playwright 剧作家		

2. In the last act, a gaoler would always come on to the stage...

act（戏）一幕	come on to the stage 上舞台
scene 一场	come into a new stage 进入新的阶段
chapter（书）一章	be at the initial stage 处于发展初期
volume（书）一卷	China is still at the initial stage of socialism.
stanza（诗歌）一节	中国仍处于社会主义的初级阶段。

3. The gaoler looked on eagerly, anxious to see if his fellow actor had at last learnt his lines.

look on 观望	fellow actor 搭档
stand by 观望	fellow worker 工友
looker-on 观望者	fellow passenger 同车人
stander-by 观望者	fellow traveler 同路人；志同道合者
stand with arms crossed 袖手旁观	fellow countryman 同胞, 同乡

learn one's lines 熟记台词	learn sth. by rote 死记硬背
know one's parts 熟记台词	learn sth. by analogy 举一反三
learn sth. by heart 用心牢记	

Ⅱ.现身说"法"：insist与虚拟语气

> He always insisted that it should be written out in full.
> 他总是坚持要求将信的全文写在信纸上。

insist表"要求、命令"时，后面要接虚拟语气，形式是insist that sb./sth.(should)+动词原形。美国英语中常常省略should. 例：

The workers insisted that the management (should) give them a pay rise.

工人们坚持要求管理层给他们提高工资。

如果insist不表"要求，命令"，则要用虚拟语气。例：

I insisted he was wrong. 我坚持认为他错了。

Ⅲ.说"文"解"字"

1. Some plays are so successful that they run for years on end.

译文：有些剧目非常成功，以致连续上演好几年。

解析：1) successful一词多义，熟练掌握将对阅读、写作极有好处。例：

His business is very successful. 他的生意很红火。

a successful writer 颇有建树的作家

a successful banker 飞黄腾达的银行家

a successful film 大受欢迎的影片

2) for years中间省略了数词。一般而言，如果数词是表不精确的概念，如a few、several、many等，则可以省略；如果数词是精确概念，如five、six等，则通常不省。例：

for (several) months   for five months

3) on end是固定表达，意为"连续地"，其中end意为"端口"。例：

make both ends meet 收支相抵

4) for years on end意思是"连续好几年"。以下是一些同义表达：

for many/several consecutive years 连续好几年

for five/six straight years 连续五/六年

for a few successive years 连续好几年

2. Yet this is not always the case.

译文：然而，情况并非常常如此。

解析：该句可作为套路句型使用，总结上文，引出下文，起承转合的作用。类似用法的句子如下：

This is always the case. 情况往往如此。

This is indeed the case. 情况确实如此。

The other side of the idea is just the opposite. 另一种想法恰恰相反。

3. One night, the gaoler decided to play a joke on his colleague to find out if, after so many performances, he had managed to learn the contents of the letter by heart.

译文：一天晚上，狱卒决定与他的搭档开个玩笑，看他反复演出这么多场之后，是否已将信的内容背熟了。

解析：1) play a joke on sb.意为"开某人的玩笑"，与laugh at sb.不同，后者为"嘲笑某人"，贬义性更强。试比较以下用法：

play pranks on sb. 开某人的玩笑	pull sb.'s leg 逗某人乐
tease/kid sb. 逗某人	make an ass of sb. 令某人出洋相
disgrace sb. 令某人丢脸	

2）learn sth. by heart 是固定短语，意为"熟记…，牢记…"。以下是一些相关用法：

| know sth. by heart 用心牢记 | learn sth. by rote 死记硬背 |
| learn sth. by analogy 触类旁通 | learn sth. by association 联想记忆 |

4. With this, he hurried off the stage.

译文：他一边说着，一边匆匆走下了舞台。

解析：with this在这里意为"说着这话"，需注意：with不是常规意义的"拿着"。请看with在以下例句中的不同含义：

I'm with you on this point. 这点上我和你意见一致。

The tide is with us. 形势对我们有利。

secure a job with a college 在一所大学找到了工作

With a short distance to go, he collapsed. 离目的地仅有咫尺之遥，他却支撑不住了。

He's in bed with flu. 他因患流感卧病在床。

拓 展 篇

Ⅰ.英语趣园

The heart, the organ in your chest, pumps blood through your body. But this organ once was considered as the centre of a person's thoughts, emotions, and conscience by ancient people. As a result, the phrase "learn/get/know something by heart" was born, which refers to knowing or learning something so that you can remember all of it.

Ⅱ.听力快车

People believed for a long time that _____. That is why the heart is used in so many expressions about _____. In the phrases "take heart" and "lose heat", it refers to _____. But if a person who "win your heart" does not love you, then you are sure to have a "broken heart". In your pain and sadness, you may decide that person is "hard-hearted".

You may "_____" to a friend. _____. If he does not understand how painful your broken heat is, you may ask him to "have a heart"— _____. He may, however, warn you "not to wear your heart on your sleeve". In other words, _____.

Ⅲ.补充阅读

Thunderstorm act Ⅲ（excerpt）

Inside Lu Kuei's house at No. 10, Almond Blossom Lane

First let us look at the scene outside the house:

The station clock has struck ten, and the people of Almond Blossom Lane, old and young, are talking in the air along the banks of a pond which, although it is the source of stinging inhalations drawn up by the summer sun in the daytime, provides late at night an open space where one may catch the fresh, cool breezes. Despite a sharp downpour a moment ago, it is still unbearably hot. It is the sort of weather that makes people feel parched inside and thirsting for another thunderstorm. Yet the frogs that crouch among the reeds by the pond are as untiringly strident as ever. The sound of the strollers' voices comes in desultory snatches. From time to time a silent flash of lightning splashes the starless sky with a harsh, blurred glare and for one startled moment shows us the weeping willows by the pond, drooping and trembling over the water. Then, just as suddenly, it is dark again.

Then, one by one, the strollers drift away and silence closes in on all sides. A rumble of distant thunder seems to cow even the frogs into silence; a breeze springs up again and sifts through the rustling leaves of the willows.

Presently the lightning blazes again, stark and terrifying, then a jarring burst of thunder goes shuddering across the sky. In its wake comes a close, oppressive silence, broken only by the occasional croaking of a frog and, what is louder, the sharp clack of a night watchman's bamboo "gong." A storm is about to break.

When the storm does come, it will last right through to the final curtain.

All the audience can see, however, is the interior of Ssufeng's room.

The Lus have just finished their evening meal. All four of them are in an unpleasant mood, and each of them is occupied with his or her own thoughts. Ta-hai is sitting in a corner cleaning something. Lu Ma and Ssu-feng keep an uncomfortable silence. The former, her head bent, is clearing away the bowls and chopsticks from the round table in the center of the room. A drink-fuddled Lu Kuei sits slumped back in a rickety easy-chair on the left. Monkey-like, he stares at his wife from bloodshot eyes and hiccups. He puts his bare feet on the floor with his legs wide apart. He wears a white singlet, sweatsoaked and clinging. He fans himself incessantly with a palm-leaf fan.

Ssu-feng is standing in front of the window. Her back is towards the audience as she stares anxiously out. From outside the window comes the croaking of the frogs and the lighthearted voices of the passers-by. She seems to be listening uneasily for something, and from time to time she looks around at her father and then looks swiftly away again in disgust. Beside her, standing against the left wall. Is a plank-bed covered with a mat and a spotless double quilt. A mat pillow and a palm-leaf fan are neatly arranged on it.

The room is very small and, as is always the case in the houses of the poor, the ceiling comes oppressively low over one's head. On the wall over the head of the bed hangs an illustrated poster advertising a brand of cigarettes, while on the left-hand wall is pasted an old reproduction originally put up as a New Year decoration and now very tattered and torn. A small table stands by the only chair in the room—now occupied by Lu Kuei—with a mirror, a comb and various cheap cosmetics on it: apparently Ssu-feng's dressing-table. Along the left-hand wall stands a bench, and by the table in the middle of the room there is a solitary stool. Under Ssu-feng's bed, there are several pairs of fashionable shoes. Next to the bed there is a trunk draped with a white cloth and with a teapot and several cheap bowls on it. An oil lamp with a bright red-paper lampshade stands on the round table.

The room has two doors, of which the one on the left the side where the bed is—is no more than a gaudily pattered red curtain hanging over a recess which, besides providing storage-space for a heap of coal and bits of old furniture, also serves as Ssu-feng's dressing-room. The door on the right leads to the front room. This is LuKuei's room. Just inside the door between the two rooms, leaning against the wall are several long planks for making a bed with.

When the curtain rises, Lu Kuei has just delivered a voluble and highly-colored lecture to his family. A tense silence follows this spirited outburst. LuKuei is apparently reveling in his position of authority as head of the family, judging by the gusto with which he brandishes his tattered palm-leaf fan and the way he points and gestures with it. His sweat-soaked, flesh-draped head is thrust forward and his glazed eyes swing from one member of his family to another.

Ta-hai is still busy cleaning the object in his hand, which the audience now sees to be a pistol. The two women wait in silence for Lu Kuei to launch another shrill tirade against them. The croaking of the frogs and the voices of street-singers now drift in through the window.

Still standing in front of the window, Ssu-feng now and then heaves a deep sigh.

▶ 测 试 篇 ◀

I . 单项选择

1. The work was almost complete when we received orders to _____ no further with it. (CET-4 03/6)
   A. progress   B. proceed   C. march   D. promote

2. Could you take a _____ sheet of paper and write your name at the top?
   A. bare   B. vacant   C. hollow   D. blank

3. Reading _____ the lines, I would say that the Government are more worried than they will admit.
   A. behind   B. between   C. along   D. among   (CET-4 03/6)

4. Because of his excellent administration, people lived in peace and _____ and all previously neglected matters were taken care of. (CET-4 05/6)
   A. conviction   B. contest   C. consent   D. content

5. This is not much time left so I'll tell you about it _____ . (考研91)
   A. in detail   B. in brief   C. in short   D. in all

6. The young man insists that he _____ innocent.
   A. is   B. be   C. have been   D. is to be

7. Jane's pale face suggested that she _____ ill, and her parents suggested that she _____ a medical examination.
   A. be...should have   B. was...have   C. should be...had   D. was...has

8. The suggestion that the mayor _____ the prizes was accepted by everyone. (CET-4 00/6)
   A. would present   B. present   C. presents   D. ought to present

9. Peter, who had been driving all day, suggested _____ at the next town. (CET-4 00/6)
   A. to stop   B. stopping   C. stop   D. having stopped

10. Some people criticize family doctors for _____ too many medicines for minor illnesses.
    A. prescribing   B. ordering   C. advising   D. delivering

II . 翻译

11. 一说起英语，我就磕磕巴巴。（falter）

12. 心理因素在考试的时候起到了重要作用。（play a role in）

13. 我写的诗被全文刊登了。（in full）

14. 不要无故抱怨。（without cause）

15. 学习不能靠死记硬背。（learn by rote）

拓展篇

People believed for a long time that the heart was the center of a person's emotions. That is why the heart is used in so many expressions about emotional situations. In the phrases "take heart" and "lose heat", it refers to courage and enthusiasm. But if a person who "win your heart" does not love you, then you are sure to have a "broken heart". In your pain and sadness, you may decide that person is "hard-hearted".

You may "pour out your heart" to a friend. Telling someone about your personal problems can often make you feel better. If he does not understand how painful your broken heat is, you may ask him to "have a heart"— to show some sympathy. He may, however, warn you "not to wear your heart on your sleeve". In other words, do not let everyone see how lovesick you are.

测试篇

1-5 BDBDB   6-10 ABBBA

11. When it comes to speaking English, I begin to falter.

12. Psychological factors play a key role in exams.

13. My poem was published in full.

14. Don't complain without cause.

15. You cannot learn by rote.

Lesson 23. One man's meat is another man's poison

积累篇

I.振振有"词"

1. <u>Your stomach would turn at the idea of</u> frying potatoes in <u>animal fat</u>.

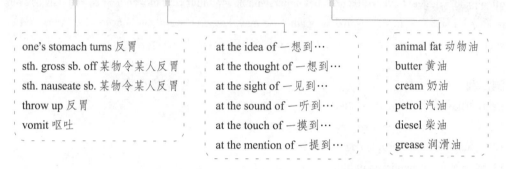

one's stomach turns 反胃	at the idea of 一想到…	animal fat 动物油
sth. gross sb. off 某物令某人反胃	at the thought of 一想到…	butter 黄油
sth. nauseate sb. 某物令某人反胃	at the sight of 一见到…	cream 奶油
throw up 反胃	at the sound of 一听到…	petrol 汽油
vomit 呕吐	at the touch of 一摸到…	diesel 柴油
	at the mention of 一提到…	grease 润滑油

2. Snails are a great <u>luxury</u> in <u>various</u> parts of the world.

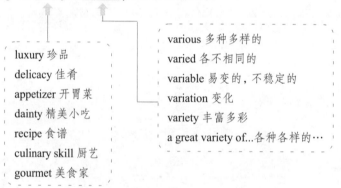

luxury 珍品	various 多种多样的
delicacy 佳肴	varied 各不相同的
appetizer 开胃菜	variable 易变的, 不稳定的
dainty 精美小吃	variation 变化
recipe 食谱	variety 丰富多彩
culinary skill 厨艺	a great variety of...各种各样的…
gourmet 美食家	

3. There are <u>countless</u> people who...have learned to <u>associate snails with food</u>. ·

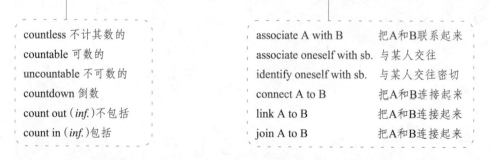

countless 不计其数的	associate A with B	把A和B联系起来
countable 可数的	associate oneself with sb.	与某人交往
uncountable 不可数的	identify oneself with sb.	与某人交往密切
countdown 倒数	connect A to B	把A和B连接起来
count out (*inf.*)不包括	link A to B	把A和B连接起来
count in (*inf.*)包括	join A to B	把A和B连接起来

4. Acting <u>on a sudden impulse</u>, I collected several <u>dozen</u>.

impulse 冲动
impulsive 冲动的
on a sudden impulse 一时冲动
on（an）impulse 一时冲动
impulse buying 冲动性购买
panic buying 抢购

dozen 一打
Six of one and half a dozen of the other. 半斤八两。
a dozen of... 一打…
dozens of... 几打…
hundreds of... 数百…
thousands of... 数千…
tens of thousands of... 数万…

Ⅱ. 现身说"法"：No...more...than... 表示的最高级

> No **creature has received** more **praise and abuse** than **the common garden snail.**
> 没有一种生物受到的赞美和厌恶能超过花园里常见的蜗牛了。

no（或其他否定词）...more...than... 表示最高级，即比较级表示最高级。例：

Nothing illustrates his selfishness more clearly than his attitude toward his wife.

没有什么比他对待妻子的态度更能表明他的自私。

There is no quicker method of disposing of patients than by giving them what they are asking for. (《新概念英语》4册）病人要什么就给他们什么，没有比这样处理病人更快的方法了。

此外，最高级意义的表达方式还有：

1. 否定词+so/as+原级+as...。例：

Nothing impressed me so deeply as my first trip to Xi'an.

没有什么比我初次西安之行给我留下的印象更深刻的了。

2. 比较级+than any other+名词。例：

He is more successful than any other classmate. 他比其他同学更成功。

Ⅲ. 说"文"解"字"

1. One man's meat is another man's poison.

译文：各有所爱。

解析：这是英文的一句谚语。这里采用了意译法。相似意义的句子还有：

One man's breath is another man's death. 各有所爱。

All things fit not all persons. 一物难称万人心。

Beauty is in the eye of the beholder. 情人眼里出西施。

> ★★★ 注 意 ★★★
>
> 一般而言，在英汉互译的过程中，首要原则是能直译则直译；无法直译，则用意译。例：
>
> the game is not worth the candle 得不偿失　　to bring a hornet's nest about one's ears 惹是生非
>
> as regular as clockwork 有条不紊　　to drink the cup of joy 花天酒地
>
> to shoot at a pigeon and kill a crow 声东击西

2. People become quite illogical when they try to decide what can be eaten and what cannot be eaten.

译文：在决定能吃什么不能吃什么的时候，人们往往变得不合情理。

解析：彩色部分可以改写为when it comes to deciding...（当谈论/涉及到…）。When it comes to sth. / doing sth. 是一固定句型，也可作为写作的开篇句加以模仿。例：

When it comes to the medical reform, opinions are abundant.

对于医疗改革，人们意见纷纷，莫衷一是。

When it comes to the slowing economy, Ellen Spero isn't biting her nails yet.（2004年考研）

当谈到衰退的经济状况，Ellen Spero并没有感到无计可施。

When it comes to the quality of life, more prognosticators are fairly cautious.（2001年英专八级）

谈及生活质量，更多预言家出言谨慎。

3. The idea never appealed to me very much.

译文：我并不喜欢这个想法。

解析：appeal to sb.意为"吸引某人"。但是，appeal to sb. to do sth.则是"恳求/呼吁某人做…"之意。例：

The delegates appealed to the local government to take some strict measures to tackle pollution.

代表们呼吁当地政府采取更加严厉的措施解决污染问题。

4. But one day, after a very heavy shower, I happened to be walking in my garden when I noticed a huge number of snails taking a stroll on some of my prize plants.

译文：后来有一天，一场大雨过后，我在花园里游逛，突然注意到许许多多蜗牛在我心爱的花草上悠闲地散步。

解析：1）notice属于感官动词，taking a stroll是宾语补足语。notice sb. do sth.意为"注意到某人做…"（强调过程），notice sb. doing sth.意为"注意到某人正在做…"（强调动作）。

以下几个感官动词的用法相同：

see sb. do sth./doing sth. 看到某人做…/正在做…

watch sb. do sth./doing sth. 观察到某人做…/正在做…

hear sb. do sth./doing sth. 听到某人做…/正在做…

此外，该句子也可改写为when I noticed a huge number of snails were taking a stroll on some of prize plants, 则notice之后接宾语从句。

2）take a stroll应译作"悠闲地散步"，这里采用了拟人手法，轻松诙谐的情调跃然纸上。类似表达有：

go for a walk 散步　　　　　　　　　　take a walk 散步

stroll the street 逛街　　　　　　　　　hang around 无事闲逛

▌ 拓 展 篇

I. 英语趣园

"One man's meat is another man's poison" was spoken by Hippocrates. Hippocrates was a Greek physician born in 460 BC in Greece. He became known as the founder of medicine and was regarded as the greatest physician of his time. He based his medical practice on observations and on the study of the human body. He held the belief that illness had a physical and a rational explanation. He rejected the views of his time that considered illness to be caused by superstitions and by possession of evil spirits and disfavor of the gods. Hippocrates traveled throughout Greece practicing his medicine. He founded a medical school on the island of Cos, Greece and began teaching his ideas. He soon developed an Oath of Medical Ethics for physicians to follow. This Oath is taken by physicians today as they begin their medical practice. He died in 377 BC. Today Hippocrates is known as the "Father of Medicine".

Ⅱ. 听力快车

Health food is a general term applied to all kinds of foods that are considered more healthful than the types of foods sold in supermarkets. For example, _____, dried beans and corn oil are health food. A ____of health is_____. This term is used to distinguish between types of the same food. Raw honey is a natural sweetener, whereas_____is not. Fresh fruit is a natural food, but ___ fruit, with sugar and other ___ , is not.

Ⅲ. 补充阅读

Food provides certain chemical substances needed for good health. The substances, called nutrients, perform one or more of three functions. They provide materials for building, repairing, or maintaining body tissues. They help regulate body process. They serve as fuel to provide energy. The body needs energy to maintain all its functions.

The body breaks food down into its nutrients through the process of digestion. Digestion begins in the mouth. As food is being chewed, saliva moistens the particles. The saliva begins to break down such starchy foods as bread and cereals. After the food is swallowed, it passes through a tube that leads into the stomach. In the stomach, digestive juices speed up the breakdown of such foods as meat, eggs, and milk. The partly digested food passes from the stomach into the small intestine, other juices complete the process of digestion. They break down the food into molecules that pass through the walls of the intestine and into the blood.

The blood distributes the nutrients to cells and tissues through the body. There the nutrients are broken down to produce energy or are used to rebuild tissues or to regulate chemical processes. Some of the nutrients are stored in the body, and others are used over and over again. But most of the nutrients undergo chemical changes as they are used in the cells and tissues. These chemical changes produce waste products, which go into the bloodstream.

Some of the wastes are carried to the kidneys, which filter them from the blood. The body expels these wastes in the urine. The liver also filters out some wastes and concentrates them into a liquid called bile. Bile is stored in the gall bladder until it is needed to aid in digestion. Then the gall bladder empties bile into the small intestine. From there, any remaining bile passes into the large intestine, along with parts of the food not digested in the small intestine. The large intestine absorbs water and small amounts of minerals from this waste material. This material, along with bacteria present in the large intestine, becomes the final waste product and it is eliminated from the body.

◆▶ 测试篇 ◀◆

Ⅰ. 单项选择

1. He had an almost irresistible _____ to talk to the crowd when he entered Hyde Park. （CET-6 05/1）
   A. impulse   B. instinct   C. stimulation   D. surge

2. The traditional markets retain their _____ for the many Chinese who still prefer fresh food like live fish, ducks, chickens over packaged or frozen goods. （CET-6 05/1）
   A. appeal   B. pledge   C. image   D. survival

3. In fact, as he approached this famous statue, he only barely resisted the _____ to reach into his bag for his camera. （CET-6 03/9）
   A. impatience   B. impulse   C. incentive   D. initiative

4. Parents have a legal _____ to ensure that their children are provided with efficient education suitable to their age.
   A. impulse   B. influence   C. obligation   D. sympathy

5. Human behavior is mostly a product of learning, whereas the behavior of an animal depends mainly on _____.
   A. consciousness   B. impulse   C. instinct   D. response

6. The lady in this strange tale very obviously suffers from a serious mental illness. Her plot against a completely innocent old man is a clear sign of _____.
   A. impulse   B. insanity   C. inspiration   D. disposition

7. It wasn't so much that I dislike her _____ that I just wasn't interested in the whole business.
   （2000年考研）
   A. rather   B. so   C. than   D. as

8. Tomorrow the mayor is to _____ a group of Canadian businessmen on a tour of the city.
   A. coordinate   B. cooperate   C. accompany   D. associate

9. A healthy life is frequently thought to be _____ with the open countryside and homegrown food.
   A. tied   B. bound   C. involved   D. associated

10. They used to quarrel a lot, but now they are completely _____ with each other.
    A. reconciled   B. negotiated   C. associated   D. accommodated

Ⅱ. 翻译

11. 在对孩子能学什么不能学什么的问题上，家长往往是没有逻辑可言的。（become quite illogical）
12. 学生们一听到铃声，便成群结队地走出了教室。（at the sound of）
13. 除夕之夜守岁是中国人的传统习俗。（an accepted practice）
14. 再也没有什么比眼泪干得更快的了。（好了伤疤忘了疼）（nothing...more...than）
15. 想去喝一杯吗？（fancy doing/sth.）

拓展篇

Health food is a general term applied to all kinds of foods that are considered more healthful than the types of foods sold in supermarkets. For example, <u>whole grain</u>, dried beans and corn oil are health food. A <u>narrower classification</u> of health is <u>natural food</u>. This term is used to distinguish between types of the same food. Raw honey is a natural sweetener, whereas <u>refined sugar</u> is not. Fresh fruit is a natural food, but <u>canned</u> fruit, with sugar and other <u>additives,</u> is not.

测试篇

1-5 AABCC   6-10 BDCDA

11. Parents become quite illogical when they try to decide what their children can learn and what they can't.

12. The students trooped out of the classroom at the sound of the bell.

13. It is an accepted practice in China that people will stay up all night on New Year's Eve.

14. Nothing dries sooner than tears.

15. Do you fancy a beer?

Lesson 24. A skeleton in the cupboard

I.振振有"词"

1. We often read in novels how a seemingly <u>respectable</u> person or family has some terrible secret which has been <u>concealed</u> from strangers for years.

conceal sth. from sb. 向某人隐瞒某事
keep sth. from sb. 不让某人知道某事
keep sth. to oneself 不让某人知道某事
Between you and me. 不要外传。
reveal sth. to sb. 将某事泄露
let the cat out of the bag 泄密

respectable 可敬的
respectful 谦卑的
respective 各自的，分别的
respecting 关于
in respect of 关于
with respect to 关于，谈到
pay one's respects to sb. (礼貌地) 拜访

2. At some <u>dramatic</u> moment,... a <u>reputation</u> is <u>ruined</u>.

dramatic 戏剧般的	reputation 名声	ruin (完全) 毁坏
theatric 戏剧般的	fame 名声	spoil (抽象义) 损害
thrilling 令人激动的	prestige 声誉	shatter (猛烈) 击碎
fascinating 令人着迷的	eminence 名声	demolish 拆毁 (建筑物)
breathtaking 摄人心魄的	popularity 名望	devastate 毁坏
eye-catching 吸引眼球的		

II.现身说"法"：be about to do sth. 与将来时

> **It gave me the impression that** it was about to leap out at me.
> 我觉得它好像马上要跳出来扑向我。

1. be about to do sth.表示即将做某事，意为"正要，马上就要"，句中一般不用表将来时间的状语。例：
   He was about to leave when the alarm was sounded. 警报响时，他正要离开。
   The helicopter is about to take off. 直升飞机即将起飞。

2. be on the point of doing sth.与 be about to do sth.意思基本相同，例：
   They are on the point of departing. 他们马上出发。

3. be to do sth. 略有不同，表示按计划安排要发生之事，多见于报刊、广播，用以宣布官方的决定或计划。例：

She is to go abroad next month. 她准备下月出国。

The minister is to visit Canada next week. 部长定于下周出访加拿大。

> ★★★ 注 意 ★★★
>
> 1. 如果不是人所能安排的动作，不可用be to do sth.表示即将发生。例：
>
> I feel I'm to faint. （误）　　I feel I'm going to faint. （正）
>
> 2. be not about to do sth.意为"不愿意…"。例：
>
> She is not about to go boating. 她不想去划船。

Ⅲ. 说"文"解"字"

1. a skeleton in the cupboard

译文：家丑

解析：该短语意为"家丑"，常以以下形式出现：to show one's skeleton in the cupboard（家丑外扬）。相似意义的表达有：

to foul one's own nest 自暴家丑　　to cry stinking fish 家丑外露　　to wash dirty linen 自暴家丑

2. It is all very well for such things to occur in fiction.

译文：这种事情发生在小说中是无可非议的。

解析：It is all very well for sb. to do sth.是一固定句型，意为"某人有理由…"，其中well是形容词用法，相当于reasonable。此外，该句型包含轻微的责备、不满情绪，实际上其后面省略了but引导的转折内容。因此，补全后应是：It is all very well for such things to occur in fiction, but not in reality. 例：

It is all very well for you to criticize, but could you have done any better yourself?

你可以批评别人，但是你自己不能做得更好点吗？

3. He told me to unpack my things and come down to dinner.

译文：他让我打开行装后下楼吃饭。

解析：come down to dinner是常用短语，类似表达有：

stay to dinner 留下吃饭　　　　　　　　　invite sb. to dinner 邀请某人吃饭

bring sb. to dinner 带某人来吃饭

4. It gave me the impression that it was about to leap out at me.

译文：让我觉得它好像马上要跳出来扑向我似的。

解析：1）give sb. the impression of...意为"给某人…印象"。类似表达有：

make a（n）...impression on sb. 给某人…印象

have the impression that...具有…印象

be under the impression that...具有…印象

2）leap at...意为"朝…扑过去"。英文中许多具有"攻击，进攻"之意的短语都是"动词+at"结构：

charge at...朝…冲过去　　　come at...朝…进攻　　　fly at...朝…冲过去

拓展篇

I. 英语趣园

Saint Sebastian

Sebastian died a martyr in Rome, probably in AD 288. Two hundred years after his death a legend sprang up about his life. According to this legend, Sebastian, a Christian, decided to go into the military during a time of persecution. This decision was not to save his own life, but in order to put himself in a position to comfort the martyrs. As a member of the military, he was in ideal place to stay with them, encourage them, and even alleviate their sufferings without anyone being suspicious or keeping him out. He showed such aptitude, however, in the military life, that the emperor Diocletian made him a captain without ever guessing Sebastian was a Christian. As more and more Christians died, it was inevitable that Sebastian would be found out. Diocletian was furious at what he saw as a betrayal after all he had done for Sebastian. He ordered Sebastian to be shot by archers.

II. 听力快车

When a man has an _____ about something that happened to him in the past that he wants to hide, he is said to have a "skeleton in his cupboard or closet" or "_____".

III. 补充阅读

Arthur Ignatius Conan Doyle was born on May 22, 1859, in Edinburgh, Scotland. The Doyles were a prosperous Irish-Catholic family, who had a prominent position in the world of art. Charles Altamont Doyle, Arthur's father, a chronic alcoholic, was the only member of his family, who apart from fathering a brilliant son, never accomplished anything of note. At the age of twenty-two, Charles had married Mary Foley, a vivacious and very well educated young woman of seventeen.

Mary Doyle had a passion for books and was a master storyteller. Her son Arthur wrote of his mother's gift of "sinking her voice to a horror-stricken whisper" when she reached the culminating point of a story. There was little money in the family and even less harmony on account of his father's excesses and erratic behavior. Arthur's touching description of his mother's beneficial influence is also poignantly described in his biography, *In my early childhood, as far as I can remember anything at all, the vivid stories she would tell me stand out so clearly that they obscure the real facts of my life.*

After Arthur reached his ninth birthday, the wealthy members of the Doyle family offered to pay for his studies. He was in tears all the way to England, where for seven years he had to go to a Jesuit boarding school. Arthur loathed the bigotry surrounding his studies and rebelled at corporal punishment, which was prevalent and incredibly brutal in most English schools of that epoch.

During those grueling years, Arthur's only moments of happiness were when he wrote to his mother, a regular habit that lasted for the rest of her life, and also when he practiced sports, mainly cricket, at which he was very good. It was during these difficult years at boarding school, that Arthur realized he also had a talent for storytelling. He was often found surrounded by a bevy of totally enraptured younger students listening to the amazing stories he would make up to amuse them.

By 1876, graduating at the age of seventeen, Arthur Doyle（as he was called, before adding his middle name "Conan" to his surname）, was a surprisingly normal young man. With his innate sense of humor and his sportsmanship, having ruled out any feelings of self-pity, Arthur was ready and willing to face the world and make up for some of his father's shortcomings.

测 试 篇

I. 单项选择

1. With prices _____ so much, it is difficult for the school to plan a budget.　　　　（CET-6 03/1）
   A. vibrating　　　　B. fluctuating　　　　C. fluttering　　　　D. swinging

2. The old gentleman was a very _____ looking person, with grey hair and gold spectacles.
   A respectful　　　　B. respected　　　　C. respective　　　　D. respectable

3. The city was named _____ the first president of the U.S. , who decided upon its location in the first place.
   A. with respect to　　B. with regard to　　C. to pay respect to　　D. in honor of

4. After the collision, he examined the considerable _____ to his car.
   A. ruin　　　　B. destruction　　　　C. damage　　　　D. injury

5. They believed that this was not the _____ of their campaign for equality but merely the beginning.
   A. climax　　　　B. summit　　　　C. pitch　　　　D. maximum　　　　（CET-6 02/6）

6. Marlin is a young man of independent thinking who is not about _____ compliments to his political leaders.　　　　（99年考研）
   A. paying　　　　B. having paid　　　　C.to pay　　　　D. to have paid

7. They believed that this was not the _____ of their campaign for equality but merely the beginning.
   A. climax　　　　B. summit　　　　C. pitch　　　　D. maximum　　　　（CET-6 02/6）

8. Many patients insist on having watches with them in hospital, _____ they have no schedules to keep.
   A. even though　　　B. for　　　　C. as if　　　　D. since

9. If I correct someone, I will do it with as much good humor and self-restraint as if I were the one _____ .
   A. to correct　　　B. correcting　　　C. having corrected　　D. being corrected

10. It seems somewhat _____ to expect anyone to drive 3 hours just for a 20-minute meeting.
    A. eccentric　　　B. impossible　　　C. absurb　　　D. unique

II. 翻译

11. 那样浪漫的爱情写在小说里是很好的，但现实和想像是不一样的。（It is all very well...）
12. 她为自己的美貌而得意。（pride oneself on...）
13. 他的事业在三十多岁的时候达到了巅峰。（reach its climax）
14. 很多人以为美国是人间天堂。（be under the impression that...）
15. 三思而后行。（leap）

答案

拓展篇

When a man has an <u>embarrassing or unpleasant secret</u> about something that happened to him in the past that he wants to hide, he is said to have a "skeleton in his cupboard or closet" or "<u>every family has got a skeleton in his cupboard</u>".

测试篇

1-5 BADCA   6-10 CAADC

11. It is all very well for such romances to occur in novels. But reality doesn't speak the same language with imagination.

12. She prides herself on her beauty.

13. His career reached its climax in his thirties.

14. Many people are under the impression that US is paradise.

15. Look before you leap.

Lesson **25.** The *Cutty Sark*

积累篇

I. 振振有"词"

1. She <u>served as</u> an impressive <u>reminder</u> of the great ship of the past.

> serve as 作为…
> function as 作为…
> act as 作为…
> be used as 被用作…
> make up as 化装成…
> dress up as 装扮成…
> disguise as 伪装成…

> reminder 令人回忆的东西
> remind sb. of...令人回忆起…
> be reminiscent of...令人回忆起…
> reminiscence 回忆
> memoir 回忆录
> memorandum 备忘录

2. This rudder would <u>be torn away</u> as well. Because of this, the Cutty Sark <u>lost her lead</u>.

> tear sth. away 刮走
> tear oneself away 依依不舍地走开
> tear sth. down 推倒
> tear sth. off 迅速生产出
> tear sth. up 撕碎

> lose one's lead 失去领先地位
> regain one's lead 重新获得领先地位
> be in the lead 处于领先地位
> take the lead 占据领先地位
> play the lead 担任主角

II. 现身说"法": 不定式作定语

The only other ship to match her was the *Thermopylae*.
惟一可以与它一争高低的是"塞姆皮雷"号帆船。

不定式若置于名词之后, 可作名词的定语。例:

Atomic power is associated in the mind with the destructive force of atom bombs, though it is claimed that there is no danger to be associated with atomic power stations. (《新概念英语》4册)

尽管有人声称原子能电站不会发生危险, 但公众通常把原子能和原子弹的破坏力联系在一起。

The best way to overcome it...is to make your interests gradually wider and more impersonal. (《新概念英语》4册) 克服恐惧心理的最佳方法……便是逐渐使你的兴趣更加广泛, 更加摆脱个人狭小的圈子。

> ### ★★★ 注意 ★★★
> 不定式作定语时, 如果和它所修饰的词构成动宾关系, 且不定式中使用的是不及物动词, 则不定式之后应加相关的介词。例:
> There is nothing for you to worry about. 你不必担心。
> We will have to find a place to put the stuff in. 我们得找个地方把东西放进去。

Ⅲ. 说"文"解"字"

1. **She** serves as an impressive reminder **of the great ships of the past.**

译文：它给人们留下深刻的印象，使人们回忆起历史上的巨型帆船。

解析：reminder意为"回忆物"，但在翻译中将其作动词处理，这是英汉互译中经常运用的词性变通原则，以使得语言更加顺畅自如。例：

She is a beautiful singer. 她唱得很美。（singer翻译为动词）

I have often tried to conceive of what those pages contain, but of course I cannot do so because I am a prisoner of the present-day world.（《新概念英语》4册）我经常试图去猜想这十几页中可能是什么内容，但我当然不能，因为我的思想被禁锢在当今这个世界里。（prisoner翻译为动词）

Few students of the Far East doubted that Japan intended to use the opportunity offered by the plight of Russia and Britain to grab the oil she desperately needed. 研究远东问题的人很少有怀疑日本打算利用俄英的困境来获取它迫切需要的石油。（students of the Far East翻译为动作概念）

2. **It** marked the end of **the great tradition of ships with sails** and the beginning of **a new era.**

译文：它标志着帆船伟大传统的结束和一个新纪元的开端。

解析：sth. mark the end of...and the beginning of...是一个经典句型，意为"某事标志着…的结束和…的开始"。例：

This event marked the end of her tragedy and the beginning of her success.

这件事标志着她的悲剧的终结和其辉煌的到来。

This novel marked the end of romanticism in his writing and the beginning of critical realism.

这部小说标志着其创作中浪漫主义风格的结束和批判现实主义的出现。

The invention of steam engine by Watt marked the end of great tradition of labor with hands and the beginning of a new era of machinery. 瓦特蒸汽机的发明标志着手工劳动这一伟大传统的结束和机器时代的到来。

类似句型有：

sth. mark the milestone of sth. 某事标志着…的里程碑

sth. is a turning point of sth. 某事是…的转折点

▎▊ 拓 展 篇

Ⅰ. 英语趣园

Greenwich, an area of southeast London, is on the river Thames. The original British Royal Observatory（=a special building from which scientists watch the moon, stars etc.）is there, and the zero meridian（=an imaginary line which divides the eastern and western halves of the world）passes through the grounds of the Observatory.

Ⅱ. 听力快车 🎧

The equator, hemispheres, Tropic of Cancer, and Tropic of Capricorn

Three of the most significant _____ running across the surface of the earth are the equator, _____, and _____ . While the equator is the longest line of _____ on the earth（the line where the earth is widest in an east-west direction）, the tropics are based on the sun's position in relation to the earth at two points of the year.

The equator is located at_____ latitude. The equator runs through Indonesia, Ecuador, northern Brazil, the Democratic Republic of the Congo, and Kenya, among other countries. It is 24,901.55 miles（40,075.16 kilometers）long. On the equator, the sun is_____ on the two equinoxes—near March and September 21. The equator divides the planet into the_____ .

Ⅲ.补充阅读

Cutty Sark

She is the world's sole surviving extreme clipper, a type of vessel that was the highest development of the fast commercial sailing ship, with the majority of her hull fabric surviving from her original construction.

- She is internationally appreciated for her beauty and is one of the most famous ships in the world.
- Her fine lines—a considerable part of her appeal—are defined by her frames which form part of the vessel's composite construction: a construction technique of which she is the best surviving example and of which she is of exceptional quality.
- She has captured the imagination of millions of people, 15 million of whom have come on board to learn the stories she has to tell.
- She is a gateway to the World Heritage Site at Greenwich and is a key asset to both the World Heritage Site and the Borough of Greenwich.
- As a tea clipper, she is tangible evidence of the importance of tea in 19th century trade and cultural life.

▶ 测 试 篇 ◀

Ⅰ.单项选择

1. Many in the credit industry expect that credit cards will eventually _____ paper money for almost every purchase.
   A. exchange   B. reduce   C. replace   D. trade

2. While people may refer to television for up-to-minute news, it is unlikely that television _____ the newspaper completely.
   A. replaced   B. have replaced   C. replace   D. will replace

3. Professor Smith and Professor Brown will _____ in presenting the series of lectures on American literature.
   A. alter   B. alternate   C. substitute   D. exchange

4. Doctors warned against chewing tobacco as a _____ for smoking.
   A. relief   B. revival   C. substitute   D. succession

5. Located in Washington D.C., the Library of Congress contains an impressive _____ of books on every conceivable subject.
   A. flock   B. configuration   C. pile   D. array

6. I have kept that portrait _____ I can see it every day, as it always reminds me of my university days in London.

A. which   B. where   C. whether   D. when

7. The sign set up by the road _____ drivers to a sharp turn.

     A. alerts   B. refreshes   C. pleads   D. diverts

8. The day before my history exam, I still hadn't _____ reading the first book on the list.

     A. as about   B. caught up with   C. got round to   D. sat for

9. I think we need to see an investment _____ before we make an expensive mistake.

     A. guide   B. entrepreneur   C. consultant   D. assessor

10. Many years had _____ before they returned to their original urban areas.

     A. floated   B. elapsed   C. skipped   D. proceeded

Ⅱ. 翻译

11. 每年都有成千上万的人前往布达拉宫。（be visited by）

12. 人们普遍认为在不远的将来，计算机作为一种信息手段将取代电视。（replace）

13.《铁达尼号》是好莱坞有史以来拍摄过的耗资最大的片子之一。（one of the most...that have ever been...）

14. 我们被车子颠得东倒西歪。（bump from side to side）

15. 二战后，日本的工业发展遥遥领先。（take the lead in）

拓展篇

The equator, hemispheres, Tropic of Cancer, and Tropic of Capricorn

Three of the most significant imaginary lines running across the surface of the earth are the equator, the Tropic of Cancer, and the Tropic of Capricorn. While the equator is the longest line of latitude on the earth (the line where the earth is widest in an east-west direction), the tropics are based on the sun's position in relation to the earth at two points of the year.

The equator is located at zero degrees latitude. The equator runs through Indonesia, Ecuador, northern Brazil, the Democratic Republic of the Congo, and Kenya, among other countries. It is 24,901.55 miles (40,075.16 kilometers) long. On the equator, the sun is directly overhead at noon on the two equinoxes —near March and September 21. The equator divides the planet into the Northern and Southern Hemispheres.

测试篇

1-5 CDBCD   6-10 BACCB

11. Potala Palace is visited by thousands of people each year.

12. There is a popular belief that computer would replace TV as a means of information in the near future.

13. *Titanic* was one of the most costly films that have ever been made by Hollywood.

14. We were bumped from side to side in the car.

15. Japan took the lead in industrial development after World War Ⅱ.

Lesson Wanted: a large biscuit tin

积 累 篇

I.振振有"词"

1. No one can <u>avoid</u> being influenced by <u>advertisements</u>.

> avoid doing sth. 不愿做…
> 后面接动名词用法的词：
> deny doing sth. 否认做…
> risk doing sth. 冒险做…
> imagine doing sth. 想像做…
> enjoy doing sth. 喜欢做…
> delay doing sth. 推迟做…

> advertisement 广告
> commercial advertisement 商业广告
> classified advertisement 分类广告
> false advertisement 虚假广告
> advertise sth. 推销…
> advertise for sth. 为…代言

2. <u>Much as</u> we may <u>pride ourselves on</u> our good taste, we are no longer <u>free to</u> choose the things we want.

> much as 尽管
> as much 同样数量
> much less 更不用说
> not much 几乎没有
> by much 极大程度
> every so much 非常

> pride oneself on...对…引以为豪
> be proud of...对…很自豪
> take pride in...对…很自豪
> hurt one's pride 伤某人的自尊
> do someone proud 给某人面子

> be free to do 自由做…
> be ready to do 乐于做…
> be pleased to do 高兴做…
> be voluntary to do 自愿做…
> be willing to do 愿意做…

3. <u>Advertisers</u> discovered years ago that all of us love to <u>get something for nothing</u>.

> advertiser 广告人
> photographer 摄影师
> program deviser 节目策划人
> fashion designer 服装设计师
> broker 经纪人

> get sth. for nothing 免费得到某物
> get sth. free of charge 免费得到某物
> get sth. at no cost 免费得到某物
> get sth. gratis 免费得到某物
> get sth. for free 免费得到某物

4. The <u>manufacturers</u> had to pay more money than they had <u>anticipated</u>.

manufacturer 制造商	anticipate 预料，预期
manual 体力的	antique 古董
manipulate 操纵，控制	antecedent 前事，先例
manicurist 美甲师	anterior 前面的
manuscript 手稿，草稿	antedate 先于，早于
manacle 手铐	antechamber 前厅，外室

II. 现身说"法"：much as引导的让步状语从句

Much as we may pride ourselves on our good taste, we are no longer free to choose the things we want. 尽管我们可以自夸自己的鉴赏力如何敏锐，但我们已经无法独立自主地选购自己所需的商品了。

实际上，much是修饰provide的，其原始位置应在ourselves之后，前置是为了强调，再加上as，则构成固定短语，引导让步状语从句。例：

Much as I admire David as a poet, I don't like him as a man.（CET-4 /04）

尽管戴维作为诗人我很景仰，但他的为人我却不喜欢。

Much as he likes her, he does get annoyed with her sometimes.（CET-4 /04）

尽管他很喜欢她，有时他却对她很恼火。

> **补充**
>
> 在由although/though引导的让步状语从句中，可去掉although/though，而将所要强调的词置于句首，再加上as，构成特殊的让步状语从句。例：
>
> Although he is rich, he spends a cent on charity. ➡ Rich as he is, he spends a cent on charity.
>
> 尽管他很富有，却很吝啬。
>
> Though he tries, he never seems able to do the work beautifully. ➡ Try as he does, he never seems able to do the work beautifully. 尽管很努力，他从未把工作干得很出色。

III. 说"文"解"字"

1. For advertising exerts a subtle influence on us.

译文：因为广告给我们施加了一种潜移默化的影响。

解析：1）advertising与advertisement稍有不同。前者表动态行为，意为"广告的理念、手段等"；而后者侧重静态，指 "广告宣传片" 等，所以advertising前一般不加a，而advertisement前则可以。例：

This advertisement（advertising ✗）is appealing. 这部广告片很精彩。

Various advertising（advertisement ✗）techniques were employed to attract consumers.

为了招揽顾客，各种广告促销手段都用上了。

2）exert sth. on sb.是一个常用结构，意为"给某人施加…"，exert 也可用impose替换。例：

exert/impose a strong fascination on sb. 极其吸引某人

exert/impose much pressure on sb. 给某人施加极大压力

此外，exert若后接反身代词，则表示"努力做…"。例：

She exerts herself for the welfare of her children. 她尽力为孩子们创造幸福。

The host exerted himself for the guests. 主人尽心尽力地招待客人。

2. **An advertisement which** begins with **the magic word FREE can rarely** go wrong.

译文：凡是用"免费"这个神奇字眼开头的广告很少会失败的。

解析：1）begin with...意为"以…开头"。例：

The novel begins with a brief depiction of the hero's early years.

小说开头简要描述了主人公的早年生活。

> **联想记忆**
>
> ①be headed with...篇首是…
>
> The newspaper is headed with a striking illustration of the road accident.
>
> 报纸的篇首是一幅令人震惊的车祸场景。
>
> ②sth./sb. makes the headline/frontpage 占据头条

2）go wrong中的go是系动词用法，其他类似用法有：

go bad 变质   go mad 疯了

go bald 秃顶   go insane 精神失常

3. **They offered to pay $10** a pound **for the biggest biscuit baked by a listener.**

译文：他们许诺以每磅10美元的价格买下由听众烘制的饼干。

解析：a pound在句中充当状语，也可用by the pound替换。一般而言，英文中表时间、重量等的名词短语可充当状语，与加by的短语意义相同。例：

earn 100 yuan a day/by the day; run 90 miles an hour/by the hour

拓 展 篇

Ⅰ. 英语趣园

Madison Avenue, a street in New York City is famous as the center of the advertising business. Its name is sometimes used to mean the US advertising business in general.

Ⅱ. 听力快车

Choose the best answer for each of the following questions.

1. How long had the speaker realized the occurrence of advertisement?

   A. Since childhood.   B. Since his teenage.

   C. Over the past 30 years.   D. After 1966.

2. What was the second change thing in speaker's mind?

   A. The variety of daily life.   B. The use of new media.

   C. The difficulty to find ads.   D. The simplified form of presses.

3. Advertising techniques have _____ become more persuasive and more sophisticated.

   A. initially   B. successfully

   C. directly   D. psychologically

III. 补充阅读

Having fun can exhaust one's bank account. By the time a person drives to the city and pays the tired-looking parking attendant the hourly fee to park, there is little money left to buy movie tickets, let alone popcorn and soft drinks to snack on. As a result, people have turned from wining, dining, and moviegoing to the nearby free-parking, free admission shopping malls. Teenagers, couples on dates, and the nuclear family can be observed having a good time at this alternative recreation spot.

Teenagers are the largest group of mallgoers. The guys saunter by in sneakers, T-shirts, and blue jeans, complete with package of cigarettes sticking out of their pockets. The girls stumble along in high-heeled shoes and daring tank tops, with hairbrushes tucked snugly in the rear pockets of their tight-fitting designer jeans. Traveling in a gang that resembles a wolf pack, the teenagers make the shopping mall their hunting ground, Their raised voices, loud laughter, and occasional shouted obscenities can be heard from as far as half a mall away. They come to "pick up chicks," to "meet guys," and basically just to "hang out."

Lovers make up the second largest group of mallgoers. They spend their dates at shopping malls, walking hand in hand, stopping to sneak a quick kiss after every few steps. Those people would first pause at jewelry store windows so they can gaze at diamond engagement rings and gold wedding bands. Then, they wander into furniture departments in the large mall stores. Whispering happily to each other, they imagine how that five-piece living room set or brass headboard would look in their future home. Finally, they drift away, their arms wrapped around each other's waists.

Apart from teenagers and lovers, nuclear family members can also be identified as the largest group of mallgoers. Mom, Dad, little Jenny, and Fred, visit the mall on Friday and Saturday evenings. Mom walks around looking at various things until she discovers that Jenny is no longer attached to her hand. Dad is admiring the products he would love to buy. Jenny is seeing some of the special mall exhibits geared toward little children and Fred is heading for the place that young boys find appealing. Indeed, the mall provides something special for every member of the nuclear family.

The teenagers, lovers on dates, and the nuclear family make up the majority of mallgoers. These folks need not purchase anything to find pleasure at the mall. They are shopping for inexpensive recreation, and the mall provides it.

▶ 测 试 篇 ◀

I. 单项选择

1. We are interested in the weather because it _____ us so directly—what we wear, what we do, and even how we feel. (CET-4 91/6)

   A. affects   B. benefits   C. guides   D. effects

2. How close parents are to their children _____ a strong influence on the character of the children.

   A. have   B. has   C. having   D. to have

3. In Australia the Asians make their influence _____ in businesses large and small.

   A. feeling   B. feel   C. felt   D. to be felt

4. Parents have a legal _____ to ensure that their children are provided with efficient education suitable to their age.

   A. impulse   B. influence   C. obligation   D. sympathy

5. Tryon was extremely angry, but cool-headed enough to _____ storming into the boss's office.

   A. prevent   B. prohibit   C. turn   D. avoid

6. You will see this product _____ wherever you go.　　　　　　　　　　(CET-4 00/6)

A. to be advertised　　B. advertised　　　C. advertise　　　D. adverting

7. The house was very quiet, _____ as it was on the side of a mountain.　　(CET-4 99/6)

A. isolated　　　　　B. isolating　　　C. being isolated　　D. having been isolated

8. _____, he does get annoyed with her sometimes.　　　　　　　　　(CET-4 00/6)

A. Although much he likes her　　　　B. Much although he likes her

C. As he likes her much　　　　　　　D. Much as he likes her

9. Anyone not paying the registration fee by the end of this month will be _____ to have withdrawn from the program.

A. contemplated　　B. deemed　　　C. acknowledged　　D. anticipated

10. Louis Herman, at the University of Hawall, has _____ a series of new experiments in which some animals have learned to understand sentences.

A. installed　　　B. equipped　　　C. devised　　　D. formatted

Ⅱ．翻译

11. 孔孟之道对我们社会的形成有着深远的影响。（exert a profound influence on）
12. 我在网上登了旧车出售的广告。（advertise sth.）
13. 在竞争如此激烈的社会，没有人能避免受到英语对我们的影响。（avoid being influenced by）
14. 尽管卢梭作为一个哲学家让我很崇拜，然而他作为一个人本身，我并不喜欢。（Much as I...）
15. 我们学校刚建立的时候是一个很小的学校。（to begin with）

答案

拓展篇

　　1. A　2. B　3. D

　　I was born in Britain in 1966, so I suppose advertising has always been part of my life. As a child, I was always aware of ads in magazines and newspapers, and on boardings in the street, on posters in public transport and so on. But there have been changes in advertising in Britain over the past 30 years or so.

　　The first thing that comes to mind is the amount of advertising we live with nowadays. There is, quite simply, a lot more advertising than there used to be. Nowadays, whatever you're doing in your daily life it's quite difficult to get away from ads in one form or another. They're all around you!

　　Another noticeable change is the use of new media for advertising. I suppose I'm thinking mainly of TV, which has developed over the last 30 years and is now an integral part of life for most people. There are TV sets in most homes. TV advertising, consequently, has developed at an enormous rate and is perhaps the most important form of advertising, certainly one of the most influential in Britain today.

　　A 3rd big change has been in advertising psychology—in how advertisers aim to persuade people to buy their products. Originally, adverts were very simple. Either they simply gave straight information about a product or, if they set out to persuade, they did this in a very direct way.

测试篇

　　1-5 ABCCD　　　　6-10 BADBC

　　11. The doctrine of Confucius and Mencius has exerted a profound influence on the making of our society.

　　12. I advertised a second-hand car for sale on the Internet.

　　13. In such a competitive society, no one can avoid being influenced by English.

　　14. Much as I admired Rousseau as a philosopher, I don't like him as a man.

　　15. Our school was quite a small one to begin with.

Lesson Nothing to sell and nothing to buy

积 累 篇

I. 振振有"词"

1. <u>In the light of</u> this <u>statement</u>, teachers <u>live by selling knowledge</u>.

in the light of 按照…	statement 声明	live by doing sth. 靠…谋生
in terms of 依据…	personal statement 个人陈述	live on sth. 以…为食
according to 根据…	bank statement 银行结算表	live off sb. 靠某人养活
in respect of 关于，至于…	announcement 通告	live on 继续活着
with regard to 关于…	communiqué 公告	live through sth. 经历…
	bulletin 告示	live out sth. 实现…

2. Yet we might <u>grudge paying</u> a <u>surgeon</u> a high <u>fee</u> for offering us precisely this service.

grudge doing sth. 不愿做…	surgeon 外科医生	fee (付给医生、律师等的) 劳务费
grudge sb. sth. 不舍得给某人某物	physician 内科医生	tuition 学费
loathe doing sth. 讨厌做…	physicist 物理学家	toll 过路费
detest doing sth. 厌恶做…	surgery 外科手术	membership dues 会员费
resent doing sth. 痛恨做…	plastic surgery 整容术	commission 佣金
		compensation money 赔偿金

3. He has <u>deliberately</u> chosen to lead the life he leads and <u>is fully aware of</u> the <u>consequences</u>.

deliberate 故意的	be aware of 意识到…	consequence 后果
intentional 刻意的	be conscious of 意识到…	consequent 随后发生的
intentional murder 蓄意谋杀	be sensible of 意识到…	consequential 意义重大的
on purpose 故意	be unaware of 没有意识到…	in consequence of 由于
purposefully 故意地	be unconscious of 没有意识到…	as a consequence of 由于
go out of one's way to do sth. 特意做某事	be ignorant of 不知…	take the consequence 承担后果

4. We often speak of <u>tramps</u> with <u>contempt</u> and <u>put them in the same class as beggars</u>.

tramp 流浪汉
wanderer 流浪者
vagrant（尤指因贫困而无家可归的）流浪者
roamer 闲逛者
dolittle 游手好闲者

put A in the same class as B 将A与B归为一类
bracket A with B 把A与B相提并论
be tarred with the same brush 一丘之貉
Birds of a feather flock together.
物以类聚，人以群分。

contempt 蔑视　　disdain 鄙视
despise 藐视　　belittle 小看
disparage 轻视　　slight 瞧不起

Ⅱ. 现身说"法"：**in doing**结构

In seeking independence, **they do not sacrifice their human dignity.**
在追求独立自由的同时，他们并不牺牲人格尊严。

　　in doing结构中的介词in具有when或while之意。如果将in去掉，则该结构变成了分词结构，意思上没有什么不同。此外，on doing结构中的on具有as soon as或when之意。试比较：

In talking（=When we talk）about imagination, we invariably talk of the poet.
谈及想像力时，我们总会谈谈起那位诗人。

In making（=When he makes）a dictionary, he displays a special skill.
对于编字典，他有特殊技能。

On entering（=As soon as we entered）his room, we at once perceived that he was a man of taste.
一走进他的房间，我们就看出来他是一个风雅的人。

On arriving（=As soon as he arrived）in Britain, he received a visit from a college professor.
刚到英国，一位大学教授就来拜访他。

Ⅲ. 说"文"解"字"

1. There are times when **we would willingly give everything we possess to save our lives.**
译文：有时，我们为了挽救生命，愿意付出我们所拥有的一切。
解析：There are times when... 是一个常用结构，功能上近似于sometimes，但前者更正式，更适合写作中延展句型。例：
There are times when/Sometimes we want to achieve a goal beyond attainment, but it is better to be realistic. 有时，我们会渴求某个难以企及的目标，但务实一点儿是更好的选择。

2. But he **is free from the thousands of anxieties** which afflict other people.
译文：但他不像有些人那样被诸多的烦恼所困扰。
解析：1）be free from sth.表"远离…，不受…困扰"。一般后接带有"灾祸，痛苦，危险"之意的名词，如：poverty、trouble、pain、danger等。例：

Even the wise are not free from error. 智者千虑，必有一失。

2）the thousands of anxieties是夸张手法，以表现烦恼之多。实际上，夸张是英文中常用的写作手段。例：

a mountain of work 大量的工作

a thousand and one jobs about the house 成堆的家务活

Under freezing skies a million creatures contend in freedom. 万类霜天竞自由。

3. His few material possessions make it possible for him to move from place to place with ease.

译文：他几乎没有什么财物，这使他能够轻松自如地游走四方。

解析：move from place to place是固定表达，两个place前面不加冠词。其他类似短语有：

laugh from ear to ear 大笑

read sth. from cover to cover 读完…

sell sth. from door to door 挨门挨户推销…

vary from person to person 因人而异

4. But how many of us can honestly say that we have not felt a little envious of their simple way of life and their freedom from care?

译文：但是，我们中有多少人能坦率地说我们对流浪汉简朴的生活和无忧无虑的境况不感到有些羡慕呢？

解析：该句的结构是疑问句，但实际上起到了加强语气的陈述句作用，这种疑问句被称为修辞疑问句，其中的否定形式常表肯定意义，而肯定形式表否定意义。例：

Didn't I tell you this proposal was impractical?（I told you...）

我难道没告诉你这项计划不合实际吗？

Could any spectacle, for instance, be more whimsical than that of gunners using science to shatter men's bodies while, close at hand, surgeons use it to restore them?（《新概念英语》4册）

例如：枪手利用科学摧毁人体，而外科医生就在附近利用科学抢救被枪手摧毁的人体，难道还有什么场景比这更加荒诞吗？

拓 展 篇

Ⅰ. 英语趣园

　　Tramps or vagabonds are those who give up everything they are. Some who do so are fond of freedom and most probably cannot conform to society, while others may be depressed by their setbacks and cannot return to society. Whatever the reason and however the result, their lives are full of interest, providing them with opportunities to experience and taste real life.

Ⅱ. 听力快车

　　The number of homeless people in the United States has been a _____. Advocates for the homeless claim that there are several million homeless people; however, recent studies suggest that the homeless number from _____. Precise numbers are impossible to collect because _____in different ways and because the homeless are transitory. The number of people predicted to become homeless in any given year is estimated to be_____ the number of people who are homeless at any given moment. The US Census Bureau _____ in the 1990 census. However, most analysts regard this attempt as a failure.

III. 补充阅读

Whistling Dick's Christmas stocking

by O. Henry

The two surly tramps made a collection of all the matches in the party, Whistling Dick contributing his quota with propitiatory alacrity, and then they departed...

It was with much caution that Whistling Dick slid back the door of the boxcar, for Article 5716, City Ordinances, authorized（perhaps unconstitutionally）arrest on suspicion, and he was familiar of old with this ordinance. So, before climbing out, he surveyed the field with all the care of a good general.

He saw no change since his last visit to this big, alms-giving, long-suffering city of the South, the cold weather paradise of the tramps. The levee where his freight-car stood was pimpled with dark bulks of merchandise. The breeze reeked with the well-remembered, sickening smell of the old tarpaulins that covered bales and barrels. The dun river slipped along among the shipping with an oily gurgle. Far down toward Chalmette he could see the great bend in the stream outlined by the row of electric lights. Across the river Algiers lay a long, irregular blot, made darker by the dawn which lightened the sky beyond. An industrious tug or two, coming for some early sailing ship, gave a few appalling toots, that seemed to be the signal for breaking day. The Italian luggers were creeping nearer their landing, laden with early vegetables and shellfish. A vague roar, subterranean in quality, from dray wheels and street cars, began to make itself heard and felt; and the ferryboats, the Mary Anns of water craft, stirred sullenly to their menial morning tasks.

Whistling Dick's red head popped suddenly back into the car. A sight too imposing and magnificent for his gaze had been added to the scene. A vast, incomparable policeman rounded a pile of rice sacks and stood within twenty yards of the car. The daily miracle of the dawn, now being performed above Algiers, received the flattering attention of this specimen of municipal official splendour. He gazed with unbiased dignity at the faintly glowing colours until, at last, he turned to them his broad back, as if convinced that legal interference was not needed, and the sunrise might proceed unchecked. So he turned his face to the rice bags, and, drawing a flat flask from an inside pocket, he placed it to his lips and regarded the firmament.

Whistling Dick, professional tramp, possessed a half-friendly acquaintance with this officer. They had met several times before on the levee at night, for the officer, himself a lover of music, had been attracted by the exquisite whistling of the shiftless vagabond. Still, he did not care, under the present circumstances, to renew the acquaintance. There is a difference between meeting a policeman on a lonely wharf and whistling a few operatic airs with him, and being caught by him crawling out of a freight-car. So Dick waited, as even a New Orleans policeman must move on some time—perhaps it is a retributive law of nature—and before long "Big Fritz" majestically disappeared between the trains of cars.

Whistling Dick waited as long as his judgment advised, and then slid swiftly to the ground. Assuming as far as possible the air of an honest laborer who seeks his daily toil, he moved across the network of railway lines, with the intention of making his way by quiet Girod Street to a certain bench in Lafayette Square, where, according to appointment, he hoped to rejoin a pal known as "Slick," this adventurous pilgrim having preceded him by one day in a cattle-car into which a loose slat had enticed him.

As Whistling Dick picked his way where night still lingered among the big, reeking, musty warehouses, he gave way to the habit that had won for him his title. Subdued, yet clear, with each note as true and liquid as a bobolink's, his whistle tinkled about the dim, cold mountains of brick like drops of rain falling into a hidden pool. He followed an air, but it swam mistily into a swirling current of improvisation. You could cull out the trill of mountain brooks, the staccato of green rushes shivering above chilly lagoons, the pipe of sleepy birds.

Rounding a corner, the whistler collided with a mountain of blue and brass.

▶ 测 试 篇 ◀

I . 单项选择

1. The medicine _____ his pain but did not cure his illness. （CET-6 02/6）
   A. activated   B. alleviated   C. mediated   D. deteriorated

2. Every man in this country has the right to live where he wants to _____ the color of his skin.
   A. with the exception of   B. in the light of
   C. by virtue of   D. regardless of

3. _____ their differences, the couple were developing an obvious and genuine affection for each other.
   A. But for   B. For all   C. Above all   D. Except for

4. Over a third of the population was estimated to have no _____ to the health service.
   A. assessment   B. assignment   C. exception   D. access

5. These two areas are similar _____ they both have a high rainfall during this season.
   A. to that   B. besides that   C. in that   D. except that

6. Many people believe we are heading for environmental disaster _____ we radically change way we live.
   A. but   B. although   C. unless   D. lest

7. _____ the help of their group, we would not have succeeded in the investigation.
   A. Besides   B. By virtue of   C. But for   D. Regardless of

8. Five minutes earlier, _____ we could have caught the last train.
   A. and   B. but   C. or   D. so

9. The fire has caused great losses, but the factory tried to _____ the consequences by saying that the damage was not as serious as reported.
   A. decrease   B. subtract   C. minimize   D. degrade

10. Melted iron is poured into the mixer much _____ tea is poured into a cup from a teapot.
    A. in the same way like   B. in the same way which
    C. in the same way   D. in the same way as

Ⅱ. 翻译

11. 作为一名作家，我以写作为生。（live by）

12. 根据《圣经》，亚当和夏娃是赤身裸体的生活在伊甸园。（In the light of）

13. 就智力而言，人和人之间并没有不同。（in terms of）

14. 伊拉克长期以来一直饱受饥荒和战争之苦。（be afflicted by）

15. 他的演讲激起了我们的极大兴趣。（arouse interest）

拓展篇

The number of homeless people in the United States has been a <u>matter of considerable dispute</u>. Advocates for the homeless claim that there are several million homeless people; however, recent studies suggest that the homeless number from <u>600,000 to 700,000</u>. Precise numbers are impossible to collect because <u>researchers define homelessness</u> in different ways and because the homeless are transitory. The number of people predicted to become homeless in any given year is estimated to be <u>3 to 5 times</u> the number of people who are homeless at any given moment. The US Census Bureau <u>attempted to count homeless people</u> in the 1990 census. However, most analysts regard this attempt as a failure.

测试篇

1-5 BDBDC   6-10 CCACD

11. As a writer, I live by pens.

12. In the light of the Bible, Adam and Eve lived naked in the Garden of Eden.

13. In terms of intelligence, we are not different.

14. Iraq has long been afflicted by famine and wars.

15. His speech aroused great interest in us.

Lesson 28. Five pounds too dear

积 累 篇

I.振振有"词"

1. Small boats loaded with wares sped to the great liner as she was entering the harbour.

be loaded with 装满…	speed to…快速驶向…	harbour 港口（较小）
be filled with 充满…	accelerate to…加速驶向…	seaport 海港（较大，从事贸易）
be packed with 挤满…	rush to…匆匆去往…	dock 码头
be stuffed with 塞满…	hasten to…匆匆赶往…	marina 小船坞
be covered with 铺满…	hurry to…匆匆赶往…	

2. Many of the tourists on board had begun bargaining with the tradesmen.

be on board 在船/车/飞机上
be above board 光明正大的
go by the board 被遗弃，被忽视
tread the boards 当演员
sweep the boards 获得压倒性胜利

tradesman 商人
merchant（批发）商人
dealer（专营某项的）商人
peddler 小贩

bargain with sb. 与某人讨价还价
negotiate with sb. 与某人谈判
hold dialogues with sb. 与某人举行对话
converse with sb. 与某人谈话

联想记忆：（单词中间均有s）
tradesman 商人
statesman 政治家
spokesman 发言人
craftsman 工匠

a good bargain 便宜货
a real bargain 便宜货
a bad bargain 不合算的物品
bargain counter 廉价商品部
bargain day 减假日

3. <u>At the base of</u> the gold cap, the words "made in the U.S.A." had been <u>neatly</u> <u>inscribed</u>.

at the base of 在…的底部
on the basis of 以…为基础
at base 本质上
a military base 军事基地
a training base 培训基地

neat 整洁的
tidy 整齐的
neat as a new pin 非常整洁
neat but not gaudy 朴实无华

inscribe 刻字
engrave（在木、石等上）雕刻（字、图案）
carve 雕刻
sculpt 雕塑（多指人像）

4. The man acted as if he found my <u>offer</u> <u>outrageous</u>.

offer 出价
demand a price（卖家）要价
offer a price（买家）出价
bargain with sb 讨价还价

outrageous 令人不悦的
It's outrageous！岂有此理！
unspeakable 难以启齿的

indescribable 难以言表的
unutterable 难以言传的
inexpressible 难以表达的

II. 现身说"法"：**no sooner...than...**引导的时间状语从句

> I had no sooner got off the ship than I was assailed by a man who wanted to sell me a diamond ring. 我刚下船，就被一个人截住，他向我兜售一枚钻石戒指。

no sooner...than...结构说明一件事紧接着另一件事发生，意思上等同于as soon as...结构，但用法上略有不同。as soon as结构中，主从句的时态一致。而no sooner...than...结构中，主句多用过去完成时，从句多用一般过去时。例：

As soon as I checked into the hotel he arrived.

I had no sooner checked into the hotel than he arrived. 我刚住进宾馆他就到了。

no sooner...than...结构中no sooner经常置于句首，助动词had提前，句子倒装。

补充

1. 与as soon as用法、意义完全相同的结构有：

The moment...   The instant...   The minute...

Immediately...   Instantly...   Directly...

2. 与no sooner...than...用法、意义完全相同的有：

hardly...when...   scarcely...when...

III. 说"文"解"字"

1. But I <u>decided not</u> to buy anything until I had disembarked.

译文：但我打定主意上岸之前，什么也不买。

解析：decide to do sth. 的否定式是decide not to do sth.，而非not decide to do sth.。hope的否定用法也是如此：

hope not（✓）   not hope（✗）

2. The man went to great lengths to prove that the diamonds were real.

译文：那人想竭力证明那些钻石是真货。

解析：go to great lengths是固定短语，意为"竭尽全力"。而go to the length of doing sth.意为"竟然会…"。试比较：

He went to great lengths to prove he was sincere. 他努力想证明自己很真诚。

He went to the length of taking drugs. 他竟然吸毒。

> **联想记忆**
>
> nothing is spared to do sth. 不遗余力做…
>
> go all out to do sth. 全力以赴做…
>
> use every ounce of one's energy to do sth. 竭尽全力做…

3. I felt especially pleased with my wonderful bargain—until I got back to the ship.

译文：在回到船上之前，我一直为得到的便宜货而洋洋得意。

解析：bargain本是"讨价"之意，但本句活用作"便宜货"讲。例：

a bargain 便宜货   a wonderful/good/real bargain 便宜货

a bad bargain 价高质次的商品   He is no bargain. 他不太好说话。

4. No matter how hard I tried, it was impossible to fill this beautiful pen with ink.

译文：不管我如何摆弄，那支漂亮的钢笔就是吸不进墨水。

解析：beautiful在这里显然是反语用法，以增强行文的轻松幽默的色彩。实际上，反语在英文中的运用十分频繁，例：

This caused the construction of gigantic buildings where too large masses of human beings are crowded. Civilized men like such a way of living. (《新概念英语》4册) 这样就导致了许多摩天大楼拔地而起，大厦内众多的人拥挤在一起。文明人喜欢这样的生活方式。

拓展篇

Ⅰ.英语趣园

> Unlike Chinese people, westerners are not likely to bargain in the department store. They may bargain at flea market, but to point out the bad quality of the product is considered rude.

Ⅱ.听力快车

Match the gestures with their messages. Choose the appropriate letters A-I from the right.

1. crushing handshake   A. no message

2. half handshake   B. confidence

3. quickly released handshake   C. lack of confidence

4. long handshake   D. lack of interest

FOR AUSTRALIAN WOMEN   E. arrogance

5. half handshake   F. competence

6. full, firm handshake   G. competitiveness

FOR BOTH SEXES   H. mutual liking

7. no eye contact during handshake   I. recognition

III. 补充阅读

Body positions

People often show their feelings by the body positions they adopt. These can contradict what you are saying, especially when you are trying to disguise the way you feel. For example, a very common defensive position, assumed when people feel threatened in some way, is to put your arm or arms across your body. This is a way of shielding yourself from a threatening situation. This shielding action can be disguised as adjusting one's cuff or watchstrap. Leaning back in your chair especially with your arms folded is not only defensive, it's also a way of showing your disapproval, of a need to distance yourself from the rest of the company.

A position which betrays an aggressive attitude is to avoid looking directly at the person you are speaking to. On the other hand, approval and desire to cooperate are shown by copying the position of the person you are speaking to. This shows that you agree or are willing to agree with someone. The position of one's feet also often shows the direction of people's thoughts, for example, feet or a foot pointing towards the door can indicate that a person wishes to leave the room. The direction in which your foot points can also show which of the people in the room you feel most sympathetic towards even when you are not speaking directly to that person.

▶ 测 试 篇 ◀

I. 单项选择

1. They're going to build a big office block on that _____ piece of land.　　　（CET-6 05/12）
   A. void 　　　　B. vacant 　　　　C. blank 　　　　D. shallow

2. Although he was on a diet, the delicious food _____ him enormously.　　　（CET-6 04/6）
   A. distracted 　　B. stimulated 　　C. inspired 　　D. tempted

3. If you want this painkiller, you'll have to ask the doctor for a _____.　　　（CET-6 01/6）
   A. transaction 　　B. permit 　　C. settlement 　　D. prescription

4. You should _____ to one or more weekly magazines such as *Time*, or *Newsweek*.　　（CET-6 01/6）
   A. ascribe 　　　B. order 　　　　C. reclaim 　　　　D. subscribe

5. When a psychologist does a general experiment about the human mind, he selects people _____ and ask them questions.
   A. at length 　　B. at random 　　C. in essence 　　D. in bulk

6. The board of the company has decided to _____ its operations to include all aspects of the clothing business.
   A. multiply 　　B. lengthen 　　C. expand 　　D. stretch

7. In the advanced course students must take performance tests at monthly _____.
   A. gaps 　　　　B. intervals 　　C. length 　　　　D. distance

8. Students or teachers can participate in excursions to lovely beaches around the island at regular _____.
   A. gape 　　　　B. rate 　　　　C. length 　　　　D. intervals

9. ＿＿＿＿＿ I admit that there are problems, I don't think that they cannot be solved.

    A. Unless   B. Until   C. As   D. While

10. She would have been injured ＿＿＿＿＿ stopped her.

    A. if I had not   B. unless   C. if I would not   D. unless I

Ⅱ. 翻译

11. 还没等人们来得及找个位子坐下，"葛底斯堡"演讲已经结束了。（before）

12. 我刚一进考场，大脑就一片空白，因此，我考砸了。（no sooner...than）

13. 吸毒的人很难戒掉毒瘾。（get rid of drugs）

14. 在西方人看来，道歉的时候，面带微笑是一种侮辱。（indicate）

15. 1935年，波斯更改国名为伊朗。（until）

 答 案

拓展篇

    1. G   2. C   3. D   4. H   5. A   6. F   7. E

    How you shake hands is almost as important as the act itself. How you shake hands tells the other person a lot about you. It's true, and especially so of men!

    Here's what I mean. A limp or weak handshake by a man has the same meaning as no handshake at all. The message is: "I'm not very interested in you." Think about this, because I know that some of you may come from cultures that accept limp handshakes as normal. Here, even if you don't intend to, you may send the wrong message.

    Is the best way, then, to use all your muscles and crush—and possibly hurt—the other person's hand? Man-to-man handshakes in Australia are sometimes like this. The message behind this kind of handshake is aggressiveness and a desire to compete. Unless you specifically want to communicate these feelings to the other person, you don't have to shake hands with all your strength. One more type of male handshake that can send the wrong message is the half handshake. Here, only the front half of the fingers is offered to the other person's hand. The message is that you have little confidence, that you're shy. "I'm not a strong or courageous person." That's what a half handshake says.

    Until recently, women in Australia felt no great need to shake hands during introductions. That's changed as more and more women are working in business, government and academia. The way that women used to shake hands with men was to give only half the hand—that is, the fingers only. This gave little impression or message, at least to men. Nowadays, women are having to learn again how to shake hands. Now, women are beginning to offer all of the hand—the fingers and palm. The other person's hand is held and shaken firmly but not too hard. This communicates to the other person more of a feeling of competence or strength than the old-fashioned way of doing it.

    How long should you shake hands? That's right; the length of time you shake hands also says something about you. If a man lets go of the other person's hand too quickly, what kind of message do you think that sends? Releasing your hand quite soon indicates that you don't want to get too involved or you're not very interested in the other person. That goes for both men and women. However, it's both more acceptable and more common for two men to shake hands for a longer time, even as long as six or seven seconds. The message in this case is "I like you" and generally indicates that the two men think they'll get on well.

Finally, what do you do with your eyes when you are shaking stranger's hand? In this society at least, you should look at the other person straight in the eyes. If you look somewhere else, like looking down or to the side, this sends a negative message to the other person. The other person may think you are being arrogant, that your action says "I am better than you". Another unpleasant message that comes across when there is no eyes contact is: "you don't exist or I don't recognize your existence."

So you see, there really is quite a lot to consider when shaking hands in this culture. As silly as it may sound, practicing handshaking, say with a friend, may be a good way to become confident so that the next time you need to introduce yourself in a formal setting here in Australia, you'll feel comfortable knowing you did it the right way.

测试篇

1-5 BDDDB   6-10 CBBDA

11. The whole speech of Gettysburg finished before people had time to find themselves to sit down.

12. No sooner had I come into the exam room than my mind went blank. As a result, I poorly performed.

13. It's hard for addicts to get rid of drugs.

14. To apologize with a smile indicates insult, according to westerners.

15. Iran was called Persia until 1935.

Lesson ㉙ Funny or not?

I.振振有"词"

1. The <u>sense of humour</u> <u>is mysteriously bound up with</u> national <u>characteristics</u>.

> sense of humour 幽默感
> sense of honor 荣誉感
> sense of pride 自豪感
> sense of morality 道德是非感
> sense of superiority 优越感
> sense of inferiority 自卑感

> be bound up with 与…有联系
> be associated with 与…有联系
> be relevant to 与…有关
> be pertinent to 与…密切相关
> have some bearing on 与…有关

> characteristic 特色
> character 性格；人物
> personality 个性
> performance 性能
> function 功能

2. <u>In the same way</u>, a Russian might fail to see anything <u>amusing</u> in a joke which would make an Englishman <u>laugh to tears</u>.

> in the same way 同样地
> in like manner 一样地
> accordingly 同样地
> equally 类似地

> laugh to tears 笑出眼泪
> laugh from ear to ear 咧开嘴笑
> convulse with laughter 大笑不止
> split one's sides with laughter 开怀大笑

> amusing 可笑的
> joking 好笑的
> funny 有趣的
> farcical 滑稽的

> in a way 有点
> in many ways 这样看来
> in a big way 大范围地
> in a small way 小范围地
> in a fair way 很可能地
> in a general way 一般地

> amazing 奇妙无比的
> terrific 绝妙的
> fabulous 美妙绝伦的
> fantastic 不可思议的

3. However, a new type of humour, which <u>stems largely from</u> the U.S., has recently <u>come into fashion</u>.

> stem from...源自…
> result from...由于…
> originate in...起源于…
> set about...引发…
> bring about...引起…
> result in...导致…

> come into fashion 开始流行
> come into popularity 开始盛行
> come into vogue 开始流行
> come out of fashion 不再流行
> come out of date 过时

II. 现身说"法": whether与if之区别

> Whether we find a joke funny or not largely depends on where we have been brought up. 我们觉得一则笑话是否好笑,很大程度上取决于我们是在哪儿长大的。

whether作为连词作用甚广,但时常与if相混。以下是两者的主要区别:

1. whether可引导让步状语从句或名词从句(主语从句、宾语从句、表语从句等),而if则引导条件状语从句或宾语从句。例:

All countries, whether they are big or small, should be equal.(whether引导让步状语从句)

所有国家,无论大小,都一律平等。

Whether he comes or not makes no difference.(whether引导主语从句)他来不来无所谓。

The question is whether he comes.(whether引导表语从句)问题是他来不来。

2. 引导名词从句时,if不和or not直接连用,即不说if or not。但可以说if...or not, whether无此限制。例:

I don't know if or not she is right.(×)

I don't know whether or not she is right. 我不清楚她是对还是错。

3. if不用在介词之后。例:

The committee has not discussed the question of if he will be chosen.(×)

The committee has not discussed the question of whether he will be chosen.

委员会还未讨论他是否被选中的问题。

4. if不用在不定式之前。例:

I haven't decided if to go with him.(×)

I haven't decided whether to go with him. 我还没决定是否和他一起去。

III. 说"文"解"字"

1. A Frenchman, for instance, might find it hard to laugh at a Russian joke.

译文:譬如,法国人听完一则俄国笑话可能很难发笑。

解析:1)laugh at在这里不是"嘲笑"之意,因为逻辑不通。laugh应与at拆开,at sth.意为"听到/看到…"。例:

You would find it difficult not to laugh at, say, Charlie Choplin's early films.

你看了查理·卓别林的早期影片很难不发笑。

At these words, she felt a little embarrassed. 听到这番话,她显得有些尴尬。

2)with有"说到…"之意,与at相对。例:

With these words, he left hurriedly. 说完这番话,他匆匆离开了。

2. On Christmas Day, the man still had his right leg in plaster.

译文:圣诞节那天,他的右腿还打着石膏。

解析:have sth./sb.+介词/副词表示"让…处于某种状态"。翻译时应灵活处理。例:

Let me have Mr. Wang over. 我去请王先生过来吧。

We'll have the decorators in next week. 我们准备让装修工下周过来。

He was had up for exceeding the speed limit. 他因开车超速被起诉。

149

3. He spent a miserable day in bed thinking of **all the fun he was missing.**

译文：他在床上闷闷不乐地躺了一天，想着他错过的种种欢乐。

解析：本句中spend...doing sth.结构不是"花时间做…"，因为逻辑不通。即thinking不是动名词用法，而是现在分词，表伴随，spend应理解为"度过"。

拓 展 篇

Ⅰ.英语趣园

The word "humor" had its origin as old French from Latin, which means "moisture". The original sense was "bodily fluid"（fluid in the eyeball）. This led to the 16th century meaning "state of mind, or mood". "Good humor" is the ability to remain cheerful, especially in situations that would make some people upset or angry. It's an attitude to life rather than the mere ability to laugh at jokes.

Black humor, in literature, drama, and film, refers to grotesque or morbid humor used to express the absurdity, insensitivity, paradox, and cruelty of the modern world. Ordinary characters or situations are usually exaggerated far beyond the limits of normal satire or irony. Black humor uses devices often associated with tragedy and is sometimes equated with tragic farce. For example, Stanley Kubrick's film *Dr. Strangelove*; or, *How I Learned to Stop Worrying and Love the Bomb*（1963）is a terrifying comic treatment of the circumstances surrounding the dropping of an atom bomb, while Jules Feiffer's comedy *Little Murders* （1965）is a delineation of the horrors of modern urban life, focusing particularly on random assassinations. The novels of such writers as Kurt Vonnegut, Thomas Pynchon, John Barth, Joseph Heller, and Philip Roth contain elements of black humor.

Ⅱ.听力快车

If you intend using humor in your talk to make people smile, you must know _____. Your humor must be _____ and should help to show them that _____ or that you understand their situation and are _____ their point of view. Depending on whom you are addressing, the problems will be different. If you are talking to a group of managers, you may refer to the disorganized methods of their secretaries; alternatively if you are addressing secretaries, you may want to _____.

Ⅲ.补充阅读

My country and my people (excerpt)

by Lin Yutang

Humor is a state of mind. More than that, it is a point of view, a way of looking at life. The flower of humor blooms whenever in the course of development of a nation there is an exuberance of intellect able to flay its own ideals, for humor is nothing but intellect slashing at itself. In any period of history, when mankind was able to perceive its own futility, its own smallness, and its own follies and inconsistencies, a humorist appeared, like Chuangtse of China, Omar Khayyam of Persia, and Aristophanes of Greece. Athens would be infinitely poorer had there been no Aristophanes, and the Chinese intellectual heritage would be infinitely less rich had there been no Chuangtse.

Since Chuangtse lived and wrote, however, all Chinese politicians and bandits have become great humorists, because they have been imbued, directly or indirectly, with the Chuangtse view of life. Laotse had laughed before him, a thin, shrill yet cataclysmic laughter. He must have been a bachelor all his life, or he could not have laughed so roguishly. Anyway there is no record that he ever married or had any progeny. The last coughs of Laotse's laugh were caught up by Chuangtse, and he, being a younger man, had a richer voice, and the ring of his laughter has reverberated throughout the ages, we still cannot resist a chance to laugh, yet sometimes I feel we are carrying the joke too far, and laugh a little out of season.

The abysmal ignorance of the foreigner about China and the Chinese cannot be more impressive than when he asks the question: Do the Chinese have a sense of humor? It is really as surprising as if an Arab caravan were to ask: Are there sands in the Sahara desert? It is strange, however, how little a person may see in a country. Theoretically, at least, the Chinese people should have humor, for humor is born of realism; and the Chinese are an unusually realistic people. Humor is born of common sense, and the Chinese have an overdose of common sense. Humor, especially Asiatic humor is the product of contentment and leisure, and the Chinese have contentment and leisure to a supreme degree. A humorist is often a defeatist, and delights in recounting his own failure and embarrassments, and the Chinese are often sane, cool-minded defeatists. Humor often takes a tolerant view of vice and evil and instead of condemning them, laughs at them, and the Chinese have always been characterized by the capacity to tolerate evil. Toleration has a good and a bad side, and Chinese have both of them. If the characteristics of the Chinese race we have discussed above—common sense, toleration contentment and old roguery—are true, then humor is inevitable in China.

Chinese humor, however, is more in deeds than in words. The Chinese have their words for the various types of humor, but the most common type, called huach'I, in which sometimes the Confucian scholars indulge under pseudonyms, really means to me only "trying to be funny". Such writings are only literary relaxations of a too rigorous classical tradition, but humor as such had no proper place in literature. At least there was no open acknowledgment of the role and value of humor in literature. Humor, indeed, abounds in Chinese novels, but novels were never accepted as "literature" by the classicists...

▶ 测 试 篇 ◀

I . 单项选择

1. The relatives of those killed in the crash got together to seek _____. （CET-6 04/6）
   A. premium   B. compensation   C. repayment   D. refund

2. The _____ they felt for each other was obvious to everyone who saw them. （CET-6 04/6）
   A. affection   B. adherence   C. sensibility   D. sensitivity

3. Texas, the second largest state of America, is _____ in natural resources. （CET-6 89/6）
   A. wealthy   B. abundant   C. scattered   D. deposited

4. To _____ for his unpleasant experiences he drank a little more than was good for him.
   A. commence   B. compromise   C. compensate   D. compliment

5. We'll _____ you for any damage done to your house while we are in it.
   A. compensate   B. remedy   C. supplement   D. retrieve

6. Some companies have introduced flexible working time with less emphasis on pressure _____.

A. than more on efficiency   B. and more efficiency

C. and more on efficiency   D.than efficiency

7. There ought to be less anxiety over the perceived risk of getting cancer than _____ in the public mind today.

   A. exists   B. exist   C. existing   D. existed

8. These proposals sought to place greater restrictions on the use and coping of digital information than _____ in traditional media.

   A. exists   B. exist   C. existing   D. existed

9. More families consist of one-parent house holds or 2 working parents; consequently, children are likely to have less supervision at home than _____ common in the traditional family structure.

   A. was   B. were   C. is   D. are

10. A healthy life is frequently thought to be _____ with the open countryside and homegrown food.

   A. tied   B. bound   C. involved   D. associated

Ⅱ. 翻译

11. 在中国做生意很大程度上取决于建立良好的人际关系。（largely depend on）

12. 他强烈的自卑感源自他不幸的童年。（stem from）

13. 不要给小孩子太多的钱。（more than）

14. 我刚好来得及赶最后一趟车回家。（in time for）

15. 我从看到她的那一刻开始，就爱上了她。（the moment）

答案

拓展篇

If you intend using humor in your talk to make people smile, you must know <u>how to identify shared experiences and problems</u>. Your humor must be <u>relevant to the audience</u> and should help to show them that <u>you are one of them</u> or that you understand their situation and are <u>in sympathy with</u> their point of view. Depending on whom you are addressing, the problems will be different. If you are talking to a group of managers, you may refer to the disorganized methods of their secretaries; alternatively if you are addressing secretaries, you may want to <u>comment on their disorganized bosses</u>.

测试篇

1-5 BABCA   6-10 CABCD

11. Doing business in China largely depends on building good relationship.

12. His strong sense of inferiority stemmed from his unfortunate childhood.

13. Children should not have more money than is needed.

14. I was just in time for the last train home.

15. I fell in love with her the moment I saw her.

Lesson The death of a ghost

Ⅰ. 振振有"词"

1. For years <u>villagers</u> believed that Endley <u>Farm</u> was <u>haunted</u>.

> villager 村民
> migrant worker 民工
> farmhand 农工
> farm labourer 农工
> seasonal worker 短工

> on the farm 在农场干活
> on the soccer team 在足球队踢球
> on the delegation 成为代表团成员
> on the committee 在委员会任职

> be haunted 闹鬼
> haunt the theatre 常去看戏
> haunt the rich 常同有钱人来往
> a holiday haunt 度假胜地

2. Fearing the <u>authorities</u>, Eric <u>remained in hiding</u> after the war as well.

> authorities (复) 政府, 当局
> an authority on sth. ⋯的权威
> the ruling party 执政党
> the party in wilderness 在野党
> authoritative 有权威的
> authoritarian 专制的

> remain in hiding 一直躲着
> go into hiding 躲藏起来
> keep sb. in hiding 将某人隐藏起来
> come out of hiding 从躲藏处出来

Ⅱ. 现身说"法": **none other than**及其他

> **Everyone went to the funeral, for the "ghost" was** none other than **Eric Cox.**
> 大家都去参加了葬礼, 因为那"鬼"不是别人, 正是埃里克·考科斯。

1. none other than结构中, none即 no one, other than等同于except/but (介词), 因此该结构可以转化为no one except/but。
2. 四个否定词nothing, no one, nobody, nowhere与but连用表only或just之意。例:
   He accepted my favor with nothing but pleasure. 他非常愉快地接受了我的帮助。
   The man standing on the rostrum was no one but our president. 站在演讲台上的那人正是我们校长。
   He has been to nowhere but his mother's hometown. 他只是去过母亲的老家。

Ⅲ. 说"文"解"字"

1. Every time a worker gave up his job, he told the same story.

译文：*每次雇工辞职后都讲述着同样的故事。*

解析：1）every time在本句中引导时间状语从句，相当于when，因此其后一般不再加when或while。

2）every moment, the moment, the instant用法相同。例：

Every moment I sing the national anthem, I'm filled with patriotism.

每次唱起国歌，我的心中都会涌起爱国之情。

The instant he saw the robber, he called the police. *他一看到那个抢劫犯，就立刻报了警。*

2. A farm worker, who stayed up all night, claimed to have seen a figure cutting corn in the moonlight.

译文：*一个彻夜未眠的工友声称他看见一个人影在月光下收割庄稼。*

解析：stay up是一个固定短语，意为"熬夜"。

> **联想记忆**
>
> | | |
> |---|---|
> | sit up 熬夜 | burn the midnight oil 开夜车 |
> | stay up till the small hours 熬到后半夜 | have a white night 失眠 |
> | be sleepless 失眠 | be ill with insomnia 患上失眠症 |

3. In time, it became an accepted fact that the Cox brothers employed a conscientious ghost that did most of their work for them.

译文：*考科斯兄弟雇了一个尽心尽职的鬼，替他们干了大部分活，随着时间的流逝，这已成了人所共知的事实。*

解析：1）依据逻辑推理，in time不是"及时"，而是"随着时间流逝"。类似表达有：

with time; as time goes on; as time slips by; as time flashes by

2）fact 之后的 that 从句不是同位语从句，而是 it 所替代的真正的主语从句，这可根据上下文做出判断。

4. A third brother who was supposed to have died as a young man.

译文：*考克斯家的一位兄弟，被认为年轻时就死了。*

解析：a third brother 与 the third brother 略有不同，后者只指排行老三，而前者既可指老三，也可指兄弟三人中的任何一位，具体所指要根据上下文得出。

5. Eric had been the eldest son of the family, very much older than his two brothers.

译文：*埃里克是家里的长子，年龄比其他两个兄弟大很多。*

解析：彩色部分不是句子，可看作Eric的修饰成分，作主语补足语。实际上，这是一种省略形式，其前省略了and he had been. 这是英文行文中常用的变化手段。例：

An individual human existence should be like a river—（and it is）small at first, narrowly contained within its banks.（《新概念英语》4册，括号内为省略部分）*一个人的生命如同一条河流——起初是涓涓细流，紧紧地围于两岸之间。*

China is a promising country,（and she is）vast in territory and diverse in culture.（括号内为省略部分）*中国前途远大，幅员辽阔，文化丰厚。*

拓 展 篇

I. 英语趣园

A festival for the dead is held once a year in Japan. This festival is a cheerful occasion, for on this day, the dead are said to return to their homes and they are welcomed by the living. As they are expected to be hungry after their long journey, food is laid out for them. Specially-made lanterns are hung outside each house to help the dead to find their way. All night long, people dance and sing. In the early morning, the food that had been laid out for the dead is thrown into a river or into the sea as it is considered unlucky for anyone living to eat it. In towns that are near the sea, the tiny lanterns which had been hung in the streets the night before, are placed into the water when the festival is over. Thousands of lanterns slowly drift out to sea guiding the dead on their return journey to the other world. This is a moving spectacle, for crowds of people stand on the shore watching the lanterns drifting away until they can be seen no longer.

II. 听力快车

Stories about ghosts and other spirits have scared people through the ages. Some ghosts, however, are not to be feared. They are ghostwriters. Just as a ghost is a spirit that you cannot see, _____. A ghostwriter is a person _____. Usually that other person is famous, but not as a writer. The ghostwriter does the writing, and _____. But his name is not on the book as the writer. Instead, one sees the name of the other, more famous person. The ghostwriter exists, _____.

III. 补充阅读

Once people were very much afraid of ghosts. Their fear led them to develop elaborate rituals to ward off encounters with the dead. For example, since primitive people believed that ghosts could capture their spirit at funerals, they carried wooden images of themselves in the hope that the ghosts would be fooled into carrying off the images. Images have been popular with people from primitive times until today. Once people believed that taking a picture of someone would rob the person of his or her soul. It is possible, too, that the tradition of sitting up with the dead comes from a belief that ghosts escape in the night. Certainly the ritual of laying tombstones is derived from a superstition about the dead. People once believed that stones piled on top of a grave would keep the dead person's ghost from escaping and haunting the living. Eventually the number of stones diminished until only one stone, the tombstone, was left as reminder of the ancient superstition.

▶ 测 试 篇 ◀

I. 单项选择

1. Years after the accident he was still _____ by images of death and destruction.　　　　(CET-6 04/6)
   A. twisted　　　　B. dipped　　　　C. haunted　　　　D. submerged

2. Even though he was guilty, the _____ judge did not send him to prison.
   A. merciful　　　　B. impartial　　　　C. conscientious　　　　D. conspicuous

3. He seems to be _____ enough to climb to the mountain top in an hour.

    A. radiant   B. conscientious   C. conspicuous   D. energetic

4. The suspect _____ that he had not been in the neighbourhood at the time of the crime.

    A. advocated   B. alleged   C. addressed   D. announced

5. Mrs. Brown is supposed _____ for Italy last week.

    A. to have left   B. to be leaving   C. to leave   D. to have been left

6. What _____ would happen if the director knew you felt that way?

    A. do you suppose   B. you suppose   C. will you suppose   D. you would suppose

7. The bride and groom promised to _____ each other through sickness and health.   （CET-6 05/12）

    A. nourish   B. nominate   C. roster   D. cherish

8. As the trial went on, the story behind the murder slowly _____ itself.

    A. convicted   B.released   C.haunted   D.unfolded

9. When I go out in the evening I use the bike _____ the car if I can.

    A. rather than   B. regardless of   C. in spite of   D. other than

10. Nuclear science should be developed to benefit the people _____ harm them.

    A. more than   B. other than   C. rather than   D. better than

Ⅱ. 翻译

11. 长期以来，此人一直出没于此地。（haunt at a place）

12. 每次我见到你，你都越发漂亮了。（every time）

13. 要怪，只能怪你自己。（none other than）

14. 这位影星结了第八次婚。（for an 8th time）

15. 不做亏心事，不怕鬼叫门。（conscience）

 答 案

拓展篇

    Stories about ghosts and other spirits have scared people through the ages. Some ghosts, however, are not to be feared. They are ghostwriters. Just as a ghost is a spirit that you cannot see, <u>a ghostwriter is a writer whose name is unseen</u>. A ghostwriter is a person <u>who is paid to write a speech, report or book for another person</u>. Usually that other person is famous, but not as a writer. The ghostwriter does the writing, and <u>gets paid for it</u>. But his name is not on the book as the writer. Instead, one sees the name of the other, more famous person. The ghostwriter exists, <u>but his name is unknown by the public</u>.

测试篇

1-5 CADBA   6-10 ADDAC

11. The man has long been haunting at the place.

12. Every time I saw you, you look even more beautiful.

13. You have none to blame other than yourself.

14. The film star married for an 8th time.

15. A conscience is a soft pillow.

Lesson **31.** **A lovable eccentric**

积累篇

I. 振振有"词"

1. True <u>eccentrics</u> never deliberately <u>set out to</u> <u>draw attention to themselves</u>.

eccentric 怪人	set out to do sth. 开始做…	draw attention to oneself 引人注目
be concentric on...专注于…	set about sth./doing sth. 着手做…	draw the attention of sb. 引起某人的关注
weird 怪人	set to sth. 努力做…	pay attention to...对…很关注
outlandish 怪异的	set off sth. 引发…	be in the spotlight 受人关注
exotic 奇异的	set forth 动身	

2. For they <u>add colour to</u> the dull <u>routine</u> of everyday life.

add colour to sth. 给…增添色彩	routine 常规；惯例
add relish to sth. 给…增添情趣	practice 惯例
add grace to sth./sb. 给…增添魅力	tradition 传统
add vigour to sth. 给…增添活力	custom 风俗
add fuel to the flame 火上浇油	institution 制度

3. Dickie <u>disliked</u> <u>snobs</u> <u>intensely</u>.

dislike 讨厌	snob 势利小人	intense 强烈的
resent 憎恨	hypocrite 伪君子	intensive 密集的
abhor 痛恨	chameleon 阳奉阴违者	intensivereading 精读
abominate 厌恶	velvet paw 笑面虎	intensified 强化的
disapprove 不喜欢		intensified-training 强化培训

4. It contained £300 in pennies. He insisted on the assistant's counting the money before he left.

in pennies 用便士支付（in表示"以某种方式"） in ink 用钢笔 in pencil 用铅笔 in cash 用现金 in installment 分期付款	insist on doing... 坚持（自己的观点等）… persist in doing... 坚持做… consist of sth.... 由…组成 desist from doing... 不做… subsist on sth.... 以…为生

Ⅱ. 现身说"法"：-'s名词所有格

> He insisted on the assistant's counting the money before he left.（the assistant's是名词的所有格）他坚持让店员点清那些钱才离去。

一般而言，该类所有格有以下几种用法：
1. 表所属关系
   Smith's possessions   Linda's toy
2. 表主谓关系
   Galileo's death（=Galileo is dead）   the helicopter's landing（=the helicopter landed）
3. 表动宾关系
   Clinton's supporters（=people support Clinton） the robber's accusation（=people accused the robber）
4. 表类别
   a girl's school（=a school for girls）   a worker's hopspital（=a hospital for workers）
5. 表时间、度量等
   a moment's thought   a pound's weight
6. 表地点（表地点的所有格后面一般不跟名词，只用the加所有格）
   the buthcher's/barber's/grocer's/dentist's

Ⅲ. 说"文"解"字"

1. He was a shrewd and wealthy businessman, but most people in the town hardly knew anything about this side of his life.
   译文：他是个精明强干、家境丰裕的商人，但镇上大部分人对他生活的这个方面几乎一无所知。
   解析：this side of his life 替代上句的shrewd and wealthy，这是写作中常用的变化手法。一是行文更加简练，二是语言更加多变。望多加演练，融会贯通。例：
   He is very thrifty, but in the presence of his friends he never shows this side of his life.
   他非常节俭，但在朋友面前他从未显露。

2. One day, he walked into an expensive shop after having been caught in a particularly heavy shower.
   译文：一天，他遇上一场瓢泼大雨，就走进了一家高档商店。
   解析：expensive修饰"商店"时作"高档"解，相当于luxury，而修饰物品时则作"昂贵"解。be caught

in a shower意为"淋雨"，介词不可用by。其他表"淋雨"的短语有：

be wet all over 浑身透湿   be soaked from head to toe 从头湿到脚

like a drowned rat 湿得像落汤鸡

3. But he was in such a bedraggled condition that an assistant refused to serve him.

译文：但他弄得浑身透湿，店员不愿意接待他。

解析：in such a/an+形容词+condition that... 结构在意义上等同于so+形容词+that...，但前者更显正式。例：

His family was in such an impoverished condition that he could hardly pay his tuition. (=His family was so impoverished that...) 他的家庭非常贫困，几乎付不起他的学费。

4. Dickie left the shop without a word.

译文：迪克一声不响地离开了商店。

解析：without a word意为"一言不发"，在句中修饰left，作方式状语。近义表达有：

leave without saying goodbye 不辞而别   take French leave 不辞而别

5. It took him four years to stage this elaborate joke simply to prove that critics do not always know what they are talking about.

译文：他花了四年时间策划这出精心设计的闹剧，只是想证明评论家们有时并不知道自己在谈论什么。

解析：请注意该句中主句和后面从句的动词时态不一致，似乎违背了复合句中主从谓语时态一致的原则。其原因在于：本句是用一般现在时表达一种客观事实或真理，即用此表达对当今评论家的间接、委婉的批评。例：

The scientist claimed that the Earth is round instead of square. (用一般现在时表客观真理)

这位科学家说地球是圆形的，而不是方的。

拓 展 篇

Ⅰ.英语趣园

An eccentric is someone who behaves in a way that is different from what is usual or socially accepted, while a maverick is an unusual person who has different ideas and ways of behaving from other people, and is often very successful.

Ⅱ.听力快车

True or False Questions.

1. Only an eccentric has particular habits which others find irritating or amusing.

2. The Victorian surgeon lived at Buckland.

3. Visitors to the Victorian surgeon's house used to get bitten or even attacked by the animals that he kept there. However, the guests still liked to go back.

4. A hermit is a person who cuts himself off from the world.

5. Howard Hughes was not a hermit all his life.

6. Howard Hughes became a recluse because he was tired of high living.

7. Ever since Howard Hughs became a recluse, he cut himself off completely from the world.

8. Howard Hughs used to spend his days watching adventure films without eating anything.

III. 补充阅读

Emily Dickinson

Emily, or should I say Poetess Dickinson, was born in Amherst, Massachusetts on December 10, 1830. Emily lived secluded in the house she was born in, except for the short time she attended Amherst Academy and Holyoke Female Seminary, until her death on May 15, 1886.

Emily was an energetic and outgoing woman while attending the Academy and Seminary. It was later, during her mid-twenties that Emily began to grow reclusive. She attended almost exclusively to household chores and to writing poetry.

Many scholars have tried to understand and theorize why Emily decided to seclude herself in her home and write about the most intimate experiences and feelings of life. I think that the best of these theories is that Emily could not write about the world without first backing away from it and contemplating it from a distance.

Emily had a few friends and acquaintances from day to day. One of these acquaintances was Thomas Wentworth Higginson, to whom she sent a few pieces of her poetry. He rejected her poems, but he was eventually the first to publish her work after her death. Emily only had six or seven of her poems published during her lifetime—and those without her consent. The number is argued over because one poem was published more than once.

It was after her death that her poems were discovered. It is estimated that Emily wrote over 1,700 poems.

▶ 测 试 篇 ◀

I. 单项选择

1. If you go to the park every day in the morning, you will _____ find him doing physical exercise there.
   (CET-6 03/6)

   A. ordinarily　　　B. invariably　　　C. logically　　　D. persistently

2. The music aroused an _____ feeling of homesickness in him.　　(CET-6 03/1)

   A. intentional　　　B. intermittent　　　C. intense　　　D. intrinsic

3. Please do not be _____ by his offensive remarks since he is merely trying to attract attention.

   A. distracted　　　B. disregarded　　　C. irritated　　　D. intervened

4. _____ that the demand for power continues to rise at the current rate, it will not be long before traditional sources become inadequate.

   A. Concerning　　　B. Ascertaining　　　C. Assuming　　　D. Regarding

5. The machine looked like a large _____, old-fashioned typewriter.

   A. forceful　　　B. clumsy　　　C. intense　　　D. tricky

6. The goal is to make higher education available to everyone who is willing and capable _____ his financial situation.

A. with respect to   B. in accord with

C. regardless of   D. in terms of

7. What you say now is not _____ with what you said last week.

    A. consistent   B. persistent   C. permanent   D. insistent

8. _____ efforts are needed in order to finish important but unpleasant tasks.

    A. Perpetual   B. Persistent   C. Consecutive   D. Condensed

9. Things might have been much worse if the mother _____ on her right to keep the baby.

    A. has been insisting   B. had insisted   C. would insist   D. insisted

10. Since a circle has no beginning or end, the wedding ring is accepted as a symbol of _____ love.

    A. successive   B. consecutive   C. eternal   D. insistent

Ⅱ. 翻译

11. 幽默总是能为交流增添色彩。（add color to）

12. 伦敦又被叫做雾都。（be known to us all as）

13. 搬起石头砸自己的脚。（simply to do）

14. 他说的话在理。（make sense）

15. Helen Keller 从不向命运低头，因此她为自己赢得了别人的尊重和爱戴。（win herself the love and respect of）

答案

拓展篇

1. F   2. F   3. T   4. T   5. T   6. T   7. F   8. F

Dave: Dr. Jones, how exactly would you define eccentricity?

Dr. Jones: Well, we all have our own particular habits which others find irritating or amusing, but an eccentric is someone who behaves in a totally different manner from those in the society in which he lives.

Dave: When you talk about eccentricity, are you referring mainly to matters of appearance?

Dr. Jones: Not specifically, no. There are many other ways in which eccentricity is displayed. For instance, some individuals like to leave their mark on this earth with bizarre buildings. Others have the craziest desires which influence their whole way of life.

Dave: Can you give me an example?

Dr. Jones: Certainly. One that immediately springs to mind was a Victorian surgeon by the name of Buckland. Being a great animal lover he used to share his house openly with the strangest creatures, including snakes, bears, rats, monkeys and eagles.

Dave: That must've been quite dangerous at times.

Dr. Jones: It was, particularly for visitors who weren't used to having "pets" —for want of a better word—in the house. They used to get bitten and even attacked. And the good doctor was so interested in animals that he couldn't resist the temptation to sample them as food. So guests who came to dinner had to be prepared for a most unusual menu, mice on toast, roast giraffe. Once he even tried to make soup from elephant's trunk. Strangely, though, his visitors seemed to go back for more.

Dave: They must've had very strong stomachs, that's all I can say. Dr. Jones, what particular kind of eccentric are you most interested in from a psychologist's point of view?

Dr. Jones: I think they're all fascinating, of course, but on the whole I'd say it's the hermit that I find the most intriguing, the type who cuts himself off from the world.

Dave: Does one of these stand out in your mind at all?

Dr. Jones: Yes, I suppose this century has produced one of the most famous ones: the American billionaire, Howard Hughes.

Dave: But he wasn't a recluse all his life, was he?

Dr. Jones: That's correct. In fact, he was just the opposite in his younger days. He was a rich young man who loved the Hollywood society of his day. But he began to disappear for long periods when he grew tired of high living. Finally, nobody was allowed to touch his food and he would wrap his hand in a tissue before picking anything up. He didn't even allow a barber to go near him too often and his hair and beard grew down to his waist.

Dave: Did he live completely alone?

Dr. Jones: No, that was the strangest thing. He always stayed in luxury hotels with a group of servants to take care of him. He used to spend his days locked up in a penthouse suite watching adventure films over and over again and often eating nothing but ice cream and chocolate bars.

Dave: It sounds like a very sad story.

Dr. Jones: It does. But, as you said earlier, life wouldn't be the same without characters like him, would it?

测试篇

1-5 BCCCB   6-10 CABBC

11. Humor invariably adds color to communication.

12. London is known to us all as "Foggy Capital".

13. They lift a rock simply to drop on their own feet.

14. What he says makes sense.

15. Helen Keller never became submissive to fate. As a result, she won herself the love and respect of others.

Lesson 32. A lost ship

积累篇

Ⅰ.振振有"词"

1. The sea bed was <u>scoured</u> with powerful nets and <u>there was tremendous excitement</u> on board.

scour 彻底搜寻
comb 仔细寻找
go in quest for 寻觅
cast about for 四处寻觅
forage for 寻找
rake...for... 彻底寻找

there was tremendous excitement 欢呼雀跃
be transported with joy 欣喜若狂
be wild with joy 欣喜若狂
be in great form 兴高采烈
be in royal spirits 兴奋异常
tread on air 得意洋洋

2. The chest <u>contained</u> the personal <u>belongings</u> of a <u>seaman</u>.

形似词辨析:
contain 包含
attain 达到
obtain 获取
detain 扣留
abstain 弃权

belongings 个人财物
possessions 个人财产
property 财产
real property 不动产；房地产
real estate 房地产
asset 资产

seaman 海员
fireman 消防员
sailor 水手
mariner 船员
crew 全体船员
helmsman 舵手

Ⅱ.现身说"法": together with 与主谓一致的问题

There were books, clothing and photographs, together with letters which the seaman had once received from his wife. 其中有书籍、衣服、照片以及收到的妻子的信件。

当主语后面跟有together with、along with、as well as、in addition to、with等引导的词语时，其后的动词形式取决于主语的形式。例:

Tom, as well as his parents, is vacationing in Thailand. 汤姆及其父母正在泰国度假。

The manager, in addition to his assistants, was responsible for the accident.

经理和两位助手要对事故负责。

联想记忆

当主语后面跟有as much as、rather than、more than、no less than等引导的从属结构时，其后的动词形式也取决于主语的形式。例:

The manager, rather than his assistant, is to blame. 是经理而不是助手应受指责。

Some of the classmates, as much as the teacher, are going to plant trees. 一些同学与老师要去

植树。

My sister, more than anyone else in the family, is looking forward to the performance.

我妹妹是家里最期待看那场演出的人。

Ⅲ. 说"文"解"字"

1. For the sunken ship he was trying to find had been carrying a precious cargo of gold bullion.

译文：因为他试图寻找的沉船上载有一批珍贵的金条。

解析：a cargo of...表"…的货物"，cargo是量词，一般后跟不可数名词。若要表复数概念，则在该量词后加复数。例：

bubbles of air 数个气泡　　　　　　five bottles of beer 五瓶啤酒

three schools of thought 三派观点　hearty rounds of applause 阵阵热烈掌声

2. Though the crew were at first under the impression that the lost ship had been found...

译文：尽管船员们认为沉船已找着了……

解析：be under the impression that...可理解为"认为…，觉得…"。实际上，under一词的意义广泛，往往可表达一种正在进行的状况。例：

The patient is under treatment. (=is being treated) 病人正在接受治疗。

The building is under construction. (=is being constructed) 大厦正在建设中。

The car is under repair. (=is being repaired) 车正在修理。

The baby is under tender care. (=is being cared tenderly) 小孩正在被精心地护理。

3. Nothing of value was found, but the numerous items which were brought to the surface proved to be of great interest.

译文：没发现什么有价值的东西，不过打捞出来的众多物品还是引起了大家的极大兴趣。

解析：1) 该句中出现了两个"名词+of+名词"的结构，一般而言可以转化为"名词+（该名词衍生的）形容词"，不过前者更加正式，且中间可以添加形容词，用来延展句型。请看以下变化过程：

nothing of value=nothing valuable　　　　　　sth. of interest=sth. interesting

sth. of importance=sth. important

2) 在该句中，sth. is brought to the surface译为"将某物打捞出水面"，此外，该词组还可理解为"将某事曝光"，与sth. is brought to light同义。例：

The reporter brought the embezzlement to the surface/light. 这位记者把这桩贪污案曝了光。

试比较：The embezzlement came to the surface/light. 这桩贪污案终于曝了光。

4. The captain learnt from the letter that the name of the lost ship was the *Karen*.

译文：船长从这封信中了解到沉船名叫"卡伦"号。

解析：learnt不是和from the letter直接连用，而是接后面的that从句。from the letter插入句中作前置成分，目的在于保持句型平衡。learn from后面一般接人，即learn from sb. (向某人学习)。

拓 展 篇

Ⅰ.英语趣园

The Imperial War Museum is unique in its coverage of conflicts, especially those involving Britain and the Commonwealth, from the First World War to the present day. It seeks to provide for, and to encourage, the study and understanding of the history of modern war and "war-time experience". It is proud to be regarded as one of the essential sights of London.

Ⅱ.听力快车

_____ when, returning from the bridge, I entered my action station. I picked up the control telephone and heard, "_____." I turned my director and saw two bulky silhouettes, unmistakably King George V and Rodney, at a range of_____. As imperturbable as though they were on their way to an execution, they were coming directly towards us in line abreast, a good way apart, their course straight as a die._____._____. The nerves of our gun directors, gun captains, and range-finding personnel were steady. After the utterly hopeless night they had just spent, any action could be a release. The very first salvo would bring it. How many ships were approaching no longer meant anything:_____.

Ⅲ.补充阅读

The sink of the *Bismarck*

The report came to the British on May 21, 1941. The German battle ship Bismarck, the most powerful warship in the world, was moving out into the Atlantic Ocean. Her task was to destroy the ships carrying supplies from the United States to war-torn England.

The British had feared such news. No warship they had before could match the Bismarck in speed or in firepower. The Bismarck had eight 15-inch guns and 81 smaller guns. She could move at 30 nautical miles an hour. She was believed to be unsinkable.

However, the British had to sink her. They sent out a task force headed by their best battleship Hood to hunt down the Bismarck. On May 24, the Hood found the Bismarck.

It was a meeting that the German admiral Luetjens did not want to see. His orders were to destroy the British ships that were carrying supplies, but to stay away from a fight with British warships.

The battle didn't last long. The Bismarck's first torpedo hit the Hood, which went down, taking all but three of her 1,419 men with her.

But in the fight, the Bismarck was slightly damaged. Her commander decided to run for repairs to France, which had at that time been taken by the Germans. The British force followed her, but because of the Bismarck's speed and the heavy fog, they lost sight of her.

For two days, every British ship in the Atlantic tried to find the Bismarck, but with no success. Finally, she was sighted by a plane from Ireland. Trying to slow the Bismarck down so that their ships could catch up with her, the British fired at her from the air. The Bismarck was hit.

On the morning of May 27, the last battle was fought. Four British ships fired on the Bismarck, and she finally sank.

测 试 篇 ◀━━

I.单项选择

1. Putting in a new window will _____ cutting away part of the roof.

   A. include   B. involve   C. contain   D. comprise

2. I had just posted the letter when I remembered that I hadn't _____ the cheque.

   A. imposed   B. involved   C. enclosed   D. contained

3. Throughout his life, Henry Moore _____ an interest in encouraging art in the city of Leeds.

   A. contained   B. secured   C. reserved   D. maintained

4. Among all the public holidays, National Day seems to be the most joyful to the people of the country; on that day the whole country is _____ in a festival atmosphere.

   A. trapped   B. sunk   C. soaked   D. immersed

5. Tom is bankrupt now. He is desperate because all his efforts _____ failure.

   A. tumbled to   B. hinged upon   C. inflicted on   D. culminated in

6. It was difficult to guess what her _____ to the news would be.

   A. impression   B. reaction   C. comment   D. opinion

7. We didn't know his telephone number, otherwise we _____ him.

   A. would have telephoned   B. must have telephoned

   C. would telephone   D. had telephoned

8. You _____ her in her office last Friday; she's been out of town for two weeks.

   A. needn't have seen   B. must have seen

   C. might have seen   D. can't have seen

9. Susan has _____ the elbows of her son's jacket with leather patches to make it more durable.

   A. reinforced   B. sustained   C. steadied   D. confirmed

10. Language belongs to each one of us, to the flower-seller _____ to the professor.

    A. as much as   B. as far as   C. the same as   D. as long as

II.翻译

11. 这次"春晚"办砸了。(be a failure)
12. 两国正踏上和平之路。(on way to)
13. 古时候,人们以为彗星会带来灾难。(be under the impression that)
14. 考古学家将所有的碎片拼接起来,最终重塑了一个远古时期的雕塑。(piece together)
15. 真相最终得以水落石出。(come to light)

答 案

拓展篇

    <u>The alarm bells were still ringing</u> when, returning from the bridge, I entered my action station. I picked up the control telephone and heard, "<u>Two battleships port bow.</u>" I turned my director and saw two bulky silhouettes, unmistakably King George V and Rodney, at a range of <u>approximately 24,000 meters</u>. As imperturbable as though they were on their way to an execution, they were coming directly

towards us in line abreast, a good way apart, their course straight as a die. The seconds ticked by. Tension and anticipation mounted. The nerves of our gun directors, gun captains, and range-finding personnel were steady. After the utterly hopeless night they had just spent, any action could be a release. The very first salvo would bring it. How many ships were approaching no longer meant anything: we could be shot to pieces only once.

测试篇

1-5 BCDDD   6-10 BADAA

11. The Spring Festival Entertainment Show was a failure.

12. The two countries are on way to peace.

13. Ancient people were under the impression that comet could bring about disasters.

14. Archaeologists pieced together all the fragments and reconstructed a statue of ancient times.

15. The facts finally came to light.

Lesson 33. A day to remember

积累篇

I.振振有"词"

1. It is as if a single unimportant event set up a chain of reactions.

an unimportant event 一件小事 a trifle 琐碎小事 a triviality 琐碎细节 make a fuss over...小题大做 make a storm in a teacup 大惊小怪	set up 引发 bring about 引起 give rise to 引起 give birth to 导致 result in 导致	a chain of reactions 连锁反应 a series of reactions 连锁反应 domino effect 多米诺效应，连锁反应 ripple effect 波浪效应，连锁反应

2. This marks the prelude to an unforeseen series of catastrophes.

the prelude to sth. …的序曲 the beginning of sth. …的开端 the end of sth. …的结束 the turning point of sth. …的转折点 the milestone of sth. …的里程碑	unforeseen 不可预见的 unpredictable 不可预料的 unanticipated 不可预期的 unexpected 出乎意料的 unavoidable 不可避免的	catastrophe 大灾 disaster 灾祸 calamity 灾祸 mishap 灾难 debacle 大灾祸 tragedy 悲剧

fore-为前缀，表"在…前"之意 foretell 预言 foreword 序言 forecast 预报 forefather 祖先	astro-为词缀，表"关于天体、宇宙的" astrology 占星术 astronomy 天文学 astronaut 宇航员 asterisk 星号

3. You hang up hurriedly and attend to the baby, crockery, etc.

hang up 挂断（电话） hold up 不挂断 be on the phone 在接电话 sb. is speaking. 我是… This is...我是… You dialed the wrong number. 打错了。	attend to sth./sb. 照料… tend sb./sth. 照看… see to sb./sth. 照看… see to it that...务必… intend to do 打算做… tend to do 趋向做…

4. <u>Meanwhile</u>, the traffic <u>piled up</u> behind...to get the traffic <u>on the move</u> again.

meanwhile 同时	pile up（交通）堵塞	on the move 运动起来；奔波
in the meantime 同时	heap up（交通）堵塞	on the increase 不断增长
at the same time 同时	congest（交通）堵塞	on the decrease 不断下降
at the same moment 同时	jam（交通）堵塞	on the mend（局势、病情）逐步好转
in the process 此间	hold up（交通）堵塞	on the dodge 一直在躲藏
		on the way 在路上

Ⅱ. 现身说"法"：**what**引导的名词性从句

What invariably happens is that a great number of things choose to go wrong at precisely the same moment.（彩色部分是what引导的主语从句）

情况往往这样：许许多多的事情偏偏赶在同一时刻出差错。

what引导名词性从句时一般有以下两种用法：

1. what用作关系代词，既可表人，也可表物。这时，what可理解为"the...that/which"。what前不能再出现先行词，因为它本身已包含了一个名词的意义。例：

You can do everything what you like.（✕）　　You can do what you like.（✓）

Please hand in what you have written.（Please hand in the things that you have written.）

请把你写的东西交上来。

She was not what she was several years ago.（She was not the girl that she was several years ago.）

她已不是几年前的样子了。

2. what用作关系形容词，修饰其后的名词，此时结构为"what+名词"，意为"所有的…"。例：

You can take away what books on this project. 你可以拿走有关这个项目的所有书籍。

What people I've met are sincere and hospitable. 我遇到的所有人都很真诚好客。

I will give you what help I can. 我会尽可能地帮助你。

Ⅲ. 说"文"解"字"

1. What invariably happens is that a great number of things choose to go wrong at precisely the same moment.

译文：情况往往这样：许许多多的事情偏偏赶在同一时刻出差错。

解析：1）choose to do sth.在这里为拟人手法，相当于coincide to do sth.（碰巧做…）或conspire to do sth.（合谋做…）。

2）go wrong在本句的意思与26课略有不同，意为"出差错"，相当于"get out of control"，"get out of hand"等。

3）at the same moment是一个固定短语，意为"在同一时刻"。本文为了追求多变，使用了几个近似表达，如：

at the same time　　　　　in the process

meanwhile　　　　　　　in the meantime

2. As if this were not enough to reduce you to tears, **your husband arrives.**

译文：似乎这一切还不足以使你落泪，你的丈夫接着就回来了。

解析：reduce sb./sth. to...是一个常用结构，意即"使某人/某物成为…状况"，常常指不好的状况，其中的to为介词。例：

The rebellion swept over my home district and reduced it to ashes.

战乱在我的家乡肆虐，将其化为灰烬。

Gambling has reduced him to impoverishment. 赌博令他一贫如洗。

Big things can be reduced to small things, and small things to nothing. 大事化小，小事化了。

3. The woman immediately behind the two cars **happened to be a learner.**

译文：紧跟在两车后面的女司机恰好是个生手。

解析：immediately在本句中不是时间副词"立即地"，而是方位副词"紧挨着"，相当于closely、just。例：

immediately in the vicinity 就在附近

There is a mountain immediately north of the city. 紧靠城的北面有一座山。

one's immediate superior 顶头上司

4. As she was thrown forward, the cake went right **through the windscreen and landed on the road.**

译文：由于她身体前倾，蛋糕正好从挡风玻璃飞了出去，落在了马路上。

解析：1）As she was thrown forward之后实际上省略了by inertia（由于惯性）。例：

The container truck, though the engine failed to work, ran forward by inertia.

尽管引擎熄火了，集装箱卡车由于惯性还在向前行驶。

2）right在本句是副词，意为"恰好"。其他例证：

Speak right out! 请直说！ 　　　　　　　　　　talk just right 谈吐得体

5. A lorry driver who was drawing up alongside the car **pulled up all of a sudden.**

译文：一辆卡车正和轿车并排行驶，忽然，卡车司机紧急刹车。

解析：1）draw up意为"行驶"，pull up意为"靠边停车"。请注意与以下词组区分：

pull in（进站）停车 　　　　　draw out 开出（车站）

2）all of a sudden与suddenly意思相同，不过前者更加正式。

■ 拓 展 篇

Ⅰ.英语趣园

> Superstition is complex. Its history is too long and too old to easily understand, and indeed you will find many relics of it in modern Britain. It is unlucky, for instance, to walk under a ladder, or to spill salt, or break a mirror, or to have anything to do with number 13; whereas a horseshoe brings good luck, and people jokingly "touch wood" to prevent the return of a past misfortune.

Ⅱ.听力快车 🎧

There is still a surprising amount of interest in_____, e.g. in the form of "horoscopes" in newspapers and women's magazines which they may well be slightly_____. Fairies are pretty _____ in "fairy stories" for children, and any adult who believed in fairies or _____ would be considered slightly mad.

III. 补充阅读

There are superstition attached to numbers; even the ancient Greeks believed that all numbers and their multiples had some mystical significance.

Numbers between 1 and 13 were in particular believed to have a powerful influence over the affairs of men.

For example, it is commonly said that luck, good or bad, comes in threes; if an accident happens, two more of the same kind may be expected soon afterwards. The arrival of a letter will be followed by two others within a certain period.

Another belief involving the number three maintains it is unlucky to light three cigarettes from one match. If this happens, the bad luck that goes with the deed falls upon the person whose cigarette was the last to be lit. The ill-omen linked to the lighting of three things from one match or candle goes back to at least the 17th century and probably earlier. It was believed that three candles alight at the same time would be sure to bring bad luck; one, two, or four, were permissible, but never just three.

Seven was another significant number, usually regarded a bringer of good luck. The ancient astrologers believed that the universe was governed by seven planets; students of Shakespeare will recall that the life of man was divided into seven ages. Seven horseshoes nailed to a house will protect it from all evil.

Nine is usually thought of as a lucky number because it is the product of three times three. It was much used by the Anglo Saxons in their charms for healing.

Another belief was that great changes occurred every 7th and 9th of a man's life. Consequently, the age of 63 (the product of nine and seven) was thought to be a very perilous time for him. If he survived his 63rd year he might hope to live to a ripe old age.

Thirteen, as we well know, is regarded with great awe and fear. The common belief is that this derives from the fact that there were 13 people at Christ's Last Supper. This being the eve of his betrayal, it is not difficult to understand the significance given to the number by the early Christians.

In more modern times 13 is an especially unlucky number of a dinner party, for example. Hotels will avoid numbering a floor the 13th; the progression is from 12 to 14, and no room is given the number 13. Many homeowners will use 12 1/2 instead of 13 as their house number.

Yet oddly enough, to be born on the 13th is not regarded with any fear at all, which just shows how irrational we are in our superstitious beliefs.

▪▷ 测 试 篇 ◁▪

I. 单项选择

1. In the experiment we kept a watchful eye _____ the development and recorded every detail.

   A. in   B. at   C. for   D. on

2. The 1986 Challenger space-shuttle _____ was caused by unusually low temperatures immediately before the launch.   (CET-6 03/1)

   A. expedition   B. controversy   C. dismay   D. disaster

3. Very few people could understand his lecture because the subject was very _____.　　（CET-6 05/12）
　　A. faint　　　　　B. obscure　　　　　C. gloomy　　　　　D. indefinite
4. The Prime Minister was followed by five or six _____ when he got off the plane.　　（CET-6 02/1）
　　A. laymen　　　　B. servants　　　　C. directors　　　　D. attendants
5. The morning news says a school bus _____ with a train at the junction and a group of policemen were sent there immediately.
　　A. bumped　　　　B. collided　　　　C. crashed　　　　D. struck
6. It is of the utmost importance that you _____ here on time.
　　A. be　　　　　　B. shall be　　　　C. are to be　　　　D. must be
7. The police accused him of setting fire to the building but he denied _____ in the area on the night of the fire.
　　A. to be　　　　B. to have been　　　C. having been　　　D. be
8. Some people viewed the findings with caution, noting that a cause-and-effect relationship between passive smoking and cancer remains _____.
　　A. to be shown　　　　　　　　B. to have shown
　　C. to have been shown　　　　　D. being shown
9. Maid: Do you have any clothes _____?
　　A. to wash　　　　B. washed　　　　C. to be washed　　　D. wash
10. Hard work can often _____ a lack of intellegence.
　　A. make up for　　B. take advantage of　C. come up with　D. keep pace with

Ⅱ. 翻译

11. 通货膨胀引起了一连串的经济危机。（set up）
12. 德国入侵波兰成为二战的导火索。（mark a prelude to）
13. 先生，您需要服务吗？（attend to）
14. 美国对伊拉克发动大规模地面进攻。（on a vast scale）
15. 居安思危。（immediate）

答案

拓展篇

There is still a surprising amount of interest in fortune-telling, e.g. in the form of "horoscopes" in newspapers and women's magazines which they may well be slightly ashamed of. Fairies are pretty little winged creatures in "fairy stories" for children, and any adult who believed in fairies or magic or witches would be considered slightly mad.

测试篇

1-5 DDBDB　　　　6-10 ACACA

11. Inflation set up a series of economic crises.

12. The German invasion of Poland marked a prelude to World War Ⅱ.

13. Sir, are you being attended to?

14. USA launched a ground assault against Iraq on a vast scale.

15. Danger is the immediate neighbor to security.

Lesson A happy discovery

Ⅰ.振振有"词"

1. <u>Antique shops</u> <u>exert a peculiar fascination on</u> a great many people.

antique shop 古玩店
fashion shop 时装店
expensive shop 高档店
high-brow shop 高档店
middle-brow shop 中档店
low-brow shop 低档店
secondhand shop 二手店
flea market 跳蚤市场

exert a (n) ...fascination on sb. 对某人有着…的魅力
exert a (n) ...influence on sb. 对某人产生…的影响
exert a (n) ...pressure on sb. 对某人施加…的压力
exert control over sb. 对某人进行控制
exert one's abilities 发挥自己的才能
exert every effort 尽一切力量
exert oneself 努力

antique 古董
curiosity 古玩
rarity 珍品
masterpiece 杰作
legacy 遗产
treasure 珍宝

fascination 魅力
fascinate sb. 吸引某人
fascinating 吸引人的
have a(n)... fascination for sb. 对某人有着…的魅力
exercise a(n)... fascination over sb. 对某人有着…的魅力
be fascinating to sb. 对某人有着…的魅力

2. But one has to <u>muster up courage</u> to enter a less <u>pretentious</u> antique shop.

muster up courage 鼓起勇气
screw up courage 鼓起勇气
pick up courage 鼓起勇气
pluck up courage 鼓起勇气
call up courage 鼓起勇气
summon up courage 鼓起勇气

pretentious 自命不凡的
ostentatious 卖弄炫耀的
contemptuous 自高自大的
presumptuous 自以为是的
supercilious 目空一切的
imperious 飞扬跋扈的

173

3. Like a scientist <u>bent on</u> making a discovery, he must <u>cherish the hope</u> that... he will be <u>amply</u> rewarded.

be bent on... 专注于…	cherish the hope 怀抱希望	ample 充足的
be intent on... 专心于…	cherish a dream 怀抱梦想	sufficient 充裕的
be concentrated on... 全神贯注于…	cherish friendship 珍重友谊	adequate 足够的
be absorbed in... 专心于…	cherish peace 珍爱和平	abundant（正式）富足的
be engrossed in... 醉心于…	cherish the memory of...怀念…	plentiful 丰富的
be dedicated to... 专心致志于…	a long-cherished dream 夙愿	

Ⅱ. 现身说"法"：同位独立主格结构

The box was full of crockery, much of it broken.
货箱内装满了陶器，大部分已经破损。

彩色部分就结构而言不是句子，而是短语，且其逻辑主语与前面句子的主语不同，因此可以看作是独立主格成分。但同时much of it又和crockery指同一事物，构成同位语的概念。鉴于这两方面的原因，准确地说彩色部分为同位独立主格结构。例：

A novelist would bring his story to a conclusion by presenting his readers with a seiries of coincidences—most of them wildly probable. (彩色部分是同位独立主格结构)
小说家常常在小说结尾处给读者准备一系列巧合——大部分是牵强附会，极不可能的。

There are fifty students in this class, the youngest being a Beijing boy of 18. (彩色部分是同位独立主格结构) 这个班共有50个学生，最小的是一个18岁的北京男孩。

There are two doors in the living room, one leading to the bedroom, the other leading to the kitchen. (彩色部分是同位独立主格结构) 客厅有两道门，一道通向卧室，另一道通向厨房。

如果稍加改动，同位独立主格结构就可以变为常见的语法现象。例：

The box was full of crockery, and much of it was broken. (简单并列句)

The box was full of crockery, much of which was broken. (非限定性定语从句)

Ⅲ. 说"文"解"字"

1. a happy discovery

译文：幸运的发现

解析：happy一词多义，在这里作"幸运的"解。试比较以下例句：

He did not die happily. (happily修饰die) 他死得很惨。

Happily he did not die. (happily修饰句子) 幸运的是他没有死。

He did not tell me about it frankly. (frankly修饰tell) 他没有坦诚地告诉我那件事。

Frankly he did not tell me about it. (frankly修饰句子) 坦率而言，他没有告诉我那件事。

2. There is always hope that in its labyrinth of musty, dark, disordered rooms a real rarity will be found.

译文：在发霉、阴暗、杂乱无章、迷宫般的店堂里，总有希望找到一件稀世珍品。

解析：句中三个形容词的使用涉及到一系列形容词修饰名词时的排序问题。一般而言，以下公式适用于大多数情形：表性质状态形容词+表新旧形容词+表颜色形容词+表材料形容词+名词。例：

a broken small old gray stone bridge

a nice yellow wooden chair

3. **Frank visited an antique shop** in my neighbourhood.

译文：弗兰克去了我家附近的一家古玩店。

解析：in one's neighbourhood是固定短语，表"在某人家附近"，相当于nearby。

> **联想记忆**
>
> in the vicinity 在附近   be adjacent to...与…毗邻
>
> live a stone's throw 住得很近

4. **... but that he** could not be bothered to open it.

译文：……但他嫌麻烦不想把它打开。

解析：cannot be bothered to do sth.不可直译，应译为"嫌麻烦做…，懒得做…"。例：

He always cannot be bothered to give a helping hand. 他总是懒于帮忙。

> **联想记忆**
>
> 1. take great pains to do sth. 费尽心机做…
>
>   He always takes great pains to kiss up to his superior. 他总是费尽心机取悦上司。
>
> 2. take great trouble to do sth. 费尽气力做…
>
>   Some people always take great trouble to achieve some goals which are beyond attainment.
>
>   有些人总是追求一些力不能及的目标。

拓 展 篇

Ⅰ.英语趣园

Correggio (Antonio Allegri) (c. 1489-1534), an Italian painter, was named after the small town in Emilia where he was born. Little is known of his life, but his paintings suggest under whom he may have formed his style. Echoes of Mantegna's manner in many of his early paintings indicate that he may have studied that master's work in Mantua, and he was influenced in these works also by Lorenzo Costa and Leonardo, adopting Costa's pearly Ferrarese coloring and, in the St. John of the St. Francis altarpiece, his first documented work, Leonardo's characteristic gesture of the pointing finger. Later he initiated a style of sentimental elegance and conscious allure with soft sfumato and gestures of captivating charm. Correggio may well have visited Rome early in his career, although Vasari maintains that he never went there and the obvious inspiration of the paintings of Raphael and Michelangelo could be accounted for by drawings and prints which were known all over Italy.

Ⅱ.听力快车

Michelangelo was an _____ . He was one of the founders of _____, and in his later years, one of the principal exponents of Mannerism. Born at Caprese, the son of the local magistrate, his family returned to

Florence soon after his birth. Michelangelo's _____, as to be a practicing artist was then considered beneath the station of a member of the gentry. He was, however, eventually apprenticed in 1488 for a three-year term to _____. He is known especially for his statue of David（an ancient king of Israel）and for painting the ceiling of the Sistine Chapel in Rome with scenes from the *Old Testament* of the Bible, including the *Creation of Adam*.

Ⅲ. 补充阅读

Leonardo: Renaissance polymath

From Sister Wendy's *Story of Painting*

"There has never been an artist who was more fittingly, and without qualification, described as a genius. Like Shakespeare, Leonardo came from an insignificant background and rose to universal acclaim. Leonardo was the illegitimate son of a local lawyer in the small town of Vinci in the Tuscan region. His father acknowledged him and paid for his training, but we may wonder whether the strangely self-sufficient tone of Leonardo's mind was not perhaps affected by his early ambiguity of status. The definitive polymath, he had almost too many gifts, including superlative male beauty, a splendid singing voice, magnificent physique, mathematical excellence, scientific daring... the list is endless. This overabundance of talents caused him to treat his artistry lightly, seldom finishing a picture, and sometimes making rash technical experiments. The *Last Supper*, in the church of Santa Maria delle Grazie in Milan, for example, has almost vanished, so inadequate were his innovations in fresco preparation.

"Yet the works that we have salvaged remain the most dazzlingly poetic pictures ever created. The *Mona Lisa* has the innocent disadvantage of being too famous. It can only be seen behind thick glass in a heaving crowd of awe-struck sightseers. It has been reproduced in every conceivable medium; it remains intact in its magic, forever defying the human insistence on comprehending. It is a work that we can only gaze at in silence.

"Leonardo's three great portraits of women all have a secret wistfulness. This quality is at its most appealing in *Cecilia Gallarani*, at its most enigmatic in the *Mona Lisa*, and at its most confrontational in *Ginevra de' Benci*. It is hard to gaze at the *Mona Lisa* because we have so many expectations of it. Perhaps we can look more truly at a less famous portrait, *Ginevra de' Benci*. It has that haunting, almost unearthly beauty peculiar to Leonardo da Vinci.

A withheld identity

"The subject of *Ginevra de' Benci* has nothing of the *Mona Lisa*'s inward amusement, and also nothing of Cecilia's gentle submissiveness. The young woman looks past us with a wonderful luminous sulkiness. Her mouth is set in an unforgiving line of sensitive disgruntlement, her proud and perfect head is taut above the unyielding column of her neck, and her eyes seem to narrow as she endures the painter and his art. Her ringlets, infinitely subtle, cascade down from the breadth of her gleaming forehead（the forehead, incidentally, of one of the most gifted intellectuals of her time）. These delicate ripples are repeated in the spikes of the juniper bush.

"The desolate waters, the mists, the dark trees, the reflected gleams of still waters—all these surround and illuminate the sitter. She is totally fleshly and totally impermeable to the artist. He observes, held rapt by her perfection of form, and shows us the thin veil of her upper bodice and the delicate flushing of her throat. What she is truly like she conceals; what Leonardo reveals to us is precisely this concealment, a self-absorption that spares no outward glance.

Interior depth

"We can always tell a Leonardo work by his treatment of hair, angelic in its fineness, and by the lack of any rigidity of contour. One form glides imperceptibly into another (the Italian term is *sfumato*), a wonder of glazes creating the most subtle of transitions between tones and shapes. The angel's face, in the painting known as the *Virgin of the Rocks* in the National Gallery, London, or the Virgin's face in the Paris version of the same picture, have an interior wisdom, an artistic wisdom that has no pictorial rival.

"This unrivaled quality meant that few artists actually show Leonardo's influence: it is as if he seemed to be in a world apart from them. Indeed he did move apart, accepting the French King Francis I's summons to live in France. Those who did imitate him, like Bernardini Luini of Milan (c. 1485-1532), caught only the outer manner, the half-smile, the mistiness.

▪▶ 测 试 篇 ◀▪

I.单项选择

1. He still _____ the memory of his carefree childhood spent in that small wooden house of his grandparents'. (CET-6 05/1)

   A. nourishes   B. cherishes   C. fancies   D. scans

2. By turning this knob to the right you can _____ the sound from the radio. (CET-6 05/1)

   A. intensify   B. amplify   C. enlarge   D. reinforce

3. The microscope and telescopes, with their capacity to enlarge, isolate and probe, demonstrate how details can be _____ and separated from the whole. (CET-6 05/1)

   A. radiated   B. extended   C. prolonged   D. magnified

4. Jack is not very decisive, and he always finds himself in a _____ as if he doesn't know what he really wants to do. (CET-6 05/6)

   A. fantasy   B. dilemma   C. contradiction   D. conflict

5. It was a wonderful occasion which we will _____ for many years to come. (CET-6 05/6)

   A. conceive   B. clutch   C. contrive   D. cherish

6. It is generally known that New York is a city for _____ and a center for odd bits of information.

   A. veterans   B. victims   C. pedestrians   D. eccentric   (CET-6 04/6)

7. Most people in the modern world _____ him to act for me while I was away from office. (CET-6 03/6)

   A. embody   B. cherish   C. fascinate   D. illuminate

8. The toy maker produces a _____ copy of the space station, exact in every detail. (CET-6 02/6)

   A. minimal   B. minimum   C. miniature   D. minor

9. Doctors are often caught in a _____ because they have to decide whether they should tell their patients the truth or not. (CET-6 02/1)

   A. puzzle   B. perplexity   C. dilemma   D. bewilderment

10. I should like to rent a house, modern, comfortable and _____ in a quiet neighborhood.　（CET-4 90/1）

　　A. all in all　　　　B. above all　　　　C. after all　　　　D. over all

Ⅱ. 翻译

11. 西藏是让许多人魂牵梦绕的地方。（exert a peculiar fascination on）

12. 我们相信无论黑夜如何漫长，白昼终将到来。（there is hope that）

13. 没有人能够随随便便成功。（by chance）

14. 在大学里，学生至少要得C才能继续读下去。（at least）

15. 我在等车的时候，买了张报纸。（pick up）

拓展篇

　　Michelangelo was an Italian sculptor, painter, architect and poet. He was one of the founders of the High Renaissance, and in his later years, one of the principal exponents of Mannerism. Born at Caprese, the son of the local magistrate, his family returned to Florence soon after his birth. Michelangelo's desire to become an artist was initially opposed by his father, as to be a practicing artist was then considered beneath the station of a member of the gentry. He was, however, eventually apprenticed in 1488 for a three-year term to Domenico Ghirlandaio. He is known especially for his statue of David（an ancient king of Israel）and for painting the ceiling of the Sistine Chapel in Rome with scenes from the *Old Testament* of the Bible, including the *Creation of Adam*.

测试篇

1-5 BBDBD　　　　　6-10 DBCCB

11. Tibet exerts a peculiar fascination on a great many people.

12. There is always hope that however long the night is, the day will come in the end.

13. No one can succeed by chance.

14. In university, students have to maintain at least C in order to remain in school.

15. I picked up a newspaper at the newsstand while waiting for the bus.

Lesson 35. Justice was done

积累篇

I. 振振有"词"

1. We might say that <u>justice has been done</u> when a man's innocence or guilt has been proved <u>beyond doubt</u>.

justice is done 伸张正义
do justice to sb. 给某人伸张正义
bring sb. to justice 将某人绳之以法
Justice has long arms. 天网恢恢, 疏而不漏
treat sb./sth. with justice 秉公对待…
deny sb. justice 对某人不公平

beyond doubt 毫无疑问
beyond question 无可置疑
beyond argument 无可争辩
beyond words 无以言表
beyond description 难以描述
beyond hope/cure 无可救药
beyond measurement 无法估量

2. <u>There are rare instances when</u> justice almost <u>ceases to be</u> an abstract concept.

写作中常用的扩展句型:
There are rare instances when... (替代occasionally) 个别情况下
There are times when... (替代sometimes) 有时候
There was a time when... (替代once) 曾经

cease to do sth. 不再做…
cease doing sth. 停止做…
cease from doing sth. 不再做…
cease fire (战争) 停火
Wonders will never cease. 真是无奇不有

3. The shop assistants must have <u>found it impossible to resist the temptation to say</u> "<u>it serves him right</u>."

常用的写作句型:
find it impossible to resist the temptation to do 不由自主做…
find it hard to resist the temptation to do 不由自主做…
cannot help doing 情不自禁做…
cannot refrain from doing 禁不住做…
cannot wait to do 迫不及待做…
be impatient to do 急不可耐做…

It serves him right. 罪有应得; 活该
He deserves it. 罪有应得
He has his own fingers burnt. 自讨苦吃
stir up a nest of hornets 捅马蜂窝; 自寻烦恼
borrow trouble 自找麻烦

Ⅱ. 现身说"法"：however引导让步状语从句

Judges, however wise or eminent, are human and can make mistakes.
法官无论如何聪明显赫，毕竟也是人，也会犯错的。

however引导的是让步状语从句，且使用了省略手法，完整形式为however wise and eminent (they are)。实际上，以疑问词+ever构成的复合词都可引导让步状语从句，具有"不管"或"无论"之义。例：

Whatever happens, don't change your mind. 无论发生什么事，别改变主意。

Whenever I'm in trouble, I turn to Jack. 无论何时有困难，我都会求助杰克。

You can't come in, whoever you are. 无论你是谁，都不能进来。

Whichever you choose, I don't mind. 无论你选哪个，我都不介意。

I will follow you wherever you go. 你去哪儿，我都会跟着你。

如将上述结构转化为no matter+疑问词，则更多用于口语场合。例：

I have to purchase that instrument no matter how much it costs. (=however much it costs)

不管那件仪器有多贵，我都得买下来。

Ⅲ. 说"文"解"字"

1. The word justice is usually associated with courts of law.

译文："正义"这个词常常是同法庭联系在一起的。

解析：1）be associated with... 意为"与…有联系"，意义相近的表达有：

be connected with...   be linked to...

have something to do with...   have some bearing on...

2）courts of law结构中之所以用of law加以限定，是因为court一词多义，单用可能会产生误解。例：

The court decided against the alliance. (court朝廷) 朝廷已决定不参加该联盟。

Are the players on court yet? (court 球场) 球员们都上场了吗？

3）本句还可以作为经典句式加以模仿，例：

The word success is usually associated with diligence. 成功这个词经常与勤奋密切相连。

The word gentle is usually associated with women. 温柔这个词经常与女性相连。

2. Judges, however wise or eminent, are human and can make mistakes.

译文：法官无论如何聪明显赫，毕竟也是人，也会犯错的。

解析：human在这里作形容词，意为"人的，人类的"。试比较：

humane 仁慈的   humanistic 人道主义的   humanitarian 博爱的

inhuman 无人性的   nonhuman 非人类的

3. They located the right chimneys by tapping at the walls and listening for the man's cries.

译文：他们敲打烟囱倾听那人发出的喊叫声，由此确定了烟囱的位置。

解析：1）tap at表"轻轻击打"，如tap dance（踢踏舞）。pound at, hammer则指"重重击打"，如pound at the door（使劲敲门）。

2）listen for与listen to略有不同，前者实际上相当于listen to+look for。例：

She is listening closely for her husband's footsteps on the stairs.

她仔细倾听着楼梯上传来的丈夫的脚步声。

4. Justice had been done even before the man was handed over to the police.

译文：甚至在那人被送交给警察之前，正义已经得到了伸张。

解析：hand over意为"移交，转交"，反义词组为take over（接管）。例：

China took over Hong Kong from Britain on July, 1st, 1997.

中国于1997年7月1日从英国手中接管香港。

联想记忆

hand out sth. 分发　　　　　　hand in sth. 上交　　　　　　hand down sth. 流传

拓 展 篇

Ⅰ.英语趣园

At a trial the jury selection is made subject to the direction of the presiding judge. The names of the prospective jurors are drawn by lot by the clerk of the court. Both the defense and the prosecution may examine the jurors to ascertain whether cause for challenge in any particular case exists—that is, whether circumstances exist that might improperly influence a juror's decisions, such as bias or self-interest. The parties to the action or their attorneys may then exercise their right to eliminate undesirable members from the jury by names of challenge. After a satisfactory jury has been drawn, the jury is formed, and the trial proceeds.

Ⅱ.听力快车

At the court

Lawyer: _____?

Mary:　Yes, I did.

Lawyer: You saw a man, didn't you?

Mary:　That's right. _____.

Lawyer: Now, look around the court... can you see that man?

Mary:　Yes, he is the man I saw.

Lawyer: _____?

Mary:　No, he was with a young woman.

Lawyer: Now, look around the court again... can you see that woman?

Mary:　Yes, there! That's the woman I saw.

Lawyer: I see. Mary. Now look at the man and the woman again. This is very important. _____?

Mary:　Yes, absolutely sure. They are the people I saw.

Lawyer: Thank you, Mary.

Ⅲ. 补充阅读

Creative justice

Throwing criminals in jail is an ancient and widespread method of punishment; but is it a wise one? It does seem reasonable to keep wrongdoers in a place where they find fewer opportunities to hurt innocent people, and where they might discover that crime doesn't pay. The system has long been considered fair and sound by those who want to see the guilty punished and society protected. Yet the value of this form of justice is now being questioned by the very men who have to apply it: the judges. The reason, they say, is that prison doesn't do anyone any good.

Does it really help the society, or the victim, or the victim's family, to put in jail a man who, while drunk at the wheel of his car, has injured or killed another person? It would be more helpful to make the man pay for his victim's medical bills and compensate him for the bad experience, the loss of working time, and any other problems arising from the accident. If the victim is dead, in most cases his family could use some financial assistance.

The idea of compensation is far from new: some ancient nations had laws defining very precisely what should be paid for every offense and injury. In Babylon, around 2,700 B.C., a thief had to give back five times the value of the goods he had stolen; in Rome, centuries later, thieves only paid double. "Good system!" say the modern judges, who know what bad effects a prison term can have on a nonviolent first offender. A young thief who spends time in jail receives there a thorough education in crime from his fellow prisoners. Willingly or not, he has to associate with tough criminals who will drag him into more serious offenses, more prison terms—a life of repeated wrongdoing that will leave a trail of victims and cost the community a great deal of money; for it is very expensive to put a man on trail and keep him in jail.

Such considerations have caused a number of English and American judges to try other kinds of punishment for "light" criminals, all unpleasant enough to discourage the offenders from repeating their offenses, but safe for them because they are not exposed to dangerous company. They pay for their crime by helping their victims, financially or otherwise, or by doing unpaid labor for their community; they may have to work for the poor or the mentally ill, to clean the streets of their town, collect litter or plant trees, or to do some work for which they are qualified. Or perhaps they take a job and repay their victim out of their salary. This sort of punishment, called an alternative sentence, is applied only to nonviolent criminals who are not likely to be dangerous to the public, such as forgers, shoplifters, and drivers who have caused traffic accidents. Alternative sentences are considered particularly good for young offenders. The sentenced criminal has the right to refuse the new type of punishment if he prefers a prison term.

Since alternative sentences are not defined by law, it is up to the judges to find the punishment that fits the crime. They have shown remarkable imagination in applying what they call "creative justice".

The supporters of the new justice point out that it presents many advantages. It reduces prison crowding, which has been responsible for much violence and crime among inmates. It saves a great deal of money, and decreases the chances of bad influence and repeated offenses. It also provides some help to the victims, who have always been neglected in the past. Many judges think that alternative sentences may also be beneficial to the offenders themselves, by forcing them to see the effects of their crimes and the people who have suffered from them. The greatest resistance to the new kind of justice comes from the families of victims who have died. Bent on revenge, many angrily refuse any sort of compensation. They want the criminal locked up in the good old-fashioned way. They believe, reasonably, that the only just punishment is the one that fits the crime. And they fail to understand the purpose of alternative sentencing. What the judges are trying to find is the kind of punishment that will not only be just, but useful to society, by helping the victims and their families, the community, and those offenders who can be reformed. "This," says a "creative" judge, "is true justice."

▶ 测 试 篇 ◀

I. 单项选择

1. Nothing Helen says is ever _____. She always thinks carefully before she speaks. (CET-6 05/1)
   A. simultaneous   B. homogenous   C. spontaneous   D. rigorous

2. Fiber-optic cables can carry hundreds of telephone conversations _____. (CET-6 05/1)
   A. homogeneously   B. spontaneously   C. simultaneously   D. ingeniously

3. The meaning of the sentence is _____; you can interpret it in several ways. (CET-6 05/12)
   A. skeptical   B. intelligible   C. ambiguous   D. exclusive

4. President Wilson attempted to _____ between the powers to end the war, but neither side was prepared to give in. (CET-6 04/1)
   A. mediate   B. arbitrate   C. intervene   D. interfere

5. Professor Smith and Professor Brown will _____ in presenting the series of lectures on American literature. (CET-6 04/1)
   A. alter   B. alternate   C. substitute   D. exchange

6. They were _____ in their scientific research, not knowing what happened just outside their lab.
   A. submerged   B. drowned   C. immersed   D. dipped   (CET-6 01/6)

7. We must look beyond _____ and assumptions and try to discover what is missing.
   A. justifications   B. illusions   C. manifestations   D. specifications

8. Why this otherwise excellent newspaper allows such an article to be printed is _____ me.
   A. above   B. outside   C. beside   D. beyond

9. This book will show the readers _____ can be used in other contexts.
   A. how that they have observed   B. that how they have observed
   C. how what they have observed   D. that they have observed

10. The world's greatest sporting event, the Olympic Games, upholds the amateur ideal that _____ matters is not winning but participating.
    A. anything   B. it   C. what   D. everything

II. 翻译

11. 在中文里,"殖民"总是和侵略、占领联系在一起。(be associated with)

12. 对欧洲国家来说,殖民是重商主义理论的一部分。(part of)

13. 我等着自己的名字被叫到。(listen for)

14. 我的车子陷在泥里了。（be stuck in）

15. 车子已经不再是身份和地位的象征。（cease to be）

拓展篇

At the court

Lawyer: Now, Mary. You saw the robbery, didn't you?

Mary: Yes, I did.

Lawyer: You saw a man, didn't you?

Mary: That's right. I saw him when he went into the garage and came out.

Lawyer: Now, look around the court... can you see that man?

Mary: Yes, he is the man I saw.

Lawyer: He wasn't alone when he went into the garage, was he?

Mary: No, he was with a young woman.

Lawyer: Now, look around the court again... can you see that woman?

Mary: Yes, there! That's the woman I saw.

Lawyer: I see. Mary. Now look at the man and the woman again. This is very important. Are you absolutely sure about the man and the woman?

Mary: Yes, absolutely sure. They are the people I saw.

Lawyer: Thank you, Mary.

测试篇

1-5 CCCAB   6-10 CBDCC

11. According to Chinese context, "colony" is associated with invasion and aggression.

12. "Colony" is part of mercantilism for European countries.

13. I listened for my name to be called.

14. My car was stuck in the mud.

15. Cars ceased to be a symbol of status.

Lesson A chance in a million

积 累 篇

I . 振振有"词"

1. A novelist would <u>bring his story to a conclusion</u> by <u>presenting his readers with</u> a series of <u>coincidences</u>.

coincidence 巧合
concurrence 同时发生的事
conjunction 同时发生
correlation 相互关系
incidence（大）事件
accident（小）事件；事故

写作中常用的扩展模式：
conclude sth. 扩展为 bring sth. to a conclusion
fail in sth. 扩展为 bring sth. to a failure
succeed in sth. 扩展为 bring sth. to a success
fulfill sth. 扩展为 bring sth. to a fulfillment

present sb. with sth. 提供某人…
present sth. to sb. 提供某人…
provide sb. with sth. 提供某人…
provide sth. for sb. 提供某人…
offer sth. to sb. 提供某人…
offer sb. sth. 提供某人…

2. Yet in real life, circumstances do sometimes <u>conspire to</u> bring about coincidences which <u>anyone but</u> a nineteenth century novelist would find <u>incredible</u>.

incredible 不可置信的
unbelievable 难以相信的
incredulous 表示怀疑的
suspicious 疑心的；令人起疑的
superstitious 迷信的

conspire to do 合谋做…
join hands to do 联手做…
make concerted efforts to do 齐心协力做…
collaborate with sb. 与某人合作

anyone but sb. 除了某人
none but sb. 正是某人
none other than... 正是…
anything but... 除了…
nothing but... 正是…

3. Mrs. Bussman <u>commented on</u> the workman's close <u>resemblance</u> to her husband...

comment on...对…评论
make a comment on...对…评论
make a remark on...对…评论
air one's opinion on...对…发表观点
state one's opinion on...对…发表看法

resemble sb. 与某人相似
bear/take close/strong resemblance to sb. 与某人酷似
take after sb. 与某人相似
look like sb. 与某人相似
be similar to sb./sth. 与…相似

II. 现身说"法"：**suggest** 与虚拟语气

> **Mrs. Bussman... even** suggested **that he might be his brother.**
> 巴斯曼夫人甚至猜测他可能就是她丈夫的兄弟。

1. suggest 如果表建议、命令或要求时，其后要接虚拟语气，形式是 should+动词原形，美国英语中经常省略 should。以下动词都是这种用法：

   表建议：suggest, move, recommend, propose, advise；

   表要求：require, request, demand, insist, urge；

   表命令：direct, command, order；例：

   They suggested that the project（should）be suspended. 他们建议停止这个项目。

   Many students insisted that they（should）have more literature classes. 许多学生要求多开设一些文学课。

   He recommended that I（should）go traveling. 他建议我去旅游。

2. 如果这些动词不表示命令、建议和要求，则不用虚拟语气，而用陈述语气，本文的例句即是这种情况。请看其他例句：

   The expression on her face suggested that she had made it clear. 她脸上的表情表明她已明白了此事。

   He insisted that we were wrong. 他坚持认为我们错了。

III. 说"文"解"字"

1. **We are less credulous than we** used to be.

   译文：我们不再像以前那样轻信别人了。

   解析：use to do 是固定短语，表"过去常常…"。to 之后是实义动词时，可省略该动词；若是 be 动词，则不可省。例：

   He earns less than he used to（earn）. 他挣得比以前少。

   She is more introverted than she used to be. 她比以前更内向了。

2. While on a walking tour with is wife, **he stopped to talk to a workman.**

   译文：一次，他与妻子徒步旅行，途中停下来与一个工人交谈。

   解析：1）彩色部分运用了省略手法，补全后应是 While he was on a walking tour with his wife，这符合状语从句的省略原则。

   2）be on a walking tour 意为"徒步旅行"，相关的表达有：

   go for a walk 散步   take a walk 散步   go for a stroll 溜达

3. **Mrs. Bussman** commented on the workman's close resemblance to her husband.

   译文：巴斯曼夫人说那工人与她丈夫相貌相似。

   解析：1）comment on 用法上相当于 air one's opinions on 或 state one's views on（对…发表看法）。此外，no comment 经常在外交场合出现，意为"无可奉告"。

   2）resemble sb. 意为"很像某人"，但若转化为名词，则其后要加介词 to，一般形式为：

   have/take/bear a close resemblance to sb. 这种结构对于写作极为有效，使句型更加饱满，意义更加充实。

4. **Franz** poured scorn on the idea, **pointing out that his** borhter had been killed in action **during the war.**

译文：弗朗兹对此不屑一顾，说他兄弟已经在战争中阵亡了。

解析：1）pour scorn on sth./sb.意为"对…大加嘲讽"。可将scorn换成其他表观点、看法或感情方面的词，则衍生出以下短语：

pour criticism on...对…大肆批评　　　　　pour praise on...对…大肆称颂

pour love on...对…倍加宠爱　　　　　　　pour hatred on...对…非常痛恨

2）be killed in action意为"阵亡"，注意在action之前不可加a或the。

拓 展 篇

I.英语趣园

East Germany, also the German Democratic Republic, was a former country in northeast Europe which in 1990 joined again with West Germany to become Germany.

West Germany, also the Federal Republic of Germany, was a former country in Western Europe, between France and East Germany, whose capital city was Bonn. In 1949 Germany was split into two countries: the western part became the Federal Republic of Germany, and the eastern part became the German of Democratic Republic, a communist country. The two countries joined together again in 1990 to become Germany, after the fall of the Berlin Wall.

II.听力快车

_____

_____

_____

_____

III.补充阅读

The date father didn't keep

It happened in one of those colorful Danish inns which offer service specially for tourists and where English is spoken. I was with my father on a business-and-pleasure trip, and in our leisure hours we were having a wonderful time.

"I wish Mother were here," said I.

"If your mother had come with us, it would have been wonderful to show her around."

He had visited Denmark when he was a young man. I asked him, "How long is it since you were here?"

"Oh, about thirty years. I remember being in this very inn, by the way." He looked around, remembering. "Those were pleasant and enjoyable days..." he stopped suddenly, and I saw that his face was pale. I followed his eyes and looked across the room to a woman who was setting a tray of drinks before some customers. She might have been pretty once, but now she was stout and her hair was untidy. "Do you know her?" I asked.

"I did once," he said.

The woman came to our table. "Drinks?" she asked.

"We'll have beer," I said. She nodded and went away.

"How she has changed! Thank heaven she didn't recognize me," Father said in a low voice, mopping has face with a handkerchief. "I knew her before I met your mother," he went on, "I was a student, on a tour. She was a lovely young thing, very graceful. I fell madly in love with her and she with me."

"Does mother know about her?" I said suddenly, without thinking.

"Of course," father said gently. He looked at me a little anxiously. I felt embarrassed for him.

I said, "Dad, you don't have to..."

"Your mother would tell you if she were here. I don't want you wondering about this. I was a foreigner to her family. I was dependent on my father. If she had married me, she wouldn't have had any prospects. So her father objected to our romance. When I wrote to my father that I wanted to get married, he cut off my allowance. And I had to go home. But I met the girl once more, and told her I would return to America, borrow enough money to get married, and come back for her in a few months."

"We knew," he continued, "that her father might stop and seize our letter, so we agreed that I would simply mail her a slip of paper with a date on it, the time she was to meet me at a certain place; then we'd get married. Well, I went home, got the loan and sent her the date. She received the note. She wrote me: 'I'll be there.' But she wasn't. Then I found that she had been married a bout two weeks before, to a local innkeeper. She hadn't waited."

Then my father said, "Thank God she didn't. I went home, met your mother, and we've been completely happy. We often joke about that youthful love romance. I suggest that one day you write a story about it."

The woman appeared with our beer.

"Are you from America?" she asked me.

"Yes," I said.

She smiled happily, "A wonderful country, America."

"Yes, a lot of your countrymen have gone there. Did you ever think of it?"

"Not me, not now" she said, "I thought so one time, a long time ago. But I stay here. It's much better here."

We drank our beer and left. Outside I said, "Father, just how did you write that date on which she was to meet you?"

He stopped, took out an envelope and wrote on it. "Like this," he said, "12/11/63 which was, of course, December 11, 1963."

"No!" I exclaimed, "It isn't in Denmark or any European country. Over here they write the day first, then the month. So that date wouldn't be December 11 but 12th of November!"

Father passed his hand over his face. "So she was there!" He exclaimed, "and it was because I didn't show up that she got married." He was silent for a while. "Well," he said, "I hope she's happy. She seems to be."

As we resumed walking, I said, "It's a lucky thing it happened that way. You wouldn't have met Mother."

He put his arm around my shoulder, looked at me with a heartwarming smile, and said, "I was doubly lucky, young fellow, for otherwise I wouldn't have met you either!"

测 试 篇

I. 单项选择

1. It was such a(n) _____ when Pat and Mike met each other in Tokyo. Each thought that the other was still in Hong Kong.　　　　　　　　（CET-6 05/6）

   A. occurrence　　　　B. coincidence　　　　C. fancy　　　　D. destiny

2. At present, it is not possible to confirm or to refute the suggestion that there is a casual relationship between the amount of fat we eat and the _____ of heart attacks.　　　　　　（CET-6 04/1）

   A. incidence　　　　B. impetus　　　　C. rupture　　　　D. emergence

3. It is no _____ that a large number of violent crimes are committed under the influence of alcohol.　　　　　　　　（CET-6 03/9）

   A. coincidence　　　　B. correspondence　　　　C. inspiration　　　　D. intuition

4. It is fortunate for the old couple that their son's career goals and their wishes for him _____.

   　　　　　　　　（CET-6 03/9）

   A. coincide　　　　B. comply　　　　C. conform　　　　D. collaborate

5. Very few people could understand the lecture the professor delivered because its subject was very _____.

   　　　　　　　　（CET-6 03/6）

   A. obscure　　　　B. indefinite　　　　C. dubious　　　　D. intriguing

6. The results are hardly _____ ; he cannot believe they are accurate.

   A. credible　　　　B. contrary　　　　C. critical　　　　D. crucial

7. Often such arguments have the effect of _____ rather than clarifying the issues involved.　　（CET-6 03/1）

   A. obscuring　　　　B. prejudicing　　　　C. tackling　　　　D. blocking

8. The author of the report is well _____ with the problems in the hospital because he has been working there for many years.　　　　　　（CET-6 01/6）

   A. acquainted　　　　B. informed　　　　C. accustomed　　　　D. known

9. Comparison and contrast are often used _____ in advertisements.

   A. intentionally　　　　B. pertinently　　　　C. incidentally　　　　D. tiresomely

10. It took me a long time to _____ the disappointment of losing the match.

    A. get through　　　　B. get over　　　　C. get off　　　　D. get down

II. 翻译

11. 他一点儿也不穷。（anything but）

12. 缺乏适应能力、被动消极，以及情感的孤独，这一切都不可避免地导致了他的自杀。（conspire to do）

13. 我是两年前认识他的。（make one's acquaintance）

14. 大会圆满成功。（bring to a conclusion）

15. 这么多年来，她一直默默无闻地生活着。（in obscurity）

答案

拓展篇

There are lots of idioms connected with numbers in English. For example: "A chance in a million" means no chance at all or a very slim chance, a tremendous fluke. "Not one chance in a million" refers to completely impossible. "I have told you a hundred times!" means I have told you over and over again. "I've made a thousand and one apologies" is used in the same meaning here.

测试篇

1. 1-5 BAAAA   6-10 AAAAB

11. He is anything but poor.

12. Inability to conform, passivity and emotional isolation conspired to make his tragic suicide inevitable.

13. I made his acquaintance 2 years ago.

14. The conference was brought to a successful conclusion.

15. For years, she lived in obscurity.

Lesson 37. The westhaven express

Ⅰ.振振有"词"

1. Most of us have <u>developed an unshakable faith in</u> railway <u>timetable</u>.

develop an unshakable faith in... 对…形成不可动摇的信念
place high hopes on... 对…充满希望
pin high expectations on... 对…期待很高
have a high ideal of... 对…期待很高
have much belief in... 对…非常信任

timetable〈英〉时刻表
schedule〈美〉时刻表
time sheet 考勤表
agenda 日程
syllabus 教学大纲
curriculum 课程

2. It is all too easy to <u>blame</u> the railway <u>authorities</u> when something does <u>go wrong</u>.

blame 责怪
get oneself to blame 怪自己
be to blame for sth. 为…受责备
reprimand（严厉）训斥
reproach（难过、失望地）责怪
condemn 谴责
denounce 斥责

authorities（复）政府，当局
authority 权威
authoritative 权威的
authoritarian 专制的
authorization 授权书
authorship 作者身份

go+adj. 结构：
go wrong 出差错
go bad 变质
go insane 失去理智
go bald 秃顶
go slow 怠工

3. <u>It suddenly dawned on me that</u> this express was not <u>roaring down</u> the line at ninety miles an hour.

It dawns on sb. that... 某人想起…
It occurred to sb. that... 某人想到…
sth. crosses sb.'s mind 某人想到某事
sth. reminds sb. of... 使某人想起…
sth. strikes sb. as... 某人觉得某事…

roar down...轰鸣着驶过…
thunder along...轰隆隆地驶过…
lumber through...轰隆隆地驶过…
rumble through...轰鸣着驶过…
hoot（汽车、火车）鸣笛

II. 现身说"法": too... to...结构

> **It is all** too easy to blame **the railway authorities when something does go wrong.**（彩色部分中too... to...结构不含否定意义）一旦铁路出了问题，人们便不假思索地责备铁路当局。

一般而言，凡在too之前出现only、all、not、but，句中的不定式不具有否定意义。all too表very或exceedingly。此外，若在too之后出现easy、apt、eager、inclined、willing、glad等词，则不定式也不具有否定意义。例：

You know but too well to hold your tongue. 你深知少说为妙。

I'm only too glad to help you. 我很乐意帮助你。

She is too ready to suspect. 她爱猜疑。

People are too apt to do so. 人们都爱这样做。

Beginners are too inclined to make mistakes. 初学者易犯错。

He is too eager to get promoted. 他太想得到提拔。

III. 说"文"解"字"

1. **After** consulting **my railway timetable, I** noted **with** satisfaction **that there was an** express train **to Westhaven.**

   译文：我查看了列车时刻表，满意地了解到有一趟去威斯特海温的快车。

   解析：1）consult是及物动词，例：

   consult a lawyer 请教律师 　　　　consult a doctor about one's illness 找医生看病

   consult a dictionary 查字典 　　　　consult one's watch 看表

   2）with satisfaction相当于satisfiedly（参看11课相关内容）。

   3）express train意为"直达列车"，其中express是形容词。以下是该用法的其他例子：

   an express bus 特快公共汽车 　　　　an express elevator 直达电梯

   work at express speed 高速度工作 　　　　an express consignment 快件

   an express highway 高速公路

2. **At the time,** this did not strike me as odd.

   译文：一开始，我并不感到奇怪。

   解析：strike sb. as...意为"给某人以…印象"。例：

   His story stuck us as incredible. 我觉得他的故事不可信。

   The joke didn't strike me as ridiculous. 我觉得这个笑话不可笑。

   Their discussion struck me as pointless. 我认为他们的讨论毫无意义。

   His arrival didn't strike them as surprise. 他的到来并没有令他们感到奇怪。

3. I reflected that there must be a great many people besides myself who wished to take advantage of **this excellent service.**

   译文：我想除我之外，想利用快车之便的人一定大有人在。

   解析：1）take advantage of意为make good use of（充分利用）。例：

   take advantage of all educational opportunities 利用一切教育机会

2）该词组还有"剥削"之意。例：

Some businesses took advantage of their customers. 有些商家欺骗消费者。

> **联想记忆**：avail oneself of "利用"，例：
> I will avail myself of this precious opportunity to express my heartfelt thanks.
> 我想借这个难得的机会表达我衷心的感谢。

4. There was a note of triumph in my voice when I told him that it was there in black and white.

译文：我带着一种胜利者的口吻告诉他那趟车明明白白印在时刻表上。

解析：1）a note of triumph意为"胜利者的腔调"，其中note指"说话的语调"。例：

There was a note of desperation in what he said. 他的话中带有一种绝望的口气。

She noticed a note of sarcasm in his voice. 她注意到他的话中有几分讥讽。

His voice rose to a note of passion. 他的嗓门高起来，语气变得十分激动。

2）in black and white在本句中表"确实，明白无误"，相当于clearly、indeed、no doubt。例：

You should keep this down in black and white. 你应该清清楚楚地把这记下来。

Everything is black and white to Tom; if you are not his friend, you are his enemy.

在汤姆看来，一切都是绝对的；你不是他的朋友，就是他的敌人。

■ 拓 展 篇

Ⅰ.英语趣园

Located on 1,500 acres, Westhaven is off Highway 96 on the West side of Franklin, Tennessee, the county seat of Williamson County just south of Nashville.

Ⅱ.听力快车 🎧

The railway across the roof of the world

They said_____. There were_____, _____, _____that could never support tracks and trains. How could anyone tunnel through rock at -30℃, or_____? But that's the sort of challenge today's China relishes. Next month, three years ahead of schedule, _____will link the garrison town of Golmud in China's "wild west" and the Tibetan capital of Lhasa, strengthening the regime's grip on this troublesome corner of the empire and _____.

Ⅲ.补充阅读

The biggest railroad station in the world

"Yes, the biggest of the hundred great terminal stations of the world." Thus spoke President Cassatt, of the Pennsylvania Railroad, in reply to my question as to whether he "would call it the biggest."

Mastodonic in area, of course, and multimillioned in cost and yearly passenger capacity is this new depot, the largest of the more than one hundred thousand railway stations in civilization. It is the Pennsylvania's new terminal in the heart of New York. The general progress of the whole country made necessary this Titanic structure for passenger traffic, and hence the traveling public will accept it as a matter of course.

A giant of giants

Railroad men, however, see it with eyes more specific, regarding it as a monument erected by the far-seeing administration of President A. J. Cassatt. The new station is one-third larger than the present largest station in the world—Liverpool Street Station, London; one-half larger than the present largest station in the United States—South Station, Boston; and one-quarter larger than the new Grand Central Station now being built for the New York Central in Manhattan.

You could put Madison Square Garden in one corner of the new terminal and the Waldorf-Astoria Hotel in another corner, and still the "Penn" road would have ample room left for all the traffic for which the station is designed, except that to and from Long Island. On the ground occupied by the new station and train-shed there is room for twenty-four cathedrals like that of St. Patrick's, on Fifth Avenue, or room for five hundred ordinary city dwelling-houses, for a few more than that number of dwellings were torn down to secure the site (at a cost of ten million dollars, or one million dollars more than the cost of the site for the South Station, Boston) for what railroad men call the "Great Ambition" of President Cassatt. At least three or four years may elapse before the new station is completed. Meantime, it exists only on paper—in hundreds of plans in the Pennsylvania's main offices at Broad Street Station, Philadelphia.

Only a hole in the ground

The visible beginning of the mammoth station is represented by a vast hole in the ground running from Seventh to Ninth avenues, and from Thirty-First to Thirty-Third Streets, embracing four of the largest blocks in the metropolis, equal to sixteen ordinary blocks, or three blocks larger than the site for the new Grand Central Station. Besides this main area, the company has bought several parcels of adjoining properties, notably the whole Seventh Avenue front facing the new station, just for elbowroom.

The new Pennsylvania station and train-yard will cover twenty-five acres, while the new Grand Central will cover only twenty acres, and the South Station in Boston covers only thirteen acres. Specifically, the station itself will be seven hundred and eighty feet long by four hundred and thirty feet wide, these dimensions not including the train-shed or yard, but only the station building itself. Thirty-Second Street from Seventh to Ninth Avenues will, naturally, be closed forever to the public to accommodate the train service. Everybody will have to go, as it were, around the yard.

100,000,000 passengers a year

Within the station and train-shed will be standing-room for fully three hundred thousand persons, a number equal to five armies like that of the regular military force of our country. Two hundred thousand persons can occupy the same space without any dangerous crowding. To put the passenger capacity of the station in another way, the engineers estimate that the accommodation will be equal to a maximum traffic of one hundred and thirteen thousand arriving and departing travelers per hour, or over a million per day of ten hours.

This would mean a maximum capacity of over three hundred and fifty million a year, or two thousand a minute, or thirty each second, but in their conservative way the engineers divide the maximum by three, thus attaining what will probably be the actual traffic, namely, thirty thousand passengers an hour, or five hundred each minute, or eight each second, which means three hundred thousand in a ten-hour day, or about one hundred million a year.

Therefore, in the first year of the station's existence, the entire populations of the United States, Canada, and Mexico could use it in the ordinary course of travel without discomfort to a single individual patron of the road. Meantime the annual passenger traffic at the South Station, Boston, is less than twenty-five million, while the estimate for the new Grand Central is not more than forty million yearly, or thirteen thousand an hour. Were all the travelers who are to use the Pennsylvania Station in the course of one year to form in line of procession, four abreast, the line would reach from New York to Panama, and it would require a period of three years to pass through the station, stepping at regular military pace.

▪▶ 测 试 篇 ◀▪

I . 单项选择

1. My grandfather, a retired worker, often _____ the past with a feeling of longing and respect.

   （CET-6 05/1）

   A. considers   B. contemplates   C. contrives   D. contacts

2. Failure in a required subject may result in the _____ of a diploma. （CET-6 01/6）

   A. refusal   B. betrayal   C. denial   D. burial

3. Attempts to persuade her to stay after she felt insulted were _____.

   A. in no way   B. on the contrary   C. at a loss   D. of no avail

4. There were no tickets _____ for Friday's performance.

   A. preferable   B. considerable   C. possible   D. available

5. Visitors are asked to _____ with the regulations.

   A. contrast   B. consult   C. comply   D. conflict

6. Salaries for _____ positions seem to be higher than for permanent ones.

   A. legal   B. optional   C. voluntary   D. temporary

7. In my opinion, he's _____ the most imaginative of all the contemporary poets.

   A. in all   B. at best   C. for all   D. by far

8. Convenience foods which are already prepared for cooking are _____ in grocery stores.

   A. ready   B. approachable   C. probable   D. available

9. In general, the amount that a student spends for housing should be held to one-fifth the total _____ for living expenses.

   A. acceptable   B. available   C. advisable   D. applicable

10. Her fluency in English gives her an advantage _____ other girls for the job.

    A. above   B. over   C. than   D. with

Ⅱ. 翻译

11. 经过多年来的适应，我习惯了北京的噪音、堵车、空气污染。（condition）

12. 一个英语好的人在找一份收入较高的工作时比其他人更有优势。（have advantage over）

13. 中国对小泉首相参拜靖国神社提出严重抗议。（lodge a serious protest against）

14. 家长会在出差错的时候，不分青红皂白地批评最大的孩子。（all too easy to do）

15. 在葬礼上，村民才恍然大悟，原来农场上的鬼是另有其人。（it dawns on...）

拓展篇

The railway across the roof of the world

They said it was impossible to build a railway to Tibet. There were 5,000m-high mountains to climb, 12km-wide valleys to bridge, hundreds of kilometres of ice and slush that could never support tracks and trains. How could anyone tunnel through rock at -30℃, or lay rails when the least exertion sends you reaching for the oxygen bottle? But that's the sort of challenge today's China relishes. Next month, three years ahead of schedule, more than 1,000 km of fresh track will link the garrison town of Golmud in China's "wild west" and the Tibetan capital of Lhasa, strengthening the regime's grip on this troublesome corner of the empire and confirming its status as a technological superpower.

测试篇

1-5 BCDDC　　6-10 DDDBB

11. After years of conditioning, I'm used to the noise, traffic jam, and air pollution in Beijing.

12. A man with a good command of English will have an advantage over others in seeking for a well-paid job.

13. China lodged a serious protest against Junichiro Koizumi's visiting Yasukuni Shrine.

14. It is all too easy for parents to reprimand their eldest kid when something does go wrong.

15. On the funeral, it suddenly dawned on the villagers that there was someone else on the farm rather than the ghost.

Lesson 38. The first calendar

积累篇

Ⅰ. 振振有"词"

1. Up to now, historians have <u>assumed</u> that calendars <u>came into being</u> with the advent of agriculture.

形似词联想记忆：
assume 认为
presume 假设；认为
consume 消费
resume 恢复
costume 服装

come into being 形成
come into existence 出现
come into sight 呈现，出现
come into fashion 流行起来
come into a fortune 继承遗产
come into one's own 发挥本领

常用的写作开篇短语：
with the advent of... 随着…的出现
with the development of... 随着…的发展
with the advance of... 随着…的进步
with the increase of... 随着…的增长
with the decrease of... 随着…的下降

2. <u>What is more</u>, they will not have to <u>rely solely on</u> the written word.

表递进关系的连接词：
what is more 而且
in addition 另外
additionally 另外
furthermore 甚至
moreover 甚至
besides 此外

rely on... 依靠…
depend on... 依赖…
bank on... 指望…
lean on... 依靠…
pin high hopes on... 对…寄予厚望
place high expectations on... 对…充满期待

Ⅱ. 现身说"法"：插入语结构

They will be able, as it were, to see and hear us in action.（as it were是独立成分，语法上称为插入语结构）他们好像能够观看我们做事，倾听我们说话。

一般而言，插入语有以下几种形式：

1. 单个词

Unquestionably, this decision is unwise. 毫无疑问，这个决定不明智。

Frankly, I don't agree with you. 说实话，我不同意你的看法。

Hence he will not trust anyone. 从此以后，他不会相信任何人。

2. -ing短语

Considering the amount she paid, he was more dear in more ways than one.
考虑到她花的那笔钱，他的珍贵就具有双重意义了。

Generally speaking, this proposal is feasible. 总体而言，这个建议是可行的。

3. 不定式短语

To do this, you must be as knowledgable as the dealer. 要做到这一点，你就得和商家一样懂行。

To be honest, I don't like this style. 说实话，我不喜欢这种样式。

4. 介词短语

To my surprise, he turned up at the party. 令我吃惊的是，他在派对上露面了。

In this way, he made a big sum of money. 他以这种方式赚了一大笔钱。

5. 短句

This project must be suspended, I argue. 我认为，这个项目必须中止。

What's more, you are expected to have responsibility. 而且，你还要有责任心。

Ⅲ. 说"文"解"字"

1. Future historians will be in a unique position when they come to record the history of our own times.

译文：未来的历史学家在写我们这一段历史的时候会处于得天独厚的地位。

解析：1）be in a position to do sth.意为"有能力、权利做…"。例：

The professor is in a position to comment on this issue. 这位教授有资格对此事做出评判。

> **联想记忆**
>
> be in a better position to do sth. 更有资格做…   be in no position to do sth. 没有资格做…
>
> be in an awkward position 处境尴尬   be in an embarrassing position 处境为难
>
> be in a subtle position 处境微妙

2）come to do sth. 表"逐步…"。例：

I come to realize that he really loves his child. 我渐渐知道他真的很爱自己的孩子。

He came to learn how important the choice was to him.

他终于认识到这个选择对于自己多么重要。

2. They will be able, as it were, to see and hear us in action.

译文：他们好像能够观看我们做事，倾听我们说话。

解析：as it were在句中作插入语，意思相似于seemingly, it appears, 与as it is（实际上）意义不同。例：

He became, as it were, a man without a country. 他似乎成了一个无国籍的人。

I thought things would get better, but as it is, they are getting worse.

我原以为情况会改善，但事实上情况越来越糟。

3. Even seemingly insignificant remains can shed interesting light on the history of early man.

译文：即使看起来微不足道的遗物，也可能揭示人类早期历史中的一些有趣的内容。

解析：shed/throw light on...表"揭示，解释，使…显现"，在light前可加形容词修饰。例：

The investigation shed/threw new light on the mystery. 调查报告使人进一步了解了这个疑案。

His hypothesis shed/threw a different light on the formation of rock.

他的假说对于岩石的形成做了不同的解释。

拓 展 篇

I . 英语趣园

History of the calendar

The purpose of the calendar is to reckon past or future time, to show how many days until a certain event takes place—the harvest or a religious festival—or how long since something important happened. The earliest calendars must have been strongly influenced by the geographical location of the people who made them. In colder countries, the concept of the year was determined by the seasons, specifically by the end of winter. But in warmer countries, where the seasons are less pronounced, the Moon became the basic unit for time reckoning; an old Jewish book says "the Moon was created for the counting of the days."

Most of the oldest calendars were lunar calendars, based on the time interval from one new moon to the next—a so-called lunation. But even in a warm climate there are annual events that pay no attention to the phases of the Moon. In some areas it was a rainy season; in Egypt it was the annual flooding of the Nile River. The calendar had to account for these yearly events as well.

II . 听力快车

_____, there were cultures, but not civilizations. _____ created societies, constructed houses, lived in villages, _____, farmed, made pottery, wove cloth, and created languages. But unlike more _____, they did not build cities, read, or write. Cities are the _____ because with them came other civilizing elements, including differentiation of classes and employment, _____, monumental architecture, and the formation of states and empires.

III . 补充阅读

Why do we study history?

Six years ago I saw the eminent historian Arthur Schlesinger Jr. speak of his theories on 30-year cycles of history. After the lecture he fielded some questions from the audience, the last one being "Why do we study history?" I sat in my chair, for his question invariably leads to a response filled with sanctimonious platitudes, or pithy quotations by George Bancroft, George Santayana, or Woodrow Wilson. Instead Schlesinger looked down and replied matter-of-factly, "First of all it's a lot of fun."

I was taken aback; in academic circles fun is not supposed to be part of the equation, rewarding, important, essential but certainly not fun. Fun trivializes the subject matter, stunts one's intellectual growth and flies in the face of our puritan tradition of grim self-determination. After all, the purpose of teaching history and social studies in secondary schools is to build a responsible citizenry for the republic—quite serious business.

I also felt exposed, for Schlesinger had found me out. I didn't become a history teacher because I thought it important; I became a history teacher because there's nothing more fun than history. I was preventing a confrontation with my great fear in life-boredom—by casting my lot with the story of humankind. And having a hell of a time, I might add.

Of course I tried to conceal my enjoyment from those in the profession who saw teaching as a mission, since exuberance in the workplace implies a lack of seriousness, making one suspect by the morally inclined. Also I did no want to make friends and relatives, who put their noses to the grindstone in more commercial pursuits, feel bad. Schlesinger confirmed my inclinations, and since then, I have never doubted what history should be.

Unfortunately history as subject matter has joined the ranks of the other disciplines in which the focus is on factual inputs and outputs. A student learns the facts and returns the information on a quiz or test. This is not all the teachers' fault, for there is much to cover.

In U.S. history we have to get from Columbus to the end of the cold war; in world history we have to follow human progress from prehistory through the modern era. This includes not only the great people and great events, but the new social history that examines how people lived. At the same time we teach skills, research, analysis, synthesis and how to support an argument in a spirited essay. The problem is that with all the knowledge we try to put into students' heads, the skills we're trying to develop are more applicable to law school—we lose the narrative, the ability to see history as story.

There is no better story than history. The cast of characters in the human race gives us plenty of sex, violence and knavery, with occasional acts of genius and nobility that propel the race forward in spite of itself. In fiction, who could come up with people as intrinsically good as Jesus, Moses, Muhammad and the Buddha? Who do we find today as noble as Socrates, Abraham Lincoln, Chief Joseph, Clara Barton or Frederick Douglass? Who has the complexities of nature that were King David or Thomas Jefferson? How can we contemplate through the imagination the horrors that befell the 14th and 20th centuries?

Yet we continue to bore students with meaningless multiple-choice quizzes and essays that emphasize cause-effect relationships such as "Examine the effects of the Enclosure Acts on the English industrial revolution," or "compare and contrast the emergence of the welfare state in 19th-century Britain and France". Who cares? Where is the story and how much fun is this?

No doubt history has to include rational analysis to strengthen one's ability to make logical conclusions, create intellectual order out of the material and to develop a healthy skepticism. However, history is also the intuitive, the visceral, and the imaginative. Otherwise it becomes just another subject geared toward inputs and outputs. No wonder we lose students.

I want a story. I want to know how Themistocles outsmarted the Persian navy at Salamis. I want to know about Henry V and his longbow men at Agincourt. Tell me about the terror one felt in looking over the one-mile field before Pickett's Charge, or being thrown out of a landing craft on a Normandy beach. Don't make it easy on me—make me fell the guilt and shame of owning slaves in the plantation South or exploiting immigrant workers in late 19th-century America. Inspire me with stories about courage and sacrifice so that when I hit my own Thermopylae somehow I can stand fast.

And don't lie to me. The slave South was not *Gone With the Wind* and the frontier was not *Dances With the Wolves*. Tell me the story with integrity like Solomon Northup's *Twelve Years a Slave*. Simon Schama's chronicle of the French Revolution, *Citizens*, as with Michael Shaara's depiction of Gettysburg in *The Killer Angels* or with Joanna Stratton's *Pioneer Woman*, on the hardship faced by families on his Civil War epic, and Steven Spielberg's version of *Schindler's List* all capture a riveting story with honesty and clarity.

We can all share in the glory and disasters that are our own. Refusing to share in either risks the loss of our own humanity, for the lens to our individual soul becomes unfocused. Kenneth Clark said that we need to learn from history because it is ourselves. But without a leap of the imagination and a willingness to be part of the collective human race, there is little that history can do for us. I want to experience that true story and to make the ultimate connection with someone in another place and time. If I'm careful, I might in the process learn a little more about who I am. And God forbid, I might have more fun than academia should allow. But don't tell anyone.

测 试 篇

I . 单项选择

1. One of the examination questions _____ me completely and I couldn't answer it.　　（CET-6 04/1）
   A. baffled　　　　　B. mingled　　　　C. provoked　　　　D. diverted
2. How much of your country's electrical supply is _____ from water power?　　（CET-6 03/1）
   A. deduced　　　　　B. detached　　　　C. derived　　　　D. declined
3. When the farmers visited the city for the first time, they were _____ by its complicated traffic system.
   　　　　　　　　　　　　　　　　　　　　　　　　　　　　（CET-6 01/6）
   A. evoked　　　　　B. bewildered　　　　C. diverted　　　　D. undermined
4. Just as a book is often judged _____ by the quality and appearance of its cover, a person is judged immediately by his appearance.
   A. previously　　　　B. uniquely　　　　C. outwardly　　　　D. initially
5. When he realized he had been _____ to sign the contract by intrigue, he threatened to start legal proceedings to cancel the agreement.
   A. elicited　　　　　B. excited　　　　C. deduced　　　　D. induced
6. It is believed that the feeding patterns parents _____ on their children can determine their adolescent and adult eating habits.　　　　　　　　　　　　　　　　　　（CET-6 05/12）
   A. compel　　　　　B. impose　　　　C. evoke　　　　D. necessitate
7. She expressed her strong determination that nothing could _____ her to give up her career as a teacher.
   A. reduce　　　　　B. deduce　　　　C. attract　　　　D. induce
8. He was proud of being chosen to participate in the game and he _____ us that he would try as hard as possible.
   A. insured　　　　　B. guaranteed　　　　C. assumed　　　　D. assured
9. Many people like white color as it is a _____ of purity.
   A. symbol　　　　　B. sign　　　　C. signal　　　　D. symptom
10. Small as it is, the ant is as much a creature as _____ all other animals on earth.
    A. are　　　　　　B. do　　　　C. is　　　　D. have

II . 翻译

11. 我被方向搞得晕头转向。（be bewildered）
12. 随着电视，尤其是因特网的问世，它们已经取代了印刷的许多功能。（with the advent of）

13. 城市儿童在入学接受教育方面处在一种让人羡慕的境况。（in an enviable position）
14. 天空仿佛被一块黑幕遮住一般。（as it were）
15. 大量信息以杂志和电视广告的方式对人们进行狂轰滥炸。（in the form of）

 答 案

拓展篇

Before about 3500 B.C., there were cultures, but not civilizations. Prehistoric men and women created societies, constructed houses, lived in villages, hunted and fished, farmed, made pottery, wove cloth, and created languages. But unlike more advanced peoples, they did not build cities, read, or write. Cities are the cornerstone of civilized life because with them came other civilizing elements, including differentiation of classes and employment, sophisticated religious and political systems, monumental architecture, and the formation of states and empires.

测试篇

1-5 ACBDD   6-10 BDDAA

11. I was bewildered at the directions.

12. With the advent of TV, especially Internet, they have taken many of the functions once served by print.

13. Urban children will be in an enviable position when they come to receive education.

14. The sky was covered, as it were, with a black curtain.

15. People are bombarded with information in the form of magazines and TV advertising.

Lesson Nothing to worry about

积累篇

I. 振振有"词"

1. Even though the road was littered with boulders and pitted with holes, Bruce was not in the least perturbed.

---

be littered with... 布满···
be covered with... 覆盖着···
be scattered with... 散落着···
be dotted with... 点缀着
be filled with... 充满···
be stuffed with... 塞满···

---

be pitted with holes
坑坑洼洼的
A fall in the pit, a gain in the wit.
吃一堑，长一智。
pit one's wits against sb.
与某人斗智

---

not in the least 一点也不
not in the slight 一点也不
not the least bit 丝毫也不
by no means 绝不
not...any more 不再

---

2. The wheels scooped up stones which hammered ominously under the car.

---

scoop up stones 卷起石头
scoop the other newspapers
比其他报纸抢发消息
winkle new meanings
挖掘新内容
tap one's potential 挖掘潜能
unearth an ancient tomb 挖掘古墓

---

hammer 重重击打
strike 击打
pound 使劲敲打
knock 敲门
tap 轻敲
pat 轻拍
click 点击

---

ominous 不祥的
auspicious 吉利的
inauspicious 不吉利的
superstitious 迷信的
suspicious 多疑的

---

3. In response to renewed pleadings, Bruce stopped.

---

in response to... 对···回应
respond to... 回答···
give feedback on... 对···做出反馈
cause tremendous concern
引起极大关注
cause great sensation
引起极大轰动

---

renew 更新
renew a book 续借书
renew a passport 续签护照
renew a driving license
更换驾照
renew a pleading
再次请求

---

plead 请求
plead for sth. 要求···
plead with sb. to do sth. 央求某人做···
plead for sb. 为某人辩护
plead guilty 认罪
make a plea with sb. for sth. 请求某人···
on the plea of sth. 以···为借口

---

4. Bruce charged at it, but in the middle, the car came to a grinding halt.

英语中表"向…猛扑, 攻击"的短语多为V+prep. 结构：

charge at... 向…冲来

fly at... 向…扑来

jump at... 向…扑来

come at... 向…袭击过来

shoot at... 向…瞄准

英语中常用的动词扩展为动词短语的模式：

halt（停止）扩展为 come to a(n) ... halt

stop（停止）扩展为 come to a(n) ... stop

end（结束）扩展为 come to a(n) ... end

fail（失败）扩展为 come to a(n) ... failure

succeed（成功）扩展为 come to a(n) ... success

Ⅱ. 现身说"法": **in the least**强调含有**not**的否定句

Bruce was not in the least perturbed.

布鲁斯一点儿也不慌乱。

1. in the least意为"一点儿", 表程度, 用于强调not否定句。与此类似的短语还有：in the slightest, the least bit, a bit等。例：

I don't really envy you in the least. 我一点儿也不羡慕你。

Neither of the assistants was the slightest repentant afterwards. 两位助手随后都不感到懊悔。

They are not a bit interested. 他们一点儿也不感兴趣。

2. 如果in the least和in the slightest与动词连用时, 要紧跟在动词之后；如果动词有宾语, 则要置于宾语之后。例：

The weather hasn't improved in the least. 天气一点儿也没好转。

I don't want her advice in the slightest. 我根本不想听她的建议。

3. the least bit和a bit只与形容词连用, 置于形容词之前。例：

She is not the least bit buoyant. 她一点儿也不开心。

I'm not a bit worried. 我一点儿也不担心。

Ⅲ. 说"文"解"字"

1. The rough road across the plain was so bad that we tried to get Bruce to drive back to the village we had come from.

译文：穿越平原的路面高低不平, 开车走了不远, 路面愈加崎岖, 我们想劝说布鲁斯开回到出发的那个小镇。

解析：get sb. to do sth.本指"让某人做某事", 根据情境可译为"劝说某人做某事", 相当于persuade sb. to do sth.. 这就是词汇在上下文中的活用现象。其他活用的例子有：

He talked me into abandoning this plan. (talk活用为"劝说", 相当于persuade)

他劝我放弃那个计划。

I spent 8 hours in the office. (spend活用为"工作", 相当于work) 我在办公室里工作了8个小时。

The two boxers met on another occasion. (meet活用为"打斗", 相当于fight)

两位拳手随后又进行了一次决斗。

2. It was not that Bruce always underestimated difficulties. He simply had no sense of danger at all.

译文：不是说布鲁斯总是低估困难，而是他根本就没有一点儿危险感。

解析：这两句话看似无关，实则是一个整体，起连接作用的是It was not that... but, 即第二句前面省略了but。因此，恢复原状的完整形式是：It was not that Bruce always underestimated difficulties, but that he simply had no sense of danger at all.这种省略多见于口语，正式写作时补全为宜。例：

It is not that she doesn't take to fashion clothes, but that she can't afford them.

不是说她不喜欢高档服饰，而是她买不起。

3. The wheels scooped up stones which hammered ominously under the car.

译文：车轮卷起石块敲击着车身，发出不祥的声音。

解析：ominous意为"不吉祥的"，本指人对于事物产生的感觉，但在这里活用在事物的身上，这种用法被称为转类现象（transferred epithet），这类形容词也随之被称为被称为转类形容词。例：

He spent a miserable day in bed.（miserable为转类现象）

他在床上度过了痛苦的一天。

The scientist made a happy discovery of a special kind of metal.（happy为转类现象）

这位科学家幸运地发现了一种特别的金属。

The man bid a sad farewell to his newly-wedded wife.（sad为转类现象）

这位男子痛苦地与新婚妻子告别。

4. What a relief it was when the boulders suddenly disappeared.

译文：突然大石块不见了，我们终于长长地舒了口气。

解析：这是一个以what引导的感叹句。也可改写为以how引导的下面两种模式：

How relieving it was when the boulders suddenly disappeared.

How relieved we were when the boulders suddenly disappeared.

5. A yellow light on the dash board flashed angrily.

译文：仪表盘上一盏黄灯愤怒地闪烁着。

解析：这里的angrily也属于上面讲解3中的转类现象。

拓 展 篇

Ⅰ.英语趣园

Detroit is a city in the US state of Michigan. It is an important center for making cars, and the Ford, General Motors, and Chrysler（or present-day Daimler Chrysler）car companies are all based there. Hence, one of the 29 NBA teams is well-known as Detroit Pistons.

Ⅱ.听力快车

Learning driving

John: First, _____. Now start the engine.

David: How do I do that?

John: _____.

David: I see. And what do I do next?

John: _____.

David: My left foot or my right?

John: Your left foot, of course.

David: And I press it down?

John: That's right. Press it down, but don't put your foot on the accelerator yet. Now...

David: _____. Oh! The car has stopped.

John: Stupid! I've already told you a hundred times._____.

Ⅲ. 补充阅读

Henry Ford（1863~1947）

Henry Ford's parents left Ireland during the potato famine and settled in the Detroit area in the 1840s. Ford was born in what is now Dearborn, Michigan. His formal education was limited, but even as a youngster, he was handy with machinery. He worked for the Detroit Edison Company, advancing from machine-shop apprentice to chief engineer. In 1893, Ford built a gasoline engine, and within a few years, an automobile, still a novelty item of the rich or do-it-yourself engineers.

In 1899 Ford left Edison to help run the Detroit Automobile Company. Cars were still built essentially one at a time. Ford hoped to incorporate ideas from other industries — standardized parts as Eli Whitney had used with gun manufacturing, or assembly line methods George Eastman tried in photo processing — to make the process more efficient. This idea struck others in his field as nutty, so before long, Ford quit Detroit Automobile Company and began to build his own racing cars. They were good enough to attract backers and even partners, and in 1903, he set up the Ford Motor Company.

He still met resistance to his ideas for mass production of a car the average worker could afford. But he stuck to his goal and finally in 1908, began production of the Model T. Ford gradually adapted the production line until in 1913, his plant incorporated the first moving assembly line. Demand for the affordable car soared even as production went up: before Ford stopped making the model T in 1927. Fifteen million had been sold, and Ford had become the leading auto manufacturer in the country. In addition to the moving assembly line, Ford revolutionized the auto industry by increasing the pay and decreasing the hours of his employees, ensuring he could get enough and the best workers. During the Model T era, Ford bought out his shareholders so he had complete financial control of the now vast corporation. He continued to innovate, but competitors (growing more powerful though fewer in number) began to cut into Ford's market share.

Ford became interested in politics and as a successful and powerful business leader, was sometimes a participant in political affairs. In 1915, he funded a trip to Europe, where World War I was raging. He and about 170 others went — without government support or approval — to seek peace. The war lasted another three years. After the war Ford ran unsuccessfully for the Senate on the Democratic ticket. He never ran again, but was always outspoken on political subjects. He violently opposed labor organizations and actively worked against the United Auto Workers trying to unionize his plants. His criticism of Jews and a certain tolerance of German nationalism during World War II have left him with the reputation of an anti-Semite.

Ford and his family spent a good deal of time and money on charitable work. They set up an historical museum in Greenfield Village, Michigan, and most notably set up the Ford Foundation, which provides grants for research, education, and development.

▪▶ 测 试 篇 ◀▪

I. 单项选择

1. The price of the coal will vary according to how far it has to be transported and how expensive the freight _____ are. (CET-6 02/1)

   A. payments   B. charges   C. funds   D. prices

2. Not having a good command of English can be a serious _____ preventing you from achieving your goals.

   A. obstacle   B. fault   C. offense   D. distress

3. Deserts and high mountains have always been a _____ to the movement of people from place to place.

   A. barrier   B. fence   C. prevention   D. jam

4. He could not _____ ignorance as his excuse; he should have known what was happening in his department.

   A. petition   B. plead   C. resort   D. reproach

5. Can you give me even the _____ clue as to where her son might be?

   A. simplest   B. slightest   C. least   D. utmost

6. Although many people view conflict as bad, conflict is sometimes useful _____ it forces people to test the relative merits of their attitudes and behaviors.

   A. by which   B. to which   C. in that   D. so that

7. There was such a long line at the exhibition _____ we had to wait for about half an hour.

   A. as   B. that   C. so   D. hence

8. The opening between the rocks was very narrow, but the boys managed to _____ through.

   A. press   B. squeeze   C. stretch   D. leap

9. It wasn't such a good dinner _____ she had promised us.

   A. that   B. which   C. as   D. what

10. It is a pity that we should stay at home when we have _____ weather.

   A. so fine   B. such a fine   C. such fine   D. so fine a

II. 翻译

11. 他的衣服上锈迹斑斑。（be pitted with）

12. 天黑得吓人。（ominously...）

13. 给车挂上低速档。（in low gear）

14. 如果你稍微迟到一会儿，一点关系也没有。（not in the least...）

15. 你这次迁就了他，他下一次会要求更多。（give way to）

答 案

拓展篇

Learning driving

John:　First, <u>make sure the car is out of gear</u>. Now start the engine.

David: How do I do that?

John:　<u>Just turn the key lightly</u>.

David: I see. And what do I do next?

John:　<u>Put your foot on the clutch</u>.

David: My left foot or my right?

John:　Your left foot, of course.

David: And I press it down?

John:　That's right. Press it down, but don't put your foot on the accelerator yet. Now...

David: <u>I've put it on the gear</u>. Oh! The car has stopped.

John:　Stupid! I've already told you a hundred times. <u>Don't take your foot off the clutch before you've put it onto the gear</u>.

测试篇

1-5 BAABB　　　　　6-10 CBBCC

11. His clothes were pitted with corrosion.

12. The sky looked ominously dark.

13. Put the car in a low gear.

14. It doesn't matter in the least if you are a bit late.

15. If you give way to him this time, he will make a further demand next time.

Lesson 40. Who's who

积 累 篇

I.振振有"词"

1. <u>It has never been explained why</u> university students seem to enjoy <u>practical jokes</u> more than anyone else.

常用的写作开篇句型：

It has never been explained why... 谁也说不清···
It is still unclear why... ···尚不清楚
It is still a mystery why... ···仍是不解之谜
It is beyond me that/why... 我对···毫不理解
It is still an unknown fact that... ···仍旧不为人知

practical joke 恶作剧
play a joke on sb. 开某人的玩笑
make a spectacle of sb. 使某人出洋相
put up a poor show 表现很差
a laughingstock 笑柄
disgrace sb. 使某人丢脸

2. Inviting the fire brigade to <u>put out</u> a nonexistent fire is a crude form of deception which no <u>self-respecting</u> student would ever <u>indulge in</u>.

self-respecting 自尊的
self-esteeming 自重的
self-reliant 自立的
self-confident 自信的
self-sufficient 自给自足的
self-supporting 自食其力的
self-disciplined 自律的

put out a fire 扑灭火焰
hand out sth. 分发···
mete out reward/punishment 给予奖励/惩罚
turn out sth. 生产···
map out sth. 制定···
lay out sth. 布局···，设计···

indulge in sth. 从事···；沉迷于···
abandon oneself to sth. 放纵于···
resign oneself to sth. 沉迷于···
be addicted to sth. 对···成瘾
give free rein to sth. 沉迷于···

3. <u>Shortly afterwards</u>, four more policemen arrived and <u>remonstrated with</u> the workmen.

shortly afterwards 随后
shortly after 不久
soon afterwards 很快
before long 不久之后
in no time 立刻

remonstrate with sb. on sth.
就某事规劝某人
persuade sb. to do sth. 劝说某人做···
talk sb. into doing sth. 劝说某人做···

sweet talk sb. into doing sth.
甜言蜜语劝某人做···
coax sb. into doing sth. 哄骗某人做···
mislead sb. into doing sth. 误导某人做···

II. 现身说"法": 关系副词引导的主语从句

> It has never been explained why university students seem to enjoy practical jokes more than anyone else. (关系副词why引导主语从句)
> 谁也说不清为什么大学生好像比任何人都喜欢搞恶作剧。

1. 能够引导主语从句的关系副词有: when, where, how, whenever, wherever, however。一般而言, 它们在引导主语从句时具有以下特点: 通常含有疑问意义; 在从句中充当状语; 均不能省略。

2. 实际情况中, 为了保持句子结构的平衡关系, 会用it作形式主语, 代替上述关系副词引导的主语从句。本文例句即是这种情况。例:

   It makes no difference whether you turn up or not. 你来不来无所谓。

   It is still unknown how the universe came into existence. 宇宙如何形成尚未有定论。

3. it作形式主语的常见句型还有:

   1) It+be+-ed分词+that从句

   It must be pointed out that the statistics are inaccurate. 必须指出的是, 那些数据不准确。

   2) It+be+形容词+that从句

   It is important that you submit these materials Thursday. 你们要在周四把材料交上来, 这一点很重要。

   3) It+名词+that从句

   It is no wonder that he won the prize. 他赢得了大奖, 这毫不为奇。

III. 说"文"解"字"

1. Students often create amusing situations which are funny to everyone except the victims.

   译文: 大学生经常制造一些可笑的场景使大家笑上一场, 当然受害者是笑不出来的。

   解析: 1) 本句中的amusing和funny属于同义词, 这是写作中常采用的同义词替换现象, 以使行文更加灵活多变。例:

   Before long a man arrived. Shortly after, an old woman came along. (before long和shortly after属于同义替换) 一会儿, 一位男士到了。不久, 一位老妇人也来了。

   2) except在本句也可替换成but, 但后者更多是和以any-开头的四个不定代词和副词构成固定用法, 即anyone but, anybody but, anything but, anywhere but。例:

   She never revealed the secret to anyone but her sister.

   除了妹妹以外, 她从未向任何人吐露过这个秘密。

   He has never been to anywhere but his hometown. 除了家乡, 他哪里也没去过。

   You can never speak about anything but money to him. 除了金钱, 你无法和他谈任何东西。

2. Both the police and the workmen were grateful to the student for this piece of advance information.

   译文: 警察与工人都对那个学生事先通报消息表示感谢。

   解析: 1) be grateful to sb. for sth.是一固定短语, 意为"因为某事感谢某人"。其同义结构有:

be thankful to sb. for sth.	be indebted to sb.
express one's gratitude to sb. for sth. (正式)	be obliged to sb. (正式)

   2) advance在这里是形容词, 意为"预先的", 注意同以下几个词的区别:

   advanced technologies (advanced为形容词) 先进的技术

Medicine has advanced greatly. (advance为动词) 医学已大有发展。

Medical advances are important to human evolution. (advance为名词)

医学进步对人类的发展至关重要。

3. At this, **the police pointed out ironically that this would hardly be necessary as the men were already under arrest.**

译文：听到此话，警察讥讽地说，这大可不必，因为他们已经被捕了。

解析：1) at this中的at表示"听到"，参看22课with this (说着话) 及29课at a Russian joke。

2) be under arrest意为"被捕"，注意under实际替代了常规用法中被动语态的表达方式。这是写作中的一种变通手段。例：

The road is under construction. (代替being constructed) 这条路正在建设。

The car is under repair. (代替being repaired) 这辆车正在修理。

The child is under ever-present attention. (代替being attended)

这个孩子得到了无刻不在的关爱。

拓 展 篇

Ⅰ.英语趣园

> *The boy who cried wolf* was taken from Aesop's Fables. A shepherd boy sounded a false alarm so many times that, when at last he sounded a genuine alarm, no one would come to his help.

Ⅱ.听力快车

The following paragraph will be read to you slowly. Listen to it twice, and while listening write as much and as closely to the original text as you can.

_____

_____

_____

_____

Ⅲ.补充阅读

> Unlike most of the other nonfoolish holidays, the history of April Fool's Day, sometimes called All Fool's Day, is not totally clear. There really wasn't a "first April Fool's Day" that can be pinpointed on the calendar. Some believe it sort of evolved simultaneously in several cultures from celebrations involving the first day of spring.
>
> The closest point in time that can be identified as the beginning of this tradition was in 1582, in France. Prior to that year, the new year was celebrated for eight days, beginning on March 25. The celebration culminated on April 1. With the reform of the calendar under Charles IX, the Gregorian Calendar was introduced, and New Year's Day was moved to January 1.
>
> However, communications being what they were in the days when news traveled by foot, many people did not receive the news for several years. Others, the more obstinate crowd, refused to accept the new calendar and continued to celebrate the new year on April 1. These backward folk were labeled

as "fools" by the general populace. They were subject to some ridicule, and were often sent on "fools errands" or were made the butt of other practical jokes.

This harassment evolved, over time, into a tradition of prank-playing on the first day of April. The tradition eventually spread to England and Scotland in the eighteenth century. It was later introduced to the American colonies of both the English and French. April Fool's Day thus developed into an international fun fest, so to speak, with different nationalities specializing in their own brand of humor at the expense of their friends and families.

In Scotland, for example, April Fool's Day is actually celebrated for two days. The second day is devoted to pranks involving the posterior region of the body. It is called Taily Day. The origin of the "kick me" sign can be traced to this observance.

Pranks performed on April Fool's Day range from the simple (such as saying, "Your shoe's untied!") to the elaborate. Setting a roommate's alarm clock back an hour is a common gag. Whatever the prank, the trickster usually ends it by yelling to his victim, "April Fools!"

Practical jokes are a common practice on April Fool's Day. Sometimes, elaborate practical jokes are played on friends or relatives that last the entire day. The news media even gets involved. For instance, a British short film once shown on April Fool's Day was a fairly detailed documentary about "spaghetti farmers" and how they harvest their crop from the spaghetti trees.

April Fool's Day is a "for-fun-only" observance. Nobody is expected to buy gifts or to take their "significant other" out to eat in a fancy restaurant. Nobody gets off work or school. It's simply a fun little holiday, but a holiday on which one must remain forever vigilant, for he may be the next April Fool!

▪▶ 测 试 篇 ◀▪

I.单项选择

1. The police set a _____ to catch the thieves.
   A. plan   B. device   C. trap   D. trick
2. I know you've got a smooth tongue, so don't talk me _____ buying it
   A. away   B. down   C. out   D. into
3. On weekends my grandma usually _____ a glass of wine.
   A. subscribes to   B. engages in   C. hangs on   D. indulges in
4. The circus has always been very popular because it _____ both the old and the young.
   A. facilitates   B. fascinates   C. immerses   D. indulges
5. Most broadcasters maintain that TV has been unfairly criticized and argue that the power of the medium is _____ .
   A. granted   B. implied   C. exaggerated   D. remedied
6. Certain programs work better for some _____ for others.
   A. and   B. than   C. as   D. but
7. Not that John doesn't want to help you, _____ it's beyond his power.
   A. but that   B. for that   C. and that   D. in that
8. He might have been killed _____ the arrival of the police.
   A. except for   B. but for   C. with   D. for
9. If you want this painkiller, you'll have to ask the doctor for a _____ .
   A. transaction   B. permit   C. settlement   D. prescription

10. Had he worked harder, he _____ the exams.

    A. must have got through   B. would have got through

    C. permitted are freshmen   D. are permitted freshmen

Ⅱ. 翻译

11. 一个寒冷的冬日，我让自己舒舒服服地小睡了一会儿。（indulge oneself in）

12. 要打扰别人的时候，提前说一声对不起。（advance）

13. 美国获得了在伊拉克境内开采石油的权利。（grant permission）

14. 谁也说不清楚为什么许多人宁愿放弃高薪，也要获得成为白领的殊荣。（it has never been explained why...）

15. 核武器对世界和平构成了威胁。（pose a threat to）

拓展篇

The boy who cried wolf

    Once upon a time there was a very naughty shepherd boy. He often fell asleep while he was watching his sheep. And he told lies. The villagers shook their heads and said, "That boy will come to a bad end."

    One day, when he was feeling very bored, the boy decided to play a practical joke on the villagers. He ran down the hill. "Wolf, wolf!" he cried. "Help, come quickly. Wolf!" All the villagers seized their spears and ran to help him. But there was no wolf. "He heard you," the naughty boy lied, "and ran away." When everyone had gone, he started to laugh.

    Three weeks later, when he was feeling very bored indeed, he decided to play the same trick again. "Wolf, wolf!" he shouted. "Help, come quickly. Wolf!" Most of the villagers hurried to help him. This time the boy laughed at them. "Ha, ha. There wasn't a wolf," he said. "What a good joke!" The villagers were very angry. "Lies are not jokes," they said.

    Two days later the boy woke up suddenly. He had fallen asleep in the afternoon sun. What was that big dark animal coming towards his flock? Suddenly it seized a lamb. "Wolf!" screamed the boy. "Wolf! Help, come quickly. Wolf!" But none of the villagers came to help him. He screamed again. The wolf heard him and licked its lips. "I like lamb," it thought, "but shepherd boy tastes much nicer."

    When the shepherd boy didn't come home that night, some of the villagers went to look for him. They found a few bones.

测试篇

1-5 CDDBA   6-10 BABDB

11. I indulged myself in a short sleep on a cold winter day.

12. "Excuse me" is used as an advance apology for troubling someone.

13. USA was granted permission to exploit oil in Iraq.

14. It has never been explained why so many people are willing to sacrifice higher pay for the privilege of becoming white color workers.

15. Nuclear weapons pose a real threat to the world peace.

Lesson 41. Illusions of pastoral peace

积累篇

I. 振振有"词"

1. Though they <u>extol</u> the virtues of the <u>peaceful</u> life, only one of them has ever gone to <u>live in the country</u>...

extol (*fml.*) 赞美	用于描述生活的优美词汇：	表示居住不同区域的短语：
eulogize (*fml.*) 称颂	peaceful 宁静的	live in the country 住在乡村
commend (*fml.*) 称赞	quiet 安静的	live in the rural area 住在农村
pedestal (*fml.*) 赞颂	serene (*fml.*) 静谧的	live in the suburb 住在郊区
praise highly 高度赞扬	tranquil (*fml.*) 幽静的	live on the outskirts 住在市郊
pour praise on 大肆赞扬	harmonious 祥和的	live in the city 住在城市
		live in the city proper 住在市区

2. Yet they always <u>go into raptures</u> at the mere <u>mention of</u> the country.

go into raptures 狂喜	at the mention of... 一提及…
go into ecstasies 欣喜若狂	at the thought/idea of... 一想到…
be transported with joy 欣喜若狂	at the sight of... 一见到…
be in high spirits 兴高采烈	at the sound of... 一听到…
be in great form 兴高采烈	at the touch of... 一接触到…
tread on air 欢天喜地，得意洋洋	

3. Even he still lives under the <u>illusion</u> that country life is <u>somehow</u> <u>superior to</u> town life.

illusion 幻想；憧憬	somehow 不知为何	以-ior结尾的形容词后接介词to构成短语：
delusion 妄想；错觉	someway（美）不知为何	be superior to... 胜过…
delusions of grandeur 妄自尊大症	somewhat 有点	be inferior to... 不及…
hallucination 幻觉	anyhow 无论如何	be senior to... 比…年长/资历深
mirage 海市蜃楼；空想	anyway 无论如何	be junior to... 比…年轻/资历浅
daydream 白日梦；空想		prior to... 在…之前

4. There is so much <u>variety</u> that you never have to <u>make do with</u> <u>second best</u>.

variety 多样性；差异性	make do with... 用…凑合	second best 二等品
variation 变化	do without... 没有…也行	shoddy goods 劣质产品
various 各种各样的	do away with... 终止，废除	imitation goods 仿冒品
varied 不同的	do with... 想要…；处理…	substandard goods 次品
varying 不同的	make away with... 谋杀…	low-quality goods 低劣产品

II. 现身说"法"：否定词+without

> **Nor is the city** without **its moments of beauty.**（彩色部分构成双重否定（参看9课），实表肯定）城市也并非没有良辰美景。

双重否定翻译时最好保留否定的语气，实比肯定更强而有力。大抵皆可译为"每…必，无…不"。这种双重否定的用法变化颇多，仅举几例以见一斑：

Not a day passed without their meeting. 他们无日不相见。

No roses without thorns. 凡物必有缺憾。

No pleasure without pain. 有乐必有苦。

No gains without pains. 无不劳而获者。

It never rains without pouring. 祸不单行。（不雨则已，雨必滂沱）

One cannot succeed without perseverance. 人无毅力不能成事。

You cannot make omelettes without breaking eggs.

不事耕耘，焉得收获。（不打破蛋就不能做煎蛋卷）

III. 说"文"解"字"

1. Nothing can be compared, he maintains, with the first cockcrow, the twittering of birds at dawn, the sight of the rising sun glinting on the trees and pastures.

译文：他认为，黎明时分第一声雄鸡啼鸣，小鸟婉转歌唱，旭日东升，尽染森林、牧场，此番美景无与伦比。

解析：1) Nothing can be compared with...是典型的"否定+比较"句式，实际表肯定（参看23课）。语义重点在句子后面的内容。例：

No complaint is more common than that of a scarcity of money.

最常见的抱怨就是说钱不够用。

Nothing is more important for the student who loves literature than to become intimately acquainted with great critics. 对于爱好文学的学生而言，最重要的是要多加了解那些伟大的评论家。

Nothing is more valuable than health. 没有比健康更可贵的东西了。

2) maintain在这里表"认为"，相当于think，但前者更加正式。以下是常用于写作中与think同义的相关表达：contend/hold/argue/deem/accept/decide

It is my belief that... 我认为…   To my belief..., 我认为…

In my view..., 我认为…   I hold the opinion that...我认为…

2. Why people are prepared to tolerate a four-journey each day for the dubious priviledge of living in the country is beyond me.

译文：人们为什么情愿每天奔波4小时以换取值得怀疑的乡间乐趣，我是无法理解的。

解析：1) 这句话的主语是从why到is为止的内容，从结构看，主语过长，显然失衡。作者这样写的目的在于强调，作为英语初学者不宜仿效。

2) sth. is beyond sb.意为"某人不了解…"，写作或口语中皆可使用。其他相似意义的表达有：

sth. is beyond sb.'s knowledge   have no notion of...

have no idea of...   can't make head or tail of...

3. If you can do without the few pastoral pleasures of the country...

译文：如果你愿意舍弃那一点点乡间乐趣的话……

解析：do在这里是实义动词，可解释为manage to live。do without可翻译为"没有…也可以"。例：

I provide a service that people can do without when they are concerned about saving some dollars.

我提供的这种服务项目，人们想要省钱的时候，可以不要。

Do without what you can't afford to buy. 买不起的不买也无妨。

4. Some of my acquaintances in the country come up to town once or twice a year to visit the theatre as a special treat.

译文：我在乡下的一些亲朋好友每年进城看一两回戏，并把此看作是一种难得的享受。

解析：come up to town意为"去商业区"，类似于go downtown，反义表达是go uptown（去住宅区）。

拓 展 篇

I. 英语趣园

Nowadays with the development of economy, existing cities are growing bigger and new cities are appearing. No doubt, this process of urbanization has brought about fundamental changes in China. More and more people begin to live a well-off life. More and more areas take on a modern look. However, some problems also emerge from the spread of urbanization.

II. 听力快车

People in big cities _____ than those who live in the countryside. Just think about those theaters, cinemas, bookstores and newspaper stands, they give the lucky citizens enough enjoyment of life while in the countryside, people can hardly find any. Secondly, life in big cities is _____. _____ and various kinds of shops provide the affluent citizens with almost everything they need to purchase. But in the countryside, especially in the remote areas, people will have to travel a long distance even for _____ such as salt and soybean paste.

III. 补充阅读

I am one of the many city people who are always saying that given the choice we would prefer to live in the country away from the dirt and noise of a large city. I have managed to convince myself that if it weren't for my job, I would immediately head out for the open spaces and go back to nature in some sleepy village buried in the county. But how realistic is this dream?

Cities can be frightening places. The majority of the population live in massive tower blocks, noisy, dirty and impersonal. The sense of belonging to a community tends to disappear when you live fifteen floors up. All you can see from your window is sky, or other blocks of flats. Children become aggressive and nervous—cooped up at home all day, with nowhere to play; their mothers feel isolated from the rest of the world. Strangely enough, whereas in the past the inhabitants of one street all knew each other, nowadays people on the same floor in tower blocks don't even say hello to each other.

Country life, on the other hand, differs from this kind of isolated existence in that a sense of community generally binds the inhabitants of small villages together. People have the advantage of knowing that there is always someone to turn to when they need help. But country life has disadvantages too. While it is true that you may be among friends in a village, it is also true that you are cut off from the exciting and important events that take place in cities. There's little possibility of going to a new show or the latest movie. Shopping becomes a major problem, and for anything slightly out of the ordinary you have to go on an expedition to the nearest large town. The city-dweller who leaves for the country is often oppressed by a sense of unbearable stillness and quiet.

What, then, is the answer? The country has the advantage of peace and quiet, but suffers from the disadvantage of being cut off; the city breeds a feeling of isolation, and constant noise batters the senses. But one of its main advantages is that you are at the center of things, and that life doesn't come to an end at half-past nine at night. Some people have found (or rather bought) a compromise between the two: they have expressed their preference for the "quiet life" by leaving the suburbs and moving to villages within commuting distance of large cities. These people generally have about as much sensitivity as the plastic flowers they leave behind—they are polluted with strange ideas about change and improvement which they force onto the unwilling original inhabitants of the villages.

What then of my dreams of leaning on a cottage gate and murmuring "morning" to the locals as they pass by? I'm keen on the idea, but you see there's my cat, Toby. I'm not at all sure that he would take to all that fresh air and exercise in the long grass. I mean, can you see him mixing with all those hearty males down the farm? No, he would rather have the electric imitation—coal fire any evening.

▶ 测 试 篇 ◀

I . 单项选择

1. Cancer is a group of diseases in which there is uncontrolled and disordered growth of _____ cells.
   A. irrelevant   B. inferior   C. controversial   D. abnormal

2. The boxer _____ and almost fell when his opponent hit him. （CET-6 04/6）
   A. staggered   B. shattered   C. scattered   D. stamped

3. This new laser printer is _____ with all leading software. （CET-6 03/1）
   A. comparable   B. competitive   C. compatible   D. cooperative

4. The magician made us think he cut the girl into pieces but it was merely an _____. （CET-6 02/6）
   A. mirage   B. illusion   C. delusion   D. impression

5. There is no doubt that the _____ of these goods to the others is easy to see. （CET-6 02/1）
   A. prestige   B. superiority   C. priority   D. publicity

6. She was so _____ in her job that she didn't hear anybody knocking at the door. （CET-4 96/1）
   A. attracted   B. absorbed   C. drawn   D. concentrated

7. It is true that _____ a wild plant into a major food crop such as wheat requires much research time.
   A. multiplying   B. breeding   C. magnifying   D. generating

8. It took him several months to _____ the wild horse.
   A. tend   B. cultivate   C. breed   D. tame

9. The problems requiring immediate solution will be given _____ at the meeting.
   A. priority   B. urgency   C. superiority   D. emergency

10. David tends to feel useless and unwanted in a society that gives so much _____ to those who compete well.

A. prestige　　　　B. regime　　　　C. superiority　　　D. humanity

Ⅱ. 翻译

11. 一提起假期，学生们都会变得欣喜若狂。（go into raptures）

12. 你可以买到百科全书的虚拟光碟。（virtual CD）

13. 麦当劳会随儿童餐提供一些优惠。（special treats）

14. 夜幕降临到城市。（descend on）

15. 这里的T恤颜色、款式应有尽有。（a fine selection of）

拓展篇

　　People in big cities _enjoy more cultural life_ than those who live in the countryside. Just think about those theaters, cinemas, bookstores and newspaper stands, they give the lucky citizens enough enjoyment of life while in the countryside, people can hardly find any. Secondly, life in big cities is more convenient. Luxury shopping malls and various kinds of shops provide the affluent citizens with almost everything they need to purchase. But in the countryside, especially in the remote areas, people will have to travel a long distance even for buying the daily necessities such as salt and soybean paste.

测试篇

1-5 DACBB　　　　6-10 BBDAC

11. Students will go into raptures at the mere mention of vacation.

12. The encyclopedia is available as virtual CD.

13. McDonald's offers special treats that go with children's meal.

14. The night descends on the city.

15. The T-shirts are available in a fine selection of colors and sizes.

Lesson 42. Modern cavemen

积累篇

I. 振振有"词"

1. Cave exploration, or pot-holing, as it has come to be known, is a relatively new sport.

pot-holing 洞穴探险	写作常用的段首句型:
pot-holer 洞穴探险者	as it has come to be known 逐步为人所知
cave exploration 岩洞探险	as it is known to all 众所周知
cave explorer 岩洞探险者	as is universally acknowledged 世人皆知
polar exploration 极地探险	as is often the case 情形往往如此
polar explorer 极地探险者	as is mentioned above 正如前述
orienteering 越野识途	as is often pointed out 正如人们所指
canyoneering 峡谷探险	

2. Perhaps it is the desire for solitude or the chance of making an unexpected discovery that lures people down to the depths of the earth.

lure sb. to sth. 吸引某人去某地	solitude 孤独；独居
lure sb. to do sth. 引诱某人做…	live in solitude 幽居独处
allure sb. to do sth. 引诱某人做…	solitary 孤独的；惟一的
tempt sb. to do sth. 诱惑某人做…	lonesome 寂寞的
seduce sb. to do sth. 诱惑某人做…	forlorn 悲凉的
dangle sth. before sb. 用…诱惑某人	desolate 凄凉的

the depths of the earth 地下深处	the depths of the sea 海洋深处
the crust of the earth 地壳	the depth of night 深夜
the mantle of the earth 地幔	the depth of one's heart 心灵深处
the core of the earth 地核	

3. They had to <u>edge their way</u> along this, sometimes <u>wading across</u> shallow streams...

edge one's way 侧身移动
elbow one's way through a crowd 挤出人群
fight one's way in life 奋斗人生
forge one's way to success 打开成功之门
work one's way through college 勤工俭学
steal one's way into... 溜进…

wade across... 蹚过…
swim across... 游过…
plunge into... 跳进…
slip through... 飞跃…
soar over... 飞跃…
leap at... 扑向…

Ⅱ. 现身说"法": 同位语短语

The pot-holers arrived at an enormous cavern, the size of a huge concert hall.(彩色部分是同位语短语,对前面的名词cavern起修饰作用)

洞穴探险者来到一个巨大的洞里,其大小相当于一个音乐厅。

一般而言,可以充当同位语的短语或词组包括:

1. 名词词组(有时以逗号间隔)

Tom is a prolific writer, a good friend of mine. 汤姆是一位多产作家,也是我的好友。

Lu Xun, one of the greatest essayists in China, played an overwhelmingly important role in Chinese literature history. 鲁迅,中国最伟大的作家之一,在中国文学的进程中起着举足轻重的作用。

2. 不定式短语(有时以逗号间隔)

His claim to have wrapped up the task is nothing but a lie. 他声称完成了工作,只是在说谎。

The problem what to do next remains unsolved. 下一步要做什么,这个问题还没解决。

3. -ing短语(以逗号间隔)

He is crazy about the game, playing golf. 他对高尔夫这项运动非常痴迷。

He enjoys the exercise, jogging in autumn. 他喜欢秋天慢跑这种锻炼方式。

4. 形容词词组(以逗号间隔)

All countries, big or small, are equal. 所有国家,无论大小,一律平等。

All the people, Chinese and foreign, must obey the law.

所有公民,无论中国人还是外国人,都应遵纪守法。

◎ 常用的同位语引导词或短语有:

that is	in particular	that is to say	such as	say
in other words	for example/instance	for short	in short	including
let us say	especially	chiefly	mostly	mainly

Ⅲ. 说"文"解"字"

1. Cave exploration, or pot-holing, as it has come to be known, is a relatively new sport.

译文:人所共知,洞穴探险,即洞穴勘探,是一项比较新型的体育运动。

解析:as it has come to be known在句中作插入语成分,位置相对灵活,可以放在句首或句末。类似表达有:

as is known to us all 众所周知   as everyone knows 世人皆知

as is known universally 人所共知

2. It can take as long as eight days to rig up rope ladders and to establish supply bases before a descent can be made into a very deep cave.

译文：有时需要花整整8天时间来搭起绳梯，建立供应基地，然后才能下到一个很深的洞穴里。

解析：1）这是一个以it引导的形式主语句，真正主语是to引导的不定式内容，将其后置是为了句子平衡。

   2）as long as在句中起强调作用，相关讲解请参看14课"说文解字"部分。

   3）注意before要根据语境活译为"然后"，相关例证请参看2课"说文解字"部分。

3. The cave might never have been discovered had not the entrance been spotted by the distinguished French pot-holer, Berger.

译文：若不是法国著名洞穴探险家伯格偶然发现了这个洞口的话，这个洞也许永远不会为人所知。

解析：该句是对过去情形假设的虚拟语气句，从句中运用了倒装语序。一般而言，由if引导的虚拟语气条件句中，如果有had, were, should这样的功能词，可以将其放在句首，并且省略if，这种用法比较正式。例：

If I had known the truth, I would not have been so unhappy. 改写为：

Had I known the truth, I would not have been so unhappy.

如果我知道了真相，就不会那么难受。

If the sun should rise in the west, he would lend you money. 改写为：

Should the sun rise in the west, he would lend you money.

假如太阳从西边升起来，他才会借给你钱。

拓 展 篇

I . 英语趣园

  Caving offers the excitement of exploration and discovery; at the same time, potholing is a dangerous sport and anyone intending to go underground should be well-equipped and in a party of which at least one member is an experienced caver. It is easy to get wet and tired underground and it can then be quite difficult to return to the surface, and cave rescue is much more difficult than mountain rescue.

II . 听力快车 🎧

  On our thoroughly satellite mapped world, _____, is the essential lure of caving. To be able to fulfill this ambition almost literally on your doorstep spells adventure of a unique kind, an outdoor pursuit that uses many other skills—_____— as tools of the trade. It is the ultimate "wild sport".

  Compared to its neighbors, Scotland is not _____ but there are _____ to provide thrills and others still _____ Caving is to give it its proper title that allows for plenty of intellectual exercise too. Few Scottish caves have been studied properly before.

III. 补充阅读

Cavemen chemistry

Half a million years ago our ancestors learned to make fire from scratch. They crafted intricate tools from stone and brewed mind-altering elixirs from honey. Their descendants transformed clay into pottery, wool into clothing, and ashes into cleansers. In ceramic crucibles they turned rock into metal, metal into colored glazes, and glazes into glass. Buildings of brick and mortar enshrined books of parchment and paper. Kings and queens demanded ever more colorful clothing and accessories in order to out-class clodhoppers and call-girls. Kingdoms rose and fell by the power of saltpeter, sulfur, and charcoal. And the demands of everyday folk for glass and paper and soap stimulated the first round of chemical industrialization. From sulfuric acid to sodium carbonate. From aniline dyes to analgesic drugs. From blasting powder to fertilizers and plastics. In a phrase, "from Caveman to Chemist."

Caveman Chemistry is an experiential exploration of chemical technology from the campfires of the Stone Age to the plastic soft-drink bottle. An experiential exploration?

The four alchemical elements are Fire, Earth, Air and Water. These archetypal characters deliver first-hand accounts of the births of their respective technologies. The spirit of Fire, for example, was born in the first creature to cultivate the flame. This spirit passed from one person to another, from one generation to another, from one millennium to another, arriving at last in the pages of this book. The spirit of Earth taught folks to make tools of stone, the spirit of Air imparted knowledge of units and the spirit of Water began with the invention of "spirits." Having traveled the world from age to age, who can say where they will find their next home? Perhaps they will find one in you.

▶ 测 试 篇 ◀

I. 单项选择

1. These excursions will give you an even deeper _____ into our language and culture. （CET-6 90/6）
   A. inquiry   B. investigation   C. input   D. insight

2. The changing image of the family on TV provides _____ into changing attitudes toward the family in society. （CET-6 99/1）
   A. insights   B. presentations   C. revelations   D. specifications

3. This is a long _____ — roughly 13 miles down a beautiful valley to the little church below. （CET-6 05/1）
   A. terrain   B. descent   C. degeneration   D. tumble

4. A number of students _____ in flats, and others live in the nearby holiday resorts, where there is a reasonable supply of competitively-priced accommodation. （CET-6 05/1）
   A. revive   B. inhabit   C. gather   D. reside

5. If businessmen are taxed too much, they will no longer be _____ to work hard, with the result that tax revenues might actually shrink. （CET-6 05/1）
   A. cultivated   B. licensed   C. motivated   D. innovated

6. The post-World War II baby _____ resulted in a 43% increase in the number of teenagers in the 1960s and 1970s. （CET-6 04/6）
   A. boost   B. boom   C. production   D. prosperity

7. All the people in the stadium cheered up when they saw hundreds of colorful balloons _____ slowly into the sky. （CET-6 02/6）

   A. ascending   B. elevating   C. escalating   D. lingering

8. The opening between the rocks was very narrow, but the boys managed to _____ through.

   A. press   B. squeeze   C. stretch   D. leap

9. Governments today play an increasingly larger role in the _____ of welfare, economics and education.

   A. scopes   B. ranges   C. ranks   D. domains

10. It is important to _____ between the rules of grammar and the conventions of written language.

    A. determine   B. identify   C. explore   D. distinguish

Ⅱ. 翻译

11. 正是对知识的渴求，使他来到了知识的世界。（It is the desire... that...）

12. 士兵们在户外支起了帐篷。（rig tents）

13. 要不是因为滑铁卢之战，这个小村子还会一直不为人知。（had it not been for...）

14. 正如达尔文发现了有机自然界的发展规律一样，马克思发现了人类的发展规律。（Just as... so）

15. 政府采取了有效的预防措施遏制了禽流感。（take precautions to...）

拓展篇

On our thoroughly satellite mapped world, <u>opportunities to set foot where no-one has ever been before</u>, is the essential lure of caving. To be able to fulfill this ambition almost literally on your doorstep spells adventure of a unique kind, an outdoor pursuit that uses many other skills—<u>camping, mountaineering, orienteering, diving</u>—as tools of the trade. It is the ultimate "wild sport".

Compared to its neighbors, Scotland is not <u>blessed with plentiful caverns</u> but there are <u>limestone caves</u> to provide thrills and others still <u>remain to be discovered</u>. Caving is to give it its proper title that allows for plenty of intellectual exercise too. Few Scottish caves have been studied properly before.

测试篇

1-5 DABDC   6-10 BABDD

11. It's the desire for knowledge that lures him into the book world.

12. Soldiers rigged tents in the open.

13. The village might have never been famous had it not been for the Battle of Waterloo.

14. Just as Darwin discovered the law of development of organic nature, so Marx discovered the law of development of human history.

15. The government took effective precautions to prevent the Bird Flu.

Lesson 43. Fully insured

I . 振振有"词"

1. If, however, you were holding an open air garden party or a fete it would be equally possible to insure yourself in the event of bad weather.

形似词用法辨析:

insure sb./sth. agaist sth. 为某人/某物保险

assure sb. of sth. 使某人对…放心

ensure sth. 保证…

ensure doing sth. 保证做…

ensure sb. from/against... 保护某人不受…的伤害

英美国家聚会一览:

garden party 游园会

costume party 化装舞会

wedding party 婚礼派对

pot-luck dinner 百乐餐

hen party 女性聚会

stag party 男性聚会

in the event of sth. 以防…

in case of sth. 万一…

in the case of sth./sb. 就…而论

for fear that... 惟恐…

lest... (用法与for fear相同) 惟恐…

2. Needless to say, the bigger the risk an insurance company takes, the higher the premium you will have to pay.

needless to say 毫无疑问

no doubt 毫无疑问

sure enough 果不其然

as is expected 不出所料

beyond doubt 毋庸置疑

beyond question 无可争论

take the risk of... 冒险做…

venture to do sth. 冒险做…

take a chance of... 冒险做…

run risks 冒风险

brave it out 拼着干下去

Nothing venture, nothing have.
不入虎穴,焉得虎子。

premium 保险预付金

compensation money 赔偿金

bonus 奖金

dividend 红利

allowance 津贴

3. <u>It is not uncommon to</u> hear that a shipping company has <u>made a claim for</u> the cost of <u>salvaging</u> a sunken ship.

常用写作句型：

It is not uncommon to do...
做某事习以为常

It is not unusual to do... 做某事并不罕见

It is customary to do... 做某事司空见惯

It is no rarity to do... 做某事不足为奇

It is no accident to do... 做某事绝非偶然

make a claim for 提出索赔

make an accusation about
就…提出控告

lodge a complaint against 投诉

report sth. missing 挂失

形似词辨析：

salvage 救助

savage 野蛮的

sabotage 故意毁坏

surcharge 额外收费

submerge 使沉没

ravage 掠夺

Ⅱ. 现身说"法"：the+比较级，the+比较级

The bigger **the risk an insurance company takes,** the higher **the premium you will have to pay.**
保险公司承担的风险越大，你付的保险费就越高。

这是一种复杂句式，前为附句，后为主句。即前句表状态，后句表结果。因此，附句中的the表to what extent、in whatever degree为关系副词；主句中的the表to the extent, in that degree为指示副词。这种句型常采用省略手法，如：

The sooner, the better.（省略主语和动词）越快越好。

有时，主句也可置于附句之前，如：

I write the worse, the more I practise.（=The more I practise, the worse I write）我越练，写得越糟。

The more he gets, the more he wants. 愈有愈贪。

The more he flatters, the less I like him. 他愈逢迎，我愈不喜欢他。

The higher a mountain is, the more people like to climb it; the more dangerous the mountain is, the more they wish to conquer it. 山愈高，人愈爱爬山；山愈险，人愈想征服它。

Ⅲ. 说"文"解"字"

1. Insuring public or private property **is a standard** practice in most countries in the world.

译文：承办公共财产或私人财产保险是世界上大部分国家的正常业务。

解析：insure sth. 意为"为…保险"，其后可接 against sth. 例：

He insured his house against fire. 他给自己的房屋保了火险。

Every father should insure his life for the sake of his wife and children.
为了替妻子和儿女着想，每个做父亲的应当给自己保人寿险。

practice 在本句属于熟词生义现象，不可照字面译为"练习，行为"等。其他例子如：

It was her practice to rise early. 她习惯早起。（practice 作"习惯"解）

office practice 办公室日常工作（practice 作"惯例"解）

conform to local practices 入乡随俗（practice 作"习俗"解）

2. **They** had no difficulty in finding it.

译文：他们没费多大劲就找到了盘子。

解析：have（no）difficulty（in）doing sth. 是一常用句型，意为"做某事很（不）费力"，其中的介词 in 可省略。与此相似的句型构造有：

have（no）trouble（in）doing sth. 做某事很（不）费力

have great fun（in）doing sth. 做某事很快乐

have pleasure（in）doing sth. 做某事很快乐

3. **It was almost impossible to** attach **hawsers and chains** to **the rim without damaging it.**

译文：要在盘子边上拴上绳索和链条而同时又不损害它是很困难的。

解析：attach... to... 是一固定词组，意为"把…连到…"。但在实际场合，它的意义非常广泛。例：

The government attaches great priority to agricultural issues. 政府对农业问题很重视。

She is sentimentally attached to her dog. 她和这条狗的感情很深。

4. **The winch was again** put into operation **and one of the men started up the truck.**

译文：绞盘机再次启动，一位工人发动了急修车的引擎。

解析：put sth. into operation 意为"使…起作用，生效"。类似表达有：

sth. come into operation   sth. is in operation   sth. take effect

例：The amended law will come into operation this week. 修正法案这周生效。

The new working system will be put into operation soon. 新的工作制度将会很快付诸实施。

拓 展 篇

Ⅰ.英语趣园

What is insurance? Insurance is not necessarily an investment from which one expects to get one's money back. Nor is it gambling. A gambler takes risks, while insurance offers protection against risks that already exist. Insurance is a way to share risk with others. Since ancient times, communities have pooled some of their resources to help individuals who suffer loss. About 3,500 years ago, Moses instructed the nation of Israel to contribute a portion of their produce periodically for "the alien resident and the fatherless boy and the widow."

The origins of insurance

Insurance has existed for thousands of years. A form of credit insurance was included in the *Code of Hammurabi*, a collection of Babylonian laws said to predate the *Law of Moses*. To finance their trading expeditions in ancient times, ship owners obtained loans from investors. If a ship was lost, the owners were not responsible for paying back the loans. Since many ships returned safely, the interest paid by numerous ship owners covered the risk to the lenders.

It was likewise in a maritime setting that later one of the world's most famous insurance providers, Lloyd's of London, was born. By 1688, Edward Lloyd was running a coffeehouse where London merchants and bankers met informally to do business. There financiers who offered insurance contracts to seafarers wrote their names under the specific amount of risk that they would accept in exchange for a certain payment, or premium. These insurers came to be known as underwriters. When people buy insurance today, they are still sharing their risk. Modern insurance companies study statistics that show the frequency of past losses—for example, losses from shop fires—to try to predict what losses their clients will experience in the future. The insurance company uses the funds paid by many clients to compensate the clients who suffer losses.

II. 听力快车

How to choose an investment professional

Let's face it—_____. That's why you want to choose an investment professional you feel comfortable with. Interview and evaluate several professionals to find the one that's right for you. Look for a qualified professional whose business style is a good match for your financial planning needs.

Think about asking:

* _____?
* What are your financial planning credentials/designations and affiliations?
* How long have you been in the business?
* _____?
* _____?
* Will you be the only person working with me?
* _____?
* _____?
* Have you ever been publicly disciplined for any unlawful or unethical actions in your professional career?

III. 补充阅读

Insurance

Insurance is a method of coping with risk. Its primary function is to substitute certainty for uncertainty as regards the economic cost of loss-producing events. Insurance may be defined more formally as a system under which the insurer, for a consideration usually agreed upon in advance, promises to reimburse the insured or to render services to the insured in the event that certain accidental occurrences result in losses during a given period.

From the standpoint of the insurer, an insurable risk must meet the following requirements:

1. The object to be insured must be numerous enough and homogeneous enough to allow a reasonably close calculation of the probable frequency and severity of loses.

2. The insured objects must not be subject to simultaneous destruction. For example, if all the buildings insured by one insurer are in an area subject to flood, and a flood occurs, the loss to the insurance underwriter may be catastrophic.

3. The possible loss must be accidental in nature, and beyond the control of the insured. If the insured could cause the loss, the element of randomness and predictability would be destroyed.

4. There must be some way to determine whether a loss has occurred and how great that loss is. This is why insurance contracts specify very definitely what events must take place, what constitute loss, and how it is to be measured.

From the viewpoint of the insured person, an insurable risk is one for which the probability of loss is not so high as to require excessive premiums. What is "excessive" depends on individual circumstances, including the insured's attitude toward risk. At the same time, the potential loss must be

---

severe enough to cause financial hardship if it is not insured against. Insurable risks include losses to property resulting from fire, explosion, windstorm, etc; losses of life or health; and the legal liability arising out of use of automobiles, occupancy of buildings, employment, or manufacture. Uninsurable risks include losses resulting from price changes and competitive conditions in the market. Political risks such as war or currency debasement are usually not insurable by private parties but may be insurable by governmental institutions. Very often contracts can be drawn in such a way that an "uninsurable risk" can be turned into an "insurable" one through restrictions on losses, redefinitions of perils, or other methods.

▶ 测 试 篇 ◀

Ⅰ. 单项选择

1. Many ecologists believe that lots of major species in the world are on the _____ of extinction. (CET-6 05/1)
   A. margin   B. border   C. verge   D. fringe

2. Some felt that they were hurrying into an epoch of unprecedented enlightenment, in which better education and beneficial technology would _____ wealth and leisure for all.   (CET-6 05/1)
   A. maintain   B. ensure   C. certify   D. console

3. The manager gave her his _____ that her complaint would be investigated.   (CET-6 02/1)
   A. assurance   B. assumption   C. sanction   D. insurance

4. As one of the world's highest paid models, she had her face _____ for five million dollars.
   A. deposited   B. assured   C. measured   D. insured

5. In case of damage, the museum had all the paintings _____.
   A. insured   B. ensured   C. assured   D. guaranteed

6. He often sat in small bar drinking considerable more than _____.
   A. he was in good health   B. his health was good
   C. his good health was   D. was good for his health

7. I cannot give you _____ for the type of car you sell because there is no demand for it in the market.
   A. an expense   B. a charge   C. a purchase   D. an order

8. _____ I admit that there are problems, I don't think that they cannot be solved.
   A. Unless   B. Until   C. As   D. While

9. He bought his house on the _____ plan, paying a certain amount of money each month.
   A. premium   B. installment   C. division   D. fluctuation

10. All their attempts to _____ the child from the burning building were in vain.
    A. regain   B. recover   C. rescue   D. reserve

Ⅱ. 翻译

11. 我给房子上了火险。（be insured）

12. 一个巨浪掀翻了我们的小船。（capsize）

13. 一个小村子坐落在陡峭的山坡上。（perch）

14. 如今普通老百姓贷款买车已经不是什么新鲜事了。（not uncommon）

15. 如遇紧急情况，打119。（in the event of）

拓展篇

How to choose an investment professional

Let's face it—talking about your finances isn't always easy. That's why you want to choose an investment professional you feel comfortable with. Interview and evaluate several professionals to find the one that's right for you. Look for a qualified professional whose business style is a good match for your financial planning needs.

Think about asking:

- What's your educational background?
- What are your financial planning credentials/designations and affiliations?
- How long have you been in the business?
- Do you have clients I can contact for references?
- What is your approach to financial planning?
- Will you be the only person working with me?
- How will I pay for your services?
- How much do you charge?
- Have you ever been publicly disciplined for any unlawful or unethical actions in your professional career?

测试篇

1-5 CBADA   6-10 DDDBC

11. My house is insured against fire.

12. A huge wave capsized our boat.

13. A tiny village perched on the steep sides of a mountain.

14. It is not uncommon nowadays for common citizens to purchase cars on loan.

15. In the event of emergency, dial 119.

Lesson 44. Speed and comfort

I.振振有"词"

1. Train <u>compartments</u> soon get <u>cramped</u> and <u>stuffy</u>.

形似词联想记忆：
compartment 车厢
department 系；部门
apartment 公寓
parliament 议会
basement 底层，地下室
pavement 人行道

cramped 窄小的
crowded 拥挤的
congested 堵塞的
jammed 堵塞的
squashy 易压碎的
packed 塞满的

stuffy 憋气的，闷气的
suffocating 令人窒息的
unventilated 不透气的
airless 憋闷的
oppressed 压抑的

2. Reading is only a partial solution, for the <u>monotonous rhythm</u>... soon <u>lulls you to sleep</u>.

monotonous 单调的
monochrome 单调的
dull 乏味的
insipid 无趣的
plodding 单调乏味的
tedious 冗长的；乏味的
tiresome 令人厌烦的

rhythm 节律
rhyme 韵
tempo（机械）速率
cadence（音乐、舞蹈）节拍
pace of living 生活节奏
melody 旋律
pulse 脉搏

与"睡觉"有关的表达：
lull sb. to sleep 令某人昏昏欲睡
doze off 打盹
take catnaps 小憩
sleep like a log 酣睡
sleep profoundly 酣睡

3. <u>Inevitably</u> you arrive at your <u>destination</u> almost <u>exhausted</u>.

inevitable 不可避免的
unavoidable 不可避免的
inescapable 不可回避的
unalterable 不可更改的
inexorable 不可变更的
irrevocable 不可撤销的

destination 目的地
terminal 终点站
transfer station 中转站
boundary 边界
target 目标
destiny 命运

exhausted（fml.）精疲力竭的
weary（fml.）疲倦的
dog-tired 累极的
fatigued 疲劳的
wear-out 疲劳的
drowsy 困倦的

230

Ⅱ.现身说"法"：广义否定词

> Hardly anyone can positively enjoy sitting in a train for more than a few hours.
> 很少有人能够真正喜欢坐几个小时以上的火车。

hardly被称为广义否定词，即半否定词，表示较大程度上的否定。常见的此类副词有：rarely, hardly, scarcely, seldom, barely等。一般而言，这些词置于句首，句子要倒装。但在本句中，hardly修饰主语anyone, 所以不倒装。例：

Hardly will the estimated sales cover the cost of making the film.
估算的票房收入几乎不够拍片的投入。

Scarcely was the family able to afford the tuition. 这个家庭几乎付不起学费。

Seldom has society offered so wide arrange of leisure time activities.
社会以前很少提供如此广泛的休闲活动。

Little did I expect such enthusiasm from so many. 我几乎没想到这么多人会有如此高的热情。

Ⅲ.说"文"解"字"

1. Hardly anyone can positively enjoy sitting in a train for more than a few hours.

译文：很少有人能够真正喜欢坐几个小时以上的火车。

解析：1）本句中hardly位于句首，但不倒装，因为它修饰主语anyone。 一般而言，若广义否定词如hardly, seldom, rarely, barely, scarcely等不修饰主语，且放在句首时，句子要进行倒装。例：

Seldom could he stand after a whole day's laborious work.

辛苦工作了一整天，他都快站不住了。

Barely can her monthly salary cover her expense. 她每月的工资几乎不够花。

2）enjoy之后必须接名词或动名词，这与以下几个动词用法相同：risk、imagine、avoid、deny等。例：

The young boy always imagines traveling to the outer space.

小男孩总想像着到外层空间去旅行。

The suspect denied having stolen the car. 这个嫌疑犯否认偷车的事实。

2. It is almost impossible to take your mind off the journey.

译文：想摆脱旅途的困扰是很难的。

解析：1）该句是it引导的形式主语句。事实上，使用impossible/possible造句时一般不能直接以人作主语，只能用it形式主语句。

2）take one's mind off...是一个常用短语，意为"从…中转移注意力"。相似表达有：

divert one's attention from...   avert one's mind from...   distract sb. from...

例：The wonderful TV program diverted my attention from the book from time to time.

精彩的电视节目时不时地吸引着我，使我无法看书。

The twittering of birds distracted me from sleeping. 小鸟的鸣叫令我睡意全无。

3. You spend half the night staring at the small blue light in the ceiling, or fumbling to find your ticket for inspection.

译文：夜间有一半时间你会盯着车顶那盏小蓝灯而睡不着觉，要不然就为查票摸索着找车票。

解析：1）这里spend half the night staring at 不是spend some time（in）doing 结构（花时间做某事），因为逻辑不通。staring应作spend的伴随状语，参看29课"说文解字"部分。

2）fumble to do sth. 或fumble for... 意为"摸索着找…"。可以与以下表达比较记忆：

look for... 寻找…   feel for... 摸索着寻找…

grope for... 摸索着寻找…   search high and low for... 到处寻找…

4. But more often than not, the greater part of the journey is spent on roads with few service stations and too much traffic.

译文：但旅行的大部分时间都花在路上，而且服务设施很少，交通也很拥挤。

解析：1）more often than not基本意思和often相同，只是更加正式。以下是关于often的容易混淆的一些短语：

every so often 有时，偶尔   as often as not 往往，多半   often and often 经常，往往

2）注意too much与much too之间的区别：前者修饰名词，而后者修饰形容词或副词。例：

There is too much traffic on the road. 路上交通很拥挤。

Let's stay at home. It's much too hot for walking. 我们还是呆在家里吧。外面太热，不能散步。

拓展篇

Ⅰ.英语趣园

In many places people have the freedom to choose whether they want to commute to work by public or private transportation. Private means can bring about a lot of agonizing problems: air pollution, difficulty in finding a parking place in the city, and consumption of too much of the earth's energy. Green traveling is thus preferred and welcomed.

Ⅱ.听力快车

The safety, efficiency, and cost of _____ are high on _____ in every developed country around the world. Freedom to travel binds the Nation together and _____. When we use the transportation system, we don't pay much attention to how it works or who makes it work—unless, of course, we are caught in a traffic jam, involved in an auto crash, or sitting in a plane delayed on a runway. But every day, and every hour—around the clock— _____!

Ⅲ.补充阅读

Means of transportation

Transportation in ancient China was difficult. People traveled mainly on foot. It took several months for a candidate who expected to take the imperial examination to be a government official to go from home to the capital on foot. People also rode horses when traveling from town to town. For short-distance trips, man-carried sedans and carriages or oxcarts were also used. Needless to say, all these means of transportation were quite slow.

Now we have trains, planes, ships, buses and bikes in China. With an aggressive effort since 1949, a comprehensive transportation system was created. It consists of railways, highways, airplanes and water transportation. Just before 1950, there were only 21,800 km of railway lines available, but by the time 1998 arrived, there were 57,600km lines of railway lines open.

At present, the train, compared with planes and ships, is still the primary means of transportation for travelers who tour between cities. Beijing is the hub for the railway line that heads north to south, consisting of the following lines: Beijing-Guangzhou Railway, Beijing-Shanghai Railway, Beijing-Kowloon Railway and Beijing-Harbin Railway. The line that heads from west to east has its hub located in Zhengzhou. Apart from domestic rail lines, trains now can also run to Moscow, Russia, Pyongyang, North Korea and Hanoi, Vietnam.

All towns and counties are easy to reach through the development of the highway system, which stretches nearly 1.278 million km across the country. Compare that to 80,000 of highways in 1949. Now, towns, counties and townships that were once inaccessible are within reach. Via major expressways such as Shenyang-Dalian, Beijing-Tianjin-Tanggu, Guangzhou-Shenzhen, Jinan-Qingdao and Yichang-Huangshi. In 1998 alone, 37,000 km of highways were built, of those 1,487 km were expressways. Roads are smooth and wide when you travel to most of the big cities, but situations are quite tough if you visit remote mountainous regions, such as those in Guizhou and Yunnan provinces.

The plane is the most convenient and fastest means of transportation, though it is also the most expensive. During the reformation, China worked hard at building and expanding airports. Between 1949 and 1978, China was willing to invest lots of money to expand and build airports. Since then, airports have been built to accommodate the needs of economic development. By 1998, there were more than 140 airports opened. The hub of domestic and international air travel is based in Beijing. Beside Beijing, people are also able to enter China by plane from Hong Kong, Shanghai and Lhasa.

People nowadays seldom choose waterways to travel between cities, but they are still and always have been an important way of moving goods through the country. The Pearl River delta is a prime river system for the movement of goods and people. The system is filled with an amazingly wide armada of boats, from barges to sampans to small fishing boats, and hovercraft. Sampans, long famous in China, are still seen in Hong Kong harbor and plying the waters around China. Barges of all types, laden with goods and materials as well as soil and rocks for many of China's development projects, can be seen floating upon the waters.

Transportation inside cities occurs by private cars, autobuses, taxis, bikes and motorbikes which are forbidden in some cities in order to protect the environment. Rickshaws can be still seen.

▶ 测 试 篇 ◀

I.单项选择

1. The _____ of finding gold in California were good in the 1840's.　（CET-6 89/6）

    A. proposals　　　　B. promises　　　　C. prospects　　　　D. privileges

2. Their demand for a pay raise has not the slightest _____ of being met.　（考研95）

    A. prospect　　　　B. prediction　　　　C. prosperity　　　　D. permission

3. Governments today play an increasingly larger role in the _____ of welfare, economics, and education.　（CET-6 05/6）

    A. scopes　　　　B. ranges　　　　C. ranks　　　　D. domains

4. He is looking for a job that will give him greater _____ for career development.　（CET-6 03/9）

    A. insight　　　　B. scope　　　　C. momentum　　　　D. phase

5. The Browns lived in a _____ and comfortably furnished house in the suburbs.　　（CET-6 03/9）

　　A. spacious　　　　B. sufficient　　　　C. wide　　　　　D. wretched

6. _____ that the demand for power continues to rise at the current rate, it will not be long before traditional sources become inadequate.　　（CET-6 03/1）

　　A. Concerning　　　B. Ascertaining　　　C. Assuming　　　D. Regarding

7. Grain production in the world is _____, but still millions go hungry.　　（CET-6 02/6）

　　A. staggering　　　　B. shrinking　　　　C. soaring　　　　D. suspending

8. San Francisco is usually cool in the summer, but Los Angeles _____.

　　A. is rarely　　　　B. rarely is　　　　C. hardly is　　　　D. is scarcely

9. It is _____ impossible to find a good educational computer program in this part of the country.

　　A. barely　　　　　B. hardly　　　　　C. merely　　　　D. nearly

10. _____ with the size of the whole earth, the highest mountain does not seem high at all.

　　A. When compared　　B. Compare　　　C. While comparing　　D. Comparing

Ⅱ. 翻译

11. 我听到有人断断续续地哭。（in snatches）

12. 健身是摆脱烦恼的好办法。（take your mind off）

13. 我感觉非常好。（not....better）

14. 作业让我忙得不可开交，根本没时间去看电视。（keep sb. occupied）

15. 在南方，清明时节，十有八九是在下雨。（more often than not）

 答 案

拓展篇

　　The safety, efficiency, and cost of <u>all modes of transportation and their impact on the environment</u> are high on <u>the list of major concerns</u> in every developed country around the world. Freedom to travel binds the Nation together and <u>links us to the rest of the world</u>. When we use the transportation system, we don't pay much attention to how it works or who makes it work—unless, of course, we are caught in a traffic jam, involved in an auto crash, or sitting in a plane delayed on a runway. But every day, and every hour—around the clock—<u>our transportation system is moving everyone and everything, everywhere</u>!

测试篇

1-5 CADBA　　　　　6-10 CCBDA

11. I heard someone cry in snatches.

12. Workout is a good way to take your mind off your anxieties.

13. I couldn't feel any better.

14. Homework kept me so occupied that I didn't have time to watch TV.

15. It rains more often than not on Bright and Pure's Day in the south of China.

Lesson 45. The power of the press

I.振振有"词"

1. In democratic countries any efforts to restrict the freedom of the press are rightly condemned.

democratic 民主的
democracy 民主
democrat 民主人士；〈美〉民主党人
democratic centralization 民主集中制
demography 人口统计学
demographics 人口统计数据
demographer 人口学家

restrict sth. 限制…
restrain sb. from doing sth.
阻止某人做…
prohibit sb. from doing
禁止某人做…
forbid sb. sth. 不让某人做…

the freedom of the press
新闻自由
the freedom of speech
言论自由
the freedom of belief 信仰自由
the freedom from poverty
免于匮乏的自由

2. They would have continued to struggle against economic odds and would have lived in obscurity.

关于"生活方式"的表达：
live in obscurity 默默无闻
live in great fame 声名显赫
live in poverty 生活贫困
live in luxury 生活奢华
live in misery 生活悲惨
live in happiness 生活幸福

economic odds 经济困境
economic plight 经济窘困
financial difficulties 经济困难
keep body and soul together 勉强维生
can not make both ends meet 入不敷出
live from hand to mouth 勉强过活

3. So lawyers had to be employed to act as spokesmen for the family at press conferences.

employ 雇用
employee 雇员
employer 雇主
employment 就业；工作
unemployment 失业
reemployment 再就业

act as... 担当…
serve as... 起…作用
function as... 起…作用
be used as... 被用作…
play the role of... 担当…角色
assume the role of... 承担…角色

press conference
记者招待会
plenary session
全体大会
convention（定期）大会

symposium
专题研讨会
seminar 专家研讨会
forum 专题论坛
rally 集会

Ⅱ. 现身说"法"：过去虚拟语气

> **If they had only had one more child, the fact would have passed unnoticed.**
> 如果他们只是添了一个孩子，这件事就不会引起任何人的关注。

1. 过去虚拟语气模式表示与过去事实相反的假设，构成公式是：条件从句：If+主语+had+V-ed...，主句：主语+would（should, could, might）+have+V-ed... 例：

   If he had taken my advice, he would not have been in trouble.
   如果他接受了我的建议，就不会遇到麻烦了。

   If he had not been promoted, he would never have remained with the company.
   如果他没有得到提升，他决不会留在这家公司。

   You would have missed the train if you had not hurried. 如果你不抓紧的话，那趟车就赶不上了。

   If she had not married, she would probably have become something special.
   如果她没有结婚，很有可能会成为了不起的人物。

2. 若该虚拟语气的条件句中出现助动词had，可省略if，将had置于句首，因此，本文例句可改写为：

   Had they only had one more child, the fact would have passed unnoticed.

Ⅲ. 说"文"解"字"

1. In democratic countries any efforts to restrict the freedom of the press are rightly condemned.

   译文：在民主国家里，任何限制新闻自由的企图都理所当然地受到谴责。

   解析：1）rightly在本句的意思相当于reasonably, right本身也可用作副词，但含义不同。例：

   If I remember right. (right意为"正确地") 如果我记得不错的话。

   Things will go right. (right意为"顺利地") 事情会变得顺利。

   She took the call and came right out. (right意为"立刻地") 她接了电话，并立刻迎了出来。

   He looked me right in the eye. (right意为"径直地") 他直视着我。

   2）condemn与criticise语义不同，前者多指"道义上的批评"，语气要重于后者；而后者多指"当面批评、指正"。例：

   The atrocity of the ruler in that country was severely condemned by many governments. (用criticise不合适) 那个国家统治者的暴行受到了许多政府的严厉谴责。

2. Acting on the contention that facts are sacred, reporters can cause untold suffering to individuals.

   译文：记者按事实至上的论点行事，有时会给当事人带来极大的痛苦。

   解析：1）这里介词on作according to或based on解。例：

   This family lives on welfare. 这个家庭靠福利救济维持生活。

   They made their own judgement on his description. 他们根据他的描述做出了自己的判断。

   2）句中that引导的内容作contention的同位语成分，起解释作用。

3. As the parents had five children, life was a perpetual struggle against poverty.

   译文：家里已有5个孩子，全家人每日都在贫困中挣扎。

   解析：彩色部分是一个很好的模仿句型。只要换掉一些关键词，便可造出众多佳句。例：

Seeking knowledge is a perpetual struggle against ignorance.

索求知识就是不断地战胜愚昧无知。

Experimenting with new ideas is a perpetual struggle against sloth.

尝试新想法就是不断地克服懒惰。

4. They would have continued to struggle against economic odds and would have lived in obscurity.

译文：他们会继续与贫困作斗，并默默无闻地活下去。

解析：1）economic odds即economic difficulties.

2）in obscurity修饰live, 作方式状语。事实上，与live搭配的方式状语许多是in引导的介词短语。例：

live in happiness 生活幸福　　　　　　　live in misery 生活悲苦

live in luxury 生活奢华　　　　　　　　live in fame 声名显赫

拓 展 篇

Ⅰ.英语趣园

There is a sharp difference between civil liberties and civil rights. The former guarantees that a person will enjoy freedom from government interference, while the latter guarantees that all people will have the freedom to be treated equally. For example, civil liberties would include freedom from government interference with a person's right to free speech. Civil rights would include everyone's freedom to receive equal protection of the law. All civil rights have limits, even in democratic counties.

Ⅱ.听力快车

Use no more than 3 words for each answer.

1. Besides reporters, who else were camped out for days outside the speaker's home? _____

2. One reporter got to the speaker's apartment pretending to pay _____.

3. The speaker believed the reporter wanted a picture of her looking _____.

4. Where is a correction to a false story usually placed? _____

5. According to the speaker, the press will lose readers unless the editors and the news directors _____.

Ⅲ.补充阅读

Newspaper and TV

No country in the world has more daily newspapers than the USA. There are almost 2,000 of them, as compared with 180 in Japan, 164 in Argentina and 111 Britain. The quality of some American papers is extremely high and their views are quoted all over the world. Distinguished dailies like the *Washington Post* and the *New York Times* exert a powerful influence all over the country. However the *Post* and the *Times* are not national newspapers in the sense that *The Times* is in Britain or *Le Monde* is in France, since each American city has its own daily newspaper. The best of these present detailed accounts of national and international news, but many tend to limit themselves to state or city news.

Like the press in most other countries, American newspapers range from the "sensational", which feature crime, sex and gossip, to the serious, which focus on factual news and the analysis of world events. With few exceptions, American newspapers try to entertain as well as inform, for they have to compete with the lure of TV.

Just as American newspapers cater to all tastes, so do they also try to appeal to readers of all political persuasions. A few newspapers support extremist groups on the far right and on the far left, but most daily newspapers attempt to attract middle-of-the-road Americans who are essentially moderate. Many of these papers print columns by well-known journalists of differing political and social views in order to present a balanced picture.

As in other democratic countries, American newspapers can be either responsible or irresponsible, but it is generally accepted that the American press serves its country well and that it has more than once courageously exposed political scandals or crimes, for instance, the Watergate Affair. The newspapers drew the attention of the public to the horrors of the Vietnam War.

▶ 测 试 篇 ◀

Ⅰ.单项选择

1. We all enjoy our freedom of choice and do not like to see it _____ when it is within the legal and moral boundaries of society. (CET-6 03/6)
   A. compacted　　　　B. restricted　　　　C. dispersed　　　　D. delayed

2. Because of the _____ noise of traffic I couldn't get to sleep last night. (CET-6 03/6)
   A. prevalent　　　　B. perpetual　　　　C. provocative　　　　D. progressive

3. Up until that time, his interest had focused almost _____ on fully mastering the skills and techniques of his craft. (CET-6 02/6)
   A. restrictively　　　　B. radically　　　　C. inclusively　　　　D. exclusively

4. It has been revealed that some government leaders _____ their authority and position to get illegal profits for themselves.
   A. employ　　　　B. take　　　　C. abuse　　　　D. overlook

5. In general, matters which lie entirely within state borders are the _____ concern of state governments.
   A. extinct　　　　B. excluding　　　　C. excessive　　　　D. exclusive

6. A visitor to a museum today would notice _____ changes in the way museums are operated.
   A. cognitive　　　　B. rigorous　　　　C. conspicuous　　　　D. exclusive

7. Creating so much confusion, Mason realized he had better make _____ what he was trying to tell the audience.
   A. exclusive　　　　B. explicit　　　　C. objective　　　　D. obscure

8. The lady dressed in the latest Paris fashion is _____ in her appearance but rude in her speech.
   A. elaborate　　　　B. excessive　　　　C. elegant　　　　D. exaggerated

9. The boy cycling in the street was knocked down by a minibus and received _____ injures.
   A. fatal　　　　B. excessive　　　　C. disastrous　　　　D. exaggerated

10. The _____ cycle of life and death is a subject of interest to scientists and philosophers alike.
    A. incompatible　　　　B. exceeding　　　　C. instantaneous　　　　D. eternal

II. 翻译

11. 空军一号是美国总统的专机。（be exclusive to）
12. 根据得到的消息，警方准备对毒贩子采取行动。（act on...）
13. 尼克松总统的垮台，形象地说明了新闻报道的威力。（illustrate...）
14. 学生们纷纷打听考试成绩。（press for）
15. 他克服重重困难之后，终于名声鹊起。（against all the odds）

拓展篇

1. cameramen 　　　　2. a personal visit 　　　　3. depressed

4. among advertisements 　　5. take firm action

When I was getting divorced in 1975, reporters and cameramen were camped out for days in the lobby and on the sidewalk outside. They came from all over the country. Foreign reporters too. It was terrible. My neighbors could barely get in and out of the building. One reporter who had been a friend of mine, got up to my apartment after persuading the doorman into believing that he was there on a personal visit. I wouldn't let him in. He just wanted to talk, he said. I was certain that he had a camera and wanted a picture of me looking depressed. I just couldn't believe this attempt to invade my privacy. TV is the worst. TV reporters present themselves as having the perfect right to be anywhere, to ask any questions. It doesn't matter how personal the matter may be.

People don't trust the press the way they used to. In most cases, stories are sensationalized in order to attract more public attention. Some papers print things that simply are not true. In many papers, if a correction has to be made, it's usually buried among advertisements. I've received hundreds of letters from people asking me how do you know what's true in the press these days. I find it difficult to respond sometimes. I tell them that there are good newspapers and serious, responsible and honest reporters. Don't judge all of us by the standards of the bad ones. Unless the guys at the top—the editors and the news directors—take firm action, pretty soon no one is going to believe anything they read in the papers or see on TV news.

测试篇

1-5 BBDCD 　　　　6-10 CBCAD

11. Air Force I is exclusive to the President of USA.

12. Acting on the information received, the police are going to take steps to deal with the drug dealers.

13. Nixon's downfall dramatically illustrated the immense power of the press.

14. The students pressed for the results of the exam.

15. He rose to fame after struggling against all the odds.

Lesson 46. Do it yourself

积累篇

I.振振有"词"

1. So great is our <u>passion for</u> doing things for ourselves that we are becoming increasingly less dependent on <u>specialized labour</u>.

specialized labour 专业劳动力
home help 家政工人
baby sitter 保姆
domestic science 家政学
household art 持家本领
household management 理家技能

have a passion for... 对…很热爱
feel a passion for... 怀着对…的酷爱
develop a passion for... 培养对…的兴趣
have a craze for... 对…酷爱
have an instinct for... 天生喜欢…
take a fancy for... 极其喜欢…

2. No one can <u>plead ignorance of</u> a subject any longer, for there are <u>countless</u> do-it-yourself <u>publications</u>.

publication 出版物
publishing house 出版社
publish sth. 出版…
keep sth. publishing 使…连续出版
illegal publication 非法出版物
publisher 出版商
issue sth. 发行…

plead ignorance of... 对不知…而辩解
be in ignorance of... 不知…
be ignorant of... 不了解…
be unaware of... 没有意识到…
be unconscious of... 没有意识到…
be in the dark 毫不知情

countless 不计其数的
countable 可数的
countable noun 可数名词
uncountable noun 不可数名词
defy enumeration 不胜枚举
beyond measurement 不可估量

3. Some really <u>keen</u> <u>enthusiasts</u> <u>go so far as to</u> build their own computers.

keen 热切的	enthusiast 积极分子	go so far as to do sth. 甚至做…
earnest 急切的	enthusiasm 积极性	go to the length of doing sth. 竟然做…
fanatic 狂热的	enthusiastic 积极的；热情的	carry things too far 做事太过分
fervent 狂热的	zealot 狂热者	go too far 太过分
passionate 激情的	fiend 癖好成瘾者	go to extremes 走极端
vigorous 充满活力的	devotee 献身者；虔诚者	

Ⅱ. 现身说"法"：部分否定

> But unfortunately not all of us are born handymen. (句中 not all of us 是部分否定)
> 但不幸的是，并非人人都是能工巧匠。

一般而言，不定代词 all, every, both 以及副词 always, quite 与 not 结合时，不是全部否定，而是部分否定，而它们的反义词 none, neither 等则表示全部否定。试比较：

All that glitters is not gold. 发光的未必都是金子。

None that glitters is gold. 发光的都不是金子。

Every man can not be a poet. 不是人人都可作诗人。

No one can be a poet. 无人可作诗人。

再列举几例：

All great truths are obvious truths. But not all obvious truths are great truths.

所有伟大之真理皆是显明之真理。但并非所有显明之真理皆是伟大之真理。

You can not fool all the people all the time. 你未必能够老是愚弄所有的人。

Opportunities come to all, but all are not ready for them when they come.

机会人人均等，但当机会来临，并不是人人都能捕捉机会。

The biographies of scientists are not always good literature, but they have immense educational value.

科学家的传记并不见得是好的文学作品，但它们具有极大的教育价值。

Ⅲ. 说"文"解"字"

1. So great is our passion for doing things for ourselves that we are becoming increasingly less dependent on specialized labour.

译文：现在我们自己动手的热情很高，对于专业工人的依赖性越来越低了。

解析：1) 该句是一个倒装句。原理为：由 so 或 such 引导的结果状语从句，主句的动词为 be；或含助动词时，可将 so 或 such 位于句首，后接形容词、副词或名词，再将 be 或助动词置于主语之前，以示强调。因此，该句复原后为：Our passion for doing things for ourselves is so great that we are becoming increasingly less dependent on specialized labour.

2) increasingly 根据情境译为"越来越…"。increasingly less 即以前常用的 less and less 的换用表

达。例：

Job-hunting is increasingly more difficult.（increasingly more即more and more）

求职越来越艰难。

With the fast growth of the Internet, it is increasingly easier to contact one far away from us.（increasingly easier即easier and easier）

随着互联网的迅猛发展，我们能更加便利地与远方的另一个人进行接触。

2. **Some really keen enthusiasts** go so far as to **build their own computers.**

译文：有些热衷于自己动手的人甚至自己组装电脑。

解析：go so far as to do sth 不可望文生义，实际上这是一个固定用法，表程度或结果。在英文中，"so... as+不定式"一般表结果或程度，相似于so... that...，而"so as +不定式"一般表目的，相似于so that。例：

Books are now so expensive as to be out of the reach of many people.（=Books are now so expensive that they are out of the reach of many people.）书籍现在非常贵，许多人买不起。

Houses should be built so as to admit plenty of light as well as of fresh air.（=Houses should be built so that they can admit plenty of light as well as of fresh air.）建筑房屋应使空气流通，阳光直射。

3. It is a question of **pride as much as anything else.**

译文：认为自己什么都行的原因就是要面子。

解析：It is a question of... 是一个固定句型，意为"是…事情/问题"。其中question也可替换成thing/issue/matter。例：

For him, to be successful is merely a matter of time. 对他而言，成功只不过是时间问题。

此外，该句正常结构应为：It, as much as anything else, is a question of pride.

4. A turn of a screw here, a little tightening up there, a drop of oil **and it would be as good as new.**

译文：这儿紧紧螺丝，那儿固定一下，再加几滴油，就会崭新如初了。

解析：彩色部分看似名词短语，实际表条件。因为英文中"名词短语/祈使句+and"结构相当于"if从句+主句"，即"名词/祈使句"充当了条件句的作用。因此，该句可改写为：If there were a turn of a screw here, a little tightening up there, a drop of oil, it would be as good as new. 例：

Work hard and you will be amply rewarded.（=If you work hard, you will be amply rewarded.）

努力工作，你会得到丰厚回报的。

拓 展 篇

I.英语趣园

Do-it-yourself is the activity of making or repairing things by yourself instead of buying them or paying someone else to do it. In Britain, highly skilled workers are paid relatively high and quite a lot of people can't afford to pay those workmen. As a result, people have to learn to depend on themselves. There are a lot of DIY shops which cater to the craze, such as B&Q in Britain, which offers a wide range of houseware departments to fill and accessorize your home.

Ⅱ. 听力快车

Choose the best answer for each of the following questions.

1. How often does Do It Yourself magazine organize a competition?

    A. Every Spring.　　　　B. Every Summer.　　　　C. Every Autumn.

2. What prize did Mr. Miller win?

    A. "Handyman of the Year".　B. "Most Popular Star".　　C. "Best Master of the Kitchen".

3. What does Mr. Roy Miller do?

    A. He is a postman.　　　B. He is a journalist.　　　C. He is a photographer.

4. What has Mr. Miller done to his house?

    A. He painted it.　　　　B. He renovated it.　　　　C. He altered it.

5. Why did Mr. Miller do something to the house?

    A. For fun.　　　　　　B. For his disabled son.　　C. For the prize he won.

6. Where did Mr. Miller learn do-it-yourself skills?

    A. From books.　　　　B. From other people.　　　C. At evening schools.

7. What does Mr. Miller say he will do with the money he has won?

    A. To buy a new house.　B. To start his own business.　C. To become an expert.

8. How much is the prize?

    A. 10,000 pounds.　　　B. 1,000 pounds.　　　　C. 100,000 pounds.

Ⅲ. 补充阅读

Before developing a plan for an interior, a designer must consider a number of things. The designer, whether a professional or nonprofessional, must first determine the purpose of the area, the life style of those who will use it, and the budget available.

Many designers begin by listing all the activities an area might be used for so that the final plan will provide the right atmosphere and the necessary facilities for each activity. The main purpose of such a room as a bedroom is obvious. But the room may also have several less obvious uses. The master bedroom, for example, might also serve as a family office, which needs a desk, desk chair, and lighting for desk work.

Like the purpose of the interior, the life style of those who use it helps determine both the mood and the specific items to be included in the design plan. For example, active children need a play area with a bright mood and with furnishings that withstand rough treatment. Most people who enjoy casual living prefer a simply furnished room to an elaborate, formal one. Individual preferences for colors and materials as well as personal interests in a sport or hobby may also help in creating the design plan.

A budget can help a designer make the best use of the money available for an interior design project. Many people seek ways to cut expenses, which permits them to spend more money on expensive parts of the design. Some people may reuse old furniture, carpets, or other items in their new design. They may also choose to save money by restoring old furniture. A budget may also be important in making a predesign analysis of the interior architecture. For instance, if a large budget is available for a project, the designer may wish to change the size or shape of an area by removing walls or by adding such features as partitions or built-in cabinets.

All the predesign considerations help establish what professional designers refer to as the design concept. The design concept may be the general mood desired for an interior; a design element, such as pattern or texture; or a specific item, such as a favorite piece of furniture or a painting. By selecting each item for the interior to harmonize with the design concept, the designer can create a unified final plan.

▪▶ 测 试 篇 ◀▪

Ⅰ. 单项选择

1. Marry and I _____ the new college life soon, but Tom didn't.

   A. saw to   B. adapted to   C. used to   D. stuck to

2. He could not _____ ignorance as his excuse; he should have known what was happening in his department.   (CET-6 05/1)

   A. petition   B. plead   C. resort   D. reproach

3. When supply exceeds demand for any product, prices are _____ to fall.   (CET-6 03/1)

   A. timely   B. simultaneous   C. subject   D. liable

4. We couldn't really afford to buy a house so we got it on _____ and paid monthly.   (CET-6 02/6)

   A. investments   B. requirements   C. arrangements   D. installments

5. Shoes of this kind are _____ to slip on wet ground.   (CET-6 02/1)

   A. feasible   B. appropriate   C. apt   D. fitting

6. This is an ideal site for a university _____ it is far from the downtown area.

   A. provided that   B. now that   C. so that   D. in that

7. Although many people view conflict as bad, conflict is sometimes useful _____ it forces people to test the relative merits of their attitudes and behaviors.

   A. by which   B. to which   C. in that   D. so that

8. Government cannot operate effectively _____ it is free from such interference.

   A. so long as   B. so that   C. unless   D. because

9. The little man was _____ one metre fifty high.

   A. almost more than   B. hardly more than   C. nearly more than   D. as much as

10. Language belongs to each one of us, to the flower-seller _____ to the professor.

    A. as much as   B. as far as   C. the same as   D. as long as

Ⅱ. 翻译

11. 他称头疼，早早地走了。（plead a headache）

12. 政府为下岗工人提供就业机会。（offer outlets for）

13. 他说话这么快，我都跟不上了。（so... that）

14. 我安装了办公软件。（have sth. installed）

15. 夏天食品很容易坏。（tend to）

拓展篇

1. B   2. A   3. A   4. B   5. B   6. C   7. B   8. A

Do It Yourself magazine organizes a competition every summer to find the "Handyman of the Year".
The winner this year is Mr. Roy Miller, a Sheffield postman. A journalist and a photographer have
come to his house. The journalist is interviewing Mr. Miller for an article in the magazine.

Journalist: Well, I'm very impressed by all the work you've done on your house, Mr. Miller. How long
        have you been working on it?

Mr. Miller: I first became interested in do-it-yourself several years ago. You see, my son Paul is
        disabled. He's in a wheel-chair and I just had to make alterations to the house. I couldn't
        afford to pay workmen to do it. I had to learn to do it myself.

Journalist: Have you had any experience of this kind of work? Did you have any practical skills?

Mr. Miller: No. I got a few books from the library but they didn't help very much. Then I decided to go
        to evening classes so that I could learn basic carpentry and electrics.

Journalist: What sort of changes did you make to the house?

Mr. Miller: First of all, practical things to help Paul. You never really realize the problems
        handicapped people have until it affects your own family. Most government buildings, for
        example, have steps up to the door. They don't plan buildings so that disabled people can
        get in and out. We used to live in a flat, and of course, it was totally unsuitable. Just
        imagine the problems a disabled person would have in your house. We needed a large
        house with wide corridors so that Paul could get from one room to another. We didn't have
        much money and we had to buy this one. It's over ninety years old and it was in a very bad
        state of repair.

Journalist: Where did you begin?

Mr. Miller: The electrics. I completely rewired the house so that Paul could reach all the switches. I
        had to lower the light switches and raise the power-points. I went on to do the whole house
        so that Paul could reach things and go where he wanted.

Journalist: What else did you do?

Mr. Miller: By the time I'd altered everything for Paul, do-it-yourself had become a hobby. I really enjoyed doing things with my hands. Look, I even installed smoke-alarms.

Journalist: What was the purpose of that?

Mr. Miller: I was very worried about fire. You see, Paul can't move very quickly. I fitted them so that we would have plenty of warning if there were a fire. I put in a complete burglar-alarm system. It took weeks. The front door opens automatically, and I'm going to put a device on Paul's wheelchair so that he'll be able to open and close it when he wants.

Journalist: What are you working on now?

Mr. Miller: I've just finished the kitchen. I've designed it so that he can reach everything. Now I'm building an extension so that Paul will have a large room on the ground floor where he can work.

Journalist: There's a £10,000 prize. How are you going to spend it?

Mr. Miller: I am going to start my own business so that I can convert ordinary houses for disabled people. I think I've become an expert on the subject.

测试篇

1-5 BBDDC   6-10 DCCBA

11. He left early, pleading a headache.

12. The government offers outlets for the laid-off.

13. So fast does he speak that I almost cannot follow him.

14. I have office software installed.

15. Food tends to go bad in summer.

Lesson **47.** Too high a price?

积累篇

I. 振振有"词"

1. Pollution is the price we pay for an overpopulated, over-industrialized planet.

pollution 污染	overpopulated 人口过多的	industrialized 工业化的
pollutant 污染物	underpopulated 人口不足的	commercialized 商业化的
contamination 感染	densely-populated 人口稠密的	mechanized 机械化的
corruption 腐败	sparsely-populated 人口稀少的	automated 自动化的
adulteration 掺假	populous 人口众多的	urbanized 城市化的
vitiation (道德)败坏	uninhabited 荒无人烟的	modernized 现代化的

2. Burglar alarms going off at any time of the day or night serve only to annoy passers-by.

burglar alarm 防盗警报	annoy 惹怒	passer-by 过路人
car alarm 汽车警报	irritate 激怒	stander-by 旁观者
alarm clock 闹钟	exasperate 惹恼	hanger-on 跟随者;食客
sound an alarm 发警报	displease 使不快	grown-up 成年人
alarmist 杞人忧天者	harry 骚扰	pedestrian 行人
	infuriate 使大怒	stroller 散步者

II. 现身说"法": every time引导时间状语从句

> You have a steady diet of pesticides every time you think you are eating fresh salads and vegetables, or just having an innocent glass of water.
>
> 当你认为在享用新鲜色拉和蔬菜或在饮用一杯纯净水的时候,实际上每次都是在吃杀虫剂。

这里every time引导时间状语从句,表过去或特定环境中经常发生的事件。相似用法的短语有:each time, next time, by the time, the day, the week等,但在这些短语后一般不再加when。例:

Every time I listen to your advice, I get out of trouble. 每次听从你的建议,我总能化险为夷。

He flinched each time he spoke to her. 他每次和她说话都是畏畏缩缩的。

Next time you come, remember to bring along your family. 你下次来的时候,记着把家人一起带来。

The day he returned, his son was brought to the world. 他回来的那一天,儿子恰好出生了。

III. 说"文"解"字"

1. There are only four ways you can deal with rubbish: dump it, burn it, turn it into something you can use again, attempt to produce less of it.

译文：我们只有4种对付垃圾的方法：倾倒、焚烧、将其变成再生材料或试图少生产一些。

解析：彩色部分作前面only four ways的同位语，ways后省略了连接词that。此外，后面举出的4种方法看似并列，实则含有递进意味。

2. But the sheer volume of rubbish we produce worldwide threatens to overwhelm us.

译文：但是，我们在世界范围内所生产的垃圾就有把我们淹没的危险。

解析：1) worldwide在本句中作副词，它也可以作形容词，例：

Bill Gates has achieved worldwide eminence. 比尔·盖茨世界闻名。

worldwide web 互联网

2) 与worldwide用法相同的是nationwide（全国范围内/全国的）。例：

The businessman flies nationwide all year long. 这位商人整年在全国各地飞来飞去。

The singer started his nationwide tour. 这位歌手开始了其全国巡演。

3) threaten to do 不宜直译，而是表"有… 凶兆"。例：

The dark clouds threaten rain. 黑云预示着大雨将近。

promise to do 有… 吉兆

A timely snow promises a bumper harvest. 瑞雪兆丰年。

3. And if you think you'll abandon meat and become a vegetarian, you have the choice of very expensive organically-grown vegetables or a steady diet of pesticides.

译文：如果你不吃肉而成为素食者，那么你可以两者择一：或是选用价格昂贵的有机培植蔬菜，或是不断地吃进杀虫剂。

解析：1) abandon在这里灵活处理为"不吃"，下面是该词的另外一些活用现象：

They abandoned that war-torn country.（abandon 译为"离开"）

他们离开了那个战乱纷飞的国家。

At that moment my memory completely abandoned me.（abandon 译为"使记不起来"）

那一刻我完全记不起来了。

She abandoned herself to the serene scenery.（abandon 译为"沉浸"）

她完全沉浸在那幽静的景色之中。

2) vegetarian意思是"素食主义者"，相关词有：

carnivore 食肉者　　　　　　herbivore 食草动物

3) organically-grown vegetables即不施化肥等的环保蔬菜，反义词是inorganically-grown vegetables（施化肥，喷洒农药等的蔬菜）

4. New technology has also made its own contribution to noise.

译文：新技术也为噪音作出了它的贡献。

解析：make one's contribution to sth. 意思是"为…作贡献"，在这里是反语用法，具有幽默效果。反语在文学作品中运用甚广，必须依据一定的语境才能准确判断。掌握这一修辞法对于提升阅读水平大有裨益。

拓 展 篇

I.英语趣园

The economic costs of noise to society are several. Airports are currently operating at less than capacity because of noise regulations which restrict their hours of operation. At Washington's National Airport, for instance no jet traffic is allowed from 7 a.m. to 11 p.m. Other airports restrict the use of central runways. One estimate is that noise restrictions reduce possible airport use by 20 percent.

II.听力快车

There can be no doubt that _____, two top US government climate experts said.

_____, they say—contradicting critics, already in the minority, who argue that _____.

"There is no doubt that the composition of the atmosphere is changing because of human activities, and today _____." Some experts said so.

The likely result is more _____, _____, extreme precipitation events, and related impacts, e.g., wildfires, heat stress, vegetation changes, and _____. They added.

III.补充阅读

Air pollution

Wherever you go, whatever you do, inside, outside, upstairs, downstairs, on top of a mountain, down in the bottom of a coal mine, you're always surrounded by a sea of gases that we call air, or the atmosphere. These gases cannot be seen and we are rarely aware of them. But they are of the greatest importance, for without atmosphere neither man, animals, nor plants can live. Of almost equal importance is the quality of the atmosphere. Whether it is pure or whether it is impure, or polluted. It is easy to understand why clean air is important to good health, for throughout life, human beings take air into their lungs about 20 times a minute. The air is drawn into the lungs through the nose or mouth. After a few seconds the process is reversed and the air is blown out of the lungs through the nose or mouth. During this process of inhaling and exhaling, the impurities in the air may be absorbed by the body or deposited in the lungs.

The atmosphere is a mixture of about one part oxygen, four parts nitrogen, very small amounts of carbon dioxide and rare inert gases, and water in the form of water vapour. Oxygen, nitrogen, and water play an essential part in man's survival. The oxygen in the atmosphere is essential for all life processes. The nitrogen is essential for the plant life that provides man with the nutrients, the needs for good health. The moisture in the atmosphere is essential for plant growth and agriculture, and for the water man requires. When air contains more than a small amount of particulate matter or gases other than the ones mentioned, the air is considered to be polluted.

Even the purest air contains small amounts of pollution. Perhaps really clean air can be found only in experimental laboratories. Even in country areas, far removed factories and heavy traffic, air may contain pollen from plants, dust from the soil, and occasional bacteria and germs. But these pollutants are generally in such small amounts that they are not important. Throughout the world, air pollution is generally present in all cities, especially those with a population of more than 50,000.

▶ 测 试 篇 ◀

I. 单项选择

1. You cannot imagine how _____ I feel with my duties sometimes. （CET-6 04/6）
   A. overflowed   B. overthrown   C. overwhelmed   D. overturned

2. The Chinese Red Cross _____ a generous sum to the relief of the victims of the earthquake in Turkey. （CET-6 03/9）
   A. administered   B. elevated   C. assessed   D. contributed

3. Please be careful when you are drinking coffee in case you _____ the new carpet.
   A. crash   B. pollute   C. spot   D. stain

4. Your story about the frog turning into a prince is _____ nonsense.
   A. sheer   B. shear   C. shield   D. sheet

5. Out of _____ revenge, he did his worst to blacken her character and ruin her reputation.
   A. perfect   B. total   C. sheer   D. integral

6. I could hear nothing but the roar of the airplane engines which _____ all other sounds. （CET-6 05/12）
   A. overturned   B. drowned   C. deafened   D. smoothed

7. Their claims to damages have not been convincingly _____.
   A. refuted   B. overwhelmed   C. depressed   D. intimidated

8. Students are expected to be quiet and _____ in an Asian classroom.
   A. obedient   B. overwhelming   C. skeptical   D. subsidiary

9. Some American colleges are state-supported, others are privately _____, and still others are supported by religious organizations.
   A. ensured   B. attributed   C. authorized   D. endowed

10. Everyone should be _____ to a decent standard of living and an opportunity to be educated.
    A. attributed   B. entitled   C. identified   D. justified

II. 翻译

11. 领土的沦丧是为了获得一个表面的和平所付出的高昂的代价。（too high a price to pay）

12. 我们办公室每天的电话量很大。（a heavy call volume）

13. 闹钟每天在6点钟响。（go off）

14. 这儿的方向让我晕头转向。（serve to do）

15. 这家宾馆是五星级的。（be rated）

拓展篇

There can be no doubt that <u>global warming is real and is being caused by people</u>, two top US government climate experts said.

<u>Industrial emissions are a leading cause</u>, they say—contradicting critics, already in the minority, who argue that <u>climate change could be caused by mostly natural forces</u>.

"There is no doubt that the composition of the atmosphere is changing because of human activities, and today <u>greenhouse gases are the largest human influence on global climate</u>." Some experts said so.

The likely result is more <u>frequent heat waves</u>, <u>droughts</u>, extreme precipitation events, and related impacts, e.g., wildfires, heat stress, vegetation changes, and <u>sea-level rise</u>. They added.

测试篇

1-5 CDDAC   6-10 BAADB

11. The loss of territory is too high a price to pay for a seeming peace.

12. Our office receives a heavy call volume every day.

13. The alarm clock goes off at 6 every day.

14. The directions here only serve to bewilder me.

15. The hotel is rated 5-star.

Lesson The silent village

I.振振有"词"

1. In this <u>much-travelled</u> world, there are still <u>thousands of</u> places which are <u>inaccessible</u> to tourists.

由much组成的复合形容词：
much-travelled 旅游频繁的
much-visited 游客众多的
much-appreciated 颇受欢迎的
much-discussed 屡次讨论的

thousands of... 数千…
hundreds of... 数百…
tens of thousands of... 数万…
hundreds of thousands... 数十万…
millions of... 数百万…
hundreds of millions of... 数亿…
billions of... 数十亿…

inaccessible 难以接近的
unreachable 难以达到的
unattainable 难以企及的
unapproachable 无法接近的
ungetatable 无法到达的
unfrequented 不常光顾的

2. We always <u>assume</u> that villagers in <u>remote</u> places are friendly and <u>hospitable</u>.

以-sume结尾的动词变名词的模式：
assume: assumption 认为；假设
presume: presumption 认为；假设
consume: consumption 消费
resume: resumption 恢复

remote 遥远的
outlying 偏远的
faraway 遥远的
godforsaken 偏僻的
isolated 封闭的
secluded 与世隔绝的

hospitable 好客的
sociable 乐于交际的
convivial 善于应酬的
gracious 殷勤的
amicable 亲切的
generous 慷慨的

3. Several <u>bus loads of</u> tourists <u>descended on</u> the town.

用load表示的数量短语：
a bus load of tourists 一车游客
a car load of passengers 一轿车乘客
a train load of passengers 一火车乘客
a truck load of coal 一卡车煤
a cart load of vegetable 一大车蔬菜

descend 降落
descend on 降临
descendible 可世袭的
ascend 上升
descendant 后代
ascendant 祖先

4. The village seemed <u>deserted</u>, the only sign of life being an <u>ugly-looking</u> black goat on a short length of rope tied to a tree in a field <u>nearby</u>.

表环境不佳的形容词：
deserted 荒凉的
bleak 凄凉的
uninhabited 荒无人烟的
insulated 封闭的
derelict 破败的
wretched 糟糕的
inclement 恶劣的

nearby 在附近
in the vicinity 在附近（正式）
neighbouring 相邻的
bordering 接壤的
close at hand 近在手边
be adjacent to... 与⋯毗邻
within an inch of... 离⋯仅咫尺之遥

表长相的复合形容词：
ugly-looking 长相丑陋的
nice-looking 长相好看的
good-looking 长相英俊的
modern-looking 长相摩登的
plain-looking 长相平平的
earthy-looking 长相土气的

II. 现身说"法"：**more than**结构

This was more than we could bear.
这简直令我们难以忍受。

more than... can意为"简直不可能"。例：

How he manages to live is more than I can tell. 我简直难以想像他是怎样生活的。

It is more than flesh and blood can bear. 这非血肉之躯所能忍受。

The beauty of the place is more than I can describe. 这地方景色之美，非笔墨所能形容。

We all complain of the shortness of time, and yet we have more than we know what to do with.

我们都在抱怨时光之短暂，然而有时时光充裕，我们却无所事事。

联想记忆：more than+动词

将more than放在动词之前，可译为"深为，十二分的，岂止"。例：

He has more than repaid my kindness. 他岂止是报答了我的帮助。

I prefer autumn to spring. What we lose in flowers we more than gain in fruits.

相比春天我更喜欢秋天。我们失去春花而以秋实补偿绰绰有余。

More is meant than meets the ear. 有言外之意。

III. 说"文"解"字"

1. Visits to **really remote villages are seldom enjoyable.**

译文：到真正偏僻的村庄去旅游并不是一件快乐的事情。

解析：visit作名词时后面要接介词to，若作动词时则不必。approach有相同用法。例：

He is longing to visit the Forbidden City.（visit作动词）

He is longing for a visit to the Forbidden City.（visit作名词）他渴望着参观故宫。

A pedlar was approaching me.（approach作动词）一个小贩朝我走来。

His best approach to the great man lay through a mutual friend.（approach作名词）

对他来说，要接近那位大人物，最好的办法是通过一位双方都认识的朋友。

2. **But we** had no idea how **we could get across the stream.**

　　译文：但我们却不知如何越过这条小溪。

　　解析：how引导的内容作idea的同位语，how前面省略了of。一般而言，当关系副词how, when, 关系代词what, whose以及whether引导从句或不定式时，其前面的of, about, as to等常可省略。例：

　　　　I had no idea (of) when he would go abroad. 我不清楚他何时出国。

　　　　He hesitated (about) what to do next. 下一步该做什么，他很犹豫。

　　　　I'm not aware (of) how he won the negotiation. 我不知道他是如何在谈判中获胜的。

3. **The village seemed deserted,** the only sign of life being an ugly-looking black goat on a short length of rope tied to a tree in a field nearby.

　　译文：村里似乎无人居住，惟一的生命迹象是附近田里一只面目可憎的黑山羊。

　　解析：彩色部分是短语，而非句子，是独立主格结构。

4. **I concluded** that they were simply **shy of strangers.**

　　译文：我认为他们只不过是怕见生人罢了。

　　解析：1）conclude在这里相当于think，参看第41课"说'文'解'字'"部分。

　　　　　2）shy本指"腼腆的，害羞的"，若后接of则表示"不喜欢的，有戒心的"。例：

　　　　　My sister is shy of publicity. 我妹妹不爱抛头露面。

　　　　　The boy is shy of books. 这个男孩不爱读书。

　　　　　Don't be shy of telling your parents what you think.

　　　　　你有什么想法尽管告诉父母，不要有顾虑。

▌　拓 展 篇

Ⅰ.英语趣园

　　The Balkans, a large area in southeast Europe, includes Greece, Romania, Bulgaria, Albania and Yugoslavia. It is an area in which there have been many wars and many changes in the borders of the countries. On the Balkan Peninsula, the "next time", when speaking of war, means a dozen or half a dozen years. Hence, we are apt to speak in a lightly contemptuous manner of these aggressive Balkan people who are forever fighting among each other. But do we ever realize with what sort of an inheritance of strife and cruelty and bloodshed and slavery and plunder and rape and arson the average Serbian or Bulgarian boy starts out upon his career through life?

Ⅱ.听力快车 🎧

　　The vast land of America was once inhabited by _____. These "Indians" had lived throughout the land for thousands of years, and they will always remain the true fathers of America. _____. Later, more European immigrants came, and _____.

　　Then, _____, the old white grandfather across the sea. The miracle of America happened, and its dynamic birth rapidly changed the entire world. _____. In a very short time, _____. The United States is a nonpareil icon, and the envy of the world.

Ⅲ. 补充阅读

The American character has some strongly-marked traits that people from other countries find very noticeable, sometimes admirable, sometimes puzzling, sometimes bothersome. Knowing something of the American character is therefore important for understanding American culture and interacting with Americans.

Americans are the descendants of immigrants, sometimes of quite recent ones. Immigrants are typically people who, for whatever reason, believe that through effort and the endurance of suffering, life can be made better. Life in a new country with a new language is not easy. Yet immigrants are constantly uprooting their lives, leaving most of their friends and family behind, and going to the US. So it is no mystery that Americans have a drive to work harder and become more successful. Children learn from their parents, and the parents of Americans were not a random sample of the Europeans （and other groups）from which they came but a self-selected group of people with particular energy and drive.

There has been a fair amount of comment recently that America is very independent and not very minded to pay attention to international opinion. Given their cultural heritage, this is unsurprising. Their ancestors cared little about the opinions of the countries that they left. What would make their descendants think differently?

The frontier spirit

The common thread that binds Americans stems from their individualism, self-reliance, independence, courage to take risks and readiness to challenge the impossible. Americans believe that no frontier was or is beyond them. Indeed, no other nation uses the word frontier in the special way Americans do. During the nineteenth century, American settlers relentlessly pushed westward, ploughing the plains, killing the Indians, crossing the Rocky Mountains, and exploring the Pacific Ocean. Then they wondered where to go next. The answer is: around the world and into outer space. Only last month President Bush announced a vastly expensive plan to send man to Mars.

One cannot deny the powerful impact settlement made on the national consciousness and pride of Americans. Stories and images of the frontier and the settling of the West have shaped American identity and values. Log cabins and wagon trains, cowboys and Indians, Buffalo Bill and General Custer. These and other frontier images pervade American lives, from fiction to films to advertising, where they attach themselves to products from pancake syrup to cologne, blue jeans to banks. There is a national preoccupation with this uniquely American image. Indeed, in his speech during his state visit to London in November, President Bush mentioned two factors which influenced the development of the American character, "the fine heritage that comes from you..." and "the spirit of the frontier".

▶ 测 试 篇 ◀

Ⅰ. 单项选择

1. There is no _____ to their house from the main road.
   A. access   B. avenue   C. exposure   D. edge

2. Only a few people have _____ to the full facts of the incident.
   A. access   B. resort   C. contact   D. path

3. The British government often says that furnishing children with _____ to the information superhighway is a top priority.

A. procedure   B. protection   C. allowance   D. access

4. For professional athletes, _____ to the Olympics means that they have a chance to enter the history books.

    A. access   B. attachment   C. appeal   D. approach

5. Over a third of the population was estimated to have no _____ to the health service.

    A. assessment   B. assignment   C. exception   D. access

6. The police were alerted that the escaped criminal might be in the _____.

    A. vain   B. vicinity   C. court   D. jail

7. The tenant must be prepared to decorate the house _____ the terms of the contract.

    A. in the vicinity of   B. in quest of

    C. in accordance with   D. in collaboration with

8. Most people tend to think they are so efficient at their job that they are _____.

    A. inaccessible   B. immovable   C. irreversible   D. irreplaceable

9. Some children display an _____ curiosity about every new thing they encounter.

    A. incredible   B. infectious   C. incompatible   D. inaccessible

10. The place did not appear to be popular, for it was completely deserted, and in any case _____ to traffic.

    A. inadequate   B. inaccessible   C. incompatible   D. insignificant

II. 翻译

11. 学校离这不远，周围有便利的地铁和公交设施。（with convenient access）

12. 我的房子就在我上班地方的附近，所以我走着去就可以。（in the vicinity of）

13. 这可不是一个普通人能够理解的。（more than）

14. 悬崖边上有座寺庙。（perch）

15. 停车场的车子一字排开。（be lined）

答案

拓展篇

    The vast land of America was once inhabited by a relatively small number of indigenous people. These "Indians" had lived throughout the land for thousands of years, and they will always remain the true fathers of America. American Indians helped the Pilgrims survive the winter. Later, more European immigrants came, and American settlement finally outgrew the Indian fathers.

    Then, on July 4, 1776, America declared its independence from England, the old white grandfather across the sea. The miracle of America happened, and its dynamic birth rapidly changed the entire world. America developed into thirteen colonies, then into the strong 50 states that she is today. In a very short time, America grew from a log cabin to the largest and most technologically powerful economy in the world. The United States is a nonpareil icon, and the envy of the world.

测试篇

1-5 AADAD   6-10 BCDAB

11. The school is near here with convenient subway and bus access.

12. My house is in the vicinity of my workplace, so it's within walking distance.

13. This is more than an ordinary man can understand.

14. There is a temple perched on the edge of the cliff.

15. The cars in the parking lot are lined head to tail.

Lesson 49. The ideal servant

积 累 篇

I. 振振有"词"

1. If she were alive today she would not be able to <u>air her views on</u> her <u>favourite</u> <u>topic of conversation</u>: domestic servants.

air one's views on... 对…发表看法	topic of conversation 话题
state one's opinion on... 对…阐述看法	theme 主题
voice one's ideas on... 对…发表观点	argument 论点
make remark on... 对…作评述	premise 前提
make comment on... 对…作评论	controversy 争论
pass judgment on... 对…作判断	center of controversy 争论焦点

以下表"极致，惟一，绝对"的形容词无比较级用法：

ideal 最理想的	perfect 完美的
favourite 最好的	excellent 杰出的
complete 完全的	

2. She was <u>sentimentally</u> <u>attached to</u> this house,...she <u>persisted in</u> living there long after her husband's death.

关于人的"情感"的词汇：	be attached to... 依恋…	persist in... 坚持…
sentimental 多愁善感的	cling to... 依附…	persevere in... 坚持…
emotional 情绪化的	adhere to... 坚持…，拥护…	stick to... 坚持…
moody 喜怒无常的	appeal to sb. 吸引某人	stand to one's gun 坚持主张
fickle 变化无常的	be glued to... 黏着在…；被…吸引	hold one's ground 坚持立场
capricious 极端任性的	take a fancy to... 极其喜欢…	face it out 坚持到底
obstinate 无比固执的		

3. Aunt Harriet <u>presided over</u> an <u>invisible</u> army of servants that continuously <u>scrubbed</u>, cleaned and polished.

preside over/at... 掌管…	invisible 看不见的	scrub 擦洗	polish 擦光
command... 统帅…	intangible 摸不到的	rub 涂抹	cleanse 清洗
take possession of... 掌控…	imperceptible 觉察不到的	scrape 刮、蹭	scour 擦拭
dominate... 统治…	indiscernible 无法辨别的	scratch 抓、挠	
supervise... 监督…	inconspicuous 不显著的		
reign over... 管理…	microscopic 极其微小的		

Ⅱ. 现身说"法": 现在虚拟语气

If she were alive today she would not be able air her views on her favourite topic of conversation: domestic servants.（该句使用了虚拟语气句型，表达现在不太可能出现的情形）如果她活到今天，她将不能就她热衷的话题"佣人"发表看法了。

1. 现在虚拟语气的构成模式是：条件从句：If+主语+were或V-ed…，主句：主语+would（should、could、might）+动词原形。此外，条件从句的was常用were替代，尤其是在if之后。例：

   If there were no air and water, nothing could live. 如果没有空气和水，任何生物将难以生存。

   If I knew Latin, I should read these materials. 如果我懂拉丁语，我就能读懂这些材料。

   If they were here, they would help me. 如果他们在这儿，他们会帮助我的。

2. 如果条件从句中有were，可以将were前置，省略if，但主句的结构顺序不变。因此，本文的例句可以改写为：Were she alive today she would not be able to air her views on her favourite topic of conversation: domestic servants.

Ⅲ. 说"文"解"字"

1. It is a good thing my aunt Harriet died years ago.

   译文：我姑妈哈丽特多年前就去世了，这倒是件好事。

   解析：这句话表面上有些不可思议，事实上作者运用了幽默手法。因为下文中说我姑妈爱对佣人大加评判，而如今DIY盛行，佣人已日见甚微，所以她的离世不失为一桩好事。

2. Before she grew old, Aunt Harriet used to entertain lavishly.

   译文：哈丽特姑妈年轻时，喜欢大摆宴席，招待宾客。

   解析：entertain lavishly中间省略了her guests，该结构已形成固定表达。类似意义的短语有：

   play host to sb. 热情款待某人   regale sb. with… 用…款待某人

   feast sb. with… 用…款待某人   keep open house 大宴宾客

3. Aunt Harriet could not find words to praise Bessie's industriousness and efficiency.

   译文：哈丽特姑妈不知该用什么言辞来赞扬贝西的勤奋和麻利。

   解析：彩色部分可以作为表达赞美的经典句型加以摹写。其他类似的句型有：

   Words fail sb. in his/her praise of…   sth. is beyond words/description.

   例：Words fails me in my praise of the beauty of the West Lake.

   The beauty of the West Lake is beyond description. 西湖之美难以言表。

4. Not only was the meal well below the usual standard, but Bessie seemed unable to walk steadily.

   译文：不仅饭菜远不如平时做得好，而且贝西似乎走起路来都东倒西歪的。

   解析：1）本句是由not only… but… 连接的并列句，因not only置于句首，句子进行了倒装。但请注意，倒装现象只出现在前面部分，but之后的内容位置不变。

   2）well在句中是程度副词，修饰below，可译为"相当，可观地"。例：

   It's well worth trying. 这很值得一试。

   I can't reach it; it's well above my head. 我够不着；它在我上方有相当一段距离。

   Let me know well in advance. 请尽量让我提前知道。

5. The guests... had had a difficult time trying to conceal their amusement.

译文：客人们努力克制才没笑出声来。

解析：彩色部分不宜直译，因此采用了意译。例：

The girl had a difficult time making herself understood.

这个女孩好不容易才让别人理解她的意思。

拓 展 篇

Ⅰ.英语趣园

Résumé tips

Students tend to focus their cover letters on their job history with a quick reference to their years at school. In doing so, they are selling themselves short. The following should be covered in it: teamwork skills, strong communication skills, organization skills, problem-solving abilities.

Ⅱ.听力快车

Do you have a vacancy for a secretary?

David's friend, Mary Lee, heard that there was a vacant position for a secretary in a company. Therefore, she went there for an interview.

Mary: I heard that you have a vacant position for a secretary. I've come to apply for the job.

Receptionist: Please wait for a second.

Mary: Okay.

Mr Graham: Who is the next applicant?

Receptionist: Miss, it's your turn.

Mary: I'm.

Mr Graham: Come this way, Please. _____.

Mary: Yes, here it is.

Mr Graham: Sit down, Miss... You're presently working at Creative Advertising Company?

Mary: Yes, _____.

Mr Graham: _____? Is it hard work?

Mary: I don't mind hard work and working overtime. It's the atmosphere that drives me crazy.

Mr Graham: It'll be tough work to be a secretary here. You must understand that. _____

_____. Have you been a secretary before?

Mary: Yes, I have. I was a pretty good secretary. I know how to handle a bad-tempered boss.

_____.

Mr Graham: Thank you for coming. _____.

Ⅲ.补充阅读

The Italian job

Every Italian mother dreams that her children, especially her male children, will achieve lo starbene—a state of well-being in their work. What this generally entails is finding a steady job and

---

259

looking good behind a big desk in the air-conditioned office of a government department or government-owned bank or company. Though not particularly well-paid, these jobs entitle their holders to 13 or 14 months' salary a year and offer all sorts of perks including almost total job security and the possibility of retiring early on a full pension. Best of all, they are usually so undemanding that their holders can concentrate most of their energies on the family business, or on whatever really interests them: watching football, collecting stamps or just sitting, sipping coffee, reading comics.

Life in the average Italian office is like Italian life in general. Style and behavior are important, and managerial and office staff should, of course, look and act the part. Punctuality has been taken a little more seriously since the advent of clocking in and out of work.

Office hours can be very long in the private sector (8: 00 a.m.—7: 30 p.m. with only half an hour for lunch). However, things are very different in the public sector: some offices are only open to the public for two hours a week, and others are never open at all.

Many of the public holidays that Italians took for Saint's Days have now been surrendered, so the practice of ponti (building "bridges" between the weekend and a national holiday) assumes greater importance. Holidays are planned long in advance so as to be able to link them to public holidays.

This is why Italian strikes usually take place on Monday or Friday.

▪▶ 测 试 篇 ◀▪

I. 单项选择

1. For more than 20 years, we've been supporting educational programs that _____ from kindergartens to colleges.
   A. move   B. shift   C. range   D. spread
2. The author of the report is well _____ with the problems in the hospital because he has been working there for many years.
   A. informed   B. acquainted   C. enlightened   D. acknowledged
3. Although it was his first experience as chairman, he _____ over the meeting with great skill.
   A. presided   B. administered   C. mastered   D. executed
4. For many years the Japanese have _____ the car market.
   A. presided   B. occupied   C. operated   D. dominated
5. They couldn't see a _____ of hope that they would be saved by a passing ship.
   A. grain   B. span   C. slice   D. gleam
6. There are other problems which I don't propose to _____ at the moment.
   A. go into   B. go around   C. go for   D. go up
7. Criticism and self-criticism is necessary _____ it helps us to find and correct our mistakes.
   A. by that   B. at that   C. on that   D. in that
8. Britain's press is unusual _____ it is divided into two very different types of newspaper: the quality press and the popular press.
   A. in how   B. in what   C. in which   D. in that
9. As far as the rank of position is concerned and associate professor is _____ to a professor though they are almost equally knowledgeable.
   A. attached   B. subsidiary   C. previous   D. inferior

10. _____ your opinions are worth considering, the committee finds it unwise to place too much importance on them.

A. As   B. Since   C. Provided   D. While

Ⅱ. 翻译

11. 还好，车钥匙在你这儿。我还以为丢了。（It's a good thing）

12. 她总是喜欢向别人诉苦。（give air to ）

13. 她和她的丈夫难舍难分。（be sentimentally attached to ）

14. 保持伤口清洁。（free from dust ）

15. 春去春来。（come and go ）

拓展篇

Do you have a vacancy for a secretary?

（David's friend, Mary Lee, heard that there was a vacant position for a secretary in a company. Therefore, she went there for an interview.）

Mary: I heard that you have a vacant position for a secretary. I've come to apply for the job.

Receptionist: Please wait for a second.

Mary: Okay.

Mr Graham: Who is the next applicant?

Receptionist: Miss, it's your turn.

Mary: I'm.

Mr Graham: Come this way, Please. <u>Do you have your resume with you</u>?

Mary: Yes, here it is.

Mr Graham: Sit down, Miss... You're presently working at Creative Advertising Company?

Mary: Yes, <u>as a sales representative</u>.

Mr Graham: <u>What makes you want to quit the job</u>? Is it hard work?

Mary: I don't mind hard work and working overtime. It's the atmosphere that drives me crazy.

Mr Graham: It'll be tough work to be a secretary here. You must understand that. <u>The boss is very touchy and hard to get along with</u>. Have you been a secretary before?

Mary: Yes, I have. I was a pretty good secretary. I know how to handle a bad-tempered boss. <u>I'm sure I'll be a competent secretary if you take me as your staff</u>.

Mr Graham: Thank you for coming. <u>I'll let you know as soon as we've made a decision</u>.

测试篇

1-5 CBADD   6-10 ADDBD

11. It's a good thing the key is with you. I had thought I lost it.

12. She is fond of giving air to her grievances.

13. She and her husband are sentimentally attached to each other.

14. Keep your wound free from dust.

15. The spring comes and goes.

Lesson 50. New Year resolutions

积累篇

Ⅰ.振振有"词"

1. Mentally, at least, most of us could compile formidable lists of "dos" and "don'ts".

at least 至少，起码	compile 编制	由非名词词汇转化的名词短语：
at most 至多	compiler 编著者	dos and don'ts 要做与不做之事
at best 最多	edit 编辑	likes and dislikes 喜欢与不喜欢之事
at worst 大不了	editor 编辑	ups and downs 沉浮
first and last 大致看来	chief editor 主编	highs and lows 兴衰
first or last 迟早	compose 创作	ins and outs of sth. 某事的来龙去脉
first and foremost 首先	composition 作文；作品	
last but not least 最后但并非不重要	garner 筛选	

2. The same old favourites recur year in year out with monotonous regularity.

recur 再现，再发生	year in year out 年复一年	表数字的前缀：
occur 出现，发生	one year after another 年复一年	mono- 一；bi- 二；tri- 三；
concur 同现，同时发生	year after year 年复一年	quad- 四；penta- 五；hexa- 六；
incur 导致	day in day out 日复一日	sept- 七；hepta- 七；octa- 八；
coincide with... 与…巧合	one day after another 日复一日	ennea- 九；deci- 十；
coexist 共存		

3. If we remain inveterate smokers, it is only because we have so often experienced the frustration that results from failure.

result from... 由于…	derive from... 来自于…	英语中"老"的不同表达：
result in... 导致…	originate in... 起源于…	inveterate smoker 老烟民 aged wine 老酒
stem form... 源于…	develop from... 产生于…	regular customer 老顾客 longtime friend 老友
		hardened smuggler 老走私犯

Ⅱ.现身说"法"：so that结构

We also make the fundamental error of announcing our resolutions to everybody so that we look even more foolish when we slip back into our bad old ways.（so that引导结果状语从句）

我们还犯一个根本性的错误，即把我们的决心向大家宣布，这样一旦再染上以前的坏习惯，在别人眼里会显得更加难堪。

1. so that可表目的，相当于in order that，其后常接may、should、could等，口语则多用can。请比较以下例句：

He spoke clearly so that everyone could hear. （表结果）他说得很清楚，每个人都听见了。

He spoke clearly, so that everyone could hear. （表目的）他说得很清楚，以便每个人都能听见。

He went early so that he got a good seat. （表结果）他去得很早，得到了一个好座。

Come early, so that you can get a good seat. （表目的）来早点，你就能得到一个好座。

可以看出，so that表目的时多以逗号与主句间隔。

2. so that在较古的用法中还可表条件，相当于if only, so long as, provided that。不过，此种用法不适宜写作，可用于阅读。例：

So that it is done, I don't care who does it. 只要做好就行，我不管谁做。

So that it is true, what matters who said it? 只要真实，管它是谁说的。

III. 说"文"解"字"

1. We resolve to get up earlier each morning, eat less... do a thousand and one jobs about the house.

译文：我们决心每天早晨起得更早，吃得少点，多做点家务活。

解析：1）get up earlier与get up early略有不同，前者是相对概念，有一个比较点，即get up（earlier than before）；而后者是绝对概念。eat less与eat little的区别同理。

2）a thousand and one 属于夸张修辞手法，目的在于制造幽默诙谐的效果。

2. I limited myself to two modest ambitions.

译文：我给自己设定了两个适中的目标。

解析：limit onself to sth. 是固定短语，意为"给自己限定…"。例：

He limits himself to 500 yuan per month. 他给自己限定每月只花500元。

She limits herself to three cups of coffee a day. 她限定自己一天至多喝3杯咖啡。

3. I applied myself assiduously to the task.

译文：我全力以赴地完成目标了。

解析：apply oneself to sth. 意为"努力做某事"，相当于devote oneself to sth.或commit oneself to sth. 例：

He applied himself to learning German. 他在努力学德语。

Due to poor health, the secretary could not apply herself to the arrangements for the upcoming conference. 由于身体欠佳，这位秘书无法全力以赴为即将召开的会议做准备。

4. But I fended off the taunts and jibes of the family good-humouredly.

译文：但我心平气和地顶住了家人的嘲笑和奚落。

解析：1）fend off 意为push away, avoid（躲避，闪开），可从fence（篱笆→起遮挡作用）推导其义。例：

He fended off the difficulties. 他避开了那些难题。

She fended off his blows with her arms. 她用胳膊挡开了他的攻击。

2）good-humoured意为"心情好的"，其中的humour不是"幽默"，而是"心情"。反义词为ill-humoured（心情坏的）。

5. I sat in my room for a few evenings with my eyes glued to a book.

译文：几上晚上我坐在房间里，眼睛盯着书。

解析：1）彩色部分是以with引导的独立主格结构。参看第6课"现身说'法'"部分。

2）be glued to是一词组，意为"黏着在…，贴在…"。例：

The child stayed glued to his mother's side because he was afraid of getting lost.

那孩子紧紧跟在母亲的身边，生怕走丢了。

She stood there as if glued to the spot. 她站在那里好像不能动弹似的。

拓 展 篇

Ⅰ.英语趣园

It's said that the Spring Festival evolved from an activity known as the winter Sacrifice. It marks the beginning of the Chinese Lunar New Year. In Chinese, we also say Guo Nian, meaning keeping off the monster of Nian. The 15th day of the New Year is called the Lantern Festival, which is celebrated at night with lantern displays and children carrying lanterns in a parade.

On new year's Eve, people usually eat jiaozi or dumplings shaped like gold nuggets, which means fortune in the next year. Everything is soaked with new year celebration: "happiness" characters, couplets, firecrackers, new year visits and calls, etc.

Ⅱ.听力快车

True or False Questions.

1. Dr. Healy is talking about a space station to be launched towards the end of the 1990s.

2. This space station is going to be built by the USA.

3. The thousands of parts which make up Freedom are going to be assembled on Earth.

4. By the end of 1995 eight people are going to be involved in the first crew to begin their space life.

Ⅲ.补充阅读

Happy New Year! That greeting will be said and heard for at least the first couple of weeks as a new year gets under way. But the day celebrated as New Year's Day in modern America was not always January 1.

Aecient new years

The celebration of the new year is the oldest of all holidays. It was first observed in ancient Babylon about 4000 years ago. In the years around 2000 BC, the Babylonian New Year began with the first New Moon（actually the first visible crescent）after the Vernal Equinox（first day of spring）.

The beginning of spring is a logical time to start a new year. After all, it is the season of rebirth, of planting new crops, and of blossoming. January 1, on the other hand, has no astronomical nor agricultural significance. It is purely arbitrary.

The Babylonian new year celebration lasted for eleven days. Each day had its own particular mode of celebration, but it is safe to say that modern New Year's Eve festivities pale in comparison.

The Romans continued to observe the new year in late March, but their calendar was continually tampered with by various emperors so that it soon became out of synchronization with the sun.

In order to set the calendar right, the Roman senate, in 153 BC, declared January 1 to be the beginning of the new year. But tampering continued until Julius Caesar, in 46 BC, established what has come to be known as the Julian Calendar. It again established January 1 as the new year. But in order to synchronize the calendar with the sun, Caesar had to let the previous year drag on for 445 days.

The church's view of new year celebrations

Although in the first centuries AD the Romans continued celebrating the new year, the early Catholic Church condemned the festivities as paganism. But as Christianity became more widespread, the early church began holding its own religious observances concurrently with many of the pagan celebrations, and New Year's Day was no different. New Year's is still observed as the Feast of Christ's Circumcision by some denominations.

During the Middle Ages, the Church remained opposed to celebrating New Year's. January 1 has been celebrated as a holiday by Western nations for only about the past 400 year's.

▶ 测 试 篇 ◀

I . 单项选择

1. His wife is constantly finding _____ with him, which makes him very angry.

   A. errors   B. shortcomings   C. fault   D. flaw

2. Every member of society has to make a _____ to struggle for the freedom of the country.

   A. pledge   B. indignation   C. resolve   D. guarantee

3. I'm _____ enough to know it is going to be a very difficult situation to compete against three strong teams.

   A. realistic   B. conscious   C. register   D. resolve

4. In Britain people _____ four million tons of potatoes every year.

   A. swallow   B. dispose   C. consume   D. exhaust

5. It is my hope that everyone in this class should _____ their errors before it is too late.

   A. refute   B. exclude   C. expel   D. rectify

6. It's already 5 o'clock now. Don't you think it's about time _____?

   A. we are going home   B. we go home

   C. we went home   D. we can go home

7. "You are very selfish. It's high time you _____ that you are not the most important person in the world," Edgar said to his boss angrily.

   A. realized   B. have realized   C. had realized   D. should realize

8. It is high time that such practices _____.

   A. are ended   B. be ended   C. were ended   D. must be ended

9. Who would you rather _____ with you, George or me?

A. going   B. to go   C. have gone   D. went

10. Mr. Smith advised us to withdraw _____.

A. so that to get not involved   C. so as not to get involved

B. so as to get not involved   D. so that not to get involved

Ⅱ.翻译

11. 教练给了我列了一大堆的该吃的和不该吃的。（dos and don'ts）

12. 我再三道歉。（a thousand and one）

13. 吃点儿饼干顶住饿。（fend off）

14. 听到下课铃声，学生们便成群结队地走出了教室。（troop out of）

15. 他的眼睛显露出他的动机。（betray）

拓展篇

1. T   2. F   3. F   4. T

Mal Carrington: Here we are again with "The Years to Come". Now I'd like to tell you about and show you the pictures of an exciting new project which is the result of the cooperation of scientists, engineers and technicians from virtually all over the world.

Towards the end of the 90s, a bright new celestial body will appear in the night sky like an immense shining star, fully visible from 38 degrees north or south of the equator. It will be a space station, Freedom. The idea for Freedom originated in the USA, but eleven other nations have agreed to contribute a few of the station's many parts.

The space station is not going to be launched into orbit in one piece—the thousands of parts which make up Freedom are going to be assembled directly in space. Twenty trips by the shuttle and two rockets will be needed to deliver Freedom, piece by piece, into a low orbit around the Earth. Then, 250 miles above the Earth, construction crews are going to bolt together the space station's many components. The first batch of parts is going to be launched in 1995. By the end of 1996, the first crew of eight is going to enter the living module to begin what NASA hopes will be a continuous human presence in space. The station has been designed to remain occupied and operational for up to thirty years—a whole generation of living in space. Considering that the first man-made object reached orbit just thirty years ago, that will be quite an accomplishment. The design of a space station must combine the excitement of space with the necessity for safety and comfort. Freedom will be the best solution to date and will also be the most complex computerized house ever built—either on Earth or in space. There will be accommodation for eight people and each crew member will have his equipment, a washing machine, a pantry, and a sick bay. Add a television, video, phone and computer to each of the eight private sleeping rooms, then top it off with the best view on Earth. Is this some wild new "luxury house" of the future? Exactly. Life on board will also be brightened by a plan to fill twenty percent of the larder with fresh refrigerated fruit, vegetable and dairy products.

Behind every space station lies the dream that is at least 120 years old: a colony in space. Freedom is not going to be that colony, for it will always depend on the Earth for supplies. But it is going to be the place where scientists discover how to establish healthy and productive human habitation in space. When new technology is developed to make it less risky, we will see more civilians in space. So an eighteen-year-old can look forward to visiting space by his or her sixty-eighth birthday, in 2050.

And that's the end of this week's programme. Tune in next week for another edition of "The Years to Come". "The Years to Come" is a Channel 5 production and this is Mal Carrington.

测试篇

1-5 CABCD   6-10 CACDC

11. I was given a formidable list of dos and don'ts by the coach.

12. I made a thousand and one apologies.

13. Eat some biscuits to fend off hunger.

14. The students trooped out of the classroom at sound of the bell.

15. His eyes betrayed his motive.

Lesson 51. Predicting the future

积 累 篇

I.振振有"词"

1. It can properly be described as the first "home computer" and it pointed the way to the future.

home computer 家用电脑
personal computer 私人电脑
desktop 台式电脑
laptop 笔记本电脑
palmtop 掌上电脑
penputer 笔触式电脑
teleputer 联网电脑

point the way to the future 指出未来的方向
the gateway to success 通往成功之路
an open sesame to success 成功秘诀 (芝麻开门)
on the threshold of the new century 新世纪伊始
at the turn of the new century 新世纪开端
mark the prelude to... 成为…的序曲

2. We have seen the development of the user-friendly home computers and multimedia machines which are in common use toady.

user-friendly 便于操作的
environmentally-friendly 利于环境的
ecologically-friendly 利于生态的
green-friendly 环保的
consumer-friendly 利于消费者的

multimedia 多媒体
multinational co. 跨国公司
multiple choice 多项选择
multiversity 综合性大学

multiracial country 多民族国家
multisense word 多义词
multiuse machine 多功能机器

3. ...when they would be used in hospitals to help doctors to diagnose illnesses, when they would relieve office workers and accountants of dull, repetitive clerical work.

与介词of搭配的动词词组：
relieve sb. of sth. 减轻某人…
deprive sb. of sth. 剥夺某人…
warn sb. of sth. 告诫某人…
inform sb. of sth. 告知某人…
remind sb. of sth. 提醒某人…

医学中的常用词汇：

diagnose an illness 诊断病情	have a medical check-up 检查身体
prognose an illness 预断病情	prescribe medicine 开药
	make one's rounds 查房

Ⅱ.现身说"法"：含蓄虚拟语气句

> Of course, Leon Bagrit could not possibly have foreseen the development of the Internet.（彩色部分属于含蓄虚拟语气句）
>
> 当然，莱昂·巴格特根本没有可能预测到互联网的发展。

1. 所谓含蓄，指含有条件从句的意味，但不显示条件从句的标志词if。该句可通过上下文推导出隐含的条件：Of course, Leon Bagrit could not possibly have foreseen the development of the Internet（, if he were still alive today）. 再看两例：

   We would have won the match.（if something unexpected had not happened）

   我们本应该赢得比赛。（如果不是出了意外）

   You might stay here for the night.（if you wanted to）你可以留下过夜。（如果你愿意）

2. 可表达隐含条件的表达方式还有：

1）分词短语

   Given more time, I would have done it better.（相当于If I had been given more time, ...）

   如果再多点时间，我会做得更好。

   The same thing, happening in those days, would amount to disaster.（相当于if it happened in those days, ...）同样的事，如发生在过去，就会酿成大祸。

2）介词或介词短语

   But for the sun, there would be no life on the earth.（相当于If it were not for the sun, ...）

   如果没有太阳，地球上将不会有生命。

   Without you, what would I have done?（相当于If I had not been with you...）

   当时若没有你，我该怎么办呢？

Ⅲ.说"文"解"字"

1. Predicting the future is notoriously difficult.

   译文：众所周知，预测未来是非常困难的。

   解析：notoriously本义"臭名昭著地"，这里活译为"众所周知"。副词在英语的行文中极其灵活，熟练掌握这些用法对于阅读、写作非常关键。例：

   The conditions are terribly inclement.（terribly本义"糟糕"，活译为"非常"）环境非常恶劣。

   She is becoming increasingly more ambitious.（increasingly本义"增加"，活译为"越来越"）

   她越来越有进取心了。

2. It can properly be described as the first "home computer" and it pointed the way to the future.

   译文：准确而言，它可以被称为第一台"家用电脑"，而且它也指出了未来发展之路。

   解析：point the way to...意为"指向…，通向…"。例：

   The conference pointed the way to further mutual cooperation between the countries.

   这次会议为两国间更加深入的合作指明了方向。

   This high-level meeting pointed the way to achieving the peaceful reunification between the two sides of the Taiwan Straits. 这次高层会议为海峡两岸的和平统一大业指明了方向。

3. This was followed, at the end of the 1970s, by a machine called an Apple.

译文：70年代末，在牛郎星之后又出现了一种被称为"苹果"的机型。

解析：注意follow一词不宜直译，且应由英文的被动语态转为汉语的主动语态，因为英文多为被动形式，而汉语多主动。以下是follow其他的活译现象：

Good results followed the treatment. 治疗之后，情况良好。

I studied until exhaustion followed. 我学到最后都学不动了。

4. Considering how recent these developments are, it is more remarkable that as long ago as the 1960s, an Englishman, Leon Bagrit, was able to predict some of the uses of computers which we know today.

译文：想想所取得的这些进步的时间这么短，英国人莱昂·巴瑞特在60年代就能预言我们今天所熟知的计算机的一些用途，这一点更加非凡无比。

解析：1）considering引导的内容不是伴随状语，而是独立主格结构，因为consider的逻辑主语与后面主句的主语不同。（参看第19课"现身说'法'"部分）

2）as long ago as the 1960s是一种强调用法，普通表达是in the 1960s。（参看第14课"说'文'解'字'"部分）

拓 展 篇

Ⅰ.英语趣园

International Business Machines（IBM）is the world's largest computer company. Based in the US, it produces both hardware and software, especially for business users. IBM is sometimes informally called "Big Blue".

Microsoft is known especially for its Windows operating system, which is used on most personal computers, for Microsoft Word, a popular word processing program, and for Internet Explorer, a popular program for searching the Internet. Bill Gates, who is chief director, started the company.

Disk Operating System is abbreviated to DOS, software that is loaded onto a computer system to make all the different parts work together.

Ⅱ.听力快车

Choose the best answer for each of the following questions.

1. This talk is about the _____ of the Internet.

   A. nearest future   B. general review   C. technical uses   D. historical outline

2. The Internet enables people to do all the following things except _____.

   A. sending e-mail   B. obtaining news   C. exchanging modem   D. Internet related chat

3. According to the later part of the talk, in the future _____.

   A. it may be hard to predict the development of the Internet

   B. the Internet may become an indispensable superhighway

   C. the Internet will be applied more technically than ever

   D. the Internet will largely combine cable stations

III. 补充阅读

A major challenge facing the continued growth of the Internet is the difficulty of providing enough bandwidth to sustain the network. As Internet applications become more sophisticated, and as more people around the world use the Internet, the amount of information transmitted across the Internet will demand very high bandwidth connections. While many communications companies are attempting to develop higher bandwidth technologies, it is not known whether the technology will be able to satisfactorily keep up with demand.

In order to accommodate the increasing number of users, the non-profit organization University Corporation for Advanced Internet Development is working on the construction of Internet 2. Internet 2 will add more bandwidth, or available communication lines, to the current information superhighway in order to accommodate larger packets of data. UCAID members include representatives from universities, the government, and the computer industry.

Another important question facing Internet growth is the issue of censorship. Because the Internet has grown so rapidly, governments have been slow to regulate its use and to pass laws regarding what content is acceptable. Many Internet users also see such laws as an infringement on their right to free speech. In 1996 the Congress of the United States passed the Communications Decency Act, which made it a crime to transmit indecent material over the Internet. This decision resulted in an immediate outcry from users, industry experts, and civil liberties groups opposed to such censorship. In 1997 the United States Supreme Court declared the act to be unconstitutional because it violated 1st Amendment rights to free speech.

Commercial use of the Internet is sure to grow dramatically as more individuals gain access to it. It may be possible in the future to order nearly any goods from Internet sites and have them delivered using the postal service. Many companies are worried about security issues and the possibility of losing money through Internet commerce. They are therefore being very cautious about doing business on the Internet. Other businesses, however, are embracing the Internet, hoping to be first in what may be a rapidly expanding market. The issue of business being conducted over the Internet raises important security issues. Companies doing business over the Internet must have very sophisticated security measures in place so that information such as credit card, bank account, and social security numbers cannot be accessed by unauthorized users. Similarly, government facilities, universities, and institutions must ensure that access to their computers over the Internet is strictly regulated.

■▶ 测 试 篇 ◀■

I. 单项选择

1. The directions were so _____ that it was impossible to complete the assignment.
   A. ingenious   B. ambitious   C. notorious   D. ambiguous
2. That part of the city has long been _____ for its street violence.
   A. notorious   B. responsible   C. historical   D. illegal
3. The poetry of Ezra Pound is sometimes difficult to understand because it contains so many _____ references.
   A. obscure   B. acute   C. notable   D. objective

4. All the ceremonies at the 2000 Olympic Games had a unique Australian flavor, _____ of their multicultural communities.

    A. noticeable   B. indicative   C. conspicuous   D. implicit

5. You need to rewrite this sentence because it is _____, the readers will have difficulty in understanding it.

    A. comprehensive   B. alternative   C. deliberate   D. ambiguous

6. Military orders are _____ and cannot be disobeyed.

    A. defective   B. conservative   C. alternative   D. imperative

7. I guess Jones didn't have a chance to win the election. Almost all of the people in the city voted for his _____.

    A. candidate   B. opponent   C. alternative   D. participant

8. The little girl was so frightened that she just wouldn't _____ her grip on my arm.

    A. loosen   B. remove   C. relieve   D. dismiss

9. Don't _____ this news to the public until we give you the go-ahead.

    A. release   B. relieve   C. relate   D. retain

10. In order to prevent stress from being set up in the metal, expansion joints are fitted which _____ the stress by allowing the pipe to expand or contract freely.

    A. relieve   B. reconcile   C. reclaim   D. rectify

II. 翻译

11. 日本地处地震带, 因此地震时有发生。(be notorious for)

12. 没有了计算机, 谁能想像未来会是什么样子。(would be...without...)

13. 中国成功发射了"神舟五号", 这标志着一个新太空时代的到来。(launch)

14. 美国第16届总统林肯只是一个平民, 出身卑微, 最终入主白宫, 成为美国历史上最伟大的总统。(from humble beginnings)

15. 尼克松由于水门事件而被解除了总统职位。(be relieved of his post)

拓展篇

1. B   2. C   3. B

    The Internet is a vast network of computers that connects many of the world's businesses, institutions, and individuals. The Internet, which means interconnected networks, links tens of thousands of smaller computer networks. These networks transmit huge amounts of information in the form of words, images, and sounds.

    The Internet has information on virtually every topic. Network users can search through sources ranging from vast databases to small electronic "bulletin boards", where users form discussion groups around common interests. Much of the Internet's traffic consists of messages sent from one computer user to another. These messages are called electronic mail or e-mail. One feature of the Internet provides graphics, audio, and video to enhance the information in its documents. These documents cover a vast number of topics.

    People usually access the Internet with a device called a modem. Modems connect computers to the network through telephone lines. Much of the Internet operates through worldwide telephone networks of fiber-optic cables. In the future, the Internet will probably grow more sophisticated as computer technology becomes more powerful. Many experts believe the Internet may become part of a larger network called the information superhighway. This network, still under development, would link computers with telephone companies, cable television stations, and other communication systems.

测试篇

1-5 DAABD 6-10 DBCAA

11. Japan is notorious for earthquake, for it lies in the seismic belt.

12. Who could imagine what the world would be without Computer in the future?

13. China successfully launched the Shen Zhou Five, which marked a new start of its Space Era.

14. Abraham Lincoln, the 16th president of USA, rose from humble beginnings as one of the common rank of people to the White House and became the greatest president in US history.

15. Nixon was relieved of his post as president due to Water Gate.

Lesson 52. Mud is mud

I.振振有"词"

1. How Harry came into the possession of this outlandish stuff makes an interesting story...

come into the possession of sth.占有某物
get possession of sth. 得到某物
take complete possession of sth. 完全占有某物
be in possession of sth. 拥有某物
sth. is in the possession of sb. 某物属于某人所有
be in possession of oneself 镇定自若

outlandish 稀奇古怪的
exotic 异乎寻常的
novel 新奇的
bizarre 怪异的
grotesque 怪诞的
weird古怪的（多指人）
eccentric 古怪的（多指人）

形似词辨析：
stuff 材料
staff 工作人员
stiff 僵硬的
fluff 抖开
tariff 关税税率
turf 草地，草皮

2. He loved to be told that one of his imaginary products was temporarily out of stock...

imaginary 虚构的
imaginative 有想像力的
imaginable 能想像到的
fictitious 虚假的
fanciful 虚幻的
illusionary 幻想的

形似词联想记忆：
temporary 临时的
temporal 时间的
contemporary 当代的
temperable（气候）温和的
temperate（人）温和的
temperish 易怒的
tempest 暴风雨

out of stock 脱销
in stock 有货
sell out sth.售罄
purchase sth. 购买
procure sth.（大量）购买
impulsive buying 疯狂购买
panic buying 抢购

3. Harry does not need to be prompted to explain how he bought his precious bottle of mud.

常用的写作句型：
does not need to be prompted to do sth.
毋庸暗示做…
cannot wait to do sth. 迫不及待做…
be impatient to do sth. 急不可耐做…
cannot help doing sth. 情不自禁做…

precious宝贵的
valuable 珍贵的
invaluable 极其珍贵的
pricey 值钱的
priceless 价值连城的
worthy 有价值的

II.现身说"法"：将来虚拟语气

If you were to ask Harry what was in the bottle, he would tell you that it contained perfumed mud. 要是你问哈里瓶里装着什么，他会告诉你是香水泥。

该句是将来虚拟语气句型。构成模式为：条件从句：If+主语+should...或If+主语+were to+动词原形...或If+主语+V-ed...；主句：主语+would/should/might+动词原形...。例：

If we were to move to a small city, we would be able to buy a bigger house.

如果我们搬到一个小城市，就能买一套大点儿的房子。

If it should rain tomorrow, what would we do? 如果明天下雨，我们怎么办？

If you succeeded, everything would be all right. 如果你将来成功了，一切都会好的。

★★★ 注意 ★★★

在正式英语中，if从句的第一个动词若为should, had或were，可将此动词置于句首，从而省略if。因此，上述例句可改写为：Were we to move to a small city, we would be able to buy a bigger house. 例：

Should it rain tomorrow, what would we do?

III. 说"文"解"字"

1. Mud is mud.

译文：实事求是。

解析：该句子的汉语译文是根据具体语境变通而来，并非英语中约定俗成的说法。固定说法是：Call a sapde a spade.（spade乃扑克牌中的黑桃，意即打牌过程中要恪守规则，不可弄虚作假。）

> **联想记忆**
>
> Tell it like it is. 实话实说。　　　Don't beat around the bush. 不要旁敲侧击。
>
> Don't make insinuations. 不要含沙射影。　Put your card on the table. 要光明磊落。

2. Despite the fact that the bottle is tinted a delicate shade of green, an observant visitor would soon notice that it is filled with what looks like a thick, greyish substance.

译文：尽管那只瓶子呈淡绿色，但细心的客人会很快发现瓶里装的是一种看上去粘稠、颜色发灰的东西。

解析：1）despite是介词，一般后面直接跟名词。但在写作过程中，有时单个名词难以表述丰富的内容，本句的模式，即despite+the fact+that同位语从句便是一种有效延展。例：

Despite her great age, she was very graceful indeed. 可改写为：

Despite the fact that she was very old, she was very graceful indeed.

尽管年事已高，她仍旧体态优雅。

2）tint 本义"色彩"，这里用作动词"染色"，如：

the tints of early morning 晨曦的五光十色　　Dusk tinted the prairie. 草原上暮色苍茫。

3. On entering a shop, he would ask for a new perfume called "Scented Shadow"....

译文：走进商店后，他会提出要一种"香影"的新型香水……。

解析："on+动名词"结构中的on意为as soon as或when，是时间状语的一种常用表达。例：

On entering the hall, I perceived that it was of magnificence.

一走进大厅，我就感到它富丽堂皇。

4. How Harry managed to keep a straight face during these performances is quite beyond me.

译文：我实在想像不出哈里在这些表演中是怎样装出一本正经的。

解析：1）keep a straight face是固定短语，也可用straight-faced, 意为"一本正经"。

2）该句的主语是以关系副词how引导的内容，谓语结构为is beyond me。整个句子看似失衡，实则是为了强调。

拓 展 篇

I.英语趣园

In describing a person, the writer should not merely give details of his appearance. He should try to reveal the person's character, thoughts, and feelings, which may be shown in what the person does and says, or in how he behaves to others. And it is important to grasp the characteristic features that distinguish him from all other people. Those features that he shares with others can be omitted. Peculiarities and idiosyncrasies of a person, if any, should be included in the description, for they usually impress the reader deeply and give life to the person described.

II.听力快车

The sight of him as he came to the ten-o'clock was in itself something that had to be recognized as dramatic. In the pleasant autumn or spring, men stood high on the steps or out on the turf in front and watched in the direction of Christ Church to see who could catch the first glimpse of him.

"There he comes!" somebody called, and then everybody who was in a position to see watched him as he hurried breezily along—_____

_____. Students used to say that he smoked an entire cigar while he walked the short distance along the iron fence of the old burying ground and across the street to Johnston Gate. But as he came through the gate _____, and the students still outside hurried in and scrambled up the long stairway in order to be in their places—as he liked—before he himself entered. If any of them were still on the stairway when he came in at the outer door like a gust, they gave way and he pushed up past them, and into the good-sized room and down the aisle to the front, _____ _____, and there was sudden silence and unrestrained expectancy.

III.补充阅读

The ugly Americans

Americans seem to live and breathe and function by paradox; but in nothing are we so paradoxical as in our passionate belief on our own myths. We truly believe ourselves to be natural-born mechanics and do-it-yourselfers. We spend our lives in motorcars, yet most of us—a great many of us at least—do not know enough about a car to look in the gas tank when the motor fails. Our lives as we live them would not function without electricity, but it is a rare man or woman who when the power goes off, knows how to look for a burned-out fuse and replace it. We believe implicitly that we are the heirs of the pioneers; that we have inherited self-sufficiency and the ability to take care of ourselves, particularly in relation to nature. There isn't a man among us in ten thousand who knows how to butcher a cow or a pig and cut it up for eating, let alone a wild animal.

The paradoxes are everywhere. We are able to believe that our government is weak, stupid, overbearing, dishonest, and inefficient, and at the same time we are deeply convinced that it is the best government in the world, and we would like to impose it upon everyone else. We speak of the American Way of Life as though it involved the ground rules for the governance of heaven. We shout that we are a nation of laws, not men—and then proceed to break every law we can if we can get away with it. We proudly insist that we base our political positions on the issues—and we will vote against a man because of his religion, his name, or the shape of his nose. The result is that we seem to be in a state of turmoil all the time, both physically and mentally. We work too hard, and many die under the strain; and then to make up for that we play with a violence as suicidal. We are self-reliant and at the same time completely dependent. We are aggressive, and defenseless. Americans overindulge their children and do not like them; the children in turn are overly dependent and full of hate for their parents. We are complacent in our possessions, in our house, in our education; but it is hard to find a man or woman who does not want something better for the next generation. Americans are remarkably kind and hospitable and open with both guests and strangers; and yet they will make a wide circle around the man dying on the pavement. Fortunes are spent getting cats out of trees and dogs out of sewer pipes; but a girl screaming for help in the street draws only slammed doors, closed windows, and silence.

▶ 测 试 篇 ◀

I . 单项选择

1. A most _____ argument about who should go and fetch the bread from the kitchen was going on when I came in.

   A. trivial   B. delicate   C. minor   D. miniature

2. The statistical figures in that report are not _____. You should not refer to them.

   A. accurate   B. fixed   C. delicate   D. rigid

3. During the process, great care has to be taken to protect the _____ silk from damage.

   A. sensitive   B. tender   C. delicate   D. sensible

4. There was a _____ drop in support for the Union in the 1974 election.

   A. delicate   B. distinct   C. distant   D. downward

5. One of his eyes was injured in an accident, but after a _____ operation, he quickly recovered his sight.

   A. delicate   B. considerate   C. precise   D. sensitive

6. Rebecca _____ me earlier if she did not like her house she bought last month.

   A. told   B. would tell   C. had told   D. would have told

7. If the ocean were free of ice, storm paths would move further north, _____ the plains of North America of rainfall.

   A. to deprive   B. deprived   C. depriving   D. deprived

8. Things might have been much worse if the mother _____ on her right to keep the baby.

   A. has been insisting   B. had insisted

   C. would insist   D. insisted

9. Finding a job in such a big company has always been _____ his wildest dreams.

A. under   B. over   C. above   D. beyond

10. Last year, these ships transported a total of 83.34 million tons of cargo, a 4.4 percent increase _____ the previous year.

A. over   B. than   C. up   D. beyond

Ⅱ. 翻译

11. 中国是联合国的常任理事国。（permanent member of）
12. 如果我能再年轻，我会更多地培养自己的毅力，决不因为事情艰难或麻烦而放弃。（If I were...）
13. 他诚恳的态度打消了我之前的所有疑虑。（dispel doubts）
14. 为什么许多人宁愿放弃高薪也要获得成为白领的殊荣是我所不能理解的。（...beyond me）
15. 没人能逃脱法律的制裁。（get away with）

拓展篇

The sight of him as he came to the ten-o'clock was in itself something that had to be recognized as dramatic. In the pleasant autumn or spring, men stood high on the steps or out on the turf in front and watched in the direction of Christ Church to see who could catch the first glimpse of him.

"There he comes!" somebody called, and then everybody who was in a position to see watched him as he hurried breezily along—a graceful, tallish man in very light gray suit and gray fedora hat, with a full square beard at least as white as his suit, who moved with energy, and smoked passionately at a big cigar. Students used to say that he smoked an entire cigar while he walked the short distance along the iron fence of the old burying ground and across the street to Johnston Gate. But as he came through the gate he tossed the remnant of his cigar into the shrubbery with a bit of a flourish, and the students still outside hurried in and scrambled up the long stairway in order to be in their places—as he liked—before he himself entered. If any of them were still on the stairway when he came in at the outer door like a gust, they gave way and he pushed up past them, and into the good-sized room and down the aisle to the front, threw his hat on the table in the corner, mounted the two steps to the platform, looked about with a commanding eye, and there was sudden silence and unrestrained expectancy.

测试篇

1-5 AACBC   6-10 DCBDA

11. China is the permanent member of the Security Council of UN.

12. If I were young again, I would practise perseverance oftener, and never give up a thing because it was hard or inconvenient.

13. His sincere attitude dispelled all my previous doubts.

14. Why many people would sacrifice higher pay for the privilege of becoming white color workers is beyond me.

15. No one can get away with laws.

Lesson **53.** In the public interest

Ⅰ.振振有"词"

1. Sweden has <u>evolved</u> an excellent system for protecting the individual citizen from <u>high-handed</u> or <u>incompetent</u> public officers.

incompetent 无能的
incapable 无能的
inexpert 不熟练的
inept 不称职的
ineffective 不起作用的
ineffectual 无效的

evolve 形成
generate 产生
engender 产生
develop 培养
breed 培育
foster 抚育

high-handed 专横的
heavy-handed 暴虐的
single-handed 单枪匹马的
bare-handed 赤手空拳的
empty-handed 空手的
off-hand 未经准备的
beforehand 预先

2. The lawyer <u>ascertained</u> that a policeman had indeed <u>dealt roughly with</u> foreigners <u>on several occasions</u>.

形似词辨析:
ascertain 确定
assure 保证
assert 断定
assess 评价
assume 假定

deal roughly with sb. 粗暴对待某人
take freedoms with sb. 对某人放肆
treat sb. with abandon 对某人无礼
rough up sb. 对某人动粗
knock sb. about 虐待某人
knock around sb. 虐待某人

on some occasions 多次
on another occasion 另一次
on occasion 有时
on no occasion 绝不
on a formal occasion 在正式场合
as occasion serves 在方便时

3. The policeman <u>in question</u> was severely reprimanded and was informed that if any further <u>complaints were lodged against</u> him, he would be prosecuted.

in question 讨论中的
come into question 被讨论
call sth. into question 对…质疑
out of question 毫无疑问
out of the question 不可能
beside the question 离题

lodge a complaint against... 投诉…
complain of/about... 抱怨…
prosecute sb. 起诉某人
accuse sb. of... 指控某人…
protest... 抗议…
grumble about... 埋怨…

279

II. 现身说"法": so+副词/形容词/动词+that

> **The system has worked** so well, that it has been adopted in other countries too.
> 由于这种制度行之有效，已被其他国家采纳。

so后接副词或形容词，多表示因果关系，其中so之后表原因，that之后表结果，本句即是如此。若so之后接副词，还可表程度。若so之后接动词，多表方式、状态、程度或目的。例：

He spoke so rapidly that we could not clearly understood him.（so之后表原因，that之后表结果）
他说话太快，所以我们没有完全听懂。

His income is so small that he can not support his family.（so之后表原因，that之后表结果）
他收入太少，不能养家。

The world is so made that men are unable to live without loving others.（so之后表状态，that之后表结果）这个世界上的人不爱他人是无法生存的。

Explanations were of no use because he was so prejudiced that he would not listen to reason.（so之后表程度，that之后表结果）解释对他无用，因为他听不进去道理。

III. 说"文"解"字"

1. in the public interest
   译文：为了公众的利益
   解析：in sb.'s interest意为"为了某人的利益"。可用于替换的表达有：
   in the interest of sb.   on sb.'s behalf
   on behalf of sb.   for the benefit of sb.

2. The Swedes were the first to recognize that public officials like civil servants, police officers, health inspectors or tax-collectors can make mistakes or act over-zealously in the belief that they are serving the public.
   译文：瑞典人首先认识到了政府工作人员如文职人员、警官、卫生稽查员、税务人员等也会犯错或者自以为在为公众服务时把事情做过了头。
   解析：1）sb. is the first to do sth. 连同sb. is the last to do sth., sb. is the only one to do sth.一起记，这些都是写作中常用于表"极致，惟一"概念的句型。例：
   The man was the first to cross the Atlantic. 这个人最早横渡了大西洋。
   He is the last person to tell a lie.（last在这里指"不可能的，不愿意的"）
   他最不可能说谎。
   This is the only way to tackle the problem. 这是解决问题的惟一办法。
   2）in the belief that...在句中作原因状语，that从句作belief的同位语。例：
   He likes to kiss up to his boss in the belief that he will be favored.
   他爱巴结老板，相信能得到重视。

3. The Ombudsman is not subject to political pressure.
   译文：司法特派员不受任何政治压力的制约。
   解析：be subject to...意为"受制于…"。其中subject是形容词，to是介词，后接名词。例：
   We are all subject to the laws of nature. 我们都要受自然规律的支配。

He is highly strung and, therefore, subject to heart attacks. 他十分容易激动，因此易发心脏病。

> **联想记忆**：be liable to...有…倾向的，易患…的
>
> We are all liable to make mistakes. 我们都会犯错。
>
> He is liable to ill health. 他经常患病。

4. There is nothing secretive about the Ombudsman's work, for his correspondence is open to public inspection.

译文：司法特派员的工作没有什么秘密可言，他的信件是公开的，供公众监督。

解析：1）形容词修饰复合不定代词nothing、anything、something等要置于这些代词之后。

2）be open to...意为"乐于接受…，对…开放"。例：

My essay is open to suggestions. 鄙人拙文，敬请斧正。

The universities in our country are open to all citizens. 我国的大学对所有公民开放。

拓 展 篇

Ⅰ.英语趣园

Scandinavia, an area of Northern Europe, consists of Norway, Sweden, Denmark, and Finland. The people of the Middle Ages, who lived in a happy world of fairy stories, knew exactly how the Scandinavian peninsula happened to have got its queer shape. After the good Lord had finished the work of creation, the Devil came along to see what he had been doing those seven long days. He had been away from Heaven. When the Devil saw our planet in the first flush of its young loveliness, he lost his temper and got so terribly angry that he heaved a large rock at Mankind's new home. That rock landed in the Arctic Sea and became the Scandinavian Peninsula.

Ⅱ.听力快车

Montesquieu argued that _____ . He thought England—which divided power between the king (_____), Parliament (_____), and the judges of the English courts (_____)—was a good model of this. Montesquieu called the idea of _____ . He thought it most important to _____ . That way, _____ . He wrote,"When the［law making］and［law enforcement］powers are united in the same person... there can be no liberty."According to Montesquieu, each branch of government could limit the power of the other two branches. Therefore, _____ . His ideas about separation of powers became the basis for the United States Constitution.

Ⅲ.补充阅读

The Spirit of the Laws（1748）

Charles de Secondat, Baron de Montesquieu（1689-1755）, was a nobleman, a judge in a French court, and one of the most influential political thinkers. Based on his research he developed a number of political theories presented in *The Spirit of the Laws*（1748）.

This treatise presented numerous theories—among the most important was respect for the role of history and climate in shaping a nation's political structure.

It was for his views on the English Constitution, which he saw in an overly idealized way, that he is perhaps most renowned.

In every government there are three sorts of power: the legislative; the executive, in respect to things dependent on the law of nations; and the executive, in regard to things that depend on the civil law.

By virtue of the first, the prince or magistrate enacts temporary or perpetual laws, and amends or abrogates those that have been already enacted. By the second, he makes peace or war, sends or receives embassies; establishes the public security, and provides against invasions. By the third, he punishes criminals, or determines the disputes that arise between individuals. The latter we shall call the judiciary power, and the other simply the executive power of the state.

The political liberty of the subject is a tranquility of mind, arising from the opinion each person has of his safety. In order to have this liberty, it is requisite the government be so constituted as one man need not be afraid of another.

When the legislative and executive powers are united in the same person, or in the same body of magistrates, there can be no liberty; lest the same monarch or senate should enact tyrannical laws, to execute them in a tyrannical manner.

Again, there is no liberty, if the power of judging be not separated from the legislative and executive powers. Were it joined with the legislative, the life and liberty of the subject would be exposed to arbitrary control, for the judge would then be the legislator. Were it joined to the executive power, the judge might behave with all the violence of an oppressor.

▪▶ 测 试 篇 ◀▪

Ⅰ. 单项选择

1. Putting in a new window will _____ cutting away part of the roof.
   A. include   B. involve   C. contain   D. comprise

2. Researchers at the University of Illinois determined that the _____ of a father can help improve a child's grades.
   A. involvement   B. interaction   C. association   D. communication

3. I had just posted the letter when I remembered that I hadn't _____ the cheque.
   A. imposed   B. involved   C. enclosed   D. contained

4. Apart from philosophical and legal reasons for respecting patients' wishes, there are several practical reasons why doctors should _____ to involve patients in their own medical care decisions.
   A. enforce   B. endow   C. endeavor   D. enhance

5. She was deeply _____ by the amount of criticism her play received.
   A. deported   B. deprived   C. involved   D. frustrated

6. Mr. Smith advised us to withdraw _____.
   A. so that to get not involved   C. so as not to get involved
   B. so as to get not involved   D. so that not to get involved

7. To be frank, I'd rather you _____ in the case.

    A. will not be involved   B. not involved
    C. not to be involved   D. were not involved

8. I told him that I would _____ him to act for me while I was away from office.
    A. authorize   B. justify   C. rationalize   D. identify

9. These teachers try to be objective when they _____ the integrated ability of their students.
    A. justify   B. evaluate   C. indicate   D. reckon

10. In our highly technological society, the number of jobs for unskilled worker is _____.
    A. shrinking   B. obscuring   C. altering   D. constraining

Ⅱ. 翻译

11. 人们对三峡工程的担心和警告也是不无道理的。（justify）
12. 谨以此片献给那些曾经为了祖国和人民的利益骁勇善战，英勇献身的战士们。（in the interest of）
13. 中国人在新年的除夕之夜会放鞭炮，因为人们相信"年"这个怪物会被吓跑。（in the belief that）
14. 我代表学校的全体员工向大家表示欢迎。（on behalf of）
15. 亨利基辛格促使越战结束，从而获得了1973年的诺贝尔奖。（put sth. to an end）

拓展篇

    Montesquieu argued that the best government would be one in which power was balanced among three groups of officials. He thought England—which divided power between the king (who enforced laws), Parliament (which made laws), and the judges of the English courts (who interpreted laws)—was a good model of this. Montesquieu called the idea of dividing government power into three branches the "separation of powers." He thought it most important to create separate branches of government with equal but different powers. That way, the government would avoid placing too much power with one individual or group of individuals. He wrote, "When the [law making] and [law enforcement] powers are united in the same person... there can be no liberty." According to Montesquieu, each branch of government could limit the power of the other two branches. Therefore, no branch of the government could threaten the freedom of the people. His ideas about separation of powers became the basis for the United States Constitution.

测试篇

1-5 BACCD   6-10 CDABA

11. Worries and warnings are justified of the 3 Gorges Project.

12. The film is dedicated to the memory of those valiant soldiers who sacrificed themselves in the interest of our country and our people.

13. Chinese people will touch off fire-crackers on New Year's Eve in the belief that the monster "Nian" will be scared away.

14. On behalf of all the stuff of our school, I'd like to express our sincere welcome.

15. Henry Kissinger won Nobel Prize in 1973 for helping put Vietnam War to an end.

Lesson 54. Instinct or cleverness?

积累篇

I. 振振有"词"

1. We <u>regard them as</u> **unnecessary creatures that** <u>do more harm than good</u>.

regard...as... 把…看作…	do more harm than good 弊大于利
conceive...as... 把…想像成…	do more good than harm 利大于弊
feel...as... 认为…是…	do harm to... 对…有害
see...as... 把…看作…	do good to... 对…有利
refer to...as... 把…称为…	do no harm to... 对…无害
mistaken...for... 把…误认为…	do no good to... 对…无益

2. We continually <u>wage war on</u> them, for they <u>contaminate</u> our food, carry diseases, or <u>devour</u> our crops.

wage war on sb./sth. 向…发动战争	contaminate sth. 弄脏…	关于"吃"的不同表述:
make war on sb./sth. 向…发动战争	pollute sth. 污染…	devour sth. 吞食…
stage war on sb./sth. 向…策动战争	stain sth. 弄上污迹	eat up sth. 吃光…
declare war on sb./sth. 向…宣战	infect sb./sth. 感染…	grab sth. to eat 抓起…就吃
go to war with sb. 与…开战	corrupt sb. 腐化某人	wolf down sth. 狼吞虎咽地吃…
be at war with sb. 与…交战中	stigmatize sb. 玷污某人	can eat a horse 饭量很大
		eat like a bird 饭量很小

3. They <u>sting or bite</u> without <u>provocation</u>; they fly uninvited into our rooms on summer nights, or <u>beat against</u> our lighted windows.

和mouth有关的动词:				与against搭配的词组:
sting 叮	gnaw 啃	provoke 挑衅	annoy 惹恼	beat against 击打
bite 咬	peck 啄	harass 骚扰	insult 侮辱	turn against 与…敌对
chew 咀嚼	munch 大口吃	pester 纠缠	disgrace 使丢脸	lean against 靠着
		offend 冒犯		argue against 驳斥
				struggle against 对抗

Ⅱ. 现身说"法": **more...than...**结构

> **We regard them as unnecessary creatures that** do more harm than good.
> 我们把昆虫看作弊多利少的无用东西。

more...than... 结构是一个常用的比较结构, 两词之间可加名词, 也可加形容词。但more+形容词...than+形容词...一般翻译为"与其…不如…", 或"不是…而是…"。例:

He is more shy than unsocial. 与其说他不爱社交, 不如说他腼腆。

She is more kind than intelligent. 她不是智者, 而是仁人。

He is more bold than strong. 与其说他刚强, 不如说他大胆。

Ⅲ. 说"文"解"字"

1. **We** have been brought up to fear insects.

译文: 我们自幼就在对昆虫的恐惧中长大。

解析: 1) bring sb. up意为"把某人抚养成人"。而grow up指"长成人", 不能用被动语态。

2) to fear insects为不定式短语, 作主语we的补足语。一般而言, be brought up to do sth.已形成固定结构, 可译为"从小到大做…"。例:

The sad truth is that most of us have been brought up to eat certain kinds of foods and we stick to them all our lives. 不无遗憾的是, 我们中的多数人生来就吃几种食品, 而且一辈子也是如此。

He has been brought up to be introverted. 他生来就很内向。

2. **They sting or bite** without provocation.

译文: 它们无缘无故地又叮又咬。

解析: provocation本指"挑衅", 但without provocation不可直译, 转译为"没有理由地", 相当于for no reason或gratuitously。例:

He often flies into a rage without provocation. 他经常发无名火。

3. Knowing that the industrious ant lives in a highly organized society **does nothing to prevent us from being filled with revulsion when we find hordes of them crawling over a carefully prepaired picnic lunch.**

译文: 即使知道勤奋的蚂蚁生活在具有高度组织性的群体里, 当看到大群蚂蚁在我们精心准备的午间野餐上爬行时, 我们也无法抑制对它们的厌恶。

解析: 这是一个复合句。主语为knowing...society, 谓语为does nothing to prevent..., revulsion作宾语补足语, when引导时间状语从句。实际上, 该句的主语结构中含有让步语气, 因此整句可以改写为: Although we know that the industrious ant lives in a highly organized society, it does nothing to prevent us from being filled with revulsion when we find hordes of them crawling over a carefully prepared picnic lunch.

4. **We enjoy staring at them,** entranced **as they** go about their business, unaware (we hope) of **our presence.**

译文: 我们喜欢盯着它们看, 看它们做事入了迷, 而它们却不知 (但愿如此) 我们就在身边。

解析: 1) entranced是形容词, 作主语we的补足语。

2）go about sth./doing sth.意为"忙于干某事"。例：

He goes about securing a respectable job. 他正忙着找份好工作。

3）unaware of...作时间状语从句中的主语they的补足语。we hope作插入语，在这里起到了幽默效果。

5. Who has not stood in awe **at the sight of a spider** pouncing on **a fly, or a column of ants triumphantly bearing home an enormous dead beetle?**

译文：当看到蜘蛛扑向一只苍蝇时，或一队蚂蚁抬着一只硕大的死甲虫凯旋而归时，谁能不感到敬畏呢？

解析：1）本句是一个修辞性问句，不需回答，只是表达作者的某种语气。例：

But how many of us can honestly say that we have not felt a little envious of their simple way of life and their freedom from care? 但是，我们多少人能够坦诚地说我们对他们的简朴生活与无忧无虑的境况不感到一丝艳美呢？

2）pouncing on...意为"扑向…"，在句中修饰spider，作宾语补足语。

■ 拓 展 篇

Ⅰ.英语趣园

Flies are an important part of the environmental food chain. There are more known flies than vertebrates. These insects are a major component of virtually all non-marine ecosystems. The economic importance of the group is immense. One need only consider the ability of flies to transmit diseases. Black flies, and mosquitoes, are responsible for more human suffering and death than any other group of organisms except for the transmitted pathogens and mankind himself! Flies also destroy our food, especially grains and fruits. On the positive side of the ledger, outside their obviously essential roles in maintaining our ecosystem, flies are of little direct benefit to man. Some are important as experimental animals and biological control agents of weeds and other insects.

Ⅱ.听力快车

It is man's nature to live together in families and tribes, and cities and nations, and therefore _____ _____ .

Of these qualities one of the most important is sympathy—fellow-feeling. If a man had no fellow-feeling, _____ he would be no true man. We think so much of this quality that_____—that is, man-like in his conduct, first to other men, and afterwards to all living things.

If you are cruel to animals, you are not likely to be kind and thoughtful to men; and _____ _____ . This is why the wise man of old wrote, "the merciful man is merciful to his beast."

Ⅲ. 补充阅读

The freedom of the fly

We can nowhere find a better type of a perfectly free creature than in the common housefly. Not free only, but brave. There is no courtesy in him; he does not care whether it is king or clown whom he tastes; and in every step of his swift, mechanical march, and in every pause of his resolute observation, there is one and the same expression of perfect egotism, perfect independence and self-confidence, and conviction of the world's having been made for flies.

Strike at him with your hand; and to him, the aspect of the matter is, what to you it would be, if an acre of red clay, ten feet thick, tore itself up from the ground and came crashing down with an aim. He steps out of the way of your hand, and alights on the back of it. You cannot terrify him, nor govern him, nor persuade him, nor convince him.

He has his own positive opinion on all matters; not an unwise one, usually, for his own ends; and will ask no advice of yours. He has no work to do—no tyrannical insects to obey. The earthworm has his digging; the bee her gathering and building; the spider her cunning network; the ant her treasury and accounts. All there are comparatively slaves, or people of business. But your fly, free in the air, free in the chamber—a black incarnation of caprice—wandering, investigation, flitting, flirting, feasting at his will, with rich variety of choice feast, from the heaped sweets in the grocer's window to those of the butcher's back yard—what freedom is like this?

▶ 测 试 篇 ◀

Ⅰ. 单项选择

1. Most people who travel in the course of their work are given travelling _____ .

   A. income   B. allowances   C. wages   D. pay

2. Computer technology will _____ a revolution in business administration.

   A. bring around   B. bring about   C. bring out   D. bring up

3. As the old empires were broken up and new states were formed, new official tongues began to _____ at an increasing rate.

   A. bring up   B. build up   C. spring up   D. strike up

4. The Space Age _____ in October 1957 when the first artificial satellite was launched by the Soviet Union.

   A. initiated   B. originated   C. embarked   D. commenced

5. Our journey was slow because the train stopped _____ at different villages.

   A. unceasingly   B. gradually   C. continuously   D. continually

6. The goal is to make higher education available to everyone who is willing and capable _____ his financial situation.

   A. with respect to B. in accord with   C. regardless of D. in terms of

7. The prospect of increased prices has already _____ worries.

    A. provoked   B. irritated   C. inspired   D. hoisted

8. The prison guards were armed and ready to shoot if _____ in any way.

    A. intervened   B. incurred   C. provoked   D. poked

9. Tryon was extremely angry, but cool-headed enough to _____ storming into the boss's office.

    A. prevent   B. prohibit   C. turn   D. avoid

10. His career was not noticeably _____ by the fact that he had never been to college.

    A. prevented   B. prevented   C. hindered   D. refrained

Ⅱ. 翻译

11. 究竟"克隆"是否弊大于利还是个未知数。（do more harm than good）

12. 美国以大规模杀伤性武器为借口，向伊拉克发动战争。（wage war on ）

13. 我陷入沉思中，没有意识到旁人的存在。（unaware of）

14. 毕业之后，我就开始自己创业了。（embark on）

15. 我们对这位民族英雄肃然起敬。（stand in awe of）

拓展篇

    It is man's nature to live together in families and tribes, and cities and nations, and therefore men have learned to prize those qualities in each other which make social life happiest and best. Of these qualities one of the most important is sympathy—fellow-feeling. If a man had no fellow-feeling, we should call him inhuman; he would be no true man. We think so much of this quality that we call a kind man humane—that is, man-like in his conduct, first to other men, and afterwards to all living things.

    If you are cruel to animals, you are not likely to be kind and thoughtful to men; and if you are thoughtful towards men, you are not likely to be cruel and thoughtless towards animals. This is why the wise man of old wrote, "the merciful man is merciful to his beast."

测试篇

1-5 BBCDD   6-10 CACAC

11. Whether clone does more harm than good is remained to be seen.

12. USA waged war on Iraq on the plea of Mass Destruction Weapon.

13. I was lost in my thought, unaware of other people's presence.

14. I embarked on launching my own business after graduation.

15. We stand in awe of the national hero.

Lesson From the Earth: Greetings

I.振振有"词"

1. Recent developments in <u>astronomy</u> have made it possible to <u>detect</u> planets in our Milky Way and in other <u>galaxies</u>.

galaxy 星系
Milky Way 银河系
the solar system 太阳系
constellation 星座
horoscope（属相）星座
satellite 卫星
planet 行星

astronomy 天文学
astrology 占星术
astrophysics 天体物理学
astrobiology 天体生物学
astronomer 天文学家
astronaut 宇航员

-tect表"遮蔽"：
detect 发现（de-去除）
detective 侦探
detector 检测器
undetected 未被发觉的
protect 保护
protectory 少年感化院

2. There is no <u>telescope</u> <u>in existence</u> that <u>is capable of</u> detecting the presence of life.

tele-表"遥远"：
telescope 望远镜
telegram 电报
telecommunication 电信

teleconference 电话会议
telepathy 心心相印
telecourse 电视课程
teleshopping 电话购物

in表"处于…状态中"：
in existence 现存的
in good condition 状态良好
in excitement 很激动
in difficulties 身处困境
in liquor 喝醉了
in flower 开花

be capable of...有能力做…
be competent for...有能力做…
be adequate for...有资格做…
be eligible for...有资格做…

be qualified for...够资格做…
be proficient in...在…方面很纯熟
be expert at...在…方面很在行

3. As <u>Earth-dwellers</u>, we always <u>cherish the hope</u> that we will be visited by little green men.

Earth-dweller 地球居民
city-dweller 城市居民
country-dweller 乡村居民
cliff-dweller（喻）住高楼者
cave-dweller 穴居者
forest-dweller 森林动物

cherish the hope 满怀希望
cherish peace 珍视和平
cherish the memory of sb. 怀念某人
cherish one's native land 爱祖国
cherish illusions about...对…抱有幻想
cherish affection for sb. 喜欢某人

Ⅱ. 现身说"法"：rather than与other than之不同

> **We would be looking for plant life,** rather than **"little green men".**
> 我们要寻找植物，而不是"小绿人"。

一般而言，rather than连接的是两个并列成分，它们属于并列关系，本句中plant life和little green life即是此理；other than相当于different from，连接的两个成分属于所属关系。例：

I will persevere rather than give up.（persevere和give up属于并列关系）我要坚持而非放弃。

All students other than Jack took the exam.（all students和Jack属于所属关系）

除了杰克，所有学生都参加了考试。

This mechanism is designed to harness energy from water rather than from animals.（from water和from animals属于并列关系）这种机械装置是用来利用水能而非动物能的。

This mechanism is designed to harness energy from a source other than from animals.（from a source和from animals属于所属关系）这种装置是用来利用除了动物能以外的能源的。

Ⅲ. 说"文"解"字"

1. **Only the Earth provides** ideal **conditions.**

   译文：只有地球提供了理想的条件。

   解析：only修饰主语the Earth，所以句子未倒装。ideal为表达极致的形容词，所以无比较级和最高级，参看第9课"振振有'词'"部分。

2. **Whether a planet can support life depends on the size and brightness of its star,** that is its **"sun".**

   译文：一颗行星是否能够维持生命取决于它的恒星——即它的"太阳"——的大小和亮度。

   解析：1）关系副词whether引导主语从句，谓语动词为depend on。

   　　　2）that is表引出同位语，可译为"即，就是"，相当于that is to say, namely, i.e. 等。

3. **Imagine a star** up to **twenty times larger, brighter and hotter than our own sun.**

   译文：设想一下，一颗恒星比我们的太阳还要大，还要亮，还要热20倍。

   解析：1）原形动词直接放在句首就是祈使句的一般标记。例：

   　　　Strike while the iron is hot. 趁热打铁。

   　　　Make hay while the sun shines. 晒草要趁早。（抓紧时机）

   　　　Don't judge a book by its cover. 不要以貌取人。

   　　　2）up to表"数目上达到…"。例：

   　　　The factory turns out up to 2,000 cars per month. 这家工厂月产轿车达到2,000辆。

   　　　Please count from 1 up to 100. 请从1数到100。

4. **..., because** the dust becomes thinner the further we travel towards the outer edges of our own solar system.

   译文：……，因为我们越是接近太阳系的边缘，尘埃就越稀薄。

   解析：这个句子属于"the+比较级，the+比较级"的模式，其中，前半部分一般为附句，后半部分一般为主句（参看第9课"说'文'解'字'"部分）。但本句中主句部分（the dust becomes thinner）和附句部分（the further we travel towards the outer edges of our own solar system）互换了位置。

以下是一些主句和附句位置互换的例证：

I sing the worse, the more I practise. (=The more I practise, the worse I sing.)

我愈练习，唱得愈差。

The stone gets the harder, the longer it is exposed to the weather. (=The longer the stone is exposed to the weather, the harder it gets.) 愈是在空气中暴露得长久，石头就愈坚硬。

拓 展 篇

I.英语趣园

Mercury, the second smallest planet in our solar system, is closest to the sun and the fastest moving planet. It was the name of the messenger of Zeus who had wings on his feet. Venus is so bright and beautiful that ancient Romans named it for their female god of love and beauty. Ancient Babylonians wrote about a red star that moved slowly through the sky and named it Nergal, after their god of war. Later, ancient Romans gave the planet its present name—Mars—after their own god of war. Jupiter was king of the gods and ruler of the universe. It also king of planets, because it is one and a half times bigger than all the other planets put together. We have known about Saturn for at least twenty-five centuries. The early Greeks named it after the first ruler of the gods.

II.听力快车

_____. Until in the 17th century, Italian scientist Galileo galilei _____and on March 13,1781, William Herschel discovered something in the sky that had not been recorded before. Johann Bode, writer of the Astronomical Yearbook of Berlin, said it should be named Uranus, _____, as Jupiter is the father of Mars. Neptune is the 8th planet of our solar system._____. So _____. On March 13, 1930, the 75th anniversary of the birth of Percival Lowell, Clyde Tombaugh had found the 9th planet. After the discussion, scientists chose a name for the new one: Pluto,_____. It seemed the right name for such distant, dark place. Also, the planet could then be represented by its first two letters, P- L. And these, of course, were the same first letters of the mane of Percival Lowell.

III.补充阅读

The Greeks had observed that certain stars were forever moving across the skies while others apparently stood still. They therefore called the former "planets" or "wanderers" and the latter "fixed stars" because, having no telescopes, they could not follow them on their peregrinations. As for the word "star", we do not know its origin but it probably has something to do with a Sanskrit root which was in turn connected with the verb "to strew". If that be true the stars would then be the little flames "strewn" all over the heavens, a description which is quite pretty and fits the case admirably.

The earth turns around the sun and depends upon the sun for its light and heat. As the sun is more than seven hundred times as large as all the planets put together, and as the temperature of the sun near the surface is about 6000℉, the earth need not feel apologetic about borrowing her humble little portion of comfort from a neighbor who can so easily spare these few charitable rays and will never know the difference.

In the olden days the people believed that the earth was situated in the center of the universe, a small, flat disc of dry land entirely surrounded by the waters of the ocean and suspended in the air like the coffin of Mohammed or a toy balloon that has escaped the hand of a child. A few of the more enlightened Greek astronomers and mathematicians seem to have had a very definite suspicion that this theory must be wrong. After several centuries of very hard and very straight thinking, scientists came to the conclusion that the earth was not flat, but round, and that it did not hang quietly suspended in the air and in the exact center of the universe, but that it floated through space and was flying at a considerable rate of speed round a much larger object which was called the sun.

In the first place, there was the fact that when we approach a mountain or a ship at sea, we first of all notice the summit or the top of the mast and only very gradually, as we come nearer, are we able to see the rest of the objects under observation.

Secondly, no matter where we are, the scene all around us appears to be a circle. Our eyes therefore must be equally removed from every part of the land or sea under observation and the further we get away from the surface of the earth in a balloon or on top of a tower, the larger that circle gets. If the earth happened to be egg-shaped, we would find ourselves in the middle of a large oval. If it were a square or a triangle, the horizon would be a square or a triangle too.

Thirdly, when a partial eclipse of the moon takes place, the shadow of the earth on the moon is a circle and only a ball will cause a circular shadow.

In the fourth place, the other planets and stars too are spheres and why should we alone among so many billions be an exception?

In the fifth place, when the ships of Magellan had sailed long enough in a westerly direction, they finally returned to the place from which they had left and when Captain Cook did the same thing, going from west to east, the survivors of his expedition also came back to the port from which they had sailed.

And finally, when we travel northward towards the poles, the familiar constellations of the stars disappear lower and lower below the horizon, but they arise again and come higher and higher, the nearer we return to the equator.

▪▶ 测 试 篇 ◀▪

I . 单项选择

1. Communication is the process of _____ a message from a source to an audience via a channel.
   A. transmitting   B. submitting   C. transforming   D. switching

2. Some diseases are _____ by certain water animals.
   A. transplanted   B. transformed   C. transported   D. transmitted

3. Workers in the fine arts _____ thoughts and feelings through their creative works.
   A. transmit   B. elaborate   C. convey   D. contribute

4. The coming of the railways in the 1830s _____ our society and economic life.
   A. transformed   B. transported   C. transferred   D. transmitted

5. Sometimes patients suffering from severe pain can be helped by "drugs" that aren't really drugs at all _____ sugar pills that contain no active chemical elements.
   A. or rather   B. rather than   C. but rather   D. other than

6. At first, the speaker was referring to the problem of pollution in the country, but halfway in her speech, she

suddenly _____ to another subject.

    A. committed   B. switched   C. favoured   D. transmitted

7. Young adults _____ older people are more likely to prefer pop songs.

    A. other than   B. more than   C. less than   D. rather than

8. This crop does not do well in soils _____ the one for which it has been specially developed.

    A. outside   B. other than   C. beyond   D. rather than

9. In no country _____ Britain, it has been said, can one experience four seasons in the course of a single day.

    A. other than   B. more than   C. better than   D. rather than

10. We preferred to postpone the meeting _____ it without the presence of our president.

    A. rather than hold   B. than to hold   C. rather than held   D. to holding

II. 翻译

11. 国内考试还停留在笔考阶段；而国外考试大多实现了机考。（paper-based/ computer-based）

12. 他在自己的研究领域做出了一些重大的突破。（in his realm of）

13. 神舟五号的成功发射让国民激动不已。（generate）

14. 君子动口不动手。（rather than）

15. 尊重别人的人才会被别人尊重；反之，不尊重别人，别人也不尊重他。（alternatively）

拓展篇

    For thousands of years of recorded history, our solar system ended at Saturn. Until in the 17th century, Italian scientist Galileo galilei developed the telescope and on March 13,1781, William Herschel discovered something in the sky that had not been recorded before. Johann Bode, writer of the Astronomical Yearbook of Berlin, said it should be named Uranus, who was the ancient Roman god of the sky and father of Jupiter, as Jupiter is the father of Mars. Neptune is the 8th planet of our solar system. It is the blue-green color of the sea. So it was named after the ancient god of the sea. On March 13, 1930, the 75th anniversary of the birth of Percival Lowell, Clyde Tombaugh had found the 9th planet. After the discussion, scientists chose a name for the new one: Pluto, which was the ancient Roman god of the dead, the ruler of the underworld. It seemed the right name for such distant, dark place. Also, the planet could then be represented by its first two letters, P- L. And these, of course, were the same first letters of the mane of Percival Lowell.

测试篇

1-5 ADCAC   6-10 BDBAA

11. Domestic exams are still paper-based while foreign ones almost completely turn to computer-based.

12. He made some important break-through in his realm of study.

13. The successful launching of Shen Zhou Five greatly generated our nation's excitement.

14. Gentlemen use their mouths rather than their fists.

15. He who feels the respect which is due to others can't fail to inspire in them regard for him; alternatively, he who disrespects other people will inspire hatred against himself.

Lesson 56. Our neighbour, the river

积累篇

I. 振振有"词"

1. We know <u>instinctively</u>...that <u>misfortune</u> might <u>overtake</u> us if the important events were not related to it.

表人特征的形似词：

instinctive 本能的
impulsive 冲动的
sensitive 敏感的
plaintive 忧伤的
passive 消极的，被动的
authoritative 有权威的
conservative 保守的

以mis-(表错误、否定)开头的词：

misfortune 灾难
mischance 噩运
mischief 灾害
misconduct 行为不轨
misdeed 恶行
misadjustment 失调
misstep 过失

形似词辨析：

overtake 突然降临
undertake 承担
stake 利害关系
evoke 唤起
provoke 挑衅
hitchhike 搭便车

2. This is a rare <u>occurrence</u> as <u>our climate seldom goes to extremes</u>.

occurrence 偶然事件
incidence 事件
accident (小)事件
coincidence 巧合事件

trifle 琐碎细节
triviality 琐碎小事
detail 细节
technicality 技术细节

描述天气的句子：

The climate seldom goes to extremes. 气候很少异常。
The weather is agreeable. 气候宜人。
The weather is mild. 温度适宜。
The weather is inclement. 天气恶劣。
The weather is inhospitable. 天气糟糕。
The weather is noticeably changeable. 天气异常多变。

3. ..., but other farms are less favorably <u>sited</u>, and flooding can sometimes <u>spell disaster</u> for their owners.

be sited in...位于…（多为人为因素）	spell 导致（尤指灾祸）	由词缀-aster（表star）构成的单词：
be located in...坐落于….	invite 招致（尤指灾祸）	disaster 灾难
be situated in...位于…	evoke（*fml.*）引起	astronaut 宇航员
station 驻扎	bring about 引起	astronomy 天文学
settle 定居	give birth to（文雅）引发	asteroid 小行星
inhabit 居住于…	give rise to（文雅）引发	astrology 星象学
populate 落户于…	set up 引起	astrospace 宇宙空间
park（在停车场）停车	result in 导致	astrophysics 天体物理学

Ⅱ. 现身说"法"：in之后接that从句

> **We are lucky** in that **only the lower fields, which make up a small proportion of our farm, are affected by flooding.**
>
> 值得庆幸的是，只有低洼地受到洪水影响，而低洼地在我们农场比例很小。

一般而言，大部分介词之后不能接that引导的宾语从句，只在in, but, except, save, besides, beyond等几个介词之后这种情形才能出现。这种用法已形成固定搭配，具有了特定意义，如：

in that 由于　　　　　　but that 若不是　　　　　　except/save/besides/beyond that 除了

例：He was in a bad mood in that he failed in the exam. 他考试不及格，心情不佳。

But that you helped I could not have survived. 若不是你的帮助，我不会渡过难关的。

I know nothing besides that he was from Beijing. 我只知道他来自北京，其他一无所知。

The essay was perfect except that there were some misprints. 这篇文章除了一些打印错误，非常完美。

I saw nothing in the street save that a man was hanging around. 我在街上只见到一个人在闲逛。

Ⅲ. 说"文"解"字"

1. Without it we could not make a living.

译文：若是没有这条河，我们就无法生存下去。

解析：1）without在本句引导虚拟语气的条件句，相当于but for, if it were not for, were it not for等。例：

Without your kind help we would not overcome the difficulty.

没有你的帮助，我们就无法克服困难。

2）由于without是介词，其后引导的内容无法断定时态，所以主句中可能出现不同时间的虚拟状态。如上句也可改写为：

Without your kind help we would not overcome the difficulty.（对现在状况的虚拟）

没有你的帮助，我们就无法克服困难。

Without your kind help we would not have overcome the difficulty.（对过去状况的虚拟）

没有你的帮助，我们就无法克服困难。

2. We welcome the seasons by the riverside... giving thanks for the harvest in the autumn.

译文：我们在河边迎接四季……秋天为丰收而感恩。

解析：句中的give thanks 实际是指西方传统的感恩节，即感谢上帝赐予的丰收。感恩节定于每年11月的最后一个星期四，在美国属于联邦假日。

3. **We are lucky** in that **only the lower fields...are affected by flooding.**

译文：值得庆幸的是，只有低洼地受到了洪水的影响。

解析：前面的语法部分已提及，介词in可以后接that从句，即in that引导原因状语从句。需注意的是，in that引导的从句一般置于主句之后，这一点与for引导原因从句的用法相仿。例：

Men differ from brutes in that they can think and speak.

人类之所以异于兽类，就在于能说话又能思考。

He thought the better of her in that she had a lot of imagination.

他对她评价很高，因为她想像力丰富。

The budget is unrealistic in that it disregards increased costs.

这个预算不合实际，因为忽视了增加的费用。

4. **All the cattle had been moved into stalls and we** stood to lose little.

译文：所有的牲口都已提前转移到畜圈里，没有造成什么损失。

解析：stand to do sth.不可望文生义，它是一个固定词组，意为be in a position to do sth.（注定…）。例：

Individual enterprises stand to benefit much from this new economic policy.

私营企业一定会因这个新的经济政策受益匪浅。

If we accept this provision, we stand to lose part of the market.

如果我们接受这个条款，肯定会损失一些市场份额。

▌拓展篇

Ⅰ.英语趣园

Noah, in the Old Testament of the Bible, was a man chosen by God to build an ark (=a large boat) so that he could save his family and two of every kind of animal that lived on the Earth from the terrible Flood sent by God, which covered the Earth.

Ⅱ.听力快车 🎧

We've been boating on the non-tidal part of the River Thames since 1988. It's a hobby that_____, but it's an impulse we've never regretted. At the time_____. I think we can say we know a little more now. The Thames is a fascinating stretch of inland waterway. We never tire of it.

_____. However, for us, _____. It flows through_____ and even _____. Along the river bank there is interesting architecture to look at, _____, a variety of boats passing by and of course boating people to chat to.

Life is never dull on the river.

Ⅲ.补充阅读

The Mississippi

The Mississippi is a romantic river whose relationship with man goes way back beyond its discovery by the Spaniards in the 16th century. The River Indians used it as a highway and as a source of food, and it was they who gave it its name—"mini", meaning "great" and "sipi" meaning "water".

When the length of its great tributary, the Missouri, is added to it, the Mississippi becomes the third longest river in the world. From the source of the Missouri to the tip of the delta, it is 2,480 miles long. Its head waters have been compared with a healthy, thick-branched tree, healthy because its main branches, or tributaries, are navigable for most of their length.

The Indians paddled up and down it in their canoes. The first steamer was launched in 1810. It had a single great paddle-wheel at the stern, and from then on was known as a "paddle-wheeler". Throughout the 19th century these unique ships were queens of the Mississippi. They have become part of American history and American literature. The noted writer, Mark Twain immortalized the river in his greatest novel, Huckleberry Finn, and Oscar Hammerstein immortalized it in his song, "Ol' Man River", made popular all over the world by the great black American singer and actor, Paul Robeson.

Great rivers are prone to floods. In 1927 the Mississippi swamped 26 thousand acres, sweeping away farms, town, everything in its path. In 1938 its floods drowned or killed 2000 people and made millions homeless. Today the river has largely been tamed. Levees, high banks built of earth, hold back the flood waters.

"Great Water" has also been a frontier river. Pioneers who first reached its banks wondered not only where it went, but what lay beyond. In 1764 the French founded a city on the right bank of the river, and named it after their king, Louis XV. This city, named St. Louis, became the jumping-off place for the adventurous men and women who opened up the Great Plains, and the way to the Far West.

Some 40 years earlier, at the beginning of the 18th century, the French had founded another city just above the Mississippi delta, New Orleans. It was the Mississippi that made the city what it is. New Orleans is one of the great ports of the world, and one of the greatest terminals for both sea and river traffic. Yet the "Great Water" always remains a threat, for the streets of New Orleans are below the level of the river, and at flood time, only the huge levees stand between the city and disaster.

▶ 测 试 篇 ◀

I. 单项选择

1. Doctors are interested in using lasers as a surgical tool in operations on people who are _____ to heart attack. (CET-6 03/6)

A. infectious   B. disposed   C. accessible   D. prone

2. There are occasions when giving a gift _____ spoken communication, since the message it offers can cut through barriers of language and cultural diversity.

A. overtakes   B. nourishes   C. surpasses   D. enforces

3. Arriving home, the boy told his parents about all the _____ which occurred in his dormitory.

A. occasions   B. matters   C. incidents   D. issues

4. Professor Smith explained the movement of light _____ that of water.

A. by analogy with   B. by virtue of   C. in line with   D. in terms of

5. In the _____ of the project not being a success, the investors stand to lose up to $30 million.

A. face   B. time   C. event   D. course

6. _____ much is known about what occurs during sleep, the precise function of sleep and its different stages remains largely in the realm of assumption.

A. Because   B. For   C. Since   D. While

7. I felt somewhat disappointed and was about to leave _____ something occurred which attracted my attention.

    A. unless   B. until   C. when   D. while

8. The mere fact _____ most people believe nuclear war would be madness does not mean that it will not occur.

    A. what   B. which   C. that   D. why

9. What a good listener is able to do is to process what he hears on the basis of the context _____ .

    A. it occurring in   B. occurred in it   C. occurring in it   D. it occurs in

10. Some areas, _____ their severe weather conditions, are hardly populated.

    A. due to   B. in spite of   C. but for   D. with regard to

II. 翻译

11. 我们眼看就要输了，可就在这一关键时刻，姚明大显神通，最终反败为胜。（stand to lose）

12. 一场大雪使得铁路系统中断运营。（put...out of order）

13. 心理因素在考试时起到重要作用。（play an important part in）

14. 山顶覆盖着皑皑白雪。（be crowned with）

15. 许多人在一起吃饭的时候，老外通常不会掏钱买单。（frequent occurrence）

拓展篇

    We've been boating on the non-tidal part of the River Thames since 1988. It's a hobby that <u>we took up almost on impulse,</u> but it's an impulse we've never regretted. At the time <u>we knew nothing about boats and not much about the Thames.</u> I think we can say we know a little more now. The Thames is a fascinating stretch of inland waterway. We never tire of it.

    <u>The Thames is not a particularly long river.</u> However, for us, <u>it never loses its fascination.</u> It flows through <u>a mixture of rural and urban scenery</u> and even <u>these can look different depending on the time of year.</u> Along the river bank there is interesting architecture to look at, <u>wildlife to observe,</u> a variety of boats passing by and of course boating people to chat to.

    Life is never dull on the river.

测试篇

1-5 DCCAC   6-10 DCCDA

11. It seemed that we stood to lose the game, but at the crucial moment, Yao Ming worked his magic and converted the defeat to a success.

12. A heavy snow put the railway service out of order.

13. Psychological factors play an important part in exams.

14. The mountain peaks were crowned with snows.

15. It is not a frequent occurrence for a foreigner to pay for the bill when a number of people eat together.

Lesson 57. Back in the old country

积累篇

I.振振有"词"

1. In the new country he became <u>absorbed in</u> <u>making a new life</u> for the two of us.

be absorbed in...对…投入
be engaged in...专心从事…
be immersed in...对…专注
be engrossed in...醉心于…
be concentrated on...全神贯注于…
be intent on...专注于…

make a new life 开创新生活
turn over a new leaf 翻开新的一页
blaze a new trail 开辟新天地
break new ground 开创新田地
start afresh 重新开始
start over 重新开始

2. ..., so that I was <u>positive</u> I should <u>recognize it as</u> familiar <u>territory</u>.

positive 确信的
explicit 清楚的
definite 确定的
unequivocal 明确的
indisputable 无可争辩的
irrefutable 无可辩驳的
incontrovertible 不容置疑的

recognize...as...把…看作…
conceive...as...把…想像成…
accept...as...认为…是…
mistaken...for...错认为…是…
pass for...被误以为是…
take sth. for granted 认为…理所当然

territory 领土
province 范围；领域
domain 领域
realm 王国；领域
sphere 范围
bailiwick（活动、兴趣）范围

3. So I drove back to the town and began to <u>retrace</u> the route, <u>taking frequent glances at</u> the map.

以re-开头的词：
retrace 重新寻找
renew 更新
recur 重现
retrieve 更正
reunite 团聚
redintegrate 重建
retrospect 回顾

take frequent glances at...不停地看…
throw a hopeful glance at...满怀希望地看…
steal a glance at...偷偷看…
give sb. an admiring glance 赞赏地看某人
take a glimpse at...瞥一眼…
take a look at...看…

II. 现身说"法"：复合定语从句

> I hired a car the day after landing and bought a comprehensive book of maps..., but which I did not think I should need on the last stage.（彩色部分为复合定语从句）我下飞机后租了一辆车，并买了一本详尽的地图册……但快到家的时候，我觉得它就没什么用了。

1. 复合定语从句即在定语从句的关系词后加上"主语+表意见或看法的动词"的结构。例：

   Medical experts are now racing against time to find a cure for bird flu which WHO fear may spread to even more countries.

   医学专家正在争取时间找到治疗禽流感的良方，世界卫生组织担心它会波及更多的国家。

   She has a friend whom I think is pretty reliable.

   我认为她有一个非常值得信赖的朋友。

2. 实际上，复合定语从句中的关系词作双重身份，既充当定语从句的主语或宾语，又充当"主语+表意见或看法的动词"结构的宾语。

III. 说"文"解"字"

1. When my mother had died after a tragic accident, he did not quickly recover from the shock and loneliness.

   译文：当时我母亲在一次事故中惨死，父亲未能很快从悲痛与孤独中恢复过来。

   解析：recover from意为"从…恢复（健康等）"，若单用recover，则表"挽回（损失等）"。例：

   He recovered from a serious illness. 他从一场重病中恢复了健康

   The company did not recover its losses. 公司没有挽回损失。

2. So he decided to emigrate.

   译文：于是他决定移居他国。

   解析：1）emigrate意为"移居"，表示离开本地迁往异乡，即移出。在句中省略了to引导的表地点状语的介词短语。例：

   His family emigrated from China to Canada last year. 他全家去年从中国移民去了加拿大。

   2）emigrate的反义词是immigrate，表示为定居而迁入某国，即移入。如果不太强调方向性，则可以用migrate。例：

   This scientist immigrated to China from Turkey. 这位科学家从土耳其迁入了中国。

   Many village workers migrate to big cities each year. 每年许多民工涌入大城市。

3. He always meant to go back one day, but not to stay.

   译文：他总想将来回国看看，但却不愿长期住下去。

   解析：1）mean to do 意为"本打算做…"，含有遗憾、惋惜之语气。例：

   She meant to do morning exercise, but she overslept. 她本打算去晨练，但是睡过了头。

   2）mean doing意义略有不同，表"意味"。例：

   This new order will mean working over time. 新订单一来就意味着我们要加班加点。

4. His roots and mine had become too firmly embedded in the new land.

   译文：而且他和我一样已经深深地植根于异国他乡。

解析：be embedded in是固定词组，意为"植根于…"，类似于be rooted in, take root in。例：

His inspiring speech took deep root in my mind. 他富有激情的演说深深印在了我的脑海里。

Her radiant smile is deeply rooted in my mind. 她灿烂的笑容深深留在了我的脑海里。

5. It was not that I actually remembered anything at all. But my father had described over and over again what we should see at every milestone.

译文：这倒不是我记住了地图上的所有内容，而是父亲曾数次告诉我在每一个路标处可见到什么。

解析：It is not that...but that...是一个常用句型，翻译为"不是…而是…"。本句中but大写，单列为一句，是为了加强效果。例：

It is not that I mind going out with you, but that I'm in a low mood.

我不是不愿和你出去，而是我今天心绪不佳。

拓 展 篇

Ⅰ.英语趣园

The word "hometown", for most people is agreeably associated with home, mother, face beaming with happiness and love, comfort, warmness, safety, a harbor of peace you can turn to whenever in depression.

Ⅱ.听力快车

Talking about the hometown

On a weekend, John took David to his hometown.

John: _____!

David: Well, what was this place like before, John?

John: Well, _____. Hmm. It was pretty quiet. Not many people lived here then.

David: These days, _____.

John: Yeah. _____.

David: Hey, that doesn't sound too bad.

John: No, but I'll miss the old days.

Ⅲ.补充阅读

My old neighborhood

Several years ago I returned to Washington, D.C. and visited one of my old neighborhoods. I had been on Nash Street for more than twenty years and as I walked along the street, my mind was flooded by waves of nostalgia. I saw the old apartment building where I had lived and the playground where I had played. As I viewed these once familiar surroundings, images of myself as a child there came to mind. However, what I saw and what I remembered were not the same. I sadly realized that the best memories are those left undisturbed.

As I remembered my old apartment building, it was bright and alive. When I was a child, the apartment building was more than just a place to live. It was a medieval castle, a pirate's den, a space station, or whatever my young mind could imagine. I would steal away with my friends and play in the basement. This was always exciting because it was so cool and dark, and there were so many things there to hide among. Our favorite place to play was the coal bin. We would always use it as jour rocket ship because the coal chute could be used as an escape hatch out of the basement into "outer space".

I also have memories of many adventures outside of the building. My mother restricted how far we could go from the apartment building, but this placed no restrictions on our exploiting instinct. There was a small brush in back of the building where my friends and I would play. We enjoyed it because honeysuckles grew there. We would go there to lie in the shade and suck the sweet smelling honeysuckles. Our biggest thrill was the day the police caught an alligator there. I did not see the alligator and I was not there when they caught it, but just the thought of an alligator in the brush was exciting.

This is how I remembered the old neighborhood; however, as I said, this is not how it was when I saw it.

As for the area where I used to play, it was hardly recognizable. The brush was polluted and the honeysuckles had died. Not only were they dead, but they had been trampled to the ground. The brush itself was filled with old bicycles, broken bottles and garbage. Now, instead of finding something as romantic as an alligator, one would expect to find only rats. The once sweet smelling area now smelled horrible. The stench from my once idyllic haven was heart-wrenching.

I do not regret having seen my old neighborhood. However, I do not think my innocent childhood memories will ever be the same. I suppose it is true when they say, "You can never go home again."

▶ 测 试 篇 ◀

Ⅰ.单项选择

1. Harold claimed that he was a serious and well-known artist, but in fact he was a (n) _____.
   A. alien   B. client   C. counterpart   D. fraud

2. We find that some birds twice a year _____ between hot and cold countries.
   A. transfer   B. commute   C. migrate   D. emigrate

3. The club will _____ new members the first week in September.
   A. enroll   B. subscribe   C. absorb   D. register

4. The writer was so _____ in her work that she didn't notice him enter the room.
   A. absorbed   B. abandoned   C. focused   D. centered

5. When trapped in drifting sands, do not struggle, or you will be _____ in deeper.
   A. absorbed   B. pushed   C. heaved   D. sucked

6. This book is expected to _____ the best-seller lists.
   A. promote   B. prevail   C. dominate   D. exemplify

7. One of the attractive features of the course was the way the practical work had been _____ with the theoretical aspects of the subject.
   A. integrated   B. embedded   C. embraced   D. synthesized

8. We should be able to do the job for you quickly, _____ you give us all the necessary information.
   A. in case   B. provided that   C. or else   D. as if

9. That tree looked as if it _____ for a long time.

　　A. hasn't watered　　　　　　　　　B. didn't water

　　C. hadn't been watered　　　　　　　D. wasn't watered

10. The goals _____ he had fought all his life no longer seemed important to him.

　　A. after which　　　　B. for which　　　　C. with which　　　　D. at which

Ⅱ. 翻译

11. 我完全沉浸在这本叫做《热气球上的五个星期》的科幻小说中。（be absorbed in）

12. 青少年们不是不爱他们的家庭，而是一心想独立。（It is not that...but that....)

13. 他在一场重感冒之后，很快康复了。（get a quick recovery from）

14. 许多中国华侨依然深深扎根于故乡。（be deeply embedded）

15. 胜利在望。（in sight）

答案

拓展篇

Talking about the hometown

On a weekend, John took David to his hometown.

John:　　The neighborhood sure has changed!

David:　Well, what was this place like before, John?

John:　　Well, there used to be a grocery store right here on this corner. Hmm. It was pretty quiet. Not many people lived here then.

David:　These days, the population is growing fast.

John:　　Yeah. I bet they'll tear down all these old buildings soon. In a few years, there will be just malls and high-rise apartments.

David:　Hey, that doesn't sound too bad.

John:　　No, but I'll miss the old days.

测试篇

1-5 DCAAD　　　　　　　6-10 CABCB

11. I was totally absorbed in the scientific story, *Five Weeks In A Balloon*.

12. It's not that young adults don't love their families, but that they want to be independent.

13. He got a quick recovery from a bad cold.

14. The roots of many Chinese overseas are still deeply embedded in their hometowns.

15. The victory is in sight.

Lesson 58. A spot of bother

I.振振有"词"

1. She was thinking that she must reprimand her <u>home help</u> the next morning for such a <u>monstrous</u> piece of <u>negligence</u>.

negligence 粗心大意
negligent 粗心的
negligible 微不足道的
neglectable 无足轻重的
neglectful 不注意的
neglected 被忽略的

home help 家务帮手
housekeeper 操持家务者
domestic servant 佣人
domestic worker 佣人
cleaner 清洁工
specialized labour 专业工人

形似词辨析：
monstrous 可怕的
monotonous 单调的
momentous 重大的
meticulous 谨小慎微的
melodious 乐调优美的
mysterious 神秘的

2. The <u>chaos</u> was <u>inconceivable</u>.

chaos 混乱
disorder 杂乱
confusion 纷乱
pandemonium 大混乱
turbulence 动荡
turmoil 动乱
bedlam 喧闹

nconceivable 无法想像的
imperceptible 无法察觉的
unimaginable 难以想像的
unthinkable 不可想像的
incomprehensible 难以理解的
implausible 含混不清的
unintelligible 晦涩难懂的

3. She had lived in the flat for thirty years and was a <u>veritable</u> <u>magpie</u> at <u>hoarding</u>.

veritable 实实在在的
authentic 地道的
genuine 纯正的
bona fide 真正的
trustworthy 值得信赖的
accurate 精确的

动物用于表人：
magpie 喜鹊；爱好收藏者
shark 鲨鱼；放高利贷者
wolf 狼；色鬼
lamb 羊羔；温顺之人
donkey 驴；倔强之人

hoard 囤积（多为私用）
amass（大量）积累
accumulate（长期）积累
stack（整齐）堆放
pile（杂乱）堆放
heap（杂乱）堆放

304

Ⅱ. 现身说"法"：V-ing短语作状语

> They went through the rooms, being careful to touch nothing, as they did not want to hinder the police in their search for fingerprints. （彩色部分在句中作状语，表行为方式，修饰went through）他们搜遍了每一个房间，小心翼翼地不接触任何东西，因为怕妨碍警察寻找指纹。

1. V-ing短语作状语时，其逻辑主语必须与主句的主语一致，即V-ing短语的动作和谓语的动作是由同一主语发出的。本句中being careful的逻辑主语即是主句的主语they。例：

   The children went away <u>laughing</u> and <u>whistling</u>.（划线部分的逻辑主语是the children）
   孩子们笑着、吹着口哨走了。

2. 该状语结构也可转化为和主句的并列句型，如以上例句即可改写为：

   They went through the rooms and were careful to touch nothing, as they did not want to hinder the police in their search for fingerprints.

   The children went away and laughed and whistled.

3. V-ing的一般式常表示同时发生的动作，而V-ing的完成式常用来表示先发生的动作。例：

   Brushing his teeth, Jack went downstairs. 杰克边刷牙，边下楼。

   Having brushed his teeth, Jack went downstairs. 杰克刷牙后下楼去了。

Ⅲ. 说"文"解"字"

1. Her shopping had tired her and her basket had grown heavier with every step of the way home.

   译文：购物使她筋疲力尽，在回家的路上，每走一步，就感到手里的篮子又重了一点。

   解析：1）tire在这里作使动词，意为"使…疲劳"。例：

   He tired his eyes by reading too much. 他看书太多，把眼睛都看累了。

   Her constant chatter tired everyone. 她没完没了的唠叨令大家都很烦。

   2）with every step of the way home 中with表"随着…"。例：

   With daylight I hurried there to see what had happened.

   天一亮我就赶到那里去看出了什么事。

   With these words, he left the meeting hall. 说着话，他就离开了会议大厅。

   change with the seasons 随着季节变化而变化

2. In the lift her thoughts were on lunch and a good rest.

   译文：乘上电梯后，她只想着午饭和好好休息一下。

   解析：彩色部分是英文的地道表述，而学习者一般会用think about表达。掌握这样的手法，对于提升写作技能很有益处。例：

   On his way to the office, his thoughts were on the submitted proposal.

   在去往办公室的路上，他满脑子想着那份提交的方案。

   A few days before May, 1st, my thoughts were on a wonderful trip to the West Lake.

   五一节前几天，我满脑子想着要去西湖做一次完美旅行。

3. It was as clear as daylight then that the burglars had forced an entry during her absence.

   译文：事情很清楚，在她外出时，窃贼曾闯进家门。

解析：It is as clear as daylight that 是一个常用写作句型，意为"很显然…"。其他类似句型有：

It is as clear as crystal that...…一目了然

It is self-evident that...…不言自明

It is fairly obvious that...很清楚…

4. ..., so she sat down and accepted a cup of very strong tea.

译文：……，于是她坐下，喝了一杯浓茶。

解析：accept在这里采用了灵活译法。因此，背诵单词时，多加注意简单词的多重意义可起到事倍功半的效果。例：

How is this word to be accepted? 这个单词怎么解释？

He can accept poor conditions. 他能忍受艰苦的环境。

We all accept him as a genius. 我们都承认他是个天才。

He was accepted at Oxford. 他被牛津大学录取了。

拓 展 篇

Ⅰ.英语趣园

Problems large and small confront the elderly. They are easy targets for crime in the streets and in their homes. Because of loneliness, confusion, hearing and visual difficulties they are prime victims of dishonest door-to-door salesmen and fraudulent advertising, and buy defective hearing aids, dance lessons, useless "Medicare insurance supplements", and quack health remedies. Persons crippled by arthritis or strokes are yelled at by impatient bus drivers for their slowness in climbing on and off buses. Traffic lights turn red before they can get across the street. Revolving doors move too quickly. Subways usually have no elevators or escalators.

Ⅱ.听力快车 🎧

The old lady looked everywhere for her red purse but nowhere can she find it. Then, _____. The standing-room-only bus had moved in spastic fashion, _____. A pregnant woman was standing very close behind her. In fact, she even remembered body contact. There were a few other passengers in close proximity, too. "Hold tight to me", she told the pregnant woman, concerned that she would be thrown off balance and hurt.

_____. Pickpockets ganging up to_____, particularly older ones, is not unheard of on the buses there.

Ⅲ.补充阅读

Old women fare worse than old men. Women have an average life expectancy of seven years longer than men and tend to marry men older than themselves; so two-thirds of all older women are widows. When widowed they do not have the same social prerogatives as older men to date and marry those who are younger. As a result, they are likely to end up alone—an ironic turn of events when one remembers that most of them were raised form childhood to consider marriage the only acceptable state. The income levels of older working women are generally lower than those of men; may never work outside the home until their children were grown and then only at unskilled, low-paying jobs. Others who worked all their lives typically received low wages, with lower Social Security and private retirement benefits as a result. Until 1973, housewives who were widowed received only 82.5% of their husbands' Social Security benefits even though they were full-time home-makers.

Black, Mexican-American and American Indian elderly all have a lower life expectancy than whites, due to their socioeconomic disadvantages. Although the life expectancy of 67.5 years for white men remained the same from 1960 to 1968, the life expectancy for black men declined a full year during that time. Blacks of all ages make up 11% of the total United States population, but they constitute only 7.8% of the elderly. The life expectancy for Mexican-Americans is estimated at 57 years, and for American Indians at 44 years. Most do not live long enough to be eligible for the benefits of Social Security and Medicare. Poverty is the norm. Scant attention is paid to their particular cultural interests and heritage.

Asian-American elderly (Chinese, Japanese, Korean, Filipino and Samoan) are victims of a public impression that they are independently cared for by their families and therefore do not need help. However, patterns of immigration (by Asian-Americans) to this country, cultural barriers, language problems and discrimination they have faced have all taken a toll of their elderly and their families. This is particularly true of older Chinese men, who were not allowed bring their wives and families with them to the United States or to intermarry.

测 试 篇

Ⅰ.单项选择

1. Parents have a legal _____ to ensure that their children are provided with efficient education suitable to their age.
   A. impulse   B. influence   C. obligation   D. sympathy

2. Human behavior is mostly a product of learning, whereas the behavior of an animal depends mainly on _____.
   A. consciousness   B. impulse   C. instinct   D. response

3. The lady in this strange tale very obviously suffers from a serious mental illness. Her plot against a completely innocent old man is a clear sign of _____.
   A. impulse   B. insanity   C. inspiration   D. disposition

4. During the construction of skyscrapers, cranes are used to _____ building materials to the upper floors.
   A. toss   B. tow   C. hoist   D. hurl

5. John doesn't believe in _____ medicine; he has some remedies of his own.
   A. standard   B. regular   C. routine   D. conventional

6. You will want two trees about ten feet apart, from _____ to suspend your tent.
   A. there   B. them   C. which   D. where

7. Although he knew little about the large amount of work done in the field, he succeeded _____ other more well-informed experimenters failed.
   A. which   B. that   C. what   D. where

8. I've never been to Beijing, but it's the place _____.
    A. where I'd like to visit   B. I most want to visit
    C. in which I'd like to visit   D. that I want to visit it most

9. My major is accounting, so I want a job _____ I have more responsibility for money.
    A. which   B. that   C. what   D. where

10. Let's think of a situation _____ this idiom can be used.
    A. that   B. which   C. when   D. where

Ⅱ. 翻译

11. 随着离家越来越近，我的心跳得越来越快了。（with every step of the way home）
12. 只要一提起"家"这个字，我就会想到妈妈、晚饭、温暖。（my thoughts are on...）
13. 别大惊小怪。（make a fuss）
14. 她定期去美容院。（make a regular visit to）
15. 说起购物，女性的缺点之一是常常在购物时一时冲动而买下她们不需要的东西。（on a sudden impulse）

拓展篇

The old lady looked everywhere for her red purse but nowhere can she find it. Then, it suddenly occurred to her that she may have lost the purse on the bus. The standing-room-only bus had moved in spastic fashion, throwing the passengers to and fro, left and right. A pregnant woman was standing very close behind her. In fact, she even remembered body contact. There were a few other passengers in close proximity, too. "Hold tight to me", she told the pregnant woman, concerned that she would be thrown off balance and hurt.

That was the only chance somebody could have put his hand into her bag. Pickpockets ganging up to prey on passengers, particularly older ones, is not unheard of on the buses there.

测试篇

1-5 CCBCD   6-10 CDBDD

11. My heart began beating faster and faster with every step of the way home.

12. My thoughts are on mum, dinner, and warm at the mention of the word "home".

13. Don't make a fuss.

14. She makes a regular visit to the Beauty House.

15. When it comes to shopping, one of the weaknesses of women is that they tend to buy more goods than they need on a sudden impulse.

Lesson 59. Collecting

积累篇

I.振振有"词"

1. People <u>tend to amass</u> possessions, sometimes without <u>being aware of</u> doing so.

形似词辨析:

tend to do 倾向做…
intend to do 想做…
attend to sb./sth. 照看…
tend sb./sth. 照料…
pretend to do 假装做…
suspend sth. 暂停…
amend sth. 修正…

形似词辨析:

amass 积累
bypass 回避
surpass 超越
harass 骚扰
trespass 侵占
embarrass 使尴尬

be aware of…意识到…
be conscious of…认识到…
be sensible of…意识到…
be unaware of…没有意识到…
be unconscious of…没有认识到…
have no idea of…对…一无所知
have no knowledge of…对…毫不知晓

2. The <u>chances</u> that she will ever be able to afford such <u>purchases</u> are <u>remote</u>.

chance 可能性
accident 偶然性
coincidence 巧合
hazard 风险
hap（古）机缘
fortune 运气
destiny 命运

purchase（正式）购买
purchasable 可买到的
purchaseless 无立足点的
purchasing power 购买力
purchase money 买价
purchaser 买主

a remote chance 机会渺茫
a remote village 偏远的村庄
the remote past 遥远的过去
a remote relative 远亲
remote effects 间接后果
remote eyes 漠然的眼神
remote control 遥控

3. One wants to meet <u>like-minded</u> collectors...to exchange <u>articles</u>, ..., to <u>show off</u> the latest find.

like-minded 志趣相投的
strong-minded 意志坚定的
independent-minded 有独立见解的
tradition-minded 传统观念的
safety-minded 有安全意识的
sports-minded 热衷体育的
absent-minded 思想走神的

article 物件
artifact 人工制品
accessory 附件
component 元件
ingredient 配料
constituent 成分

show off 炫耀
boast of 夸耀
talk big 说大话
talk through one's hat 胡扯
blow the trumpet 吹嘘
exaggerate 夸大其词

II. 现身说"法"：介词of与定语从句

> ..., lack of physical and mental energy, both of which are essential in turning out and throwing away. ……，体力、精力均欠佳，这二者是清理无用的东西的必要因素。

彩色部分中的of表所属关系，置于关系代词之前。一般而言，of之前可以添加限定词如some、any、both、several、enough、neither等，还可以加数字及最高级。例：

I have a large collection of books, many of which are classic novels.

我的藏书很多，其中一大部分是古典小说。

The names, some of which he remembered were all strange to me.

他记得其中一些名字，但我全都不熟悉。

I bought a book of which the author is a worker. 我买了本书，作者是一位工人。

The delegates entered the hall, seven of whom were absent. 代表们进入了大厅，其中有七位缺席。

III. 说"文"解"字"

1. They leave unwanted objects in drawers, cupboards and attics for years, in the belief that they may one day need just those very things.

   译文：他们把一些不用的物件放在抽屉里、碗柜中、阁楼上，一放就是好几年，相信总有一天会需要这些东西的。

   解析：1）for years中间省略了数词some或a few或several。一般而言，如果for引导的时间状语表达的不是确切概念，中间的模糊性数词可以省略。例：

   for（several）months 数月以来　　　　　　for（a few）days 好几天

   2）in the belief引导的内容在句中作状语，相当于believing。实际上，这种介词短语和V-ing形式的互换是写作中常常采用的手段。例：

   She was melancholy in the thought that she made a poor show in the interview.（in the thought可换为thinking）想到自己在面试中表现不佳，她就很郁闷。

   He works hard in the hope that he can make a better life for his children.（in the hope可换为hoping）他努力工作，希望能给孩子创造更美好的生活。

   3）very在句中作形容词，意为"特定的"，有强调之意。例：

   On the very day of his birthday he enrolled in the army. 就在生日那一天他参了军。

   This is the very book I am looking for. 这正是我要找的书。

2. I know someone who always cuts sketches out from newspapers of model clothes that she would like to buy if she had the money.

   译文：我认识一个人，她喜欢从报纸上剪下流行服装的图样，等有钱以后再去买服装。

   解析：1）of model clothes在句中不是修饰newspapers，而是修饰sketches。之所以出现这种分裂现象，是因为model clothes之后还接有that引导的定语从句，这样调整后结构均衡，避免头重脚轻。例：

   In the Soviet Union several cases have been reported recently of people who can read and detect colours with their fingers.（《新概念英语》4册第4课）（of people修饰several cases，因为后有who引导的定语从句，所以后置）近来苏联有一些报道，说有人能用手指阅读和察觉颜色。

2）if she had the money中money前加定冠词the表示"有了买服装的钱"，去掉the意义则不同，表示"有钱，富有"。

3. ..., but it litters up her desk to such an extent that every time she opens it, loose bits of paper fall out in every direction.

译文：……，但是她每次打开抽屉总能带出许多纸片四处飞扬。

解析：1）every time引导时间状语，相当于when，因此其后一般不再加when。

2）in every direction意为"四处"。请注意与direction搭配的介词要用in。例：

The birds flew in all directions. 鸟儿向四处飞去。

I walked in her direction. 我朝她走过去。

4. ..., since the collection is housed at home.

译文：……，因为藏品就放在家里。

解析：house在本句中作动词。这种词性转换的用法十分普遍，目的是使行文更灵活简练。例：

They vacationed in Thailand.（vacation由名词转换为动词）他们在泰国度假。

The couple honeymooned in Hangzhou.（honeymoon由名词转换为动词）

这对夫妇在杭州度蜜月。

The old man mothered his beloved pigeons.（mother由名词转换为动词）

老人精心照料着他心爱的鸽子。

拓 展 篇

Ⅰ.英语趣园

Coin collecting is one of the most popular hobbies in the world. Most coin collectors simply enjoy trying to acquire a complete set of a nation's coins or of one or more particular coins. Some people collect coins as works of art. Others collect them as an investment, to be sold later at a profit. Through coins, a collector can also learn something about certain famous people and events in a country's history.

Ⅱ.听力快车

Philately is an interesting hobby._____ and look at the stamps I've collected over the years, I learn something new. Many of them are _____, trees or flowers. Under a magnifying glass they look very beautiful, and they help to_____. On other stamps there are_____, such as Qu Yuan and Dr. Sun Yatsen, George Washington and Chester W. Nimits. Whenever I see an unfamiliar name, I will try to find some information about the person by_____. In this way I have come to know something about quite a few people who are famous_____. Some of my friends and relatives who know I am interested in stamps often show me_____. If I see a stamp which I have never seen before or I haven't got yet, I will ask them to give it to me, and it seems that they are always kind enough to oblige me. It is always a delight to add a new stamp to my collection, and the more stamp I have, the more interested I am in philately.

III. 补充阅读

Imaginative coin collectors can build many types of collections. They can specialize in coins of one country or in various kinds of coins, such as cents or dollars. They can collect coins of unusual sizes or shapes. Many collectors concentrate on coins that illustrate a certain subject, such as animals, ships, or famous women.

The collecting or study of coins is called numismatics, and a coin collector is often called a numismatist. These words come from the Greek word nomisma and the Latin word numisma, both of which mean a piece of money or a coin. Numismatics includes paper money and also medals, tokens, and similar objects. This article tells how to begin and care for a coin collection.

The best source of coins for a beginning collector is the change received when making various purchases. Friends also can help the beginning collector by giving him or her the coins they may have and swap money for any coins found that are not in the beginner's collection. Many beginning collectors go to a bank and exchange their money for rolls of coins. They then examine the rolls to find coins for their collection. A coin's value depends on two factors—its condition and how easily it can be obtained. The most valuable coins are both uncirculated (unused) and scarce. A beginner should seek easily obtainable coins at first.

As collectors learn more and more about the hobby, they can start to acquire coins of greater value from several sources. For example, coin dealers and many collectors sell, trade, and buy coins. Some collectors obtain coins through auctions held in various communities or conducted by mail. In many countries, a government agency sells uncirculated coins to collectors. A person should have some basic information about coin collecting before starting to acquire coins. Several books for beginners can be obtained at bookstores, hobby shops, and libraries.

Many collectors subscribe to a specialized newspaper, such as Coin World or Numismatic News, both of which are published weekly. The American Numismatic Association, the largest organization of coin collectors, publishes a monthly magazine, The Numismatist, with a section for young collectors. The association sponsors a program through the magazine that awards ancient coins to young people who complete certain numismatic activities. The magazine provides the names of U.S. coin clubs. These coin clubs encourage new collectors to attend their meetings and exhibitions.

▶ 测 试 篇 ◀

I. 单项选择

1. Harry was _____ by a bee when he was collecting the honey.
   A. stung   B. stuck   C. bitten   D. scratched
2. He was looking admiringly at the photograph published by Collins in _____ with the Imperial Museum.
   A. collection   B. connection   C. collaboration   D. combination
3. They are sure they have all the facts they need to _____ the existence of a black hole.
   A. obtain   B. maintain   C. verify   D. display
4. The vast majority of people in any given culture will _____ to the established standards of that culture.
   A. confine   B. conform   C. confront   D. confirm
5. By signing the lease we made a _____ to pay a rent of $150 a week.

A. conception   B. commission   C. commitment   D. confinement

6. Sir Denis, who is 78, has made it known that much of his collection _____ to the nation.

     A. has left   B. is to leave   C. leaves   D. is to be left

7. It is important that enough money _____ to fund the project.

     A. be collected   B. must be collected   C. was collected   D. can be collected

8. He has _____ strange hobbies like collecting bottle tops and inventing secret codes.

     A. gone on   B. gone in for   C. gone with   D. gone through with

9. _____ energy under the earth must be released in one form or another, for example, an earthquake.

     A. Accumulated   B. Gathered   C. Assembled   D. Collected

10. We can accept your order _____ payment is made in advance.

     A. in the belief that   B. in order that   C. on the excuse that   D. on condition that

II. 翻译

11. 如果你坐飞机去，你就能节约很多时间。（save sb. sth.）

12. 我们获胜的可能性不大。（The chances that...are remote.）

13. 赌博对他的毁灭有直接的影响。（have a bearing on）

14. 这次成功使我信心大增。（confidence grows）

15. 一次事故使他坐上了轮椅。（be confined to）

答案

拓展篇

     Philately is an interesting hobby. Every time I open my albums and look at the stamps I've collected over the years, I learn something new. Many of them are printed drawings or pictures of rare birds, animals, trees or flowers. Under a magnifying glass they look very beautiful, and they help to increase my knowledge of nature. On other stamps there are portraits of historical figures, such as Qu Yuan and Dr. Sun Yatsen, George Washington and Chester W. Nimits. Whenever I see an unfamiliar name, I will try to find some information about the person by consulting an encyclopedia. In this way I have come to know something about quite a few people who are famous for one reason or another. Some of my friends and relatives who know I am interested in stamps often show me used envelopes. If I see a stamp which I have never seen before or I haven't got yet, I will ask them to give it to me, and it seems that they are always kind enough to oblige me. It is always a delight to add a new stamp to my collection, and the more stamp I have, the more interested I am in philately.

测试篇

1-5 ABCBC   6-10 DABAD

11. You could be saved a lot of time if you chose to fly there.

12. The chances that we win the game are remote.

13. Gambling has a direct bearing on his downfall.

14. My confidence largely grows as I succeeded.

15. He was confined to a wheelchair because of an accident.

Lesson 60. Too early and too late

积累篇

I. 振振有"词"

1. <u>Punctuality</u> is a necessary habit in all <u>public affairs</u> in <u>civilized society</u>.

形似词辨析：

punctuality 准时
punctual 准时的
puncture 刺破（轮胎）
punctuate 强调
punctuation 标点
acupuncture 针灸

public affairs 公事
personal affairs 私事
current affairs 时事
state affairs 国事
day-to-day affairs 日常事务
a romantic affair 风流韵事
a love affair 恋爱事件

civilized society 文明社会
primitive society 原始社会
ancient society 古社会
modern society 现代社会
agrarian society 农业社会
industrialized society 工业化社会
commercialized society 商业化社会

2. The <u>intellectual</u>, who is working on some <u>abstruse</u> problem, has everything <u>coordinated</u> and organized for the matter in hand.

intellectual 知识分子；知识的
intellect 智力
intelligence 聪颖
intelligent 聪明的
intellective 有理解力的
intelligible 可理解的
intellection 思考；思想

形似词辨析：

abstruse 深奥的
abstract 抽象的
abusive 满嘴脏话的；虐待的
absurd 荒谬的
absonant 不和谐的
absolute 纯粹的
obtuse 愚笨的

coordinate 协调
collaborate 合作
systematize 使系统化
synchronize 使一致
harmonize 使和谐
correlate 使关联
integrate 使结合

3. ..., so they <u>are often tempted to</u> finish a job before setting out to <u>keep an appointment</u>.

常用写作句型：

be tempted to do sth. 渴望做…
can't resist the temptation to do sth. 禁不住做…
can't wait to do sth. 迫不及待做…
can't help doing sth. 情不自禁做…
can't refrain from doing sth. 忍不住做…
be impatient to do sth. 急不可耐做…

keep an appointment 赴约
break an appointment 失约
make an appointment 预约
fix an appointment 订约会
arrange an appointment 安排约会
cancel an appointment 取消约会
by appointment 按照约定

Ⅱ. 现身说"法"：without与虚拟语气

> **Without it, nothing could ever be brought to a conclusion.** 不准时将一事无成。

without短语在本句中表虚拟语气的条件，被称为含蓄条件句。它可以转化为由if引导的常规条件句或were it not for, but for等几种形式。例：

本句可转化为：If it were not for it, nothing could be brought to a conclusion.

Without Internet, the world would not be as easy as it is today.（= If it were not for Internet）

若没有互联网，世界将不会像今天这样便利。

What civilization would be like without its benefits?（=but for its benefits）（《新概念英语》第4册）

没有教育，文明将会怎样？

But for these interruptions the meeting would have finished. 如果没有干扰，会议早该结束了。

Were it not for your help, I would not have made such great progress.

没有你的帮助，我不会进步如此明显。

Ⅲ. 说"文"解"字"

1. **Without it, nothing could ever be brought to a conclusion; everything would be** in a state of chaos.

   译文：不准时将一事无成；事事将会陷入混乱不堪的局面。

   解析：1）bring sth. to a conclusion是一个常用词组，意为"完成某事"。实际上，这是conclude sth.的扩展式表达，也是练习写作的常用手法。其他例证如：

   fail in sth. ➡ bring sth. to a failure

   succeed in doing sth. ➡ bring sth. to a success

   end sth. ➡ bring sth. to an end

   2）in a state of chaos意为"混乱状态"，与in disorder, in a mess 等短语相似。

2. **Only** in a sparsely-populated rural community **is it** possible to disregard it.

   译文：只有在人口稀少的农村，才有可能忽视准时的习惯。

   解析：1）该句因only前置，采用了倒装形式，目的在于强调地点状语in a sparsely-populated rural community。一般而言，"only+状语或状语从句"位于句首表示强调时，要采用部分倒装。例：

   Only in this way is it possible to reach an agreement. 只有用这种方式才能达成协议。

   Only when you realize your mistake can we take further.

   只有当你认识到自己的错误时，我们才能进一步沟通。

   2）sparsely-populated是复合形容词，意为"人口稀少的"。相关表达有：

   densely-populated 人口稠密的　　　　　　overpopulated 人口过多的

   underpopulated 人口不足的

3. **But people are often** reproached **for unpunctuality when their fault is** cutting things fine.

   译文：但有些人不准时是因为掐点所致，因此常常受到责备。

   解析：1）reproach意为"责备"，但更加侧重表示"难过，失望"之意。例：

   It wasn't your fault—you have nothing to reproach yourself with.

   那不是你的错，你没有什么可自责的。

2）cut things fine 是固定短语，意为"掐点"，其中的fine为副词。例：

cut up the vegetables very fine 把蔬菜切得很细。

The dress suits me fine. 这衣服非常合身。

4. The only thing to do was ask them to come half an hour later than the other guests.

译文：惟一的办法就是让他们比其他客人晚来半小时。

解析：1）该句中的表语结构ask them实际上是不定式，之前省略了to。原因在于：若在该不定式前出现实意动词do，则不定式中的to可省。例：

All you can do is wait until the meeting is over.（wait前省略了to，因为前面有do）

你只能等到会议结束。

2）不定式作介词but或except的宾语时，若but或except前出现实意动词do，不定式的to可省，反之，to不可省。例：

He could do nothing but wait for the doctor to come.（to可省，因为前面有do）

他只能等医生来。

They desired nothing but to succeed.（to不可省）他们一心想成功。

拓 展 篇

I. 英语趣园

If you are invited to some one's house in Britain, and you don't know them very well, what do you take as a present? People usually take a bottle of wine or some chocolates or flowers. If they are friends, people sometimes take food—some special cheese or something.

If the invitation is for 8 o'clock, does that mean 8 o'clock exactly? Not exactly. About 10 past 8 is fine. They probably want to eat at 8: 30 or 8: 45.

When do you leave? It depends: eleven o'clock, half past 11. Leave when other people leave, but it's usually clear when people want to go to bed.

II. 听力快车

If there is one German custom you should＿＿＿, it is punctuality. ＿＿＿＿＿＿＿＿＿＿＿. Not 15 minutes earlier and not 10 minutes later. ＿＿＿＿＿is not a German custom. Germans, ＿＿＿, are sticklers about being on time. Arriving late will certainly draw a comment and, in a business situation, put you—in German eyes—＿＿＿＿.

If you realize you are not going to arrive somewhere at the appointed time, ＿＿＿＿＿＿＿＿＿＿＿.

III. 补充阅读

Punctuality

In the U.S. being on time is the rule. In other places, such as Latin America, punctuality is rare. Why? Social psychologists have ascribed the differences to deep cultural facts, religion, and "national personalities." One theory, for example, has it that the changing of the seasons in more northern latitudes induces a greater respect for time—plant a little late or early and frost will wipe out your crop.

In *Punctuality: A Cultural Trait as Equilibrium,* game theorists Kaushik Basu and Jorgen Weibull make a simple but important point. If I think you are going to be late then it's costly for me to be on time so I will choose to be late. But if I choose to be late then it makes sense for you to choose to be late also. Indeed, if I think that you think that I might be late then I will be late! In other words, lateness is a Nash equilibrium of a game. Punctuality is also equilibrium. If you are going to be on time it makes sense for me to be on time also (especially if you can punish me for not being on time). Which equilibrium is played can be as arbitrary as the forces that determine which side of the road we drive on.

Basu and Weibull write:

A social scientist who neglects the strategic aspect may be tempted to believe that if two societies exhibit sharply different behaviors, then they must have innate differences, such as different preferences or different religious outlooks on life or different genes. What we have just seen is that none of this is necessary. Some of the "cultural" differences that we observe across societies could simply be manifestations of different equilibria in otherwise identical societies.

If the theory is correct then it should be possible, with a one-time push, to change an entire people from tardy to punctual virtually overnight in much the same way that Sweden switched to driving on the right-hand side of the road (precisely at 5am, by the way, on Sunday morning, September 3, 1967).

The theory is currently being tested in Ecuador, a country where, according to some estimates, habitual lateness costs 4.3 percent of GDP! Thus a national campaign is aiming to change the equilibrium.

Hundreds of institutions ranging from local councils to airlines have signed up to a promise to keep to time. Stragglers are barred from entering meetings. Hotel-style door signs have appeared in offices and schools. On one side, they say "Come in: You're on time" and on the other "Do not enter: the meeting began on time." A local newspaper is publishing a daily list of public officials who turn up late to events.

测 试 篇

I . 单项选择

1. The Spanish team, who are not in superb form, will be doing their best next week to _____ themselves on the German team for last year's defeat.

   A. remedy   B. reproach   C. revive   D. revenge

2. He could not _____ ignorance as his excuse; he should have known what was happening in his department.

   A. plead   B. resort   C. petition   D. reproach

3. I think that I committed a _____ in asking her because she seemed very upset by my question.

   A. blunder   B. revenge   C. reproach   D. scandal

4. Tomorrow the mayor is _____ to a group of Canadian businessmen on a tour of the city.

   A. coordinate   B. cooperate   C. accompany   D. associate

5. The newcomers found it impossible to _____ themselves to the climate sufficiently to make permanent homes in the new country.

   A. suit   B. adapt   C. regulate   D. coordinate

6. It is up to the Government to tackle the air pollution problem and _____ measures in line with the council's suggestions.

   A. set about   B. work out   C. fill up   D. bring over

7. _____ a teacher in a university, it is necessary to have at least a master's degree.

   A. To become   B. Become   C. One become   D. One becoming

8. Criticism and self-criticism is necessary _____ it helps us to find and correct our mistakes.

   A. by that   B. at that   C. on that   D. in that

9. If she doesn't tell him the truth now, he'll simply keep on asking her until she _____.

   A. does   B. has done   C. will do   D. would do

10. If the whole operation _____ beforehand, a great deal of time and money would have been lost.

   A. was not planned   B. has not been planned

   C. had not been planned   D. was not planned

II. 翻译

11. 吃得苦中苦，方为人上人。（Only when... ）

12. 他是个不折不扣的"紧踩铃"。（cut things fine）

13. 泰坦尼克号刚好急转弯，躲避了正面碰撞。（in good time）

14. 在80年代，计算机远没有像今天这样普及。（as much as）

15. 你不需要自责。（reproach oneself）

 答 案

拓展篇

If there is one German custom you should learn and stick to, it is punctuality. An invitation for 4pm means exactly 4p.m. Not 15 minutes earlier and not 10 minutes later. Fashionably late is not a German custom. Germans, particularly business professionals, are sticklers about being on time. Arriving late will certainly draw a comment and, in a business situation, put you—in German eyes—in a compromised position.

If you realize you are not going to arrive somewhere at the appointed time, the custom is to call and announce you will be late.

测试篇

1-5 DAACB   6-10 BADAC

11. Only when you experience the pain of pain can you enjoy the happiness of happiness.

12. He is an irrepressible cut-things-fine.

13. The *Titanic* turned in good time to avoid a direct collision.

14. In 1980s, the computer was not as much a necessity as it is today.

15. You don't have to reproach yourself.